MW00721000

The Self-Field

In this incisive study of the biological and cultural origins of the human self, the author challenges readers to re-think ideas about the self and consciousness as being exclusive to humans. In their place, he expounds a metatheoretical approach to the self as a purposeful system of extended cognition common to animal life: the invisible medium maintaining mind, body and environment as an integrated 'field of being'.

Supported by recent research in evolutionary and developmental studies together with related discoveries in animal behaviour and the neurosciences, the author examines the factors that have shaped the evolution of the animal self across widely different species and times, through to the modern, technologically enmeshed human self; the differences between which, he contends, are relations of degree rather than absolute differences. We are, he concludes, instinctive and 'fuzzy individuals' clinging to fragile identities in an artificial and volatile world of humanity's own making, but which we now struggle to control.

This book, which restores the self to its fundamental place in identity formation, will be of great interest for students and academics in the fields of social, developmental and environmental psychology, together with readers from other disciplines in the humanities, especially cultural theory and philosophy.

Chris Abel is an award-winning author of numerous interdisciplinary publications on the built environment and identity theory. He has taught at universities around the world, most recently at the University of Sydney and the University of Ulster, Belfast.

Routledge Research in Psychology

This series offers an international forum for original and innovative research being conducted across the field of psychology. Titles in the series are empirically or theoretically informed and explore a range of dynamic and timely issues and emerging topics. The series is aimed at upper-level and post-graduate students, researchers and research students, as well as academics and scholars.

Recent titles in the series include:

Declarative Mapping Sentences in Qualitative Research: Theoretical, Linguistic, and Applied Usages
Paul M. W. Hackett

Post-Capitalist Subjectivity in Literature and Anti-Psychiatry: Reconceptualizing the Self Beyond Capitalism
Hans Skott-Myhre

A Scientific Assessment of the Validity of Mystical Experiences: Understanding Altered Psychological and Neurophysiological States
Andrew C. Papanicolaou

For a complete list of titles in this series, please visit: www.routledge.com/ Routledge-Research-in-Psychology/book-series/RRIP

The Self-Field

Mind, Body and Environment

Chris Abel

Routledge
Taylor & Francis Group

LONDON AND NEW YORK

First published 2021
by Routledge
2 Park Square, Milton Park, Abingdon, Oxon OX14 4RN

and by Routledge
52 Vanderbilt Avenue, New York, NY 10017

Routledge is an imprint of the Taylor & Francis Group, an informa business

British Library Cataloguing-in-Publication Data
A catalogue record for this book is available from the British Library

Library of Congress Cataloging-in-Publication Data
A catalog record has been requested for this book

ISBN: 978-0-367-00208-4 (hbk)
ISBN: 978-0-367-74072-6 (pbk)
ISBN: 978-0-429-40076-6 (ebk)

Typeset in Bembo
by Newgen Publishing UK

In memory of my parents, Rose and Bill, who gave me life, and for Margaret Perrin, the love of my life, who changed it.

Contents

Preface

This volume follows my previous book, *The Extended Self: Architecture, Memes and Minds*,[1] which explores the dimensions of a human self that extends beyond the limits of the physical body into the built environment – a theory that the present work builds upon, though with some crucial differences. In an earlier essay with the same title published in 2013,[2] searching for a more accurate description of the elusive self, I depicted it as a 'field of being', likening it to a magnetic field held together, 'not by any physical force, but by an *existential force* with the body at its center'.[3] I repeated the analogy in the previous volume in conclusion of a discussion on extended cognition,[4] aware by this time, however, that the idea deserved far more attention and space of its own.

The outcome is this book, in which the self-field takes centre stage, integrating many of the key ideas floated in the earlier work, together with other new developments in my approach to the subject. My decision to open up my theory of the self to include other animal species as well as humans was driven in particular by my conviction – supported by recent research cited in this book – that, in order to have evolved to its present level of consciousness, other species, and not only those from which our own is descended, must *also* be possessed of a self, if only at different levels of self-awareness. In addition, I have been motivated to advance the idea of an extended self as basic to *all* animal life, by my belief that the commonly accepted view of the self as a uniquely human attribute, directly or indirectly provides a convenient excuse for treating the lives of other creatures as having no value other than what they provide for human needs. The consequent indifference to the interests of other life forms, while surely not the only factor responsible for the catastrophic or threatened loss of so many species in our time, is certainly, in my view, at least partly responsible for the much delayed and inadequate response to that tragedy. This may be obvious to some readers, but I doubt that attitudes towards other creatures will change much until we better understand the true nature of the self and, as I argue in this book, we recognise that, contrary to what we have been led to believe, having a self at all is actually what ties animals at all levels of evolution and development together, including *Homo sapiens*.[5]

Where the former book also focused exclusively on human technological innovation and development as a vital element in the evolution of an extended self, in line with a broader concept of the self, the present work now includes coverage of the growing body of research on animal technological knowledge and skills, encompassing elaborate constructions as well as tool use and manufacture. While this book also continues some of the key discussions in the earlier work on human technologies and their environmental impacts – especially in the latter sections on systems of production and consumption – the former's extensive coverage of architecture (my original profession) and its role in identity formation, also now gives way to a closer focus on the personalisation of homes, and the significance of other artifacts and material objects in the lives of their owners.

While much of the previous book was also written on a metatheoretical level, as indeed were many of my earlier interdisciplinary works, the inclusion of other animal species in my search for a viable theory of the extended self, along with the much-enlarged evolutionary perspective that has entailed has, in turn, necessitated a higher-level approach, as reflected in the concept of the self-field and its origins. Based upon a fusion of field theory and self-organising systems, the metatheoretical framework advanced in this book thus links together the many and diverse elements of an extended self, with all its different forms and levels of expression according to whichever species is involved.

While in many ways, therefore, this volume represents a considerable development beyond my previous works in this area, my basic approach has remained much the same ever since, as an architecture student in the 1960s, I first investigated cybernetics and systems theory in the belief that such an important aspect of human development as architecture, cannot possibly be understood solely from any *single* professional or disciplinary viewpoint. Consistent themes of that earlier research, as they have been of most of my work ever since, were the underlying processes by which new forms and technologies of building evolve over time, together with the cognitive and cultural processes involved in that evolution. As I learnt from my first explorations in self-organising systems and cognitive theories of innovation during that period, new ways of building, like new ideas, do not spring miraculously into being out of nowhere, but are the fruit of some new combination of previously developed forms and ideas. The same insights underpin my theory that the self has evolved out of similar self-organising processes governing the most basic forms of self-awareness common to all sentient creatures, the individual identity of which is crucial to those processes.

Together with *The Extended Self* and the new edition of *Architecture and Identity*,[6] a collection of published essays recording my research and writings since those tentative explorations as an architecture student, the present volume thus completes a trilogy of books focused on the complex factors shaping the evolution and identity of the self and its place in a changing world. My debt to all who have supported the previous works has already been gratefully acknowledged in the first two volumes, so it just remains for me to thank the editorial and production teams at Routledge: Aiyana Curtis, Emilie Coin, Will Bateman, Swapnil Joshi, Paula Devine and Neelukiran for seeing through this third and wholly independent work of theory and scholarship into print and for the care and patience they showed during the whole process.

Chris Abel
Champigny sur Marne.

Introduction

This book addresses certain vital questions concerning the nature of the human self: what it is, how it has evolved and functions, and to what extent it makes us uniquely different, if at all, from other species; questions to which the many theories and investigations cited in the following chapters provide only partial answers. That might seem like a tall order – and it is – but, as with so many other intractable problems that have long evaded any solution, I have come to believe the reason that the self remains so little understood is that the wrong questions have been asked of it. This is partly due to the standard anthropocentric treatment of the subject, which insists on the singularity of the human self, and partly to a lack of appropriate theories which could provide an evolutionary and developmental framework for the self which encompasses other species. More recently, we have also been told that the self is an 'illusion' or 'myth' concocted by the brain to keep us happy, for which no concrete evidence has ever been found – a viewpoint I vigorously dispute, not least for the reason that it diminishes any practical or moral responsibility individuals might have for their own fate or the fates of others.

In pursuing a fresh approach, my starting point has been that, while accepting there are indeed special aspects to the human self, we shall never fully understand what makes us different from other creatures unless we also understand what we have in common. What is needed now in support of that belief, I argue, is a *metatheoretical framework* for the self that embraces what is both specific to humans and to other species, and what is common to them all. Such a framework may be found in a combination of field theory and self-organising systems I call the 'self-field', a cognitive domain extending beyond the physical body, including any artifacts as well as other selves and social factors that may be integral to a functioning, personal self. In short, the self is neither a 'thing' nor an illusion; it is a purposeful, *self-organising system of extended cognition* common to all forms of animal life, the principles of which this book sets out to establish.

Given such a framework, which intentionally covers *any* species that, as a basic matter of survival, must be able to distinguish between their own species and behaviour and that of other species, we can re-frame the differences between human self-consciousness and the self-awareness of other creatures as *relations of degree*, rather than absolute differences. We now know, for example, from the growing body of research into animal cognition and tool use cited here, that some apes, together with a handful of other creatures, are capable of forms of abstract thought and learning previously thought to be exclusive to humans. The principal question that needs to be addressed, therefore, is not whether human beings are capable of reflective and rational thought beyond anything other creatures are capable of, but *to what extent that ability is actually exercised*. To which the answer must be – as the evidence presented in this book indicates – not nearly as much as we like to think.

In raising such questions I do not wish to cast doubt upon the power of human thought and creativity; there is plentiful evidence in the history of architecture alone to prove that. Instead, my aim is to focus attention upon the reasons why, despite those ample gifts – of which language invariably figures large – individuals, as well as organisations of all kinds, are apparently so *resistant to change* to the point that, even when faced with environmental and civilisational collapse,[1] we nevertheless cannot bring ourselves to recognise our individual and collective responsibility for our fate until it is too late to change course.

Clearly, both spoken and written language offer powerful platforms for self-conscious reflection and rational enquiry, whether individually or in groups, that is not available to even our closest ancestors in the evolutionary chain, *if* they are used as such. However, except for those philosophers, scientists and other individuals who make it their business to question what the rest of us are doing and why we are doing it – and even they have their own fixations and blind spots, as recounted in these pages – most people, it would appear, are content to coast along on autopilot, rather than focus attention upon their own personal beliefs and behaviour and their whys and wherefores, unless compelled to do so.[2]

As Michael Polanyi[3] – whose thought permeates much of the present volume as it does my previous work[4] – has taught us, given the reliance we all have upon tacit as opposed to explicit knowledge, that might, in other circumstances, be regarded as perfectly normal. However, these are anything but normal times, and running on autopilot alone is no guarantor of survival, if, indeed, it ever was. Such problems, which have their origins far back in evolutionary history, require more than just an exploration of existing research and sources, though that is an essential part of a project such as this. They also require a *re-working* of key theoretical approaches. Though both field theory and self-organisation have a respectable twentieth-century history as influential theories, each of which affords a metatheoretical approach, neither has been applied directly to the idea of the human self, either separately or in combination, let alone, as in this book, to a more general theory of the self that can be applied to other species. The former has its origins in the physical sciences before being developed as a psychological theory by Kurt Lewin[5] in the 1930s, and later, by Pierre Bourdieu and others as a major theory in social psychology; their aim being to broaden the scope of enquiry from psychologists' focus on individual characteristics to *all* those factors which might affect or influence personal development in some way. The latter theory of self-organising systems grew out of the birth of cybernetics and general systems theory in the 1950s before being given new life as an evolutionary metatheory in the philosophy and science of *complexity*. It is also now commonly associated with *emergence*, as the spontaneous generation of new phenomena (i.e., chemical, biological or behavioural) out of existing systems is called; an approach that has attracted a great deal of attention across many disciplines.

Free of anthropocentric restrictions, a metatheory of the self-field, as I expound in this book, allows us to see what is now commonly described as 'tribal' behaviour in modern societies for what it is: a form of group behaviour little different from that of *Homo sapiens'* ancestors, whose identity and security was dependent upon membership of and loyalty to a group of fellow creatures. Furthermore, in asserting that all sentient creatures are possessed of a self, I argue that it is in the nature of self-organising organisms at *any* level of development that their ultimate priority is the *conservation of the self* through its transformations, no matter what internal and external pressures it might endure. The self is thus an inherently *conservative* system operating mostly at unconscious or semi-conscious levels involving tacit knowledge and skills, only reluctantly changing habits of thought and behaviour when faced with some threat to its stability that it neglects at its peril.

This can take many forms across the evolutionary spectrum, from survival-driven changes in foraging habits to the delayed conversion to a new paradigm by the tradition-bound scientists described by Thomas Kuhn.[6] Disparate as they might seem, however, I contend that the fundamental pattern of self-organisation underlying those transformations is common to *all* evolving selves. Contrary to the neo-Darwinist picture of environmental determinism, therefore, the adjustments required to maintain the organisational stability of the self through life's changes are *not* generally imposed from outside, but, as with all self-organising systems, they *emerge spontaneously* from within the self to meet these new challenges. What may at first appear to an external observer as irrational behaviour, therefore, may be judged from a self-organising perspective as being perfectively rational – at least as far as the organism *itself* perceives things at the time.

Exactly how the actual process of emergence works, however, is a source of as much contention amongst emergentists – as its advocates are called – as it is amongst its critics, and provides one of the principle themes running through this book, closely related as it is with self-organisation. What can nevertheless be said with reasonable assurance is that changes in self-organising systems emerge as a result of some mixture of *upward and downward pressures* (influences, impacts or effects) from factors arising at different *levels* within the system, from the genetic and neurological level at one end to the social and cultural level at the other. Whether explained in mechanistic or other terms, it may also be reasonably claimed from all the related investigations on evolving systems cited here, that the emergence of novel features invariably involves some *combination or re-combination* of pre-existing features. This applies as much to the self's social and technological *extensions* within the self-field as it does to the biological self at its centre; a process that begins with the acquisition of language in early childhood and the *external* manipulation of toys and other objects in a spatial environment, by which the child first learns to classify *things* as well as other living beings within that first small universe.

The same combination and recombination of personal, social and technical elements in the nascent self-field also introduces the child to a material and technological world the future adult will spend his or her entire life relying upon – a world which, the philosopher Bernard Steigler[7] argues, defines us as uniquely *technical beings*. Given the engineering skills as well as the widespread use and manufacture of tools by numerous other creatures recorded here, that claim is questionable, to say the least. However, there can be no denying that human life is saturated by and dependent upon technology to a degree that far exceeds that of any other species, the effects of which humanity now struggles to control.

For Stiegler, the primary reason for that struggle is that the *speed* of techno-logical development outstrips that of other aspects of human culture, which might otherwise contain it, but now lag behind. However, the relative speed of that development does not explain technology's momentum, which, as others argue in this book, to all extents and purposes has a life of its own. I have also written elsewhere on the idea of technological and cultural products such as building forms and automobiles evolving as *self-producing types* and *assemblages* of artifacts, the combination of which has generated whole urban patterns and ways of life – a combination, with its dependence upon fossil fuels, which has had a dire effect upon the planetary environment.[8]

In this book I go further, however, in explaining how the generally conserva-tive character of the human self has contributed to the environmental crisis. The problem lies not just with the common resistance to ideas and events that might challenge the integrity of the self, or of those groups and institutions individuals identify with most, but with the deployment of humankind's advanced techno-logical knowledge and skills to shape the natural environment *solely in favour of human interests*. While niche construction theorists have argued that other creatures also employ their technological capacities in modifying the natural environment to suit themselves, the vital difference between their relatively modest efforts and that of humankind's is that the environmental impact of other creatures is mostly confined to a small area. In stark contrast, supported by a highly effective combination of organisational and technical skills – the two factors are virtually interdependent – *Homo sapiens* has effectively turned the whole planet into a giant exercise in human niche construction, at the expense of practically every other form of life on Earth, a geological transformation which now has a name of its own: the Anthropocene Age.[9]

We must now contemplate the very real possibility, therefore, that in addition to the usual suspects – the fossil fuel industries, the corrupt politicians and a voracious global economic system – there might also be something in the fundamental nature of the human self-field and the self-organising system that holds it together, that is at least partly responsible for the crisis. Neither, as is all too clear, are there any easy solutions to hand. It is alright to suggest we have to change our modern ways and technologies to save both ourselves and the natural resources we depend upon. However, when the human self is so embedded in those same modern ways and technologies that it is nigh on impossible to separate them, this is proving more difficult to achieve than many might have assumed.

These, then, are the principle themes running through this book. Some of them will doubtless be more familiar to certain readers than others. Taken all together, however, what this book offers is a new way of looking at the self, which allows us to see and understand what we have not seen and understood clearly before – namely that the individual human self has evolved from and is driven by the very same self-organising and emergent forces that have created all living creatures on this planet: the invisible but indispensable medium, as I explain it, maintaining mind, body and environment as an *integrated field of being* throughout life's changes.

Far from being what divides humans from those other creatures, therefore, the self is actually what *unites* us with them all. What really *does* set us apart is the unprecedented accumulation of organisational and technological power that has allowed our species to dominate life on Earth, and which now threatens humans with their own destruction, together with all those other life forms already threatened with extinction, for which nature's normal checks and balances were ill prepared.

Much like the combinatorial process of innovation described in these pages, the structure of the book itself brings together concepts and theories from numerous separate disciplines, combining them in new ways, from which, step-by-step, a metatheory of the self that is common to all animal life is constructed. Some of these ideas, like extended cognition, surface repeatedly throughout the book, and, along with field theory and self-organisation, provide the mainstay of my approach. While, at this stage of the venture, such theories may fall short of a full causal explanation – not surprising, given the questions raised in this book about the very idea of causation itself – I take the longer view of the value they offer in explanation of the complex interactions between organism and environment described in the following chapters; interactions that no mechanistic explanation of the animal brain and nervous systems alone can fully account for, and may indeed *never* be able to account for.

That said, though the purpose of this book remains focused on illuminating the bigger picture, due respect is paid throughout to the significant discoveries in the neurosciences and other fields that have thrown light upon many of the more specific aspects of human and non-human animal cognition and behaviour. Discoveries such as the spontaneous expansion of personal body maps involved in the handling of tools and other objects, for example, not only open up new avenues of research into the practical nature of the self-field, but may also, as in this case, support the earlier insights of philosophers into the same phenomena – what Polanyi in particular described in remarkably similar terms as the 'absorption' of objects by the body.[10]

The accommodation of empirical research of this kind at the neurological level, together with the numerous studies of cognition at intermediary and higher levels of human and non-human behaviour referenced in this book – all of which is essential to explaining how the various pieces of the jigsaw puzzle that is the self-field come together – requires frequent shifts of perspective between the micro and macro levels of enquiry. As with the primary theories of self-organisation and emergence, the approach works somewhat like an adjustable camera lens, the focus of which can be changed from close-up to wide-angle and vice-versa, but which always returns to the latter position.

Given the very broad range of topics required of the field view of self-organisation I advocate, my selection of research is also purposefully limited to those studies, whether by famed pioneers or lesser-known researchers, which I believe best illustrate the different arguments and evidence mustered here and the problems they raise that are in need of resolution. Any attempt to provide a more complete survey of the literature on each topic would have required several more volumes, and perhaps more than one working lifetime. It would also defeat the purpose of this book, which is to provide a metatheoretical framework illustrating the various dimensions of the self-field and the processes underlying its evolution and development across animal species. I trust more specialised readers will therefore be content with the references listed here which they can mine for further research, should they so wish.

Equally, no attempt has been made to gloss over any differences of language and style of exposition in the approach and findings of individual researchers, as is often the case, especially with overviews of research where alternative epistemologies are ironed out. On the contrary, the strength of any true metatheory lies in its capacity to embrace those differences within a common schema, while at the same time questioning any anomalies in the research, as in the counter-claims, for example, made for 'mirror neurons' and what they may and may not tell us about empathy. The focus on selected researchers also has the advantage of offering more space for an explanation of their contribution than might otherwise be possible – an important consideration if the different backgrounds and approaches involved are to be understood.

Just as important, especially in a work with a strong psychological content, in the spirit of my concept of a living, vital self, it allows individual researchers sufficient room to explain their beliefs and approach to what, for all science's rigours, is still a human enterprise. As Polanyi – who was an established biochemist before he turned to philosophy – reminds us, scientists are not wholly detached from their work, but are very much personally and emotionally committed in their pursuit of knowledge, the value of which those emotions also signal:

> The personal participation of the knower in the knowledge he believes himself to possess takes place within a flow of passion. We recognise intellectual beauty as a guide to discovery and as a mark of the truth.[11]

Part I

The background

The self, as that which can become an object to itself, is essentially a social structure, and it arises in social experience.

George Herbert Mead, 1934[1]

Chapter 1

The nature–nurture debate

Many of the key issues concerning the substance of personal identities and how they evolve were first aired in what came to be known as the 'nature–nurture' debate. Predating the publication of Charles Darwin's *Origin of Species*,[1] the early debates in eighteenth-century Europe between rationalists and empiricists revolved around the nature of the human mind and associated moral qualities, and were rooted in fixed and oppositional categories of either innate or learned attributes. Darwinian evolutionary, or 'process thinking', as Michael Tomasello[2] observes, should have ended the debate: 'But it did not, and indeed the rise of modern genetics has given it a new and concretized life in the form of genes versus environment'.[3] Either, as geneticists maintained, personal characteristics were predetermined by the genetic makeup inherited from an individual's parents, or, as environmentalists countered, they could be shaped during the course of that person's development and maturation by social, cultural and other environmental factors and conditions.

Those polarised positions have since been considerably modified in the light of more recent advances in evolutionary and developmental theory as well as in theories of extended minds. However, as the following examples show, the dichotomy between approaches continues to influence debates about the different factors shaping personal development, and to guide much of the research on the subject.

Personality traits

Of those human sciences most affected by these debates, psychological studies of behaviour have historically varied widely between those which offer a philo-sophically based and expansive approach covering both individual and social dimensions, and those more common research and clinical approaches that have typically focused on specific cognitive and behavioural characteristics. Each approach also carries with it an associated methodology of empirical research, whether it involves the clinical study or treatment of individual behaviour or some broader statistical investigation, fueling further debate about the relative merits of one approach over another.

For much of the last century, however, practicing and research psychologists have mostly been concerned with tabulating what they identify as key indicators of personal differences likely to affect individual development, and the relative influence of genetic and environmental factors on that development. As with the studies of other human characteristics described below, research into personality traits, for example, rests upon statistical measures of 'heritability', a concept referring to that proportion of individual differences or 'variance' in a population that can be *directly attributed* to genes, while other possible variations are more generally treated as the outcome of environmental influences.

Genetic and environmental factors

Amongst numerous similar studies, Thomas Bouchard[4] lists five commonly accepted traits measured for variance: introversion–extroversion; neuroticism; conscientiousness; agreeableness; and openness. However, up until the early 1980s research into the influence of genetic factors on personality traits was confined to relatively small samples of identical twins living with their biological parents, compared to twins living with adoptive parents. Environmental influences were also generally equated with those experienced within the home environment. The heritability of traits amongst twins due to genetic factors was typically estimated at around 50 per cent, while the influence of a shared home environment on personality was found to be small down to negligible.

Recent research using more sophisticated techniques and much larger samples of twins reared separately by different parents, as well as those who have been reared together by biological or adoptive parents, has since modified those earlier findings somewhat, allocating 7 per cent of heritability to shared environmental influences, while confirming a far stronger influence of genetic factors of just over 40 per cent, from which Bouchard concludes:

> The similarity we see in personality between biological relatives is almost entirely genetic in origin. If we wish to study environmental influences on personality development in families, we must look for influences that operate differentially among children in the same family.[5]

However, while acknowledging the importance of genetically inherited traits in shaping personalities, Bouchard also suggests that people are nevertheless *not* necessarily limited by their genetic inheritance, but may 'help to create their own environments' as they develop and adapt themselves to life in the wider social world. In turn, he predicts that 'unraveling the role human individual differences play in evolution is the next big hurdle, and its solution will turn the behaviour genetics of human personality from a descriptive discipline to an explanatory one'.[6]

Cognitive abilities

In addition to personality traits, comparative tests of intelligence feature prominently in the nature–nurture debate. However, beyond the broad measures of general intelligence, better known as IQ tests, the value of which has been frequently disputed,[7] intelligence is more precisely expressed as a set of distinctive cognitive abilities that also vary greatly within the population.

As with the above studies of personality, twin studies provide the mainstay of research into genetic versus environmental influences on cognitive abilities. However, despite initial assumptions by researchers in this field that environmental factors were more important in cognitive achievements than genetic histories, the findings also indicate the importance of those histories – not so much, however, as the ultimate determinant of those achievements, but more as a *moderating influence* on the learning process. Writing on their investigations into verbal and spatial abilities, Robert Plomin and John DeFries,[8] for example, observe that, while psychologists had previously favored environmental explanations for individual differences in learning, viewpoints have since changed:

> Most psychologists have begun to embrace a more balanced view: one in which nature and nurture interact in cognitive development. During the past decades, studies in genetics have pointed to a substantial role for heredity in molding the components of intellect, and researchers have even begun to track down the genes involved in cognitive function. These findings do not refute the notion that environmental factors shape the learning process. Instead they suggest that *differences in people's genes affect how easily they learn* [emphasis added].[9]

Verbal and spatial performance

Plomlin and DeFries compared the verbal and spatial performance of genetically identical twins raised in the same family household with the performance of twins raised separately, one with the biological family and the other in an adoptive home, together with studies of genetically unrelated children raised together in the same adoptive home. Tests of verbal ability covered vocabulary, fluency and understanding of categories. Tests of spatial ability included recognising which geometrical figures combined to form a given whole, and identifying which of a number of alternative figures could be mentally rotated to produce another, pre-selected figure.

The two researchers observe that twin studies of verbal and spatial ability involving both identical and fraternal twins[10] spread over several decades and countries have produced 'remarkably consistent results', indicating markedly higher similarities of performance between identical twins than between fraternal twins. More surprising, however, was the discovery that resemblances between identical and fraternal twins *continued well into old age*, contradicting assumptions that the influence of genes reduced with the accumulation of personal experience through time. Extrapolated for the general population, the combined results suggest that 'genetics accounts for about 60 percent of the variance in verbal ability and about 50 percent of the variance in spatial ability'.[11]

Related cognitive studies of adopted twins have yielded similar findings, supporting the view that family environments generally do not contribute to cognitive similarities amongst family members. Moreover, during the very period when one might expect newly learned skills to have their greatest impact on cognitive development '*genetic influence increases* [emphasis added] during childhood, so that by the mid-teens, heritability reaches a level comparable with that seen in adults'.[12]

Epigenetic factors

Along with the technical miracles of recombinant DNA technology in the 1970s and the Human Genome Project in the 1990s, 'the century of the gene',[13] as it has been called, also saw other advances in molecular biology pointing to a far more complex picture of the interaction between genetic and environmental factors, undermining the privileged position of the gene.[14] By the end of the century, it could be confidently asserted that: 'nearly all responsible researchers agree that human traits are *jointly determined* [emphasis added] by both nature and nurture, though they may disagree about the relative contributions of each'.[15]

Nessa Carey[16] vividly describes epigenetics, as the new approach is known,[17] in more familiar terms: 'We talk about DNA as if it's a template, like a mould for a car part in a factory [...] But DNA isn't really like that. It's more like a script'.[18] A script, moreover, that can be interpreted and later *reinterpreted* in significant ways, in much the same way as any drama or movie script.[19] Amongst the earliest evidence of epigenetic inheritance effects, Carey cites the groundbreaking studies in Holland on the long-term health impact of the infamous Dutch Hunger Winter of 1944–1945, when the population under wartime German control starved, resulting in 20,000 deaths before the country was liberated and food supplies were restored to normal.[20] The survivors included many pregnant women, and, due to the well-kept records of the Dutch health service, epidemiologists were able to track the after-effects of the famine on those womens' children. While short-term impacts on the health of the foetus and new born might have been expected, they also found that, depending on whether the women suffered the most from malnutrition early or late in the pregnancy, there were differential and *permanent* effects in the health of their growing children, including abnormal body sizes and weights.[21] Though having inherited their mother's normal genes, the health records show their children never fully recovered from the terrible environmental conditions in which they were conceived and born. In some instances, the same characteristics were even passed on to the next one or two generations in the same family. Given such examples, Carey writes:

> There has to be a mechanism that brings out this mismatch between the genetic script and the final outcome. These epigenetic effects must be caused by some sort of physical change, some alternations in the vast array of molecules that make up the cells of every living organism […] In this model, epigenetics can be defined as the set of modifications to our genetic material that can change the way genes are switched on or off, but which don't alter the genes themselves […] Crucially, *we are finally starting to unravel the missing link between nature and nurture, how our environment talks to us and alters us, sometimes forever* [emphasis added].[22]

Transgenerational effects

In the case of the Dutch famine the epigenetic changes had all taken place during pregnancy and were triggered by the metabolic effects of the mothers' malnutrition. However, later human studies supported by numerous and more exacting experiments with animals in controlled conditions point to epigenetic changes of yet broader significance. One such human study, also cited by Carey, focused on an isolated group of Swedish men and their sons and grandsons following a similar drastic period of food shortages. Based on historical records, researchers found that if the fathers suffered from malnutrition during their own early childhood, followed by restoration of a normal diet, their sons would be less likely to die from cardiovascular disease. Conversely, access to plentiful food during a father's early childhood followed by extended malnutrition *increased* the likelihood of such disease in their offspring. In this case, since, as Carey puts it, 'men don't get pregnant [so] they can't contribute to the developmental environment of the fetus',[23] epigenetic mechanisms responding to the lack or surfeit of food available to the fathers would be more likely to be the cause of any phenotypic changes in their children.

A different but equally significant study into the transgenerational health effects of severely unbalanced diets involved numerous laboratory experiments with overfed and overweight male rats (males were chosen to eliminate the pregnancy factor) with Type 2 diabetic symptoms, mated with females on normal diets. The resultant progeny across two generations had normal body weights like their mothers, but, like their fathers, suffered from diabetes-type abnormalities. Although not conclusive, 'the most likely explanation is that diet induces epigenetic effects that can be transmitted from father to child'.[24]

Gene regulation

Richard Francis,[25] who also examined the research on the Dutch famine case together with many other related studies of epigenetic effects across family generations, stresses the key role of cells in mediating between environment and genes:

> Different kinds of cells respond differently to the same environmental factor, whether it is social stress or food deprivation in the womb. As such, and despite the fact that all of the cells in our body have the same genes, *any environmental effect in you is cell-specific* [emphasis added].[26]

Other research suggests the impact of still-wider environmental factors of both a social and cultural nature. For example, explaining how gene regulation works, i.e., what controls the *expression* of genes, Francis writes:

> Some of the most fascinating forms of gene regulation are *initiated outside of the body* [emphasis added]. Social interactions are a particularly important source of gene regulation. For example, in animals from fish to humans, the outcome of competitive interactions can influence testosterone levels, with all the consequent effects on gene activity.[27]

As an example, Francis relates the story of Jose Canseco, a Cuban-American, Major League Baseball star and whistle-blower, who, after retiring in 2001, wrote a book exposing the widespread use of anabolic steroids throughout the sport, later admitting he was and remained a regular user. Now common knowledge due to numerous related sporting scandals, anabolic steroids are synthetic forms of androgens: male sex hormones, particularly testosterone, used for muscle building. However, the regular use of steroids produces numerous physical and psychological side effects, including loss of fertility, low libido, aggression and depression, during which the normal production of testosterone shuts down, causing users like Canseco to compensate by taking other synthetic hormones, for which he was eventually arrested after his retirement.

The reasons for these wildly differing side effects have to do with those genetic control functions described by Francis. Androgens, like testosterone, are examples of what are called 'transcription factors': chemical agents responsible for activating genes in their cells. However, they can only bind to a gene by first binding to the cell's 'receptors', and while all cells have the same genes, different types of cells have different receptors responding to different signals. Any synthetic steroids absorbed in the body only activate genes in those specific cells with androgen-sensitive receptors. Some of those receptors reside in brain cells, including parts of the brain controlling libido and emotions like aggression. Since anabolic steroids of the kind taken by Canseco circulate widely through the body, some of those steroids also reach the brain, hence the diverse psycho-logical as well as physical side effects.

New terms of debate

A full half-century after Rachel Carson[28] published *Silent Spring*, her epochal exposé of the wanton destruction of wildlife by the uncontrolled use of pesticides, the chemical saturation of the environment she and other environmentalists have fought against, continues to wreak havoc on human lives as well as other species. A recent study cited by Carey, for example, into the impact of harmful toxins in the environment on testosterone levels and their epigenetic effects suggests wider implications. The specific toxin studied was Vinclozolin, a fungicide com-monly used in the wine industry. If absorbed by mammals it can block signals from testosterone hormones to related cells, with deleterious consequences for sexual development and fertility rates. Given to pregnant rats when the male embryos were developing testes, 90 per cent of the offspring were found to have both testicular defects and reduced fertility. Still more significant, the same negative effects endured for as many as three subsequent generations. Pointing to other, equally vexed issues of environmental quality, Carey writes:

> Effects such as these are one of the reasons why some authorities are begin-ning to investigate if artificial hormones and hormone disrupters in the environment (from excretion of chemicals present in the contraceptive pill, to certain pesticides) have the potential to cause subtle, but potentially transgenerational effects in the human population.[29]

As participants on both sides of the nature–nurture debate are coming to realise, the mounting evidence of epigenetic inheritance mechanisms oper-ating at different stages and levels of human development undermines the basic oppositional premises of the argument, transforming the terms of debate.[30] In place of development being primarily driven by *either* nature *or* nurture, it is now increasingly seen as being shaped by something more like a dialogue – recall Carey's genetic 'script' metaphor – between *both* forms of development. Hilary and Steven Rose[31] highlight the radical implications for evolutionary theory of epigenetic 'switches' in activating genes:

> Alterations in the timing of these switches may result in huge changes in the adult phenotype, producing new variations on which evolution can act. Genes are no longer thought of as acting independently but rather in constant interaction with each other and with the multiple levels of the environment in which they are embedded.[32]

Notably, they argue, molecular genetics supports the argument that 'natural selection must work on entire lifecycles, not just on the adult', something which was well understood by Darwin himself, they suggest, but which was mostly ignored by his followers, 'fixated as they were on genes rather than organisms'.[33]

Neural plasticity

Advances in the neurosciences now also proffer new insights into the biological mechanisms underlying human cognition and behaviour, with important implications for the nature–nurture debate. Writing of the impact of these developments on that debate, Stephen Kosslyn[34] observes:

> The old 'nature versus nurture' argument is being revived, and proponents on both sides are often making use of new tools from a number of related disciplines, including cognitive psychology, developmental neurobiology, brain imaging and computer science.[35]

The discovery by neuroscientists that the brain is capable of 'rewiring' itself far into adult life is of special interest to much else in this book as it challenges previous assumptions concerning the *malleability* of neural circuits, with profound implications of the effects on the brain of technological and cultural changes in how it is actually *used* – crucial factors examined in more detail in later parts of this book. Defined in 1991 by the neurobiologist Marcus Jacobson, 'neural plasticity' as it is called, refers to certain types of adjustments of the nervous system to external or internal changes, such as changes to the environmental milieu picked up through the sensory systems in the normal course of development,[36] or internal changes that might occur as a result of brain injury. Though there is evidence from both human and animal studies that some degree of neural plasticity is probably common to the nervous systems of all animal species, it appears to be most marked, Kosslyn explains, in specific regions of the human cerebral cortex – the frontal part of the brain – in areas that serve the higher brain functions: 'including language, mathematical ability, musical ability, and "executive functions"'.[37]

Malleability through adulthood

However, while it was known that the human brain is more malleable during infancy and early childhood than in later life – the crucial period of language acquisition as well as other basic patterns of behaviour – recent research also suggests that malleability of the nervous system persists throughout adulthood and even into old age:

> The ability of the brain to mold itself in response to changed environmental conditions does not end with puberty. The brain, and especially the human brain, undergoes important changes in its organization *throughout the lifespan* [emphasis added].[38]

As a result, the subject of adult plasticity in human development is now the focus of intense study. Amongst the well-established cellular mechanisms by which the adult brain adjusts to changes in the environment, the *frequency of activation* of neural connections is known to facilitate learning. Thus, *repeated practice* of given tasks leads to increases of both speed and accuracy in performing those tasks. The findings confirm the theory postulated by the French neurobiologist JP Changeux, who contends that, as large as the human genome is, it is simply not large enough to provide an exact specification of each of the billions of synapses – the electrical contacts between neurons – that are formed during brain development, many of which in the early stages seem to grow at random. The discrepancy poses the question: 'How can organized function emerge from a nerve network with random connections?'[39] Changeux's answer, Kosslyn explains, is that such organisation could emerge from inputs to the nervous system that have *recurrent patterns*. Repeated inputs of this kind during development, Changeux proposes, lead to some of the randomly formed synaptic contacts being incorporated into functioning neural circuits and persisting as *stabilised components* of those circuits. Those synaptic contacts that are not stabilised and utilised this way just disappear, while new neurons fill the gaps so the overall numbers remain steady.

Summarising the research, Kosslyn concludes that plasticity is mainly a feature of complex neural systems that are more responsive to environmental inputs than simple nervous systems, which 'develop entirely according to fixed genetic programs'. This applies as much, however, to differences in the complexity of nervous systems within the *same* individual being, as between different species, such as between primates and other animals. Thus plasticity is generally thought to be limited in those regions of the human brain controlling motor actions and sensory functions, and stronger in those cortical regions responsible for the higher functions like speech. Moreover, many higher brain functions do not develop *at all* without extensive external pressures and support, of which *human literacy*, he suggests, offers a good example: 'The child learns to read *only if taught* [emphasis added], and a person may go through life without ever acquiring this skill'.[40] In the latter case, the cortical region in the illiterate brain normally handling such skills simply cannot process written letters and words at all.

Embodied development

In contrast to Kosslyn's focus on the neural mechanisms of development, Willis Overton[41] offers what he describes as a relational metatheory of 'embodied development' inspired by the phenomenological psychology of Merleau-Ponty,[42] which he suggests renders the nature–nurture debate redundant. Setting out his case within the broader historical debate between reductionist and holistic approaches to understanding human behaviour, Overton argues that embodied development represents a movement away from conventional research based on splitting variations in behavioural scores between genetic and environmental influences, towards an approach that places the active human body at the centre of developmental experience:

> Embodiment is the claim that perception, thinking, feelings, desires – that is, the way we behave, experience and live the world – is contextualized by our being active agents with this particular kind of body. In other words, the kind of body we have is a precondition for our having the kind of behaviors, experiences and meanings that we have.[43]

From the perspective of embodied development, any approach that treats genes as independently operating units having direct causal effects on psychological functions is therefore based on a conceptual confusion. Genes and their cellular counterparts are *themselves*, Overton argues, the product of biological–environmental interactions – a developmental process which continues until body and environment achieve their ultimate relationship, as with the relation of individual to culture, and is thus synthesised as the psychological person.

Against the splitting of genes and environment which characterises the nature-nurture debate, a relational metatheory based on holistic principles as Overton defines it, stipulates that 'the whole is not an aggregate of discrete elements but an organized and self-organizing system of parts, each part being defined by its relation to other parts and to the whole'.[44] Similarly, for Overton the resolution of opposite identities implicit in the gene-environment debate lies in moving 'away from the extremes to the centre and above the conflict and to here discover a novel system that will coordinate the two conflicting systems'; that novel system being the relational theory of embodied development Overton expounds.

Systems approach

Richard Lerner,[45] who writes in the same volume of essays as Overton, likewise argues that studies on the influence of genetic histories on psychological and behavioural traits, or 'behaviour genetics' as it is called, are conceptually and methodologically unsound, based as they are on an outdated view of genetic determinism. However, despite the well-published criticisms from within psychology and the lack of support coming from molecular geneticists themselves, research in the genetic heritability of such diverse behaviours as morality, temperament and even television viewing continues to be well funded and widely published. While competition between rival approaches is a normal part of scientific development itself, the problem in this case, as Lerner writes, is that the findings of behaviour genetics are too often and too easily taken up as prescriptions for social policy, with the result that other, more complex and difficult strategies to improve the *conditions* of human development are regarded as a waste of time:

They could be construed, in fact, as inhumane exercises that falsely elevated the hopes of people whose problematic plights were not due to their social circumstances (e.g., social injustice or the absence of opportunity, equity, or democracy) but rather to their fixed and immutable genetic inheritances.[46]

Like Overton, Lerner argues that the conceptual frames separating nature from nurture have no foundation in reality and proposes a 'developmental systems' approach in their place, in which 'neither genes nor context by themselves cause development'.[47] Instead, it is the *relations amongst variables* that are responsible for the fusion between levels within the integrated developmental system, and which drive the developmental process, an argument he supports by numerous references across disciplines to research along related lines.

Relational approaches of this kind in the way human behaviour is viewed are a far cry from the narrow focus and related statistical methodologies governing the research programmes on the heritability of personality traits and other personal characteristics described at the beginning of this chapter. In promoting his approach, Overton also cites the relevant work of leading neuroscientists on a mind–body synthesis, together with research on embodied action at what he describes as the three principle levels of development: biological, cultural and person-centred embodiment, each of which involves a meeting of different disciplines and perspectives.

However, while both Overton and Lerner provide cogent critiques of the treatment of nature and nurture as opposing concepts, with all its negative consequences, their expositions stop well short of a functional explanation of their systems approach or of the self-organising system that Overton briefly refers to, and how it might actually work to bridge the different levels of development he describes. Given the difficult philosophical and scientific issues at stake and the rapid evolution of theoretical developments in this area, that is hardly surprising, but it leaves many vital questions unresolved. In particular, Overton's suggestion that a 'synthesis of wholes' entails a movement from opposite extremes towards some kind of centre ground hardly explains the self-referential character of self-organising systems, or the spontaneous emergence of new structures in response to external and internal pressures – vital, interrelated issues that, as explained below, also have long histories in the metatheoretical literature, as does the systems approach itself, from which there is much more to learn.

Chapter 2

Inheritance systems

Though titled *The Origin of Species,*[1] it has been pointed out that Darwin's original work did not actually deal explicitly with the subject of his title at all. For Darwin, the endless variety of species he and his followers identified and gave names to in their explorations were, as Massimo Pigliucci and Gerard Muller[2] describe it, no more than 'arbitrary demarcation lines imposed by the human mind on an otherwise continuous process of diversification'[3] driven by natural selection – the real focus of the book. It was only much later in the mid-twentieth century, as a key element in the formulation of the Modern Synthesis (MS) of evolutionary science, that the concept of species itself was accepted as the fundamental unit of the biological hierarchy. Henceforth, the process of *speciation*, by which each biological species evolved as an identifiable entity, similar to yet also separate in distinctive ways from its nearest relatives, was to be a major focus of evolutionary biology.

However, while the focus on speciation took evolutionary theory a major step beyond neo-Darwinism, further issues of the identification and evolution of species, with all their variations and traits, and how different inheritance systems interact, have generated new bodies of research in themselves. The question of *innovation* in particular, and of how novel traits or even whole species arise – a problem for which neo-Darwinism had no answer – is paramount in the following discussions. From the idea that many organisms themselves are perfectly capable of modifying their environments in favour of their own survival, to the cumulative impacts of learning and cooperative behaviour, the complex picture that emerges of gene-culture coevolution, and the evolution of mind itself, is a far cry from the one-way Darwinist picture of environmental determinism. As Michael Tomasello, whose work on those cumulative impacts is discussed in a later chapter, writes: 'Organisms inherit their environments as much as they inherit their genomes – this cannot be stressed too much'.[4]

Evo–Devo

Since the 1970s, the problem of species evolution and, in particular, understanding the combined genetic and developmental processes that generate changes in the morphology or 'phenotype' of an organism from generation to generation, has been the special subject of evolutionary developmental biology, or 'Evo–Devo' as it is called. According to classical neo-Darwinian theory, physical characteristics can only be inherited through the DNA codes of the gene line, a one-way procedure reinforced by the so-called 'Weismann's barrier', a principle of cellular development named after its discoverer that restricts the flow of information from the body to the gene line. Any variations of the phenotype from that line are due to chance mutations, creating the necessary variety upon which natural selection can work, leaving only those variations best suited to their environments. Population genetics and the molecular discoveries later encompassed by the MS also unveiled the specific biochemical mechanisms involved in genetic inheritance and variation within whole populations of species, advancing our knowledge in those vital areas. However, as Marc Kirshner and John Gerhart[5] write, they left the basic question of what drives phenotypic variation open: 'What was still missing were the cellular and molecular mechanisms underlying the generation of the phenotype, particularly the anatomy, physiology, and behaviour of multicellular organisms'.[6]

Dismissing the orthodox unilateral picture of environmental selection pressures dictating phenotypic changes, Kirshner and Gerhart assert: 'Novelty arises from an interplay between the properties of the organism and mutation under selection'.[7] This does not of itself undermine the importance of genetic variation and mutation in the generation of new species. However, according to the authors' theory of 'facilitated variation', it spreads the burden of creativity in evolution more widely, allocating a significant role to the *existing* phenotype and affiliated developmental patterns in determining the outcome of selection pressures. Robust physiological characteristics already present in the phenotype may therefore modify the effects of genetic variation which, in turn, generates still more variation in populations, increasing the rate of evolutionary change in an ever-widening circle of innovation.

Innovation and novelty

Gerd Muller[8] is equally critical of the shortcomings of the MS in his investigations of the effects of epigenetic innovation on evolving body forms. Despite implicit prior recognition of the importance of innovation in evolutionary theory, the MS, he contends, overlooks the problem of how morphological traits and their combinations originate and stabilise into reproducible forms. Since the 1990s, however, research on phenotypic and epigenetic evolution has focused attention on previously neglected issues concerning the origins of structural complexity, rapid changes of form and associated physiological matters. Hitherto, all changes of phenotypic form, whether small or large, gradual or non-gradual, were treated as *variants*. However, the new insights afforded by Evo–Devo, with its more concentrated focus on the methods of phenotypic change, 'meant that innovation and novelty could not just be treated in the same way as variation'.[9]

Much of the research into the developmental processes affecting phenotypic innovation described by Muller involves modeling cellular behaviour, such as cell-to-cell signalling and environment-cellular interactions of the sort now common in other fields of epigenetic research described in this book. However, while accepting such mechanisms as perpetual background conditions, Muller adopts a more radical 'systems-orientated approach' toward the macroscopic outcomes of epigenetic innovation. Pointing to the assimilation of discrete new elements into established body plans and the progressive individualisation of the body features of others, Muller asks: 'Given the basic architecture, how could unprecedented elements be added if variation were the only mechanistic possibility?'[10]

The answer, he proposes, lies in the mixture of developmental systems intervening between genotype and phenotype, creating the conditions for phenotypic evolution. Typically, such systems 'are characterized by cellular self-organization, feedback regulation and environment dependence'.[11] The combination of autonomous properties, self-regulation and ability to respond to both local and global conditions ensure such systems are neither mere agents of deterministic genetic programmes nor the sole product of natural selection, but are capable of responding in *irregular, non-linear ways* to changes in the initiating conditions. While natural selection therefore retains a significant role both as an initiating cause and later stabilising factor, the morphological outcomes themselves result from developmental properties of another kind. In such cases:

> Gradual or non-gradual regimes of evolutionary change can be developmentally transformed into *discontinuous phenotypic outcomes* [emphasis added]. These may appear as losses of traits, or as combinations of previously independent traits, or as the kernels of new traits not present in the ancestral condition.[12]

Homological thinking

In his extensive study of morphological characters, or 'homology' as it is called, Gunter Wagner[13] likewise focuses on novel characters and body plans, the evolution of which, he contends, is more diverse than that allowed for by the neo-Darwinian route of genetic inheritance. As the standard MS version presents it, subject to the rigours of natural selection *all* character traits, including morphological traits, are transmitted *indirectly* from generation to generation by transmission of the genes that control phenotypic and character development. Central to this strictly functional and genetically directed picture is the idea that *character identity* is the summary product of features selected for their environmental suitability, thus ensuring the genetic survival of the organism:

> This is certainly true, at least in the short term, that is, over several generations and likely within the lifetime of a single species. Over longer

periods of evolutionary history, however, *the correspondence between genes and character identity decreases* [emphasis added].[14]

The reason for the decreasing influence of genes on character identity, Wagner explains, is that genes only produce a *limited number* of copies, the phenotypic outcomes of which are subject to the influence of developmental and other epigenetic factors at each step in the evolution of a species.[15] The older the species, therefore, the greater the proportional impact of developmental elements in the *existing* phenotype over future development of the species. However, the same epigenetic factors have the effect of *increasing* the efficiency of natural selection by limiting the possible range of phenotypic variations to only those with the best adaptive potential, and excluding weaker variations due to random mutations.

Anatomical trees

Like other key ideas in the Extended Synthesis, homology challenges entrenched conceptions of how species evolve. As pictured in the familiar Darwinian tree of descent, the genetic lineage of each distinct species follows a direct line through to common ancestors lower down in the tree. However, the elegant simplicity of the hierarchical tree, which captured popular as well as scientific imaginations, conceals a more complex network of genetic inheritance in which *homologous genes* – that is, sets of genes responsible for the development of *specific body parts* – are *duplicated* across several branches of the species tree. Other researchers cited by Wagner go so far as to suggest that individualised body parts form lineages much like species do, and can thus be analysed in similar ways with their own homologous or anatomical trees. Wagner himself takes the idea no further, but if true, then combined together, species trees and anatomical trees would form a *heterarchical* structure of interlinked branches, rather than a strictly hierarchical structure of descent – a diverse picture with many more possible outcomes than the Darwinian tree.

Accordingly, Wagner suggests that evolutionary biologists need to put aside their association of phenotypic character with body plans and features particular to a species, and rethink character identity instead in terms of *individual* body parts, or *homologs* – which may be shared between quite different species. Arguing in conclusion for an Evo–Devo approach, in addition to the focus on the developmental aspects of evolutionary change Wagner suggests a new mode of thought has emerged: 'homological thinking' as a form of historical explanation of the phylogenetic origins of body parts. Richer in biological detail and more accurate in its depiction of the diverse lineage of different body parts than functionalist explanations, homological thinking, he writes, 'may allow us to capture dimensions of organismal biology that have been obscured by other styles of thinking because they have screened out the organism and its structure from consideration'.[16]

Niche construction

The exclusive focus of the MS on genetic inheritance mechanisms and natural selection has also been criticized for holding evolutionary biologists back from integrating their own findings with potentially relevant research in other new disciplines, or engaging with the emergence of higher-level developmental processes. A major barrier to progress along these fronts, John Odling-Smee[17] argues, has been the reluctance of evolutionary biologists to acknowledge the ubiquitous significance of 'niche construction'.[18] Now a fast-growing body of theory and research, the term refers to the capacity of organisms to change their natural environments at least in part to suit themselves, including, at various levels of animal activity, the building of shelters and other constructions (i.e., nests, burrows and dams, etc.). In so doing, nature's creatures are able to modify some of the selection pressures they and their descendants may be affected by. It follows that:

> The adaptations of organisms cannot be exclusively consequences of organisms responding to autonomous selection pressures in environments. Sometimes they must involve organisms responding to selection pressures *previously transformed* [emphasis added] by their own, or by their ancestors', niche-constructing activities.[19]

Challenging the predominance of genetic theory running through the MS, niche construction theory posits two secondary inheritance systems that can influence phenotypic evolution: *niche inheritance* and *ecological inheritance*, the combination of which extends the MS into Evo–Devo territory. Odling-Smee reasons that, firstly, since niche inheritance passes on selective environments modified by populations of organisms to successive generations, evolution contributes more than genes to the development of individual organisms. Secondly, citing similar cases to those presented in the first chapter, he points to epigenetics for evidence of transgenerational inheritance of phenotypic variations acquired during the lifetime of individuals: 'the prior development (devo-) of individual organisms may influence the subsequent evolution (evo-) of populations'.[20]

Two-way picture of evolution

Niche construction theory thus effectively displaces natural selection's unidirectional picture of the evolution of passive organisms shaped by a ruthless and indifferent environment with a dynamic, two-way picture of mutual impacts. The MS assumes that, having been gifted with a set of genes from their ancestors, new organisms thereafter develop within an environment over which they have no influence themselves, but which *independently* determines which of their species survives. However, niche construction theory blesses organisms at birth with a more extensive range of gifts combining both genetic and ecological inheritances, some of the latter being the production of their predecessors' own creativity. Following Richard Dawkins' concept of an 'extended phenotype',[21] niche construction theorists also include the effects an organism *itself* has in shaping its own material environment as an integral part of its phenotypic evolution. Thus, just as Dawkins pictured the snail's shell as an extension of the phenotype, so, it may be argued, can a bird's nest or an anthill be regarded as phenotypic extensions of the creatures building those structures:

> Development therefore ceases to be the unfolding of gene programs in the context of independent environments, and becomes a matter of niche regulation by *phenotypically plastic* [emphasis added], niche-constructing organisms. Niche regulation starts at the moment of origin of a new organism, and continues for the rest of an organism's life.[22]

Furthermore, if repeated by many organisms over many generations the niche regulation activities of specific populations can have knock-on environmental effects with far wider ecological consequences, amounting to a form of *ecosystem engineering*. By altering the flow of water and nutrients through an area, beaver dams, for example, can affect not only the future well-being of the local beaver population itself, but also, depending on whether such changes modify the selection pressures on other species inhabiting the same area, they may have lasting evolutionary effects on those species. Amongst their major dam-building achievements, for example, Odling-Smee observes that beavers have created centuries-old wetlands, 'long enough, relative to the short generational turn-over of many species in riparian ecosystems, for them to evolve in response to beaver-modified selection pressures'.[23]

However, not all niche-constructing behaviours are so creative. In a previous work, Odling-Smee et al[24] were also careful to distinguish between *positive* and *negative* niche-construction efforts and their respective environmental effects. The former *strengthens* the selective advantages of niche constructing organisms over their non-niche constructing rivals by 'changing one or more factors in the environment to *enhance the match* between features of the organism and factors in their environment [emphasis added]'. By contrast, negative niche construction typically *reduces* any biological advantages of a species 'by modifying factors in the population's environment in a manner that *leads to a weaker match* [emphasis added] between the features of the organisms and the factors in their environment';[25] an outcome, as we shall see, which accurately describes the impact of humankind's own, far more extensive efforts in modifying the natural environment.

Sociocultural learning

More recently, niche construction theorists have also found evidence of *social niche construction* amongst animal populations in addition to human societies.

Odling-Smee's frequent co-researcher and author Kevin N. Laland[26] takes an ambitious stand in describing the goals of his own research group: 'We not only seek a scientific explanation for the origins of technology, science, language, and the arts, but endeavor to trace the roots of these phenomena right back to the realm of animal behaviour'.[27] Laland's principal thesis is that, in presenting the manifold forms of human culture as the product of a superior human mind that had somehow evolved ahead of its actual achievements, thus making them possible, cultural anthropologists and evolutionary theorists – as other theorists cited in this book have done – were approaching the matter from the wrong direction: 'Humanity's success is sometimes accredited to our cleverness, but culture is actually what makes us smart'.[28]

The origins of human culture, Laland argues, lie in specific patterns of animal social behaviour involving the capacity to *copy* those behaviours that favoured their survival, from rats learning to avoid poisonous foods from chemical cues left by other rats, to the now well-known variety of tool-making and using traditions amongst chimpanzees across Africa, first discovered by Jane Goodall in 1960. Developmental research has also since confirmed that such habits are acquired by young chimpanzees closely observing and then imitating their mother's tool-making and using skills; the more time spent in such lessons the more skilled the offspring become. Similarly, the tool-making behaviours of Orangutans involve such skills as making 'cups' for drinking rainwater from leaves and constructing umbrella-like shelters to protect themselves from the elements (see also Chapter 8).

Alternative learning strategies

However, if the simple imitation of behaviour amongst the same species was all there was to it, there might be as many negative as positive effects for that species. Fortunately, not all individual members of a group copy slavishly. What seems to work best from an evolutionary perspective, Laland argues, is a strategic mixture of social learning and what is called *asocial* learning, in which humans as well as other animals learn from their *own* efforts, as in trial and error. That way, the relative benefits or 'fitness' in evolutionary terms, of merely copying the behaviour of others are being constantly tested by the *alternative actions* of individual members of the group. Consequently, should there be some unexpected change in selective environmental pressures – shortages of normal food supplies compelling a change of diet or foraging habits, for example – the group would not be caught entirely unawares.

The problem for evolutionary biologists and other scientists like Laland with this orderly picture of one method of learning balancing the other is that, since there is always an unknown number of possible alternative behaviour patterns available to both individuals and groups, there is no way of putting the adaptive effectiveness of strategic learning of this kind to any sort of rigorous test. To solve the problem, inspired by the model of the 'Prisoner's Dilemma' – an economics game with two competing players designed to explore the payoffs and penalties of individual decision-making strategies – Laland and his research group created their own experimental 'social learning game'. Designed to simulate the alternative learning strategies and outcomes of groups of individuals forced to survive on a hypothetical tropical island, the computer-based game offered the voluntary players (agents) three principle moves: 'innovate' (asocial learning); 'observe' (social learning/copying), and 'exploit' (putting the lessons learnt to effective use).[29] Once familiarised with the three moves, players were invited to devise the most effective adaptive strategy from their options in response to a range of environmental scenarios.[30]

Successful strategies

Amongst the more surprising findings of the game, Laland found, was that it is possible to learn more than is needed to succeed in the game. Consequently, the most successful strategies involved a relatively *small* amount of time (5–10%) devoted to either social or asocial learning, compared to *exploiting* a learned behaviour through repeated use:

> This implied that the way to get on in life was to do a quick bit of learning and then EXPLOIT, EXPLOIT, EXPLOIT until you die. That is a sobering lesson for someone like myself who has spent his whole life in school or university.[31]

Of the two learning moves, the successful strategies also involved spending more time on copying than on innovating – another sobering result for the creatively minded. Further analysis, however, revealed more subtle processes at work amongst the players, suggesting that *too much* copying also incurred a cost penalty in the time lost on exploiting the copied behaviour. More serious still, playing 'observe' had not added any new behaviours to the agent's repertoire, thus potentially limiting the capacity of players to adapt to any changes in their environments – a defect repeated in over half of the same moves played out – whereas playing 'innovate' always produced new behaviour patterns, if not always useful ones.

The contradictory results suggest that, as with the beneficial effects of genetic mutations in generating larger pools of variants, even small amounts of copying errors would 'generate enough biological diversity to allow social learners to respond adaptively to environmental change'.[32] The number of variants so produced need not be large, but because so many copies are produced by so many individuals the variants have a good chance of surviving the death of the individuals that created them, along with the more accurate copies. Laland concludes: 'simple, poorly implemented, and inflexible social learning does not increment biological fitness, but smart, sophisticated, and flexible social learning does'.[33]

Cooperative behaviour

As sound as niche construction theory is in principle, however, aside from the decision to copy others it is hard to identify any elements in Laland's simulations that specifically address the idea of *social* niche construction that he and his team claim to be researching. In this respect, Laland's research programme may be usefully compared with that of Catherine Key and Leslie Aiello,[34] who argue that the key to the evolution of human organisation lies in *cooperation* – a concept involving a complex range of social behaviours far beyond just copying. As with the above investigations, they find supporting evidence in studies of non-human primates, including chimpanzees, which they determined have the widest repertoire of cooperative behaviours. Significantly, aside from hunting and travelling together, typical group behaviour patterns express (usually male) power structures and alliances not unlike those of human social groups:

> All members of the group are aware of who is allied with whom, and that conflict with one individual may lead to conflict with an entire coalition. Furthermore, failure to reciprocate an act of cooperation will provoke retaliation. Chimpanzees, like humans, appear to follow the rules 'you scratch my back and I'll scratch yours' and 'an eye for an eye'.[35]

Coincidentally, Key and Aiello were also inspired by the Prisoner's Dilemma as a research tool. Based on the same game, they created their own computer simulations to model the conditions under which social organisations might evolve. However, in contrast to Laland's programme, with its focus on copying and exploitation as winning strategies, Key and Aiello seized upon the most important lesson of the Prisoner's Dilemma, which is that, while it pays players to be selfish and to cheat in the *short* term, in the *long* term, players invariably achieve higher scores if they cooperate with each other. Moreover, against the former's stress on the individual gains of exploitation, the two authors point to the *feelings of security* and other psychological benefits that go with belonging to a group: 'The need to cooperate, and protect ourselves from *individuals who would exploit our cooperation* [emphasis added], appears to be part of our evolved psychology'.[36]

Energetic factors

Other similarities and differences between the two research programmes highlight the challenges involved. Both programmes employed measures of the energy expended in different behaviour patterns. However, Laland's programme equated the amount of energy expended with the amount of *time* taken in pursuing one learning strategy as against another. Key and Aiello draw instead upon empirical studies of primate behaviour for physiological and diet-related measures of the raw *energy* invested in successfully reproducing and then raising a single offspring to maturity – the aim being to see how such factors affected parental decisions as to when to cooperate with others in rearing their offspring and when not to. As might be expected, the energetic costs for reproduction and parental care are much higher for females than for males. Moreover, when modeling the social effects the authors found that:

> The likelihood of cooperation increases as the energetic costs of repro-duction increases. At very high energetic costs, cooperation in the form of reciprocal altruism, or 'tit-for-tat', evolves in almost every experiment. Furthermore, regardless of how high or how low the cost of reproduc-tion is for males, the model predicts that cooperation is *far more likely to arise between females* [emphasis added], especially when energetic costs are great.[37]

The authors cite numerous cases of female cooperation amongst mammals, including suckling and babysitting other mothers' offspring, as well as food sharing. Much of this cooperation takes place between members of the same kin, in which case the fitness effects of individual members may be spread amongst the group, increasing the benefits of cooperation. Cooperation is also common amongst female apes which move from their birth group to other groups and who are known to band together to protect each other from par-ticularly aggressive males, as well as collaborating in infant care.

However, while cooperation between females is strongly motivated by the burdens of maternity and the high energy costs involved, social exchange of this sort between male and female primates is likely to be much less common since what is being exchanged (i.e., sexual favours) is usually very different. For example, running further simulations based on the Prisoner's Dilemma, Key and Aiello found that – initially at least – despite confusions of male paternity amongst primate groups, a male may choose to share parental responsibilities for a female's young as long as such commitments did not prejudice his freedom to mate with at least one other female. For their own part, females retained their right to punish males who failed in their parental duties by not collaborating with them for extended periods. However, for the longer term:

> Once parental care arises, males will adopt strategies that increase their paternity certainty. If this occurs, simulations strongly suggest that male investment [in the relationship] will increase, even when male energetic costs are quite high.[38]

Change of diet

Pinpointing the change from a mostly vegetarian diet to an animal, meat-based diet and related physiological changes in the evolution of humans, similar ener-getic factors, they suggest, spurred the growth of higher levels of cooperative behaviour. For females in particular, the reduction in the relative size and energy requirements of the intestinal tract due to the more easily digested meat diet was balanced by an increase in body size relative to males and a threefold increase in brain size – the same as for males. The resultant increased energy load on females, the authors contend, may in turn have contributed to changes in social behaviour involving more cooperation, not only between females but also between males and females.

The parallel development of male hunting groups created further opportunities, not only for male–male cooperation but also for males to win over females with their hunting prowess. Moreover, they suggest, hunting large animals in male groups, which was frequently dangerous and relatively unsuccessful compared to hunting smaller creatures, may have been motived more by *competition* between males for females than by hunger or other social rewards. Whether such group activities are mainly driven by such factors, or, as seems more likely, by a more complex combination of male power structures and sexual needs amongst our primate forebears, is uncertain. However, the authors are in no doubt as to the psychological and cultural significance of cooperative behaviour in human evolution, nor of the part it played – boosted by an energy efficient meat diet – in the phenomenal brain growth of our ancestors:

> The development of pair-bonding and paternal care within the context of large multi-male, multi-female groups placed unique cognitive demands upon our hominid ancestors, elevating our capacity for altruism, deception, culture, communication and knowing other peoples' minds beyond anything yet observed in non-human primates.[39]

Gene-culture coevolution

According to Charles Lumsden and Edward O. Wilson,[40] the key to the further development of those higher levels of thought and behaviour lay in the evolutionary dynamics between what, for much of the last century, have been regarded as distinct inheritance systems: the genetic and the cultural. Adding their own weight to criticisms of MS researchers and their fixation on natural selection and the genetic mechanisms of evolution, they write:

> What has been missing in curious disproportion is an organized search for the origin and evolution of mind [...] To many of the wisest of contemporary scholars, the mind and culture still seem so elusive as to defeat evolutionary theory and perhaps even to transcend biology.[41]

Describing what they call the 'missing link' in human evolution that eluded anthropologists focused on the physical remains of *Homo sapiens'* predecessors, they trace the evolution of our species through each of its primary stages: from *Homo habilis*, much smaller than us with a brain half the size of ours but half again the size of a chimpanzee's; through the upright walking, hunter-gatherer *Homo erectus* about 1.5 million years ago. Over the same timespan the brain grew dramatically in size, until in modern humans the neocortex – the seat of language and other higher functions – is over three times greater than it would be in a human-sized ape. This last stage, when the human mind was formed, they suggest, constitutes no less than the most recent of 'four great steps' in the history of life on this planet, the other three being the origin of life itself, the first advanced cell structure, and the first multicellular organisms.

Yet at the time the two authors undertook to solve the mystery, the last, crucial step remained tantalisingly obscure. Rejecting the then predominant view of culture as an independent force or layer growing on top of the biological organism and explicable only according to its own laws, they write:

> Ours is a very different view. We believe that the secret of the mind's sudden emergence lies in the activation of a mechanism both obedient to physical laws and unique to the human species. Somehow the evolving species kindled a Promethean fire, a self-sustaining reaction that carried humanity beyond the previous limits of biology. This largely unknown evolutionary process we have called gene-culture coevolution: it is a complicated, fascinating interaction in which culture is generated and shaped by biological imperatives while biological traits are simultaneously altered by genetic evolution in response to cultural innovation.[42]

Underlying the linkage between genetic evolution and cultural history, they argue, are epigenetic processes rooted in human biology that influence the way culture is formed. Thus, for example, the negative genetic effects of inbreeding influence cultural traditions encouraging outbreeding, while certain colour preferences and combinations are more likely than others due to sensory rules governing the perception of colour. The other half of the equation, the translation from mind to culture, are the effects that culture has on genetic evolution. Epigenetic rules governing the manner in which the mind develops or is most likely to develop, cause individuals to adopt cultural choices ensuring their successful reproduction and survival. Thus:

> Over many generations, these rules, and also the genes prescribing them, tend to increase in the population. Hence culture affects genetic evolution, just as the genes affect cultural evolution.[43]

Anthropological approaches

While, in hindsight, there may be some confusion between cause and effect in Lumsden and Wilson's explanation of gene-culture evolution – a confusion obviated by later arguments for the spontaneous emergence of higher levels of development – they succeeded in demolishing a major barrier to progressing evolutionary theory beyond the genetic strictures of the MS. Since their groundbreaking work, other researchers from various disciplines have also shown increasing interest in the interrelations between genetic and higher-level patterns of inheritance, advancing beyond the two authors' original formulation and examples.

While anthropological research has been traditionally conducted by specialists focused on specific periods of cultural production and what they tell us about the people living at that time that, too, is changing under the influence of cross-disciplinary thought. As William Durham[44] writes, following developments in the conceptual or 'ideational theory' of human culture, anthropologists began treating culture instead as diverse 'systems of symbolically encoded *conceptual phenomena* [emphasis added] that are socially and historically transmitted within and between populations'.[45] The symbolic and historical perspective in turn opened the way to seeing human culture as a *second major inheritance system*, working in tandem with the genetic system:

> The development of ideational theory in anthropology re-emphasizes that human beings are possessed of *two* major information systems, one genetic, and one cultural. It forcefully reminds us that *both* these systems have the potential for transmission or 'inheritance' across space and time, that *both* have profound effects on the behavior of the organism, and that *both* are simultaneously co-resident in each and every living human being.[46]

The case of lactose tolerance

For Durham, a leader in gene-culture coevolution research, the key factor in common between the two systems is the historical pattern of *modified descent* from previous variations, either of which, given certain circumstances, may impact upon the other, leaving in some cases permanent traces on their future development. Amongst the well-researched cases he cites is the belated discovery in 1965 of significant variations in the physiological capacity of humans to absorb lactose, a chemical sugar compound found in fresh mammalian milk. Intensive studies over the following decades revealed that, not only did many of the world's population share the same intolerance for lactose but the phenotype of a majority also prevents them from digesting key nutrients in milk. Given the supposedly untarnished nutritional benefits of fresh milk as advertised in western cultures the discovery came as a cultural as well as a medical and scientific shock. Moreover, high levels of lactose tolerance were primarily concentrated in Northern and Western Europeans and their overseas descendants, while most of the rest of the world's population had either limited or no tolerance at all.

It is now broadly accepted that genetic differences between the lactose 'absorbers' and 'malabsorbers' are mostly responsible for the physiological anomaly. However, that left open the question as to what other evolutionary factors might be responsible for such marked genetic variations between the different populations surveyed. According to Durham, the most likely explanation lies in the early advent of agriculture in Western Europe and the Near East, and with it, the domestic raising of cattle for meat production between 9000 and 7000BC, followed by dairying between 4000 and 6000BC. Such major changes in the human diet and related social customs, so the argument goes, would have created new selection pressures over the following millennia on the genetic populations thus affected, sufficient time for:

> [...] the genetic evolution of lactose absorption among the descendants of early dairyers [...] The antiquity of dairying in the Old World is thus consistent with the idea of a *culturally mediated evolution* [emphasis added] of adult lactose absorption in human populations.[47]

Interacting dimensions

However, in making their own case for niche construction theory in providing a broader account of multi-level inheritance systems, Odling-Smee et al fault anthropologists' ideational approach to gene-culture coevolution as being 'species specific', in that it assumes that *only* human culture is strong and stable enough to create its own selection pressures:

> We think this particular human centered perspective is misleading. Humans may be unique in their capacity for cultural processes, but they are not unique in their capacity to modify their environments and hence the way in which they may be affected by natural selection.[48]

Their solution is to add a third inheritance system, *ecological inheritance*, to the genetic and cultural systems. As impacted by niche construction activities of every sort and scale – not just cultural – the inclusion of ecological inheritance in coevolutionary theory therefore challenges the ideational, anthropocentric perspective. In the *triple-inheritance* scheme of things, culturally modified selection pressures are no longer regarded as particular to the human race, but are treated as just one of a more general pattern of modified selection pressures that niche-constructing creatures of *all* kinds pass down to their descendants. Moreover, by including the specific mechanisms of niche construction, Odling-Smee et al claim their extended scheme allows for a fuller range of ontogenetic and developmental processes, including individual and social learning of the sort described earlier in this chapter, for which they prescribe detailed methods for further empirical research.

Toward a broader evolutionary pathway

In their 'four-dimensional view' of evolution Eva Jablonka and Marion Lamb[49] go further still and contend that only by examining genetic, epigenetic, behavioural and symbolic inheritance systems *all together* as interacting dimensions of a broader evolutionary pathway, can we fully understand humanity's origins and subsequent development or the reasons for the variations at each of those levels. Explaining the different information systems involved, they write: 'some of the great evolutionary transitions – from unicells to multicellular organisms, from individuals to cohesive social groups, from social groups to cultural communities – were all built on *new types of information transmission* [emphasis added]'.[50]

However, in contrast to the investigations of niche construction theorists and other researchers cited here who explore the origins of human behaviour in that of other species, Jablonka and Lamb focus on what they believe to be truly unique about human behaviour and culture: 'It is our ability to think and communicate through words and other types of symbols that makes us so different'.[51] Following the German philosopher Ernst Cassirer,[52] they stress the difference between human languages and the communication systems of other animals, including parrots, which, though they may be able to convincingly imitate specific human words and phrases, cannot grasp the *relation* between those words and other words and phrases and are thus unable to *generalise* from the use of one to another object or new item. Beyond the example of human language, like Durham, the two authors also stress the significance of symbolic systems in general as constituting 'a fourth dimension to heredity and evolution'. As with language, the key to understanding other human forms of symbolic communication lies in each symbol being part of a wider system of communication and meaning or 'network of references'. The same networks not only enable matters of specific interest to be communicated between individuals, but taken all together, may comprise a shared view of the world:

> [Symbolic] systems allow people to share a fiction, to share an imagined reality, which may have little to do with their immediate experiences. This is true of stories, of pictures, of rituals, of dances and pantomime, of music, indeed of any type of symbolic systems we can think about. *All symbolic systems enable the construction of a shared imagined reality* [emphasis added].[53]

More than just copying

Addressing the issue of the cognitive processes involved in the dissemination and understanding of cultural symbols, Jablonka and Lamb also consider Dawkins' concept of the meme as being the cultural equivalent of the gene,[54] which they reject. A sequence of DNA may be copied with the same fidelity as a photocopier, but 'other types of copying, such as that which occurs in learning, are different'.[55] Learning something new and teaching it to someone else, they argue, involves understanding the form, function and *context* of the information being transmitted. Rather than being just blindly copied, existing cultural concepts are *reconstructed* by individuals each time they are acquired or taught to others – an altogether more complex process of cognition.[56] In addition, what sets human culture apart from other animal cultures, is that 'humans are aware of and can communicate about their past history (whether real or mythical) and their future needs'.[57] Given the social and cultural need for innovation and renewal, they argue, slavish fidelity to a particular idea or element within a social system may be simply unnecessary and may even *restrict* the evolution and development of cultures. Rejecting the neo-Darwinian principles underlying the gene–meme analogy, they advocate instead a 'developmental-historical' approach to cultural variants and the diverse social environments in which they evolve:

> The important general point we want to reiterate is that the selection, generation, and transmission or acquisition of cultural variants cannot be thought about in isolation from one another; neither can they be thought about in isolation from the economic, legal, and political systems in which they are embedded and constructed, and the practices of the people who construct them.[58]

Novel behaviour

Jablonca and Lamb's persuasive arguments for a wider view of inheritance systems are endorsed by Russell Bonduriansky and Troy Day,[59] who specifically cite the former authors' works as a major influence on the development of their own concept of 'extended heredity', which, they suggest, covers both genetic and non-genetic systems of inheritance. However, while they include recent research in transgenerational epigenetics and related discoveries of the sort described above, they adopt a more conservative position than most proponents of the Extended Synthesis and claim their concept does not refute the central role genetics plays in evolutionary theory: 'We see genetic and non-genetic inheritance as hereditary processes that operate in parallel, so *extended heredity supplements rather than supplants genetics* [emphasis added]'.[60]

Comparing human and animal non-genetic systems, for example, they point out that, albeit modest by comparison with human achievements, the range of non-genetic inheritance processes in animals, including culture-like traditions, is actually much wider than is generally assumed. In addition to the more familiar examples of animal tool use, they suggest that chimpanzees, who, as previously noted, are credited with complex forms of group behaviour, are capable of limited forms of cumulative cultural innovation of the kind generally thought to be particular to humans, such as the adoption of apparently arbitrary cultural conventions. One such intriguing case involved a group of chimpanzees in Zanzibar that, following the example set by one of their members, spontaneously took up the habit of inserting a blade of grass into one ear. However, though the members of the same group continued the practice even after its inventor died, the custom was never taken up by neighbouring groups, leading

Bonduriansky and Day to speculate: 'Such arbitrary "fashions" could serve as badges of group membership in chimp societies, much as they do in humans'.[61]

Acquiring new habits

Notably, where once researchers of animal behaviour relied upon observations of their subjects in captivity, the authors argue that such discoveries can only be made by observing the behaviour of wild animals in their natural habitat. Citing a pioneering study of a group of macaque monkeys on the Japanese islet of Koshima by a team of primatologists in the 1940s, they describe how the Japanese team, whose research included feeding habits, left some sweet potatoes on the seashore for the monkeys and watched how they reacted. Soon enough they observed a young female taking her potatoes to a river nearby and dipping them in the fresh water before brushing off any sand with her hand; an action that was quickly adopted by most of the younger monkeys. Eventually, they all changed to washing their potatoes in the sea – perhaps, the researchers speculated – because the salt water might have improved the taste.

Conducting another test, the researchers scattered some wheat on the sand, whereupon the same young female – who clearly had leadership qualities – quickly learned to separate the seeds from the loose sand by throwing handfuls of the mixture into the shallow seawater and then stepping into the water, where she collected the clean seeds off the surface where they were floating. As before, the new behaviour was quickly taken up by the younger monkeys. In a third and final test the team threw some peanuts directly into the seawater, encouraging the monkeys to wade into the water – not their normal habitat – to retrieve the offering. What really surprised the researchers though, was the sight of many of the monkeys thereafter *enjoying* being in the water 'for its own sake, wading, swimming, and diving off rocks even when no food was offered. The monkey troop thus began to use an entirely new habitat'.[62]

Bonduriansky and Day offer many other examples of the spread of novel patterns of behaviour through social learning amongst non-primate species as well as primates. For all the valuable evidence such examples provide of animal group behaviour, however, the authors make no attempt to explain how the original innovations might have come about, or what the possible environmental, social or individual circumstances might have been to stimulate novel behaviour of this kind, nor how those innovations might be related to evolutionary developments at other levels of the organism. It is just these kinds of problems, however, that have vexed Evo–Devo researchers as well as many other philosophical and scientific minds striving to understand how complex systems arise out of simpler systems, and to whose work we now turn.

Part II

The metatheory

There can be no doubt that the difference between the mind of the lowest man and that of the highest animal is immense […] Nevertheless the difference in mind between man and the higher animals, great as it is, certainly is one of degree and not of kind.

Charles Darwin, 1871[1]

Chapter 3

Self-organisation

The history and philosophy of science over the latter half of the last century has been commonly presented as a contest between two principal schools of thought on what the ultimate purpose of science is or should be about, and what scientists should be searching for in their respective disciplines. On one side are the *reductionists*, who believe that all the phenomena of the world can be traced back to and explained in terms of the accumulations and interactions of its smallest components, no matter what the specific discipline involved may be. On the other side are groups of systems theorists and other *anti-reductionists*, all of whom, while differing in other respects, share a belief in a complex world comprised of multiple forms and levels of systemic development, the full explanation and description of which *cannot* be reduced to those of its smallest components, and which may vary according to each discipline.[1]

Notwithstanding entrenched beliefs on both sides, more recent theoretical and empirical developments gathered under the interdisciplinary banner of 'complexity' have blurred oppositional positions so that, like the previous debates between nature and nurture, current investigations into self-organising systems offer more nuanced approaches, from which a metatheory of the self may be constructed. Appreciation of the powers of self-organisation and the spontaneous *emergence* of differential levels of complexity in all forms of life, also resolves a major problem in defining the *boundaries* of the self-field, which by its nature may extend beyond any physical or spatial boundaries to embrace many different and fluid environmental factors.

Order of a complex sort

Among the first to promote a systems theoretical perspective, writing in a 1950 paper Ludwig von Bertalanffy[2] saw in the emergence of higher order levels of complexity a clear distinction between 'open' and 'closed' systems. According to the Second Law of Thermodynamics of classical physics, he explains, an isolated or closed system in a highly *differentiated* state will most probably be found sometime in the future in a *less* differentiated (i.e., more *homogenous*)

state. The Second Law is thus a law of increasing *entropy* or decay of structure and was generally interpreted as heralding the inevitable and irreversible
decline of information and energy.

However, Bertalanffy pointed out that, while the Second Law holds for all
closed systems, it does *not* hold for open systems which exchange energy and
materials continuously with their environments. In an open system – by which
he includes all life forms – not only does entropy increase due to the burning
up of energy and other irreversible processes, but organisms also 'feed', so to
speak, on the energy they derive from importing complex organic molecules
from other life forms, the resultant waste from which they give back to the
environment. Thus, he asserts, while the Second Law still holds for the total
amount of energy used by living systems taken together with their environments, it does *not* apply to the living system itself. In the evolutionary long run,
therefore, entropy may *decrease* in open systems, which may, in turn, develop
towards states of greater heterogeneity and complexity. In sum, Bertalanffy
argues, while in the inanimate world there appears to be a tendency toward
maximum disorder and a chaotic state, in organic development there is a contrary tendency towards states of ever higher order and differentiation.

Operational principles

Writing just a few years after the publication of Bertalanffy's foundational
paper, Michael Polanyi,[3] an early critic of the neo-Darwinist fixation on natural
selection and the biological mechanisms of genetic heredity, proffered his own
insights into the orderly workings of living systems. Polanyi argued that, beyond
the exchange of materials and energy between organism and environment, the
key to what constitutes a living system lies in the operational principles that sustain the *identity* of the individual being: 'I shall regard living beings as instances
of morphological types and of operational principles *subordinated to a centre of
individuality* [emphasis added]'.[4]

Rejecting any possible explanation of those principals in purely physical
or chemical terms, Polanyi is especially critical of neo-Darwinism's failure to
account for the appearance of *new* and more complex forms of life which
occur at quite different levels of evolution – human consciousness being the
prime example. Anticipating the language of later theorists he describes the
appearance of consciousness at differential levels of evolution: 'This great spectacle, the spectacle of anthropogenesis, confronts us with a panorama of emergence; it offers *massive examples of emergence* [emphasis added] in the gradual
intensification of personal consciousness'.[5]

Unity versus disunity

Since Bertalanffy and Polanyi published their groundbreaking works, there
have been further seismic shifts in the physical as well as the biological

sciences – changes described by Ilya Prigogine,[6] a Nobel prize winner and his co-author Isabelle Stengers, as a 'new dialogue with nature'. Probing further and deeper into what he called the 'entropy barrier', Prigogine is credited with reformulating the basic principle embedded in the Second Law which dictates that, as an irreversible process, entropy must ultimately triumph over the evolution of life. On the contrary, Prigogine claims: 'A new unity is emerging: *irreversibility is a source of order at all levels* [emphasis added]. Irreversibility is the mechanism that brings order out of chaos'.[7] Previously, reversible (organic) and irreversible (non-organic) processes were conceived as separate phenomena, in which, as in Bertalanffy's living systems, the former temporarily suspends the inevitable effects of the latter. However, breaking through the entropy barrier, Prigogine presents both as *interacting systems* within a new and broader evolutionary paradigm, where, paradoxically, order *emerges* out of disorder.

It should come as no surprise, therefore, that while scientists of all shades now acknowledge complexity in both the natural and human world as an integral factor in their work,[8] their interpretation of what it ultimately means for understanding the world, and what we can know of it, differs widely. Most, like Prigogine and Stengers, view complexity as a source of *unity* cutting across disciplines. Others however, see it as a source of *disunity* and a fundamental barrier to any hopes for a unified science, such as that to which scientists and philosophers traditionally aspired. While, as with the reductionist and anti-reductionist camps, there exist many arguable positions in between, the polar viewpoints continue to influence research. Thus Peter Coveney and Roger Highfield[9] subtitle their work on complexity as a 'search for order in a chaotic world', the essential elements of which, if not already identified, await discovery. More precisely, they define complexity as 'the study of the behavior of macroscopic collections of such units that are endowed with the potential to evolve in time', the interactions of which 'lead to coherent collective phenomena, so-called emergent properties that can be described only at higher levels than those of the individual units'. It is at these higher levels, they write, adopting a more familiar expression, that the whole is perceived as more than the sum of its component parts: 'This is as true for a human society as it is for a raging sea or the electrochemical firing patterns of neurons in a human brain'.[10]

Contrarily, in *The Disorder of Things*, John Dupre[11] denies that 'science constitutes or could ever come to constitute, a single, unified project'.[12] For Dupre, the idea of a unified science or 'scientism' as he describes it, is more of a *socially and institutionally* driven project than a truly scientific enterprise and serves no useful purpose other than according science and scientists a privileged place in society. Instead, Dupre, who advocates a viewpoint closer to the relativistic philosophy of Paul Feyerabend,[13] calls for a 'pluralistic epistemology' that embraces complexity in all its forms and levels. As a human activity itself, science, he argues, is subject to social and political pressures of many kinds and has many different facets:

Science, construed simply as the set of knowledge-claiming practices that are accorded that title, *is a mixed bag* [emphasis added]. The role of theory, evidence, and institutional norms will vary greatly from one area of science to the next.[14]

Second-order cybernetics

Approaching complex systems from what they describe as 'second-order' cybernetics and systems theory, Bruce Clarke and Mark Hansen[15] also challenge oppositional conceptions of closed and open systems:

> Whether technical or biotic, psychic or social, systems are bounded semi-autonomous entities coupled with their environments and *to* other systems. One shifts attention from isolated elements and relations to the emergent behaviors of ever-larger ensembles [...] Autonomy can never be solitary: In second-order cybernetics, *autonomy is rethought as operational self-reference* [emphasis added].[16]

Like Polanyi, therefore, Clarke and Hansen stress the operational circularity at the heart of all living systems. However, in the spirit of Prigogine's theory of order emerging out of disorder, they also go further in stressing the inherent paradox in the relations between the identity of subjects and the ever-widening networks of connections among systems and their environments. The understanding of those relations, they contend, requires a new concept of *closure* or what they call 'double closure'. By this they mean that, in addition to the primary forms of closure involved in operational self-reference, given the potentially overwhelming complexity of linkages between organism and environment, there is a constant need for all organisms and living systems to *control and reduce* those linkages to only those essential to their continued well-being and survival:

> In stark contrast to any naïve conception of autonomy as the absolute self-sufficiency of a substantial subject, this concept demarcates the paradoxical reality that environmental entanglement correlates with organismic (or systemic) self-regulation [...] Put another way, in order for a system to perpetuate itself, it must maintain its *capacity to reduce environmental complexity* [emphasis added], which is to say to process it not as direct input but as perturbation catalyzing (internal) structural change.[17]

Against Neo-Darwinian theories of passive organisms being subjected to environmental pressures, in second order cybernetics, therefore, as with niche construction and other arguments presented in these pages, living systems are instead viewed as proactively imposing *their own constraints* on those pressures.[18]

Hierarchical model

In his subsequent works of the 1960s, Polanyi also elaborated on his understanding of emergence, linking it to his influential theory of 'tacit knowing', which, he explains, underpins all forms of knowledge:

> While tacit knowledge can be possessed by itself, explicit knowledge must rely upon being tacitly understood and applied. Hence all knowledge is *either tacit* or *rooted in tacit knowledge*. A *wholly* explicit knowledge is unthinkable.[19]

Taking the example of a game of chess, he explains that, while playing the game requires tacit knowledge of the rules of the game, the *principles* controlling those rules cannot be derived from the actual rules of chess themselves. What he calls the 'two terms' of tacit knowing, the 'proximal' (i.e., the particular details of which we are only subconsciously aware) and the 'distal' (i.e., their comprehensive meaning as a game of chess) can only be properly understood as *two levels of reality*, each controlled by its own principles: 'The upper one relies for its operations on the laws governing the elements of the lower one in themselves, but these operations of it are *not explicable by the laws of the lower level* [emphasis added]'.[20]

Expanding on the idea of related but distinctive levels of reality, he offers a hierarchical picture 'of the universe filled with strata of realities, joined together in pairs of higher and lower strata'.[21] Offering numerous examples of such pairs, from hierarchies of related human skills to the distinctive levels of development found in living systems, he argues that each level in the hierarchy is subject to *dual control*, from the laws applying to the elements themselves, and from those other laws controlling the *entity as a whole* that is constituted by those elements: 'Thus the logical structure of the hierarchy implies that a higher level can come into existence *only through a process not manifest in the lower level* [emphasis added], a process which thus qualifies as an emergence'.[22]

New theory of evolution

Considering the range and diversity of all these new ideas and approaches, it may be asked whether they point to a new theory of evolution itself or simply support Dupre's call for a pluralistic epistemology? Presenting his own critique of the Modern Synthesis in a prescient 1980 paper, Stephen J Gould[23] suggests that such a theory, if not yet fully developed, is in the making, and that the theory of evolution embodied in the MS is effectively dead, despite its continued propagation in textbooks. The MS, Gould argues, is essentially founded on two basic principles: 'extrapolation of small genetic changes to yield evolutionary events *at all scales* [emphasis added] and control of direction by selection leading to adaptation'.[24] While adherents concede there are exceptions to the MS picture of gradual and consistent transformations of species spread out over millennia, Gould suggests they are always presented as minor phenomena and not important enough to disrupt or have any lasting effect on the micro-evolutionary pathway. The discovery of the DNA structure and code in turn fitted well with the prevailing orthodoxy.

Against the reductionist picture of the MS, Gould posits a hierarchical model of many semi-independent levels of evolution not unlike Polanyi's theory of emergence, the understanding of which requires a new and equally complex perspective:

> A world constructed not as a smooth and seamless continuum, permitting simple extrapolation from the lowest to the highest, but as a *series of ascending levels* [emphasis added], each bound to the one below it in some ways and independent in others. Discontinuities and seams characterize the transitions; 'emergent' features, not implicit in the operation of processes at lower levels, may control events at higher levels.[25]

In support of his approach Gould points to the new discoveries in epigenetics and other fields that undermine the MS model of evolution, drawing particular attention to the issues of speciation and macroevolution. He argues that, interpreted as a lengthy, sequential process driven by selection, the creation of new species occurs at *too high* an evolutionary level to be directly observable in nature. Consequently, theories of speciation have been mostly based on analogical thinking and inference, most famously in Darwin's own extrapolations from artificial selection and geographically based variation of populations.

Macroevolution

While analogical thinking of this kind is a normal and generally creative feature of science, as it is of other fields,[26] Gould contends that genetic level changes alone cannot explain the emergence of *new* species and that epigenetic factors may combine with natural selection and adaptation over relatively short periods to isolate and 'fix' species' phenotypic characteristics. According to these so-called 'punctuational models' of evolution, new species and subsequent evolutionary *trends* – 'the fundamental phenomenon of macroevolution' as he describes them – are the outcome, not of a continuous process of incremental adjustment to selection pressures, but of a *divergent* process in which '*species themselves must be inputs* [emphasis added], and trends the result of their differential origin and survival'.[27] The smaller, incremental changes conventionally described as speciation, however, are more likely to be the outcome of gene regulation and rearrangement than of any structurally genetic changes that could result in the production of new species, and only account for variations within the *same* species.

Looking forward, Gould concludes his thesis with a rallying call to restore a macroevolutionary concept of organism capable of *influencing its own evolution,* which he claims has been lost to biology in its obsession with the micro-level components of life:

> Organisms are not billiard balls, struck in deterministic fashion by the cure of natural selection and rolling to optimal positions on life's table. They influence their own destiny in interesting, complex, and comprehensible ways. We must put this concept of organism back into evolutionary biology.[28]

Emergentism

Since Polanyi and Gould anticipated the evolutionary significance of emergence, interest in the subject across disciplines has steadily grown, from physics and the biological and cognitive sciences to the emergence of human language.[29] However, a cross-disciplinary consensus on more precise explanations of the inter-level process itself remains stubbornly out of reach – a situation confirmed by repeated arguments for a *pluralism* of theories. Defining emergence, Antonella Corradini and Timothy O'Connor,[30] for example, offer an open description of a concept they admit is often criticized for being too vague: 'Emergent phenomena are said to arise out of and be sustained by more basic phenomena, while at the same time exerting some form of 'top down' control, constraint or some other sort of influence upon those very sustaining processes'.[31]

Beyond that general definition lies a broader and familiar debate about the nature of emergence in the larger scheme of things, and whether all the phenomena of life can be explained at the level of physical systems and their basic components or if the appearance of novel phenomena at different levels of evolution and development requires separate, perhaps novel forms of explanation of its own. Also straddling these positions are those who attempt to reconcile the idea of distinctive emergent processes and properties with the causal explanations of physics; an approach which, the two authors opine, 'can seem to deflate emergence of its initially profound significance',[32] but which offers a promising, if uncertain, way forward.

Common ground

In dissecting the many positions and arguments of philosophers and scientists of both camps, Carl Gillett[33] notes that, while science still claims many reductionists among its ranks, growing numbers of scientists also now describe themselves as emergentists. In contrast, though reduction in philosophy is now vigorously rejected, few philosophers espouse an alternative emergentism and most discount such positions as 'incoherent', a situation he believes deprives both science and philosophy of potentially useful exchanges of knowledge.

However, looking beyond the stereotypical positions, Gillett finds common ground amongst scientific reductionists and emergentists in that each group accepts the importance of 'inter-level mechanistic explanations' which explain the composition of higher-level by lower-level entities. He also finds convincing empirical evidence for a new approach in the very sciences where one might expect the strongest opposition to emergentism. Taking an example from the neurosciences, Gillett describes how Roderick MacKinnon won the Noble prize for explaining the key role a particular chemical agent, potassium ion, plays as a 'voltage-sensitive gate' in activating a neuron, and how the molecular components involved and their properties interact and change during the process. Significantly, Gillett notes, the *compositional relations* between the various components and properties at different levels of the procedure are all *synchronous*. They neither occur between wholly distinct entities, nor do they entail any mediation of force or transfers of energy.

Based on those perceptions, Gillett presents a fresh interpretation of scientific reductionism that, while being founded in mechanistic explanation, allows for the emergence of *qualitative* differences at higher-levels of development from the composition of lower level components, concordant with the different sciences: 'Given their interconnections, the various "packages" of powers, properties, individuals, and mechanisms studied by lower-level sciences *together* compose the qualitatively different powers, property instances, individuals and mechanisms studied by higher-level sciences'.[34] By such reasoning, Gillett suggests, it may be argued that 'there really are no composed entities – that "Wholes are nothing but their parts"',[35] meaning there are no entities *that can be separately described* from the composition of their component parts; a compromise position Gillet calls 'compositional reductionism'.

Strong versus weak emergence

However, there remain those scientists who actually *do* describe themselves as emergentists and who take a more radical position. Exploring their case, Gillett goes on to explain that, against compositional reductionism and other relatively weak variations of emergence, an argument can also be made for 'strong emergence' or the emergence of properties that *cannot* be adequately explained as the simple aggregate of component properties, but are the product of a process of 'conditioned aggregation'. Quoting from another Nobel Prize winner, Robert Laughlin, a condensed-matter physicist, Gillett finds support for the latter view in Laughlin's work on 'symmetry breaking':

> The idea of symmetry breaking is simple: matter *collectively and spontaneously* [emphasis added] acquires a property or preference not present in the underlying rules themselves. For example, when atoms order into a

crystal, they acquire *preferred positions* [emphasis added], even though there was nothing preferred about these positions before the crystal formed.[36]

Though the example is taken from his own specialised field of physics, Laughlin argues that similar phenomena are to be found in other areas, including chemistry and biology: 'These effects are important because they prove that organizational principles can give primitive matter a mind of its own and empower it to make decisions'.[37]

Constructive alternative

Such cases provide vital support for the systems theorists' aforementioned mantra that a whole is more than the sum of its parts, now supplemented, Gillet writes, by scientific emergentists' claim that parts, however, 'behave differently in wholes'. Nevertheless, while advocates of conditioned aggregation may differ in this and other respects from those supporting compositional reductionism, unlike the outright rejection of any form of reductive explanation of physical phenomena by most philosophers, Gillet explains, both camps of scientific emergentism include mechanistic explanations in their approach whilst retaining the essential idea of emergent properties. Consequently, he concludes, they offer a constructive alternative to the philosophers' 'false dichotomy' between reductionist and anti-reductionist theories of the physical world. What scientists pursuing the idea of Strong emergentism have been especially concerned with, he argues, is a kind of 'non-compositional, non-causal determination' overlooked by philosophers, for which he suggests we need a new term altogether: '*machresis*', a combination of the Greek words for 'macro' and 'chresis' ('use'). Speculating on the wider implications for related research into different level systems, Gillet writes:

> Obviously, it is an intriguing, and very important, question whether we find this type of Strong emergence in the 'emergent phenomena' scientists have recently highlighted, whether superconductivity, the phases of matter, symmetry breaking of all kinds, Bernard cells in chemistry, the shoaling of fish and flocking of birds, and many, many more examples. Similarly, it is interesting how machresis relates to the cases of so-called 'self-organization' found with 'emergent' phenomena in chemical systems, biological systems like ant colonies or social systems such as traffic patterns, amongst others.[38]

Levels of description

Like Gillet, Michele Di Francesco[39] also identifies several key interpretations of emergentism, the two principal varieties of which she describes in similar terms as 'moderate' and 'radical' emergentism. The first is built upon the 'causal inheritance principle' or the idea that the causal powers of emergent properties are the outcome of the causal powers of more basic properties. The second, however, simply accepts as a 'brute fact' that new kinds of causal organisation derive from new properties that *only become detectable* at the higher levels where they actually function. While both Gill and Di Francesco find common ground between different positions in the general acceptance of mechanistic (causal) principles operating at specific levels, the difference between moderate and radical emergentism, Di Francesco cautions, should not be underestimated. While the former subscribes to a reductive physicalism or the belief that all forms and levels of phenomena and their interactions can be explained in terms of their physical properties, radical emergentism 'collects together a family of positions that either reject the causal inheritance principle or give it a non-physicalistic reading'.[40] Such an interpretation, Di Francesco asserts, implies that, 'mental properties cannot be reduced to physical properties; *a purely physical reading of the world is not complete* [emphasis added]'.[41] However, anticipating objections to a possible Cartesian division between mind and matter, Di Francesco insists that emergence should not be confused with dualism and that, while not explicable as the direct consequence of the actions of lower level properties, emergent properties are nevertheless '*grounded in them*'.

Pluralistic universe

At this point, an impartial researcher might be forgiven for thinking that, in accepting that emergent properties, while not being causally determined by more basic components are nevertheless in some sense 'grounded in them', radical emergentists might just be wanting to have their cake and eat it, so to speak.[42] While both the upward and downward *effects* of emergent properties may have causal explanations, the spontaneous appearance of the qualitatively different properties themselves, if no longer shrouded in mystery, remains inexplicable in purely physical and causal terms.

Di Francesco's answer to this dilemma is to accept that, *as physical objects and processes*, the subjects of emergentism obey the same universal laws of physics as those that apply to any other physical objects or processes, but to accept equally that emergent properties cannot *all* be explained the same way, but may also require other, non-causal and non-physicalistic types of description. Echoing Dupre's plea for a 'pluralistic epistemology', Di Francesco shifts the burden of explanation of emergence to the ontological level of being or that which is simply *known*, pointing to a 'pluralistic universe' of many levels and kinds of explanation, for which he quotes from Jerry Fodor, a leading critic of neo-Darwinism:

> The world, it seems, runs in parallel, at many levels of description. You may think that perplexing; you certainly aren't obliged to like it. But I do think we had all better learn to live with it.[43]

However, Di Francesco also cautions that a pluralistic or 'patchwork' perspective of this kind could lead, in its more extreme versions at least, to a denial of any kind of unified theory or worldview. Nevertheless, he is more optimistic than Dupre about the search for unity in science. There is an alternative, he suggests, to either theoretical disunity or reductive physicalism, and that is 'to look for the unity of the world, not at the bottom, but at the top of it, so to speak; *it is at the emergent level that all causal powers merge together* [emphasis added]'. Such a position, he concedes, entails accepting a fundamental ambiguity in the idea of emergence between physicalistic and non-physicalistic explanations: 'The thesis that the unity of our world is gained at the emergent level and not the physical is quite unusual, and seems to reverse the traditional explicative route from everyday experience and its (physical) basis'.[44] In conclusion, Di Francesco advises us that we should see this as an opportunity to consider emergentism 'as a flexible conceptual tool' and be open to alternative models linking different levels of reality according to the particular way we experience them.

Questioning causation

A collection of essays by Peter Anderson et al[45] on downward (epigenetic) pressures and their effects on development in multi-level systems supports the idea that emergent properties in evolving systems may ultimately not be describable in conventional physicalistic terms, as in genetic and other microscopic processes. It is not just that *downward causation*, as it is called, is a slippery concept, the very idea of causation itself, as we have seen, is as open to question by emergentists of different shades from within the physical sciences, where it has been most influential, as it is from other disciplines. As H. H. Pattee[46] observes, causation is a 'gratuitous concept' invented for events described by the laws of physics, with a disputatious philosophical history that has yet to produce a firm consensus as to what it means. The 'naïve concept of causation', as he describes it, which is endemic to natural language (i.e., 'John kicked the ball') assumes that any event linked to another, preceding event in a time-related sequence is assumed to be causally explained by that event – an assumption, however, which requires the inclusion of another concept such as Isaac Newton's 'force'. Otherwise the only 'explanation' on offer would be that the two events are linked together in time, which by itself yields no further explanation at all but merely points to the possibility or *probability* of some *other* reason for the linkage.

Relations between events or phenomena in time itself, therefore, and especially the abstract mathematical concept of time, which Pattee suggests is particularly remote from the actual *experience* of time, are insufficient for a causal explanation of events. This does not mean, however, that we can dispense entirely with either the concepts of cause or force, since natural language requires their use even when describing science's formal models – as, for example, in the frequent and ambiguous use of the word 'force' by many writers, including your author, in this book. What it all comes down to, Pattee argues, is that the concepts of causation have quite different meanings in statistical models – which measure the *probabilities of events* – and in deterministic models, such as those which reductionists assume explain physical events at the microscopic level as the ultimate source of order. In either case, he concludes, what counts is the actual *process of measurement* employed, which is, in turn, a product of our own role as observers:

> Hence our concepts of causation *arise from our being observers or controllers of events* [emphasis added], not from the events themselves. Consequently concepts of causation are subjective insofar as they cannot be separated from the observer's choice of observables and the function of measuring devices.[47]

Complementary models

Furthermore, Pattee asserts there is no point in pretending the differences between the two levels of observation – the microscopic and the statistical – can be glossed over, since, in the sense of physicist Niels Bohr's description of complementary models,[48] they are logically irreducible: 'That is, complementary models are *formally incompatible but both necessary* [emphasis added]. One model cannot be derived from or reduced to, the other'.[49]

As a concept in everyday language, Pattee argues that causation serves the essentially *pragmatic* purpose of focusing attention on those events that might be *controllable* in some way, and is commonly used in engineering and the use of all machines, the power of which can be directly controlled by us or by mechanisms designed by us. However, since the invariant laws of physics deal precisely with phenomena that *cannot* be controlled or changed by any external force or being, causation affords no useful explanatory purpose *at that level*. Instead, he suggests we look for *other levels of organisation* where the concept might be better employed, as in living organisms, where the genotype and phenotype are separately described by upward and downward forms of causation – the primary difference between the two being that *genetic control is heritable*, while the latter involves dynamic, epigenetic, factors that are neither strictly heritable in the same form or as localised within the organism. More like a *collective and distributed* process: 'Downward causation is ubiquitous and occurs continuously at all levels, but is usually ignored simply because it is not under our control'.[50]

Such systems, he suggests, may be better explained by models of self-organisation of the kind discussed in this book, but which have been difficult to simulate by either statistical or artificial intelligence models, there still being an 'enormous gap', as he describes it, between such methods and the observable phenomena. Reiterating the idea of complementary deterministic and dynamical models, the current controversy, Pattee concludes, 'is over how much of evolution and development results from genetic control and natural selection and how much from self-organizing nonlinear dynamics'.[51]

Autopoiesis

No less controversial, Humberto Maturana and Francisco Varela's theory of self-producing systems, *Autopoiesis and Cognition*,[52] published in 1980, questions some of the most widely accepted constructs of evolutionary and systems theorists, including conventional distinctions between 'organism' and 'environment', 'wholes' and 'parts', and 'open' and 'closed'. Named after *poiesis*, the Greek for 'creation' or 'production', Maturana and Varela claim their approach provides what they say evolutionary and systems theorists have failed to provide – an explanation of how the acclaimed *unity* of organisms arises:

> The greatest hindrance in the understanding of the living organization lies in the impossibility of accounting for it by the enumeration of its properties; it must be understood as a unity.[53]

Central to their theory is a biological conception of cognition as a circular, *self-referential* process, the sole purpose of which is to sustain the *individual identity and development* of the organism. In so far as Maturana and Varela's attention is therefore firmly focused on the genesis and identity of individual organisms as complex wholes, their approach accords well with that of other systems theorists. Their interpretation of cognition as a 'biological phenomenon', however, together with their characterisation of living systems as being entirely self-referential, sets them apart. Whereas cognition is generally treated as a *mental* process in the development of ever-more complex and higher forms of life – important but *supplementary* to other forms of evolution and development – Maturana and Varela present the acquisition and use of information as the very essence of *all* forms of life, from the most basic to the most complex: 'Living systems are cognitive systems, and living as a process is a process of cognition'.[54]

It follows that the unity of organisms and their interactions with other organisms can therefore only be fully understood from an ontological viewpoint of what *knowing* involves: 'Thus cognition as a biological function is such that the answer to the question, "What is cognition?" must arise from understanding knowledge and the knower *through the latter's capacity to know* [emphasis added]'.[55] Accordingly, a biological theory of cognition should provide insight into the functional organisation of organisms that ultimately gives rise to such cognitive phenomena as 'conceptual thinking, language, and self-consciousness'.[56]

Circular organisation

The cellular metabolism of a single-celled organism (such as an amoeba), they explain, offers a prime example of autopoiesis and the circular organisation it describes. The cell has a spatial boundary (membrane) within which the bio-chemical components that sustain the life of the cell are produced in the course of development, which, in turn, produce more of the same components in a continuous cycle of mutual production. As the *active medium* between the components of the system and the external world, the membrane participates in the cell's development, importing basic chemicals as needed for the produc-tion of its constituents and excreting some molecules as waste.[57] The important thing about the membrane, they stress, is that it neither comes before nor after the formation of the cell and its components, but is intrinsic to its creation and maintenance as an individual entity. As a living system a cell is therefore *spatially distinct* from other living systems, but *alike* in its circular organisation, which is arranged so as to produce the *same* elements of which it is comprised and thus ensure its continued life. In short, it is self-producing: 'This circular organiza-tion constitutes a homeostatic system whose function it is to maintain this very same circular organization by determining that the *components* that specify it be those whose synthesis or maintenance it ensures'.[58]

Structure and organisation

Although conceived independently, Maturana and Varela's equation of the indi-vidual identity of organisms with their circular organisation thus also closely mirror's Polanyi's 'operational principles subordinated to a centre of individu-ality'. However, the two authors go further than Polanyi in specifying the pre-cise nature of those principles, drawing a clear line between what they describe as the 'structure' and 'organisation' of living systems. The former refers to the nature and composition of the system's components, which may *change* in the course of development in response to changes in the system's environment. The latter, on the other hand refers to the circular pattern of organisation itself, which *holds the system together throughout any structural changes* and which defines the organism as a member of a specific class. However, while the pattern of circular organisation never changes, this is not meant to imply any kind of sys-temic isolation. On the contrary, Maturana and Varela assert that neither the environment with which an organism interacts nor the organism itself can ever be defined separately from each other:

> Living systems are *units of interactions* [emphasis added]; they exist in an ambi-ence. From a purely biological point of view they cannot be understood independently of that part of the ambience with which they interact: the niche; nor can the niche be defined independently of the living system that specifies it.[59]

Limitations of autopoietic systems

Amongst the key points of autopoietic theory it is the clarity of Maturana and Varela's concept of identity that has made the greatest impact, but which also raises serious questions about the limitations of the theory. For the pioneering cybernetician Stafford Beer, writing in his preface to *Autopoiesis and Cognition*, the invariant circular organisation of living systems proposed by the two collaborators 'solves the problem of identity which two thousand years of philosophy have succeeded only in confounding'.[60] The main point of contention is the inability of the theory to account for evolutionary *change* and emergent phenomena of the sort previously discussed in this chapter. According to the two collaborators, the structural coupling between individual organism and environment limits the organism's responses to changes in its environment to those requiring modification of its *existing* components. Only the human observer, gifted as he or she is with the unique analytic and descriptive powers of language, is able to perceive and describe the broader interactions between organism and environment – which includes other organisms with similar organisations and structures – from an historical perspective:

> An observer beholding an autopoietic system as a unity in a context he also observes, and which he describes as its environment, may distinguish in it internally and externally generated perturbations, even though these are *intrinsically indistinguishable for the autopoietic system itself* [emphasis added]. The observer can use these distinctions to make statements about the history of the autopoietic system which he observes, and he can use this history to describe an ambience (which he infers) as the domain in which the system exists.[61]

Whilst an observer may therefore *represent* in one form or another his or her historical account of a living system and its interactions, Maturana and Varela are adamant that such representations lie *outside* the scope of a living system's own homeostatic structure and organisation:

> To talk about a representation of the ambience or the environment, in the organization of a living system may be metaphorically useful, but it is inadequate and misleading to reveal the organization of an autopoietic system.[62]

So far as the organisation of the system itself is concerned it therefore remains blind, as it were, to the effects and consequences of either internal or external changes, other than its success or failure in maintaining its own identity through those changes. As portrayed by the two authors, therefore, the history of a living system can hence only be perceived by an observer in *hindsight* as a causal sequence of linked states, a process that would seem to specifically *exclude* the possibility of emergence: 'A historical phenomenon is a process of change in which each state of the successive states of a changing system arises as a modification of a previous state in a *causal transformation* [emphasis added], and not *de novo* as an independent occurrence'.[63]

Despite its authors' vaunted claims of explaining how the organisation of living systems gives rise to such cognitive phenomena as 'conceptual thinking, language, and self-consciousness', autopoiesis therefore presents us with yet another conundrum, not so different in kind from the inconclusive debates on emergence outlined previously. Though the principle of circular organisation underpinning autopoietic theory appears close to Polanyi's own operational concept of living systems, Maturana and Varela's limited characterisation of an historical process, in strictly causal terms, is a world away from Polanyi's resounding celebration of emergence 'in the gradual intensification of personal consciousness' in anthropogenesis or, indeed, from later critiques of causal explanations by other emergentists cited in this book.

Diachronic emergence

However, as John Protevi[64] explains in his sympathetic critique of the theory, the main difficulty with autopoiesis as it was originally formulated by Maturana and Varela was not that its authors had no interest in emergence at all, but that their biological concept of circular organisation is limited to *synchronic emergence* (i.e. to the 'relation of part and whole') in which 'the research focus is on identifying an essence of life'.[65] As such, their prime example of cellular production is perfectly adequate to the task. However, strictly defined as a *homeostatic* system, autopoiesis cannot generate the conditions for the *diachronic emergence* of novel patterns of behaviour from the undoing of preceding patterns typical of the temporal dynamics of social systems, the understanding of which calls for a different historical perspective.

Following his collaboration with Maturana on autopoiesis, Varela himself, Protevi recounts, cast doubt on the wisdom of using it as a model for living systems above the cellular level and came to see it as only an example of organisational closure as a more 'general mode of being'. As a political refugee along with Maturana following the 1973 military coup in Chile, Varela had grown particularly wary of the actual and potential misuse of biological models of human development in support of authoritarian and discriminatory policies:

> History has shown that biological holism is very interesting and has produced great things, but it has always had its dark side, a black side, each time it's allowed itself to be applied to a social model. There's always slippages toward fascism, toward authoritarian impositions, eugenics, and so on.[66]

Emergence of the virtual self

Over and above the specific shortcomings of autopoiesis as a biological theory, however, Varela came to believe the more complex dynamics of social and political systems required a new approach: 'the historical changes and multiple causation of political systems *must be thought of in terms of a field* [emphasis added]', the dynamics of which lie 'beyond the scope of autopoietic thought'.[67] Henceforth, though he remained in close contact with his former collaborator, Varela went his own way. There followed a period of intense personal creativity focused on developing a concept of diachronic emergence out of several new strands of thought, culminating in 1993 with *The Embodied Mind*, which he wrote with Evan Thompson and Eleanor Rosch.[68] Described by Protevi as 'the manifesto of the "enactment" school of cognitive science', Varela and his co-authors present the act of projecting our worldviews outwards as 'only one perspective, that it is a *relative frame* [emphasis added], that it must contain a way to undo itself'.[69] Contrary to the closed, self-producing identities of autopoietic systems, epistemological flexibility of this kind involving a repertoire of behaviours and multiple resources, is characteristic of what Varela describes as a 'virtual self'. Breaking with the synchronic perspective of autopoiesis (which he thereafter restricted to cellular production only), Varela identifies two *temporal levels* of cognition – or 'cognitive registers' as he calls them – underlying the emergence of the virtual self, the neurological and the organismic, each of which, Protevi writes, also operates at 'two temporal scales', fast and slow:

> On the fast scale in the neurological register, we find resonant cell assemblies, which arise from chaotic firing patterns; on the fast scale in the organismic register, we see the arising of behavioural modules or 'micro-identities' from a competition among competing modules.[70]

Significantly, Protevi adds, Varela's concept of micro-identities was influenced by phenomenological thought focused on tacit personal skills and 'the concrete life of the everyday', in which self-conscious reflection and verbal reasoning play little if any part. Only when regular patterns of life are *severely disrupted* by unexpected social encounters or other challenges leading to 'breakdowns' in routine behaviour, Varela asserts, does reflective thought and decision making come into force, modifying or replacing deficient behaviours or skills. Whereas the neurological correlates for micro-identities are the resonant cell assemblies (RCAs) themselves, the equivalent correlates of such breakdowns are a retreat into chaotic firing, 'out of which emerges a new RCA'. At no time, however, Protevi observes, is any conscious 'choice' involved as the whole process of a new RCA emerging occurs *too quickly* for conscious reflection – which only happens anyway in 'temporal chunks' – so the emergence of a new RCA arises hidden, so to speak, from reflective consciousness.

Upward and downward effects

As with autopoiesis, Protevi also notes that, in so far as the engagement of an individual being with the world brings forth the world, as perceived by that being, with all its multiple identities, we see in Varela's new diachronic schema something resembling a 'structural coupling' between the virtual self and environment, though with greater scope for the neurological processes involved. The slow temporal scale involves the development and maturation of specific skills and other behavioural modules in the two cognitive registers during the lifetime of the individual. As a 'distributed and modular system' operating at both neurological and organismic levels of cognition, however, the virtual self emerges over time as a 'meshwork of selfless selves' the correlate for which, 'with its multiplicity of micro-identities, is the enacted world',[71] that is to say, the world into which individuals project themselves.

Here Protevi adopts a more critical stance towards Varela's conception of diachronic emergence, which, he argues, stresses the upward effects (upward causation) of the interactions of individuals with others on the creation of social regularities, at the expense of the downward effects (downward causation) of those regularities on those same individuals, which commonly take the form of *institutionalised systems* of social and political control. In addition to governing access to the training and development of many of those unspoken, tacit skills Varela alludes to as shaping everyday life, the downward effects of those systems, Protevi argues, may well include other behavioural modules or micro-identities *more beneficial to the institution concerned* than to the person so affected. Adopting an opposite and equally extreme position regarding downward versus upward effects, Protevi suggests we need to focus more attention on:

> [...] the way this socially enacted world structurally couples with, and guides, the ontogeny of the individual person. It's the pre-personal social world that needs to be thought. Persons are resolutions of the differential social field, concretions of the social field that form the effective topology of the person: the patterns, thresholds, and triggers of basic emotions or affective modules of fear, rage, joy and so on as they interact with the cognitive topology of the person, the cognitive modules or basic coping behaviors that make up the everyday repertoire of the person.[72]

However, it is not necessary to accept Protevi's passive portrait of individuals at the mercy of institutionalised society to agree that the downward effects of emergent properties, whether they be biological or social factors, merit as much attention as their upward effects, as other writers on the mysteries of emergence cited in this chapter have argued.[73] Astute as Protevi's critique is, whilst directing critical attention toward the social and political implications of emergent thought, Protevi also accepts without question Varela's post-autopoietic, fragmentary conception of a 'virtual self' comprised of 'behavioural modules', 'micro-identities' and a 'meshwork of selfless selves' – a far cry, indeed, from the unambiguous statement by his earlier collaborator Maturana quoted earlier, that the living organisation 'must be understood as a unity'.

Emergence on the global scale

Lastly, at the opposite scale to Varela's micro-identities, there has been much recent interest amongst architectural theorists and designers in the application of theories of emergence to architecture. Most of this work has been focused upon the research and development of autonomous or semi-autonomous, computer-based techniques of architectural design, supplanting the traditional human architect's role.[74] In *The Architecture of Emergence*, Michael Weinstock,[75] a leading figure in such research, goes a great deal further however, in offering a planetary-wide view of how diachronic emergence has shaped the systemic interactions between the forces of nature and human civilisation, including the formation of settlement patterns and building morphologies. While, in comparison with the highly abstract quality of the arguments over emergence cited above, Weinstock's impressive account involves relatively concrete matters of the historical expression of those processes on the ground, it comes at the cost of neglecting any direct or purposeful role for any human or other animal agency in the whole story. For Weinstock, the evolution of form in nature and civilisation is the emergent outcome of primal exchanges between matter, energy and evolving informational systems, which he describes in considerable detail, covering both living (plants and animals) and non-living (geological formations, climate) systems, as well as the appearance of early-to-late forms of human habitation, up until modern times, in which civilisations come and go in the same fateful cycles as geological era.

In respect of the general impact of changing information systems on the evolution of all forms of life, Weinstock's approach therefore accords with Jablonka and Lamb's argument that key evolutionary transitions 'were all built on new types of information transmission'. A strong case can also be made for technologies and building morphologies as having virtual 'lives of their own', as argued in this book and elsewhere. However, missing altogether in Weinstock's perspective is any *mediating role* for a living self of any kind in influencing the emergent phenomena he describes. As Polanyi and others have explained, the operational principles underlying all living systems function to *sustain the identity* of the individual being – all else is subservient to that primary function, from the most primitive to the most advanced forms of life. Put another way, possession of a *knowable* identity and a sense of self – knowable, that is, not just by observers but at a minimum level by the organism's *own* nervous system – by which it orientates itself in its environment and controls its interactions, consciously or unconsciously with other organisms, *is critical to the evolution of form in living systems.*

Leave those operational principles of organic life – including possibly plant life too,[76] although that is another story – out of the picture and you not only omit a vital factor in maintaining stable relationships between living systems and their environments, but you also omit any plausible explanation of why things can also go badly wrong in those relationships when a species *misjudges*, consciously or not, the effects of modifying the environment in its favour.

The implications of omitting any living self in Weinstock's perspective are most apparent in his concluding discussion of climate change and its disastrous impacts upon life on this planet, for which humankind, in pursuit of its own exclusive interests, is alone responsible. However, in contrast to the urgent cries by other observers for radical change in the way we live to avert those impacts, Weinstock writes with dispassionate detachment of what the future likely holds:

> It is clear that the world is within the horizon of a systemic change, and that transitions through multiple thresholds will cascade through all the systems of nature and civilization. New forms will emerge down through all the generations to come, and they will develop with new connections between them as they proliferate across the surface of the earth.[77]

There has always been the danger, as Varella reminds us, of the distortion of evolutionary thought and the objectification of living beings, from the simple Darwinian slogan, the 'survival of the fittest', to the dangers he clearly saw in the abstraction of autopoiesis from the social and political realities of human life – a common detachment that has affected the way all forms of life are viewed. However, taking a more inclusive view in the spirit of Bohr's complementary modes of thought,[78] if we accept that self-organisation and emergence are manifest at *all* levels of evolution, then we can more fruitfully encompass the expression of their workings from the most abstract and general level of analysis to the most concrete personal and social matters of the self, the creative tensions between which are a vital part of science, as they are of life.

Chapter 4

The invisible self

In challenging popular unitary conceptions of a personal self, Varela et al heralded many later critiques of what is now frequently described by philosophers, scientists and popular writers alike as the 'myth' or 'illusion' of the self.[1] Whether, like Varela et al below, they fall back upon Buddhist interpretations of a non-self, or subscribe to the idea that the brain simply *deludes* us into thinking we are the authors of our own life stories,[2] or just dismiss the self as an assorted bunch of memes,[3] none attach any importance to the commonsense idea of a self as expressed in everyday language, other than it being an illusion in need of exposing. Designations like 'myself', 'yourself', 'herself', 'himself', 'themselves', 'ourselves' and, above all, the pervasive 'I', are all, we are told, just mental window dressing for the real mechanics of thought and behaviour.

However, the self cannot be so easily dismissed. There are very good reasons, as set out in this book, for the persistence of the idea of a self in everyday language, which go beyond the familiar positions staked out by philosophers and scientists, and which anchor humans and all other animals together in the same fundamental evolutionary processes. Paradoxically, those same systemic, self-organising processes, which are responsible for the successful evolution of all nature's creatures, are also responsible for the rise and domination of *Homo sapiens* and the consequent breakdown in nature's normal regulatory constraints.

Science and common sense

The commonsense idea of the self is important not only for our understanding of the nature and very existence of a self, but also for much else in scientific discourse and its relation to ordinary language and life at large which affects our understanding of human behavior. In calling for a pluralistic epistemology in place of sciences' customary pursuit of a unified project, Dupre, for example, questions scientists' presumption that the language of science, and especially science's way of classifying things – whether they be humans themselves or any organisms – into groups of the same *kind*, or 'natural kinds' as they are called, differs significantly from the commonsense classification of things in ordinary language. The problem with the idea of natural kinds, Dupre argues, is not that some things are perceived as sharing common characteristics that distinguish them from other kinds of things – which is obvious enough – but the assumption that membership of a particular kind signifies 'that it *possesses a certain essential property* [emphasis added], a property that is both necessary and sufficient for a thing to belong to that kind'.[4] The effect, he suggests, is thus to impart an objective status to the thing described and its 'essential' properties *independent* of any specific context or purpose, which can then be compared with other kinds of things similarly devoid of context.

Contesting the essentialist approach to the classification of things with its assumptions of objectivity, Dupre asserts that such questions 'can be answered only in relation to some *specification of the goal* [emphasis added] underlying the intent to classify the object'.[5] Neither is classification just a part of the professional practice of science. It pervades any descriptive use of language. Taking the example from ordinary language of common biological names for creatures and plants such as 'cat', 'cow', 'dandelion', etc., Dupre asks whether, if such commonsense names were to be taken as scientific terms instead, the designated objects would change their fundamental character in significant ways, which would then suggest a 'truly unbridgeable gulf' between science and the rest of human knowledge. However, Dupre argues there is no such gulf between science and common sense and that classifications of this sort are the product of a 'highly pluralistic' ontology shared between the two viewpoints that 'imposes order on the buzzing, blooming confusion of phenomena not by unifying them under a relatively simple structure of fundamental concepts, but *by piecemeal extension of knowledge* [emphasis added]'.[6]

The self that won't go away

In the case of Varela and his collaborators on *The Embodied Mind*, the apparent disregard of familiar terminology for the self in ordinary language and its meaning is all the more odd given that, in challenging the traditional assumption of science that 'the world is independent of the knower', they claim to have been inspired in particular by the phenomenology of Maurice Merleau-Ponty and duly acknowledge the importance to cognitive science of common sense:

> If we are forced to admit that cognition cannot be properly understood without common sense, and that common sense is none other than our bodily and social history, then the inevitable conclusion is that knower and known, mind and world, stand in relation to each other through mutual specification or dependent co-origination.[7]

Earlier in the same book, however, much like the other sceptics cited above, they firmly reject what they describe as the 'naïve sense of self' as it is commonly expressed:

We wish to make a sweeping claim: all of the reflective traditions in human history – philosophy, science, psychoanalysis, religion, meditation – have challenged the naïve sense of self. No tradition has ever claimed to discover an independent, fixed, or unitary self within the world of experience.[8]

Nevertheless, they grant that everyone behaves *as if* such a self does indeed exist, jealously guarding it and, as we all tend to do, projecting their favoured self-image into the world. The task for cognitive scientists, they suggest, therefore comes down to explaining the origins of that illusion, if that is indeed what it is, together with the cognitive mechanisms involved in sustaining it. In addition to citing Merleau-Ponty as a major influence upon their own quest in search of those origins and mechanisms, they also discuss in some detail Buddhist conceptions of a 'decentred self', a key feature of which are the so-called 'five aggregates' of experience. Beginning with 'Forms' – including the human body – which have a purely physical and material basis, they range through four levels of mental experience, from 'feelings/sensations', through 'perceptions/discernments/impulses' and 'dispositional formations', to the very highest level of 'consciousnesses'. Each of the latter four levels includes the previous levels, culminating in consciousness, which includes them all.

Dead end

Eventually however, the authors conclude they have run into a dead end, since even 'consciousness' as presented in Buddhist schools of thought amounts to no more than the sum of its parts and, try as they might, they can find no trace of a self beyond the different aggregates. Moreover, though the co-authors make no direct comment on the anomaly, the lowly status of the human body in the Buddhist hierarchy ill accords with the phenomenological approach of *The Embodied Mind*, as clearly expressed in their introduction: 'For Merleau-Ponty, as for us, *embodiment* has this double sense: It encompasses both the body as a lived, experiential structure and the body as the context or milieu of cognitive mechanisms'.[9]

Varela et al also discuss self-organisation and emergence as promising lines of research, particularly in resolving key issues of cognitive science for which the orthodox 'general problem solving' approach has proven to be inadequate, not only for psychologists but also for research in artificial intelligence. In a chapter titled 'Selfless minds', they explore the work of Marvin Minsky and Seymour Papert on the new 'cognitive architecture' revealed by neuroscience. Rejecting the failed search for cognitive procedures capable of providing 'global solutions' to large problems, Minsky and Papert instead offer a 'connectionist' view of minds consisting of many agents, each of which operates solely in its own micro-world of limited problems, which are necessarily small scale since a single network could not possibly manage them all if they were any larger. The principle task then becomes that of organising all these specialised agents into larger systems of 'agencies' operating at higher levels, from which the human mind 'emerges as a kind of society'.

The difficulty with this approach, as Minsky himself concedes along with all the other sceptics who present the self as an illusion, is that, while it allows no room in cognitive science for the concrete existence of a personal self, we just can't give up on the idea. Neither are Varela et al able to provide a more satisfactory answer to the problem, other than falling back again, in the same chapter, on Buddhist traditions and further lists of the 'basic elements' of consciousness. Similarly, while they offer numerous detailed examples in another chapter of emergent phenomena in artificial intelligence, they get no closer to providing an explanation for the common human belief in an individual self.

Psychological connectedness

Given the fact that so many knowledgeable minds have expended so much effort in decrying what all concede is a persistent idea of the self as embedded in ordinary language, it is fair to wonder if they might not be asking the right questions. What if, say, the statement above by Varela et al on the importance of common sense to cognitive science was to be taken at face value? Following Dupre's line of argument, one might then be inclined to believe there *is*, in fact, something more behind the use of the word 'self' in everyday language than the 'naïve sense' accorded to it by Varela and other sceptics, and that the search for a more substantive self is no more nor less than yet another manifestation of the same essentialism that has misdirected so many other scientific and philosophical quests before. In this case the sceptics' error has been to assume that, in order for the commonly expressed idea of the self to be taken seriously as a scientific or philosophical concept, there must be a *clearly definable essence* underlying that idea, for which the 'necessary and sufficient conditions' may be clearly specified; in other words, logically speaking, either an individual self belongs to a certain class or type of phenomena or it does not – there is no room in essentialist thought for ambiguities or 'in-betweens'.[10]

Were the concept of the self to be confined to a purely physical description of the bodily self, then it is conceivable – though still debatable, as Dupre suggests – that an account of the individual self could be provided that would meet the strict conditions of essentialism. It should nevertheless be evident from the previous discussions on the multitude of internal and external influences on the evolution and development of the individual that no purely physical description could ever resolve the question of what it is that creates and sustains a self, let alone deal with the emergence of new characteristics over time. Neither is any enumeration of the 'aggregates of experience' or other components of a self ever likely to produce any clearer answer, any more than they can explain the unity of the relatively restricted organisation of the autopoietic system originally described by Maturana and Varela.

Mistaken criteria

One prominent philosopher who has offered a novel solution to such problems is David Parfit. In his 1971 paper, 'Personal identity',[11] followed in 1984 by his major work, *Reasons and Persons*,[12] Parfit argues against the prevalent habit of confusing the *psychological* concept of identity with the *logical* 'either-or' concept. Citing a common discrepancy between the criteria of identity applied to individuals over the lifespan, for which an unambiguous answer is generally expected, and the criteria applied to ideas like 'nation', for which such answers are *not* expected, Parfit writes:

> Some people believe that in this respect they are different. They agree that our criteria of personal identity do not cover certain cases, but they believe that the nature of their own identity through time is, somehow, such as to guarantee that in these cases questions about their identity must have answers. This belief might be expressed as follows: 'Whatever happens between now and any future time, either I shall still exist, or I shall not. Any future experience will either be *my* experience, or it will not'.[13]

In attacking that belief and its psychological and physical corollaries, Parfit deploys various counter arguments of which the best known is a thought experiment inspired by the popular TV science fiction series 'Star Trek'. In that series, avoiding the inconveniences of normal space travel Captain Kirk and his intrepid crew members make frequent use of their spaceship's 'teletransporter' – a sort of molecular 'disassembler' – to be immediately and faithfully reassembled on another planet or other remote location and occasionally, in another time period. In what sense, Parfit asks, can we say that a molecularly reassembled individual is really the *same* person, rather than say, just a *replica* that, once 'reborn' at a different place and time, might thereafter pursue a different life than the original person would?[14]

The problem with trying to answer such questions, Parfit reasons, is that, in using the *language* of identity, which implies an exact, one–one relationship of equality between two states or entities, we mistakenly apply criteria that are *inappropriate to the subject* in question. What really matters in understanding continuities of personal characteristics, he states, is personal *survival*, '[and] most of the relations which matter in survival are, in fact, *relations of degree* [emphasis added]. If we ignore this, we shall be led into quite ill-grounded attitudes and beliefs'.[15] What actually survives, Parfit continues, is not any kind of separate mental being of the Cartesian sort, but a chain of overlapping 'experience-memories', enough at least to ensure *psychological connectedness* through one personal change or event to the next. While this may not satisfy a strictly logical or physicalistic interpretation of identity, Parfit claims that 'what it provides is *as good as* personal identity'.[16]

Successive selves

According to Parfit, it follows that, if what underpins our sense of personal identity is psychological connectedness between different personal states as they evolve over time, then we should rethink the individual in terms of 'successive selves' rather than a logically defined, single self. Moreover, since such connectedness is a matter of degree, then the connections between those selves would also vary in strength:

> On this way of thinking, the word 'I' can be used to imply the greatest degree of psychological connectedness. When the connections are reduced, when there has been any marked change of character or style of life, or any marked loss of memory, our imagined beings would say, 'It was not I who did that, but an earlier self'. They could then describe in what ways, and to what degree, they are related to this earlier self.[17]

While it might seem unlikely that many individuals would take such a detached view of their own personal history, Parfit suggests that making distinctions of this kind between successive selves is 'surprisingly natural' and quotes from Marcel Proust as one of several authors who have done just that in their writings: 'We are incapable, while we are in love, of acting as fit predecessors of the next persons who, when we are in love no longer, we shall presently have become'.[18] On a different level, the ongoing research on neuroplasticity also helps to answer a vital question regarding the transition process between selves not addressed by Parfit – namely, just how is it, given the varying levels of connectivity between successive selves from weak to strong, that the nervous system is able to cope with the considerable burden of never-ending change placed upon it throughout the lifespan? Similarly, while neither the philosophy nor science of emergence has yet come up with a full explanation of that process, they offer a language and theoretical basis with which to address changes in levels of cognition and development that might occur between distinct selves.

Field theory

Nevertheless, while all these developments and discoveries help to fill in important gaps in the tantalising jigsaw puzzle that is the self, the most important question of all remains unanswered, which is: *What is the integrating force that holds all the constituent elements of an individual self together during its transformations from one state to the next?* And no less important, what, if any, *evolutionary function* might that integrating force be acting out?

A related body of theory, known as the 'field view' of self-organisation,[19] gets us closer to answering those questions, though it has not until now been applied explicitly to the problem of the self.[20] Predating cybernetics and systems theory with which it is now associated, field theory has its origins in the same fundamental shift in science from mechanistic to *relational thinking* that began early in the last century in physics and mathematics and which subsequently spread out, albeit unevenly, into the biological and human sciences.[21] In biology, for example, Brian Goodwin[22] contrasts the field view of self-organisation, which stresses the *whole organism* as the fundamental biological entity, subject to general laws of form and structure, against the standard neo-Darwinian, atomistic view of the gene and natural selection as the principle mechanisms of inheritance, which 'is determined not by rational law, but by historical accident, by contingency'.[23] Moreover, Goodwin recounts that, though largely forgotten since Darwinism swept the board, an alternative, pre-Darwinian tradition of thought had been promoted by a group of prominent eighteenth-century morphologists, 'who were animated by a belief in the possibility of a rational, intelligible ordering or classification of organisms that would provide an insight into the laws of organic creation (i.e., generative rules)'.[24]

Organising rules

However, it was the pioneering embryologist H. Driesch, Goodwin explains, who, in reviving that lost train of thought, first introduced the field concept into embryology in the late 1920s: 'Driesch assumed, as did the rational morphologists, that there are organising rules operating within organisms to *constrain or limit the forms that can be generated* [emphasis added]'. In particular, Driesch's research demonstrated that the *relative position* of a cell in the whole embryo 'is a primary determinant of cell fate and the parts that emerge during individuation and differentiation come into being as a result of *local and global ordering principles* [emphasis added], generating a structural and functional unity'.[25] According to this view, Goodwin writes, which stresses both the *conservative* as well as the dynamic aspects of self-organisation, 'the organism is not so much a self-organising system that generates an ordered state from more or less disordered parts; it is more a self-organised entity that *can undergo transformations preserving this state* [emphasis added]'.[26]

Following Driesch's example, Goodwin's own mathematically supported studies of the so-called 'cleavage process' typical of embryogenesis – the process by which cells, starting with the two-cell stage following the first division of the egg, continue splitting into ever larger but equally regular numbers of cells – confirms the complex picture of internally constrained, self-organising fields. Summarising his findings, Goodwin writes:

> The fertilized egg is *both a cell and a developing organism* [emphasis added]. It is an organism insofar as it is totality describable by a field; it is a cell insofar as it embodies the specific constraints (e.g., binary subdivision) characteristic of such an entity. As cleavage proceeds, the organism continues to be identified with the whole field (the embryo), while cells are identified as parts that play specific roles within a transforming context.[27]

Thus, while the organism replaces the common definition of the cell as the unit of life, conceptual ambiguities between 'cell' and 'organism' are resolved in the field view of self-organisation by a 'decentred structure' and *reciprocal process* of emergence, in which the organism, defined as the global field, 'continues to impose organizational constraints upon the whole, while the parts impose reciprocal constraints so that a specific form arises'.[28] A field description of developing organisms of this sort, Goodwin suggests, allows the *parts* of organisms to retain active properties of their own, while describing their organisation *within the whole* as an expression of distributed influences.

Psychological fields

In the same period that Driesch introduced the field concept to embryology, the German psychologist Kurt Lewin[29] formulated his theory of the 'total psychological field' of an individual as the combined interactions of individual and environment, which he called the 'life space'. Also described as the 'founder of social psychology' for his pioneering work on group dynamics and organisational development, Lewin studied first biology and then behavioural psychology at the University of Berlin where, as a young lecturer in psychology and philosophy in the inter-war years, he was influenced by the gestalt school of psychology, with its focus on the perceived whole. It was also during this turbulent period in Germany, before Lewin moved to the United States, that he began setting out his thoughts on a new kind of psychology, publishing several articles in German, which were later collected and translated in the US under the title, *A Dynamic Theory of Personality*.[30] Refuting the generally accepted belief amongst psychologists of his time that individuals behave similarly because they have similar psychological characteristics, the nature of which can be separately classified and analysed,[31] Lewin argued the approach overlooks finer individual differences of *degree* and was based on outdated Aristotelian modes of thought which treated all such features as isolable phenomena - the scientific value of which rested entirely on proving they applied to large numbers of subjects. Against the Aristotelian approach, Lewin posits what he describes as an emergent, 'Galileian mode' of thinking in some disciplines:

> As in physics, the grouping of events and objects into paired opposites and similar logical dichotomies is being replaced by groupings with the aid of *serial concepts which permit of continuous variation* [emphasis added], partly owing simply to wider experiences and the recognition that transition stages are always present.[32]

At the heart of this new mode of thinking, Lewin explains, which shaped the outlook of such luminaries of the night skies as Johannes Kepler and Galileo himself, is the idea of a 'comprehensive, all-embracing unity of the physical world',[33] in which the orbits of the planets, a free-falling stone and all manner of other physical phenomena that would previously have been treated separately, were now understood to be governed by the very same laws. Similarly, the differences between orbiting planets and free-falling objects, as great as they might appear, could now be seen as *variations* of a law – the law of gravity in this case – and its effects.

The change of viewpoint turns scientists' attention from finding whatever characteristics fit with the largest group of objects or other phenomena as the measure of its importance, to a deeper focus on *concrete case studies* and the degrees to which those individual cases may vary, according to the particular laws and conditions involved. At the same time, Lewin cautions against treating field theory on the same level as a general law of physics, though it might have been inspired by such theories. Field theory, he suggests, can hardly be called correct or incorrect in the same manner as the Newtonian laws. Rather, he advises: '*Field theory is probably best characterized as a method*: namely, a method of *analyzing causal relations and of building scientific constructs*',[34] that can be expressed in the form of certain general statements about the 'nature' of the conditions of change.

Boundary conditions

Though existing applications of the new mode of thought in psychology were few and far between at the time Lewin set down his theory of personality, he found encouraging signs of change in what he describes as the sensory areas of psychology, such as optics, acoustics and smell (what would now probably be bracketed under neuropsychology); particularly with regard to the relations between individual and environment. Pursuing his Galilean approach to the problem, he criticizes Aristotelian logic for treating each of the senses separately from each other and from the 'ground' or situation in which they all operate: 'Rather, the whole dynamics of sensory psychological processes depends upon the ground and beyond it upon the structure of the *whole surrounding field* [emphasis added]'.[35]

In addition to advances in the sensory areas he also found indications of new approaches in those fields of study concerned with the higher mental processes. Regarding the subject of human feelings, for example, he credits Sigmund Freud in particular for abolishing the boundaries between the normal and unusual or pathological, thereby advancing the integration of the different fields of psychology. Similarly, many of his early studies focused on child behaviour for the evidence they offered of the changing dimensions of the psychological field according to age. In a key section titled, 'Boundaries of the self', he writes:

> The individual is dynamically a *relatively closed system* [emphasis added]. How strongly the environment operates upon the individual will be determined (apart from the structure and forces of the situation) by the functional *firmness of the boundaries* between individual and environment.[36]

Thus, each step of the developmental process involves a progressive discovery and stabilisation of those boundaries, with the 'I' of the self only emerging in the second or third year: 'Not until then does the concept of property appear, of the belonging of a thing to [his or her] own person'.[37] In one of Lewin's many prescient insights, he notes that the relative firmness of the boundary between the self and environment during these formative years depends, not only upon the age of the child and his or her individual characteristics, but also upon their *interactions* with other key persons, and even *significant objects* in their lives:

> Not only other persons but other objects may have a close psychological relation with the self of the child. To the 'I' in this sense there belong not only the child's own body but certain toys, a particular chair, etc. Such objects are dynamically somewhat like his own body in that they represent points of special sensitivity to invasions by environmental forces.[38]

Lewin only uses the term 'life space' sparingly in these early essays, perhaps aware of possible confusions with the physical concept of space. Nevertheless, inspired by the mathematical precision with which the laws of physics are laid down – a precision which enables the generality of a law to be tested against concrete case studies and vice versa – he devotes much of his work to creating a formal language with which to express the spatial character of the psychological field. For this he drew upon topology, then a relatively new form of non-metric mathematics, for exploring spatial dimensions, illustrating his essays with numerous topological diagrams of the relations between different elements in the psychological field and the forces or 'vectors' acting upon them. In a later collection of theoretical papers, Lewin[39] also clarified his concept of psychological space and its importance in field theory:

> The basic statements of a field theory are that (a) behaviour has to be derived from a totality of coexisting facts, (b) these coexisting facts have the character of a 'dynamic field' is so far as the state of any part of this field depends on every other part of the field. The proposition (a) includes the statement that we have to deal in psychology, too, with a manifold, the *interrelations of which cannot be represented without the concept of space* [emphasis added].[40]

Psychological space, as conceived by Lewin, therefore, is fundamentally a *relational concept*; it refers to the interactions *between* the psychological factors and other possible elements affecting the outlook and behaviour of an individual, rather than just the factors themselves. Accordingly, given the attention Lewin also pays to childhood development in his work, it might be assumed that the life space includes the normal life span and its changes – at one point in *Dynamic Theory* he specifically heads a section describing the effects of education on the growing child with the title: 'Extension of Psychological Life-Space and – Time'.[41] However, defining the time scale encompassed by the life space in a later essay, Lewin writes: 'Any behavior or any other change in a psychological field depends only upon the psychological field *at that time*'. The more limited time-scale, he concedes, 'has been frequently misunderstood and interpreted to mean that field theorists are not interested in historical problems or in the effect of previous experiences',[42] which is certainly the case according to some.[43] However, Lewin insists, nothing could be further from the truth. The confusion arises, he explains, from:

> [...] the fact that the psychological field which exists at a given time contains also *the views of that individual about his future and his past* [emphasis added]. The individual sees not only his present situation; he has certain expectations, wishes, fears, daydreams for his future. His views about his own past and that of the rest of the physical and social world are often incorrect but nevertheless constitute, in his life space, the 'reality-level' of the past.[44]

For all that, the inclusion of what individuals remember about their past or think about their future at a particular point in time offers little or no explanation for any *longer-term patterns of thought and behaviour*, such as are influenced by epigenetic factors inherited by the individual, along with their genetic inheritance. As Lewin suggests, what an individual thinks about the world around him or her at a particular time may, in fact, be quite mistaken, at least in terms of what a more detached observer of his or her behaviour might conclude from a broader social or historical perspective. Surely, one might be permitted to think, such issues should be taken into account in defining the life space, if only in outline, as an *essential prerequisite* for understanding whatever may be going on in the mind of a person at a more specific time. This does not mean to say that Lewin excludes such factors entirely. On the contrary, in accounting for the non-psychological elements that might affect the boundaries of the life space, he goes to some lengths to include them in a broader, ecological framework, albeit they remain firmly tied to a fixed time period:

> Theoretically, we can characterize this task as discovering what part of the physical or social world will determine *during a given period* [emphasis added] the 'boundary zone' of the life space. This task is worth the interest of the psychologists. I would suggest calling it 'psychological ecology'.[45]

Social dimensions

The outcome is that, as interpreted by Lewin, field theory is treated effectively as a *synchronic* or ahistorical theory – a description shared with Maturana and Varela's original formulation of autopoiesis – rather than the truly dynamic metatheory promised in Lewin's allusions to Galilean thinking. The need for a broader historical perspective and time scale is especially apparent when it comes to dealing with any social dimensions of the life space. Lewin acknowledges as much in pointing to the growing interest in the social aspects of personal life amongst psychologists in his time, who had previously emphasised the biological character of the individual:

> These psychologists recognize that the child from his first day of life is objectively *a part of a social setting* [emphasis added] and would die within a few days if he were to be withdrawn from it. Also, the so-called 'subjective' world of the individual, his life space, is influenced in a much earlier stage by social facts and social relations than anyone would have expected a few decades ago.[46]

Offering the same meticulously detailed approach to social psychology as he takes in dissecting the individual life space, he warns that the variety of divergent facts social psychologists have to deal with might appear overwhelming, requiring: 'The integrating of vast areas of very divergent facts and aspects [and] the development of a scientific language (concepts) which is able to treat cultural, historical, sociological, psychological, and physical facts on a common ground'.[47] Staying within his own comfort zone, however, Lewin's explorations in this direction are limited to a particular period in an individual's life – namely adolescence – fraught as it is with enough personal changes to keep most field psychologists busy.[48]

Relational approach

Lewin died prematurely in 1947 before he was able to pursue the social aspects of field theory any further. However, others have since taken up the challenge, prominent amongst which Pierre Bourdieu's[49] studies of 'social fields' cover a broad range of social behaviours and institutions, including the political, scientific, economic, artistic and religious fields, the character of which is largely governed by subconsciously assimilated principles: 'Thinking in terms of fields requires a conversion of one's entire usual vision of the social world, a vision interested only in those things which are visible'.[50]

According to Bourdieu, a sociologist, anthropologist and philosopher whose own work on field theory has been as influential in the social sciences as Lewin's, each social field is governed by its own specific rules but shares invariant factors in common, such as *relative autonomy* from other fields and increasingly specialised knowledge, languages and structures of power that shape them and control participation. As with Lewin's concept of the life space, the epistemological roots of Bourdieu's social field theory, Mathieu Hilgers and Eric Mangez[51] write, like that of other later field theorists, lie in a relational approach:

What characterizes field theories, regardless of the discipline, and therefore constitutes their common epistemological background, is that they reject the existence of an absolute (social or physical) space and consequently of individual objects or agents existing independently of a set of relations. *Space, whether social or physical, is relational* [emphasis added]. The field implies the existence of an indivisible dynamics between a totality and the elements that constitute it. The field does not designate an entity but a *system of relations* [emphasis added].[52]

Critically, at the most general level, the diverse applications of field theory also feature systems with *organisational closure*, the purpose of which is to *maintain the integrity of the field, and with it, its characteristic identity*. Recall that, preceding Maturana and Varela's original definition of autopoiesis by many years, Lewin himself describes the individual as a 'relatively closed system' with dynamic characteristics of its own. Field theory thus offers what is generally missing from the specific examples of emergent properties in various phenomena described in the previous chapter and elsewhere in this book, which is a systemic *reason* for their emergence. That said, if field theory therefore shares with autopoiesis the principle of organisational closure, there remains a world of difference between the strictly closed, circular organisation of autopoiesis that later compelled Varela himself to restrict the theory to cellular reproduction, and the practice-based, tacitly acknowledged contract between the historically evolved social fields and their human agents described by Bourdieu:

The cognitive structures which social agents implement in their practical knowledge of the social world are *internalized, 'embodied' social structures* [emphasis added]. The practical knowledge of the social world that is presupposed by 'reasonable behaviour' within it implements classificatory schemes [...], historical schemes of perception and appreciation which are the product of the objective division into classes (age groups, genders, social classes) and *which function below the level of consciousness and discourse* [emphasis added].[53]

The habitus

Taken altogether, the multiple viewpoints from which *ordinary agents themselves* see the social world, Bourdieu writes, constitute 'the habitus', or the social space of life styles, as he describes it: 'Social space is to the practical space of everyday life [...] what geometrical space is to the travelling space of ordinary experience'.[54] Moreover, employing the language of homological thinking described previously in this book, he argues that the 'generative schemes of the habitus' (i.e., the logical division into oppositional classes and perspectives) are homologous to otherwise quite different areas of social practice. While he suggests that art offers possibly the greatest scope for such expressions, Bourdieu also asserts there is no area of the habitus where 'the stylization of life', that is to say, 'the primacy of form over function', does not have the same effects on the behaviour and manners of its actors. In language, for example, there is the typical opposition between popular outspokenness (e.g., on sexual matters) on the one hand, and the more restrained, censored language of the bourgeois. The same restraint is apparent, he suggests, in the body language of the elevated classes, where slowness and impassivity are opposed to the more agitated and hasty gestures of other classes.

Expressive as they are of fundamental structures in society, however, such principles of division and the roles and positions they create within a social field 'are common to all the agents of the society and make possible the production of a common, meaningful world, a common-sense world'.[55] Similarly, each social field also has its own systemic rituals and rewards, which not only maintain the identity of the field, but also serve to create the identity of the agents themselves:

> Social functions are social fictions. And the rites of institution create the person they institute as king, knight, priest or professor by forging his social image emphasis, fashioning the representation that he can and must give as a moral person, that is, as a plenipotentiary, representative or spokesman of a group. But they also create him in another sense. By giving him a name, a title, which defines, institutes, and constitutes him, *they summon him to become what he is, or rather, what he has to be* [emphasis added]; they order him to fulfil his function, to take his place in the game, in the fiction, to play the game, to act out the function.[56]

As Hilgers and Mangez explain, the evolution and continuation of a complex social field of the kind described by Bourdieu requires the active participation of 'a corps of specialists' or elites knowledgeable in the field's practices, who are both recognised and rewarded for their knowledge and skills. The more autonomous the field of activity is, they write, the more control these specialists will exert over those practices, leading to ever-more stringent forms of organisational closure:

> In becoming more autonomous, the functioning of a field also *increases the closure effects* [emphasis added]. The greater its autonomy, the more the field is produced by and produces agents who master and possess an area of specific competence [...] As the field closes in on itself, the practical mastery of the specific heritage of its history, objectified and celebrated in past works by the guardians of legitimate knowledge, is also autonomized and increasingly constitutes a minimum entry tariff that every new entrant must pay.[57]

Given their different theoretical origins, what is especially striking about Bourdieu's theory of social fields closing in on themselves is the extent to which they resemble the conservative system of 'double closure' described in the previous chapter as a key principle of second-order cybernetics. Much like that former process, progressive organisational closure in the social realm, as Hilgers and Mangez write, operates to *reduce or adapt* the possible interpretations of the world in which a field evolves to those which best accord with the field's *own* purposes and criteria: 'The more autonomous the field, the more it produces an autonomous language, representations and practices, and the more *the perception of realities is subject to the logic specific to the field* [emphasis added]'.[58]

The self as a self-organising system

Concepts like double closure, which are applicable to all forms of self-organisation, not only help us to understand the practical operation of Bourdieu's social fields, but also go a long way to resolving some major questions concerning the nature of the self as a self-organising system of extended cognition proposed here, namely: How do you define the *boundaries* of that system, with all its diffuse elements, and what are the cognitive and social processes involved in setting out and maintaining those boundaries?

The problem with the concept of boundaries, as Lewin defines them above in his psychological field theory, is that, described in terms of the relative 'firmness' of the boundaries between self and environment, they suggest something more of an 'edge condition' between 'inside' and 'outside' rather than any deeper form of spatial or organisational structure that one might expect from Lewin's approach. Neither does Bourdieu himself offer much help on such issues. For Bourdieu, the human agents populating social fields only exist in so far as they serve to play out their assigned roles in each field. To all intents and purposes, viewed from Bourdieu's perspective, agents *have* no other lives, except perhaps, in so far as they might participate in overlapping social fields.

Nevertheless, as far apart as they might seem, a clear parallel can be drawn between the *reduction of environmental complexity* in the case of social fields and similar systems of double closure operating within the self-field. More commonly discussed in later parts of this book under the rubric of 'cognitive dissonance' or 'confirmation bias', much like the subjection of realities to the prevailing logic within a social field that Bourdieu describes, cognitive dissonance essentially functions to *filter out* events and viewpoints that do not conform with well-established personal beliefs and values. There is a drawback, however, to conservative systems of organisational closure of this kind, whether they apply to the individual self-field or larger social fields. That is, in reducing environmental complexity, self-organising systems may also filter out any environmental signals warning of a potentially dangerous mismatch between system and environment, which could, if ignored, lead to pathological conditions and eventually, psychological or systemic collapse – not only of individual lives, but of whole societies.

Commonalities between human and non-human animal behaviour

Similar regulatory conditions, it can be argued, apply across all forms of sentient life no matter how simple or complex, undermining anthropocentric concepts of the individual self and blurring conventional divisions between species in favour of *variations and gradations* of difference. That might appear to be glossing over huge differences in levels of self-awareness. However, in so far as much, if not the greater part, of human cognition and the playing out of every day behaviour and skills is conducted on a tacit level, or is reliant upon tacit knowledge, as Polanyi and others cited in this book argue, it is not unreasonable to suggest that the differences between humans and other life forms, if not exaggerated, have, in turn, glossed over significant commonalities. Like most creatures, humans operate much of the time well *below* the level of reflective self-consciousness, and only occasionally surface to contemplate their condition, as Varela and others have also argued, when prompted by some obvious failure of perception or confrontation between differing viewpoints.[59]

Like many other creatures, humans have also worked hard to modify the natural environment in pursuit of what they perceive as their own best interests. However, for all the motivational similarities, there remains a very big difference between other creatures' niche construction efforts, limited as they are by both cognitive and technological skills as well as by geographical habitat, and the negative environmental effects of human efforts along those lines – an ecological transformation that had already begun, as Spencer Wells[60] persuasively argues in *Pandora's Seed*, millennia before the industrial revolution, with agriculture and settled lifestyles. Now compounded, however, by accelerating climate change and species extinction, those efforts look increasingly destructive, and even self-destructive; a development against which the celebrated human capacity for critical self-reflection has so far proven ineffective.[61] It behooves us therefore, to better understand what has brought us to this dire state, and if there might not be something in the conservative nature of the human self-field that encourages us to ignore what may appear to be only distant threats to our personal survival, or worse, makes us simply incapable of saving ourselves from ourselves.

Some propositions

With that urgent quest in mind, some basic propositions are listed below as theoretical guidelines to the more detailed discussions of the self-field and its many expressions presented in the remaining parts of this book. Where necessary, as with Parfit's important concept of 'successive selves', key ideas and approaches outlined in these pages have been adapted to better fit with the metatheory advanced here; the reason in this case being that the term's connotations of the *displacement* of one personal self by another overly tips the balance of meaning in the direction of fragmentation.[62] In correcting that balance, it is proposed that Parfit's interpretation of the self as a chain of overlapping 'experience-memories' would be better served by the alternative term 'serial selves' offered below – a concept which, while incorporating the fact of significant changes from one developmental phase to the next, preserves the essential integrity and continuity of the self, without which it cannot survive.

For the sake of brevity, while other features of the metatheory also have wider applications to all life forms, in addition to *homo sapiens* their application is mostly restricted to other animal species – and particularly, but not exclusively, mammalian species – for which there is an accumulating body of evidence of tool use and other aspects in common with humankind. Roughly speaking, they have also been arranged in order of generality from those features applicable to all creatures, to those specifically applying to our own species.

(1) The essentialist search for an autonomous personal self that, logically speaking, exists in a class of its own independent of any specific purpose, is misguided. That does not mean, however, that there is no such thing as a coherent, living self. Like the source of the invisible magnetic field that only becomes visible through its effects, the existence and purpose of the self is revealed in many different ways *through the field effects of the self-organising system* that creates and sustains it.

(2) All nature's creatures depend for their existence and survival upon a sensory capacity, no matter how primitive, to *distinguish between members of their own species and those of other life forms*, which may include predators as well as edible organisms sharing the same environment. The ability to make such distinctions – which varies with the nervous systems of the species involved – constitutes the most basic form of *self-awareness* common to all living creatures.

(3) The self-field is a *relational and diachronic concept*. It covers *historically inherited* genetic and epigenetic factors, together with those acquired in the lifetime of the individual that may affect its development. Any study of the current self-field of an individual, whether of a human or other animal, must therefore take account of those earlier influences, which may be presently expressed in significant behavior patterns.

(4) The *level of self-awareness* is relative to the *complexity* of the nervous system of the species and its interactions with its environment. Such interactions include both positive and negative responses from creatures of the same or different species to an individual's behaviour, the combination of which affirms the *identity of the individual*. A further basic level of self-awareness, called 'self-agency', enables all creatures to distinguish between their *own bodily actions* and similar actions, such as vocalisations, by members of the same species.

(5) *Awareness of any challenges* to the identity and survival of the self, whether actual or potential, may begin at an unconscious level and surface at a

conscious or semi-conscious level as *emotions or feelings*. However, such feelings and the self-regulating subsystems that monitor them *cannot be understood in isolation from each other*, but operate *within* the self-organising system that sustains the self.

(6) The *totality of interactions* between the individual self and environment, including both reciprocal and non-reciprocal relations with other individuals, constitutes the self-field. The *components* of that field, in addition to specified individuals and groups, include all those physical, spatial, and behavioural elements comprising the *experiential domain* of an individual.

(7) At more advanced levels of development, belonging to a specific *social group* and participation in *group activities* is fundamental to the evolution of the self for most animal species, through which individuals acquire much of their personal identity. The capacity of the group to *confirm or disconfirm* that identity constitutes a vital *boundary condition* for the self, which may change during the lifespan as the individual matures. At the systemic level, such boundary conditions may coalesce in a form of *organisational closure* similar to that of all living systems.

(8) Individual beings or groups in the process of establishing manageable boundary conditions may also activate a more specific form of organisational closure, called 'double closure', in which a living system purposefully *reduces* environmental complexities to more particular and *simpler levels* appropriate to its own interests. In so doing, they may also create in some measure their *own realities* – a pragmatic but potentially dangerous strategy, that may reduce the capacity of that being or organisation to recognise and respond to environmental changes that could threaten its ultimate survival.

(9) All creatures have at the spatial centre of their self-field a *body image*, which is the nervous system's internal representation of the physical body and functions as the *operational focal point* of the experiential domain. The body image, however, is not a fixed representation and may be adapted and *spatially extended* to incorporate tools or other external elements into an integrated mind-body entity, either temporarily or for longer periods if experience requires it.

(10) Changes to the self-field in the normal course of development may switch between those that can be explained as the outcome of prior conditions and the *emergence* of new properties and characteristics that cannot be so explained, but are the outcome of *spontaneous internal changes* to the self-field, the primary function of which is to *preserve the continuity of the whole*.

(11) The technical self-field of many creatures extends beyond tool making and use to the construction of nests, burrows and other shelters to protect themselves and their offspring from climatic extremes and predators, thus enhancing their chances of survival. However, at its most extreme, for much of humankind the self-field is now *saturated by technology*, to the

extent that it has largely *displaced the natural environment* in which we live, creating new and unanticipated dangers to survival.

(12) Durable and complex animal constructions such as termite mounds are comparable with many human building traditions, and, like animal tool making and use, constitute *externalised forms of cultural and technological knowledge* previously thought exclusive to humans. However, no other species matches *Homo sapiens* for the complexity and sheer *speed* of cultural and technological development, or the range of *technical media* available for the reproduction and dissemination of personal and collective knowledge, creating with it the possibility of higher levels of *historical and reflective consciousness*.

(13) For all the sophistication of human cultural and technological achievements, however, higher levels of self-consciousness are neither universal nor are they continually available to individuals, but are dependent upon personal social and cultural backgrounds, levels of education and the *situation of the moment*. For much, if not all of the time, even the most highly educated person will be reliant upon his or her tacit knowledge and skills – whether of the social or technical sort – to get through the day and will be subject to unconscious biases of one kind or another. In short, *consciousness is a variable factor* rather than the invariant concept of Cartesian dualism.

(14) While modern forms of travel and communication have *extended the spatial boundaries* of the human self-field, affirmation of an individual's self-perceptions *by others* remains essential to maintaining organisational closure, just as it was in earlier stages in the evolution of our species, reinforcing a loose but effective system of self-regulation. Similarly, such affirmations are sought and found in human societies through family and other personal relationships, but also from members of wider social groups through work and other social activities, the opinions of whom may matter greatly to the individual concerned.

(15) Many vital elements of the human self-field, including personal relationships and possessions, habitat, workplace and social standing as well as body images, are *encapsulated in a self-image*, the consciousness of which may vary from low to high, especially when any of those key elements is threatened or changes in some way. Such changes may occur in the course of development and maturation from childhood through adult life and are normally absorbed as *emergent factors* in the evolution of the self-field, resulting in new self-images. Established self-images may, however, also be severely *disrupted* by unexpected events, social or neuropsychological breakdowns.

(16) The considerable physical, psychological and social *transformations* a human being normally undergoes in the course of a lifetime requires a rethinking of *personal identity*, away from its association with a single individual to a *sequence of linked selves*, dependent for its continuity by *psychological connectedness and the development of autobiographical memory*. More complex and

frequent, however, than the common distinctions between 'childhood', 'adolescence', 'adulthood' and 'old age' suggest, each stage of development shares key elements with other stages, such as spatial habitat or durable relationships with other individuals or groups. Altogether, they form a *series* of overlapping self-fields characterised by *relations of degree* rather than the strict logical meaning of identity.

(17) *Resistance to change* that might challenge the identity of the self is an endemic feature of human behaviour at both conscious and unconscious levels, depending upon individual and group circumstances. Often described in psychological terms as *cognitive dissonance* or *confirmation bias*, such responses are, however, the *symptoms* of deeper, systemic processes of organisational closure described above as 'double closure'. What may also be regarded as a normally pragmatic evolutionary strategy has, in the case of human development, effectively divorced humanity from nature, the devastating consequences of which many still refuse to acknowledge.

Thus equipped, we can now proceed to elaborate on these fundamentals, which are all bound together. However, rather than take them one by one in the same order or attempt to present examples specific to each one, which would deny the holistic spirit in which they are conceived, the topics discussed in the following chapters are purposefully selected for the way they touch upon several key features of the metatheory, the relations between which are critical to understanding the complex nature of the self-field.

Chapter 5

Mapping the field

Of the possible features of any self-field equivalent to the consistent features described in the last chapter as characteristic of all field theories, the human body would appear to be the most obvious. Yet, aside from the physical changes every person experiences as they grow and mature, formerly clear distinctions between mind, body and environment have made way for a complex and changeable synthesis of visible and invisible elements extending beyond any obvious physical or spatial boundaries. The understanding and mapping of these mixed elements have created new research fields and techniques of their own, often involving both human and non-human subjects, particularly in the neurosciences. Taken together they offer fresh insights into the similarities and differences between the behaviour of humans and other animal species, highlighting controversial issues of consciousness and comparable cognitive and technical achievements.

The following sections cover the most relevant of these developments to understanding the self-field and its spatial and social extensions, and the light they throw upon the complex interactions between what have previously been regarded as separate neuronal functions and sensory systems. Some discoveries, as in the case of mirror neurons, have, in turn, stirred much controversy about their possible impacts on human behaviour and development at higher levels, arguments that will doubtless continue well into the future. Finally, we examine what such research can teach us about the roots of our emotions, and the vital part they play in monitoring the self and its interactions with the people and world about us.

Brain–body schemas

The discovery by Wilder Penfield, a Canadian surgeon and pioneer of modern neurology, of the role specific parts of the brain play in the formation of body schemas – mental images or 'maps' we all have of our bodies and their component parts – set the course in brain science for future revelations of a mind–body synthesis.[1] Penfield made his discovery during a series of experimental operations he conducted in the 1940s and 1950s on patients being treated for epilepsy. Searching for abnormal tissues, each patient's physical responses to the touch of an electrode on different parts of the exposed cerebral cortex were carefully noted.[2] From there, Penfield built up a comprehensive picture of which parts of the brain were linked to which parts of the body.

Combining his findings, Penfield created a complete neurological 'touch map' of the body, which he named the 'homunculus' after the Latin for 'little man'. Contrary to expectations, instead of being located in the brain in a similar spatial relationship to that of the body, the linked brain and body parts are shown *upside down* on Penfield's map. Notably, the part of the brain linked to the face is located just *below* rather than above the part linked to the hand, while both face and hand parts occupy disproportionately large areas of the map compared to other parts, indicative of their relative sensitivity to touch.[3]

Phantom limbs

However, Penfield's body-mapping techniques proved to be more durable than his colourful picture of the neurological equivalent of a human map-maker. In his research into the source and treatment of so-called 'phantom limbs', V. S. Ramachandran,[4] a neuroscientist and prominent critic of the idea of a unitary self, argues that, not only is the *normally* functioning body a temporary but useful phantom the brain constructs for individual convenience, but that the personal self is similarly constructed out of not one, but a *multitude of neural maps* in the brain: 'If so, your concept of a single "I" or "self" inhabiting your brain may be simply an illusion – albeit one that allows you to organize your life more efficiently, gives you a sense of purpose and helps you interact with others'.[5]

Ramachandran recites the case of a male subject called Tom who had lost an arm in an accident, but continued to feel 'itching' and painful sensations in his phantom fingers. Stroking different parts of Tom's body skin with a simple swab, Ramachandran asked him each time what he felt, until he finally reached Tom's face, whereupon, after responding (unsurprisingly) that he felt his cheek being touched, he added that it felt as though Ramachandran was touching his missing (phantom) thumb at the same time. Touching other parts of Tom's face elicited similar responses, each part being identified with a different finger, providing, Ramachandran writes: 'a complete map of Tom's phantom hand – on his face!'[6] The explanation for these odd sensations, he deduces, lies in the way particular body parts are mapped in the brain, in which the face and hand are mapped adjacent to each other. Following the loss of Tom's hand, the sensory fibres normally activating the facial area of the brain had now also taken over the vacated job of activating the area of the brain normally linked to the hand, so that, when Ramachandran touched Tom's face, it seemed as though he was also touching his missing hand.

Investigations with other amputees using modern neuroimaging techniques confirmed the accuracy of Penfield's original map and produced comparable results. For Ramachandran, the implications were 'staggering'. The combined findings not only pointed to the actual cause of phantom limbs, which had hitherto been the source of many misguided theories and treatments, but also revealed the extraordinary *plasticity* of neural connections at a time when it was still generally believed that, once laid down in infancy, they remained fixed for the rest of life.[7]

Spatial extensions

More remarkable still, neuroscientists have also found that, in addition to those more familiar body schemas described above, other body- and space-mapping functions of the brain *reach beyond the actual physical body* to take in surrounding spaces both close into and at further distances from the body. Reviewing the research in this field, which includes studies of extended brain–body functions in humans as well as other animals, Guiseppe di Pellegrino and Elisabetta Ladavas[8] explain:

> In everyday life, we experience the space around us as a unitary and seamless whole. Yet, a growing body of evidence in contemporary neuro-science reveals that the brain constructs not one but various *functionally distinct representations of space* [emphasis added].[9]

Those spaces close enough to the body for objects to be easily reached and handled, called the 'peripersonal space', are represented by one set of brain functions, while those surrounding spaces containing objects which are out of immediate reach are represented by the brain as 'extrapersonal space'. Though the authors' review, like much of the research itself, is generally couched in the mechanistic, 'stimulus-response' terminology of classical behaviorism, the distinction between the two kinds of peripheral space-mapping functions and their related multi-sensory systems is important for the different actions and levels of behaviour they encompass. The former describes the direct interactions between body and objects such as those involved in the use of tools and the handling of other objects, entailing the neural linkage and integration of visual, tactile and auditory senses targeted on the peripersonal space, as well as the control of movement – all being indicative of explorative and *goal-directed* activity.[10] It has also been found that, rather than taking in the whole space around the entire body surface, these multi-modal brain–body systems are coded for *specific body parts* such as a hand, arm or face, each of which is identified by its own neuronal 'receptive field'; a particular reference frame Pelligrino and Ladavas describe as being 'extremely appropriate for organizing head and arm movements toward or away from visual objects'.[11]

Close encounters with others

Against the more limited reach of peripersonal space, which does not extend further than grasping distance, extrapersonal space encompasses more *distant objects* in the surrounding space requiring further visual exploration, including an individual's engagements with other persons close by, adding a vital *social* dimension to those interactions. However, the distinction between the two forms of bodily spatial extension in this regard may not be as clear as the authors first suggest.[12] While their review is mostly focused on studies of interactions with three-dimensional objects within the peripersonal space, they also argue that 'the space close around us is not only the privileged region of space for grasping and manipulating objects but also for *interacting with other individuals* [emphasis added]'.[13] Citing related research on 'mirror neurons' – an important class of neurons associated with feelings of empathy that fire up in simulation of the actions of others – the authors explain that the brain areas involved in encoding peripersonal space are located immediately next to or are 'coextensive with' regions containing mirror neurons, and that these neurons are selectively activated whenever another individual enters the peripersonal space; a discovery the authors find 'of great interest, as it suggests that individuals might encode the body parts of others *using a representation of their own body parts*, a "matching" mechanism that is functionally similar to how mirror neurons encode one's own actions and the actions of others'.[14]

Other related discoveries the authors cite reveal the dynamic character of the processing systems governing peripersonal space in the behaviour of other animals as well as humans, reflective, as with the above case of phantom limbs, of the broader plasticity of neural connections. For example, research shows that increases in the velocity of approaching objects produces a concurrent *expansion* of the visual depth of peripersonal receptive fields, a property the authors suggest 'could be critical for facilitating the preparation and/or execution of actions in response to fast-moving objects'.[15] Similarly, underlining the flexibility of peripersonal space, it has been found that frequent use of the same tools can *change* the way individuals interact with their environment, shrinking perceived distances between body and object, so that 'far becomes near'.[16]

Finding one's way about

Neither are the brain's space mapping functions restricted to peripersonal or extrapersonal space, the variable extent of which always remains firmly anchored to the body, wherever it may be situated. Experiments with rats and other mammals exploring their local environment have also uncovered sets of specialised neurons called 'place cells' and 'grid cells' located in the region of the brain called the hippocampus, where memories are formed. According to Edvard and May-Britt Moser,[17] who are credited with the more recent discovery of grid cells, the functional embedding of both these cell types in the hippocampus is central to understanding how they work. Taken together with the brain's powers of memory, place and grid cells provide a dynamic, map-like representation of the space in which an animal is moving, enabling it to locate itself in that space, and, most importantly, to *memorise any significant previous locations and other landmarks* in its environment, so that it can return to those places if so desired.

There are significant differences, however, between the two types of cell. First discovered in the 1970s, place cells fire up whenever the animal is in a certain place in the local environment – the so-called 'place field' specific to that cell – while adjacent place cells were activated at other locations so that, 'throughout the hippocampus, the whole environment was represented in the activity of the local cell population'.[18] By contrast, though most place cells have a *single* firing location, each grid cell has *multiple firing fields* tracing an animal's changing position step by step, forming a 'triangular array', or grid of signals in its wake as it does so, mapping out the entire environment being explored with geometric precision.

While the precise functional relations between the two kinds of space mapping cells remains unclear, together they provide what the authors describe as the 'possible elements of a metric system for spatial navigation'.[19] Moreover, it is thought that the functional integration of memory with place and grid cells creates the potential for locating *experienced events* as well as landmarks at points within the same spatial system, thus laying the groundwork for higher level spatial behaviour and cognition – though this also remains to be confirmed by further research. The last word for the time being on this intriguing issue goes to Elizabeth Marozzi and Kathryn Jeffery,[20] who, having contributed their own concise account of related research, wonder why nature would use the same basic neuronal structure for both space and memory, when they seem so different:

> An intriguing possibility is that the cognitive map provides, in a manner of speaking, the stage upon which the drama of recollected life events is played out. By this account, it serves as the mind's eye not only for remembering spaces, but also the events that happened there and even – according to recent human neuroimaging evidence – imagination.[21]

Unity of perception and action

Other research on the integration of the visual and motor systems involved in perception and action, may help to answer the kind of question regarding imagination posed by Marozzi and Jeffery. It was once widely accepted that perception and action were each catered for by separate brain functions and sensory systems. That idea, as Gabriele Ferretti and Mario Alai[22] explain, is now pretty much dead. In its place, the aforementioned 'enactivist' school contends that cognition is founded upon a *unity* of perception and action. The visual and/or tactile perception of an object not only involves its recognition *as* an object, enactivists argue, it also involves *understanding the possibilities which that object affords for action*, or what we *imagine* we might be able to actually *do* with it.

However, while they accept the fundamental unity of perception and action, the two authors contest a commonly stated premise of enactivists that, since it is the *purpose* of an object that influences how it is perceived, perception must accordingly be *direct*, and not dependent upon any inner representations of the external environment in which the object is situated. Ferretti and Alai argue instead that, though a *detailed* internal representation of everything 'out there' may not be required, the very detection of the action possibilities, or 'affordances' of the object, as they are called, involves specific representational processes at the neural level.

For evidence of those processes, the authors point to studies of the motor systems of monkey's brains focusing on a particular area named F5. The area is of special interest because as well as being directly connected with the primary motor cortex controlling bodily movement, it also receives nervous signals from an adjacent part of the brain called the parietal lobe, which for a long time was regarded as an area only involved in sensory operations. However, other studies have shown that the motor cortex influences those operations of the parietal lobe so much that it is now treated as part of the motor brain, suggesting that, far from only being involved in actions, the motor cortex is also essential for sensory operations. Similarly, the F5 area is also special in that although most F5 neurons are exclusively concerned with actual motor *acts* – coordinated movements with specific goals – the area contains another large group of so-called 'visuomotor neurons', which not only have properties indistinguishable from those of their purer motor cousins, but also demonstrate peculiar 'visual' properties. While more specialised motor neurons only fire up in experiments during an actual motion, as when a monkey grasps an object, visuomotor neurons also fired significantly *during the visualisation of the object*, irrespective of whether the sighting was followed by an actual grasping action.

Canonical neurons

Visuomotor neurons are, in turn, comprised of two further groups: 'canonical neurons', which are activated whenever an object is visualised, regardless of whether any detectable action aimed at the object is actually carried out; and the mirror neurons mentioned previously with regard to intrusions of peripersonal spaces, about which more will be said later in this chapter. According to Ferretti and Alai, canonical neurons respond to *groups or types of objects*, which, although differing in shape and/or material, call for the same manoeuvre. Significantly, canonical neurons are triggered upon visual recognition of a given type of object *in anticipation* of the action itself. In the experiments with monkeys, the authors recount, immediately upon *looking* at an object the animal's motor neurons fired up, activating the programme that *would* be involved were the observer to actually engage with the object. It follows that:

> The identification of an object is a *preliminary form of action* [emphasis added], a call to agency, characterized on the basis of its (visuo) motor opportunities, independently of whether an execution occurs or not. This shows that in the recognition of objects agency and perception are two sides of the same coin: the sight guiding the hand is a kind of capacity to watch through the hand.[23]

There is further evidence that, in grouping different objects together according to their affordances for action, the F5 area of the brain functions as a kind of 'motor vocabulary' of groups of canonical neurons, each group or 'word' in the vocabulary referring to a particular kind of motor act. Such 'words' can signify different levels of generality, from the goal of the action (i.e., grasping an object) to the precise manner in which it should be held, but they always refer to different *kinds or classifications of action* in which motor acts are represented as *wholes* rather than to any particular movement included in the sequence.

In answer to the question as to whether any internal representations are involved in the process, Ferretti and Alai argue that the very fact that *recognition* of an object can automatically trigger a motor programme without actually executing that programme, indicates the generation of an intermediary representation *detached from the actual execution* of the action, which is to say, it has an existence of its own. However, contrary to the kind of classical mental representations of a conceptual sort enactivists looked for but could not find, the integration of visual and motor systems *converts* sensory information into *neural simulations*, or 'motor imagery' of the possible actions associated with the object. In effect, the authors suggest, enactivists have all along been looking for the *wrong form* of representation, leading them to believe that the unity of perception and action does not involve internal representations at all. Instead, 'sensory information is *directly mapped on motor areas* [emphasis added], so allowing us to perceive the environment in terms of possible motor acts'.[24]

Social cues

The integrative functions of neural sub-systems, however, do not stop with the versatile canonical neurons. Along with providing efficient systems for tracking spatial movement and integrating perception and action, it would seem that evolution has also provided animals with a group of other versatile cells specially geared to handling social cues. Called 'von Economo' neurons (VENS) after the Austrian anatomist Constantine von Economo, who first described and mapped the unusually large neurons in 1926, they are located in just two regions towards the front of the brain: the anterior cingulate cortex (ACC) and the frontal insula (FI). They were found again in the chimpanzee brain a year later, but were thereafter ignored on account of their small numbers and rarity until they were rediscovered by chance in the late 1990s by Patrick Hof, an American neuroanatomist.[25] His consequent collaborations with fellow neuro-anatomist John Allman revealed that the brains of *all* species of great apes had functioning von Economo cells, but *not* those of monkeys and other lesser primates. This suggested to the researchers that these cells had evolved in a common ancestor about 13 million years ago, after the great apes diverged from other primates but well before human and chimpanzee lineages diverged, and had therefore played a possible key role in the development of higher-level brain functions in humans and the great apes.

Functional relations between self-awareness and social awareness

What is so special then, about these relatively rare neurons, which have since been found in other mammalian species endowed with large brains, including elephants and whales? Brain-scanning studies have established that both the above brain regions are important for self-monitoring functions, such as registering pain and hunger or instinctively recognising errors in an animal's own behaviour. However, while the ACC region seems to be involved in most mental or physical efforts, the FI region seems to have a more specific *social pur-pose* in generating emotions like empathy, trust, guilt, embarrassment, love and even humour, and becomes active, for example, when an individual scrutinises another's face for signs of the other's intentions: 'The basic proposition that I'm advancing', Allman asserts, 'is the notion that self-awareness and social awareness *are part of the same functioning* [emphasis added], and the von Economo cells are part of that'.[26]

Allman also speculates that the consistently large brain size of all the animals equipped with VENS explains the presence and equally impressive size of the cells themselves. Brain cell size, he explains, generally relates to their speed of operation, that is, the bigger the brain the faster the cells need to be to relay their information from one part of the brain to any other regions to which it may be linked. Given their location in the socially sensitive regions of large brains, Allman hypothesises that the super-sized, speedy VENS would facilitate rapid, intuitive readings of and responses to volatile social situations – especially those requiring split-second judgements about who to trust – giving our larger primate ancestors an evolutionary advantage over other, smaller-brained species.

Allman's speculations about the social functions of VENS are borne out by studies of whales and elephants which, much like humans and great apes, have large brains as well as large bodies, together with a prolonged post-natal rearing period during which their young have ample time to learn the basics of life from their parents. As highly social creatures, whales and elephants recognise each other by both sight and sound – the latter being particularly important for whales – and develop life-long group relationships and patterns of collab-orative behaviour. Killer whales, for example, hunt in well-coordinated groups, while elephant society is governed by matriarchs who guide their herds to watering holes they have located on earlier visits, and rally the herd to rescue any endangered members – all complex social activities requiring higher-level brain processing hitherto regarded as unique to humans.

Lastly, further human evidence to support Allman's claims has been found in studies of the damaging effects of frontotemporal dementia – a particular form of the now all-too-familiar neurogenerative disease – on the sufferers' self-awareness and social capacities. Symptoms include insensitive, erratic and irre-sponsible behaviour and a general inability to empathise with others. Hearing a lecture by Allman on VENS, William Seeley, a neurologist specialising in the disease, had noted they were located in the same brain regions affected by the disease. Working together on the brains of deceased patients, the two researchers discovered that the majority of VENS in those regions had, in fact, been destroyed by the disease, while other neighbouring brain cells were not affected, from which Allman concludes: 'It is very clear that the original target of the disease is these cells, and when you destroy these cells you get a whole breakdown of social functioning'.[27]

Self-agency

Another researcher who has sought and found evidence of the neurological roots of self-awareness in patients whose normal brain functions have been similarly impaired, is Anil Ananthaswamy,[28] who, unlike Ramachandran, is an unabashed supporter of the 'I' in the self:

> We often hear of how the self is an illusion, that it is nature's most sophisticated sleight of hand. But all this talk of tricks and illusions obfuscates a basic truth: remove the self and there is no 'I' on whom a trick is being played, no one who is the subject of an illusion.[29]

This is not to say, he explains, that the self is a simple matter of subjectivity. There are many faces of the self that are not readily encompassed by the 'I' of everyday speech, including the 'material', 'social' and 'spiritual self', each of which covers a different set of personal values and experiences.[30] Underlying the elusive nature of the self and its many faces is the difficult problem of con-sciousness, for which he notes, despite all the insights into the more specific mechanisms of the brain that neuroscience provides us with, there are, as yet, no firm solutions. However, rather than looking for evidence of the self in the behaviour of healthy individuals, he suggests we turn instead for 'windows to the self', as he puts it, to studies of people whose functional sense of self has been severely disrupted by neuropsychological disorders of one kind or another, for which he draws upon the neuroscience of schizophrenia:

Each such neuropsychological disorder illuminates some sliver of the self, one that has been disturbed by the disorder, resulting at times in a devastating illness [...] These maladies are to the study of the self what brain lesions are to the study of the brain. They are cracks in the façade of the self that let us examine an otherwise almost impenetrable, ongoing, unceasing neural process.[31]

Effects of schizophrenia

Among the most revealing examples for what it tells us of the roots of self-awareness, schizophrenia can 'fragment a person – and part of this fragmentation is due to a compromised sense of agency, the feeling we all have that we are agents of our actions'.[32] This feeling of being in control of one's own actions, or 'self-agency' as it is known, is the most direct and familiar expression of the 'I' of everyday experience and a crucial aspect of the self. The contrary feeling, that one's actions are *not* of one's own volition but may be controlled by someone or something else, is one of the classic and most disturbing symptoms of schizophrenia. For example, Ananthaswamy relates the case of Laurie, whose disorder was first manifested in repeated acts of self-harm, during which she felt as if some 'outside force' was possessing and controlling her. These acts were later accompanied by 'voices' telling her to cut deeper and kill herself, which she eventually attempted to do twice, but was fortunately prevented from doing.

The many and varied symptoms of schizophrenia complicate diagnosis – in Laurie's case she was first treated for depression followed by 'borderline personality disorder', before her doctors finally settled on more appropriate treatments. However, citing further research on self-agency, Ananthaswamy finds strong support for viewing Laurie's condition as a neuropsychological disorder. In addition to his discoveries of body mapping, Penfield had conducted a further series of experiments involving stimulations of the motor cortex of his subjects' brains. Though the stimulation caused an arm to move, the subjects insisted that it was Penfield who had been responsible. Inspired by Penfield's work, Irwin Feinberg's research on neural signals emanating from the motor cortex suggests direct links with subjective feelings of self-agency. Other previous experiments with animals had shown that motor actions produced a duplicate or 'corollary signal', prompting Feinberg to enquire whether such signals might be used to distinguish self from non-self. If, for example, a person's arm moved, might that person's brain employ corollary signals to tell if the arm moved because he or she *wanted* to move it, or whether it moved due to some *external* cause.

Since no motor commands were wilfully initiated by Penfield's subjects, Feinberg deduced there would have been no corollary signal, hence the brain attributed the movement not to the self but to some other, external, agency from which he concluded the subjective experience of the neural discharges corresponded with the *experience of will or intention*. Going further still, Feinberg speculated that *thoughts* as well as motor actions might involve a similar neural mechanism by which they could be identified as one's *own* thoughts, and not those of others, any failure in the normal functioning of which could result in many of the symptoms of schizophrenia. Summarising the implications, Ananthaswamy writes:

> Thus, if corollary discharge, in permitting the distinction of self-generated from environmental movement, thereby contributes to the distinction of self and other, its impairment might produce the extraordinary distortions of body boundaries reported by schizophrenic patients.[33]

A voice in the crowd

While the above discoveries are all linked to studies of self-agency in humans, evidence of similar neural mechanisms enabling other animal species to distinguish self from non-self have been found down to the level of single neurons, supporting the view that self-awareness is fundamental to animal life. Though other species are similarly endowed, including some worms, songbirds and marmoset monkeys, the star in this case, Ananthaswamy recounts, is the noisy cricket, whose chirps reach an astonishing sound level of 100dB. Given the discordant chorus emitted by countless other crickets in the same area, he asks: 'How does a cricket – whose ears remain sensitive at all times – distinguish between its own chirps and external sounds?' The answer lies in the synchronisation of chirps and wing movements, each cricket generating its own pulses of sound as it closes its wings, for which the corollary discharges from just one neuron are responsible:

> This corollary discharge interneuron (CDI) fires in synchrony with the motor neuron that's controlling wing movement; it fires as the wings close. The CDI's firing then inhibits the auditory neurons responsible for processing sound – so the cricket is deaf to the sounds it generates on the wing's downbeat. When the CDI doesn't fire, and there is no corollary discharge, *incoming sounds are deemed external or non-self, and the cricket tunes in* [emphasis added].[34]

Mirror images

The discovery in 1990 of the mirror neurons referred to above also offers insights into the neurological mechanisms underlying the reflected images of other minds, and, according to some, much else besides. As recounted by Christian Keysers in *The Empathic Brain*,[35] the discovery was made almost accidentally during a now famous research programme using animal subjects conducted by Giacomo Rizzolatti and his team of neuroscientists at the University of Parma. Using standard procedures similar to those used by Penfield on his human patients and many researchers ever since, a fine electrode was placed on part of a monkey's brain for an experiment investigating brain cell functions in simple actions like grasping food, for which a tray of raisins was supplied. However, during the experiment, one of the team had taken a raisin from the monkey's tray for himself, triggering an unexpected neurological response from the monkey, amplified and made visible through the electrode and attached laboratory equipment. What astonished Rizzolatti and the team was that the remote – but to the monkey clearly visible action by one of the team – had fired the same cell in the monkey's brain they had previously observed when the monkey helped *itself* from the tray. Just to make sure, the team repeated the action, drawing the same response from the monkey and the same reactions from the team.

From their observations, the team deduced that the functions of perception and action, which had previously been associated with different parts of the brain, namely the premotor and primary motor cortex, are combined in a single type of neuron – a conclusion later supported by the related studies described by Pelligrino and Ladavas and by Ferretti and Alai above. Nevertheless, as Keysers relates, it was some time before the full implications of the team's discovery sank in, which he claims shows the way the brain works in understanding others. In so doing, he argues, they also enable people to work together on coordinated tasks, an ability he believes, like others cited in this book, is one of the keys to humankind's extraordinary development:

> What links our brains is the way mirror neurons lead both to actions and the perception of the other's actions [...]. Millions of years of evolution have come up with this exquisite system that enables us to make the great evolutionary leap of doing together what we could never have done alone.[36]

Imitative behaviours

According to Keysers, the scope of the discovery does not stop there. In addition to helping us to understand others and supporting collaborative behaviour, it has been suggested that mirror neurons are also involved in imitative behaviours of every kind, from learning how to use simple tools by copying others, to the acquisition of language and any other practical or social skills that entail simulating the thoughts and behaviour of others. As such, Keysers claims, mirror neurons play a vital part in all forms of cultural transmission.[37] However, unlike the blind copying of ideas and fragments of cultural knowledge which typify the assimilation and transmission of memes described by Dawkins, Keysers argues that, for example, mirror neurons, help us to understand learning by observation as a focused, *goal-orientated* activity. Essentially, he suggests, what mirror neurons do is activate those motor neurons in the observer's brain that best match what he or she interprets as the *purpose* of the other person's perceived actions:

Mirror neurons activate the observer's way of performing an action while observing someone else perform a similar action, and this is particularly important while reproducing the actions of other individuals. What is even more important, though, is knowing that the mirror system is goal oriented suggests that during observation we do not so much learn the arbitrary details of how the demonstrator achieved the goal, *but rather what he has achieved or tried to achieve* [emphasis added].[38]

Questionable claims

It is not necessary to accept everything that Keysers claims mirror neurons do for us in order to appreciate that, like other major discoveries neuroscientists have made over the past century, they add another important dimension to understanding the workings of the human mind and body. The implications for higher levels of behavior, however, are far from certain, resting as they do, like Allman's plausible hypotheses for the power of VEN's, on evidence obtained at a mechanistic level. When Keysers writes above, for example: 'knowing that the mirror system is goal oriented', the supposition is based on *assumed connections* between a subject's *interpretation* of another's motivated actions and their own specific neural responses.

However, the only hard evidence provided in the original or subsequent experiments Keysers describes involve the subject's neural simulation of the *actions* of another, for which the subject, whether monkey or human, is *already* well-prepared; that is to say, subjects would have had a comparable previous experience *of their own* inscribed in a ready-to-be-activated set of neurons. As Keysers himself records above: 'Mirror neurons activate *the observer's way* [emphasis added] of performing an action while observing someone else perform a similar action'. Likewise, the implied condition Pelligrino and Ladavas point to above for 'matching' representations of body parts between individuals is that there are significant *similarities* between the body schema of one individual and that of another to provide for an effective neural simulation of the other's actions.

It is, of course, perfectly possible that a particular sequence of actions taken by one individual might be connected by *habit* with a specific motivation. But that alone does not imply any psychological or social *understanding* of that motivation by another individual, or their ability to connect it more generally with other related actions. Like the researchers who originally gave mirror neurons their name, the mirror analogy is deployed by Keysers and others to describe an *outward-looking* process by which one animal's brain – be it human or ape – reflects the actions of another.

Action understanding versus action copying

In *The Myth of Mirror Neurons*, Gregory Hickok's[39] provocatively titled counterblast to what he describes as the exaggerated claims being made for mirror neurons, the author explains that, like many other cognitive scientists, he also was initially intrigued by the discoveries by Rizzolatti and his team at Parma. However, on closer examination of the researchers' findings from the original experiments with monkeys and subsequent published research on the subject, Hickok, whose own research is focused on language development, could trace no firm links to either language acquisition or any other human capabilities to support the claims being made for mirror neurons described by Keysers. Anomalies in the research were also overlooked on the assumption they would eventually be ironed out by later evidence, but which he found were not resolved. Expressing a rare but welcome prudence on what he concludes are basically unsupported claims for mirror neurons, Hickok writes:

> Let me be clear: there is nothing wrong with a strong, interesting, and creative hypothesis. And there is nothing wrong with pursuing that hypothesis even in the face of a few empirical anomalies, *as long as the research program proceeds with extreme caution*. This was not the case with mirror neuron research.[40]

Hickok's critique revolves around the difference between non-human and human forms of imitative behaviour, or, put another way, between *action copying* and *action understanding*. Humans, he argues, are capable of understanding the actions of another and what their purpose is in complex ways that other primates are not. The Italian team's assumptions that the behaviour of their primate subjects was indicative of a similar capacity to that of humans and a pathway to higher level functions were, as suggested above, just that: assumptions that have never since been verified.

So how, Hickok asks, could such a misunderstanding have come about? He suggests that the answer lies partly in the manner in which, preceding the actual experiments monitoring the monkeys' neural responses, the animals were trained to receive food from the experimenters, who they were encouraged to watch, thus exposing them to just the kind of actions of reaching for and interacting with objects they enacted themselves in the experiments. In watching the experimenter's behaviour, what their subjects were actually doing, he argues, was recording and then repeating for themselves *associations* they had made between one action and another in the same sequence, which Hickock describes as just 'classical conditioning'. While both humans and non-human primates possess mirror neurons, he suggests that something in the evolution of the human mirror system is causing it to *operate differently* to other primate mirror systems; that 'something' being the neural networks supporting 'complex conceptual understanding, language, theory of mind, and the rest'. From that perspective, 'what we see when we look at the behavior of the mirror system is the *reflection* of the information processing streams that plug into it',[41] instead of just the mirror system on its own.

Moreover, pursuing his case, Hickock suggests that, rather than imitation *preceding* and providing the evolutionary launchpad for the development of human cognitive abilities, as is generally assumed, imitation is itself the *outcome* of the human evolution of cognitive skills. So, while primates may have the mirror neurons required for imitative behaviour, as do humans, the more advanced cognitive systems of humans enable them to get *more out of imitation* than their primate cousins; for example, by *inferring the goal of an action* and being able to communicate with others in complex ways that, according to Hickok, have been wrongly claimed to originate with primate mirror neurons.

However, that still leaves open the question of just how all those cognitive abilities which differentiate the operation of human mirror neurons from other animal variations – what Hickok describes as the 'dark matter' of the empathetic mind – actually evolved, for which Hickok himself has no clear answer. Pointing instead towards more recent research exploring alternative perspectives on the subject, he concedes that, while mirror neurons may have been oversold, they have spurred a rethinking of how the mind works, how it is supported by the brain and how it might have evolved.

Emotional signals

Amongst those other vital aspects of the self-field that might well be described in similar terms, is the 'dark matter' of the emotional self, which has also attracted increasing attention from neuroscientists eager to move the subject from the psychoanalyst's couch to the research laboratory. While, as the discipline requires, researchers generally approach the subject from a reductionist perspective, their discoveries can also offer, as we have seen, valuable, if sometimes controversial, insights into human and non-human animal behaviour. In *The Emotional Brain*,[42] for example, Joseph LeDoux's record of his work mapping the neuronal pathways of emotions, the author employs a range of approaches, from Darwinian perspectives to animal experiments using classical methods of behavioural conditioning – common methods amongst other neuroscientists as we have seen – each of which bears the marks of its own epistemology and scientific values. Starting out as a research student in the mid-1970s with Mike Gazzaniga – renowned for his earlier studies with Roger Sperry into the effects on brain functions of split-brain surgery[43] – LeDoux recounts there was little interest in the emotions amongst brain scientists at that time. A few scientists like himself, however, thought differently:

> Emotions, after all, are the threads that hold mental life together. They define who we are in our own mind's eye as well as in the eyes of others. What could be more important to understand about the brain than the way it makes us happy, sad, afraid, disgusted, or delighted?[44]

The experiments LeDoux worked on continued Gazzaniga's investigations into the different language handling functions of the two hemispheres of the brain, including one that involved presenting verbal stimuli with emotional connotations to a particular patient known as P.S. Unlike most patients who had undergone split-brain surgery, P.S. was able to *read* words with both halves, although, as with similar patients, he could only *voice them* with the left hemisphere. When emotional stimuli, such as the words 'mom' and 'devil', were separately presented, in turn, to each hemisphere of P.S.'s brain, his responses were revealing. While the left, 'speaking brain' could tell whether the words presented to the right brain signified something *good or bad*, the left brain could not discern what the stimuli actually were. No matter how hard the team encouraged P.S. to actually *name* the words to which he had responded emotionally, he could not. Somehow the emotional significance of each word had 'leaked' across the two hemispheres, even though their identity had not. In short, the left hemisphere was making emotional judgements, but without knowing exactly what it was judging.

Emotions are not uniquely human

To LeDoux, the experiments pointed to a fundamental dichotomy between thinking and feeling or between cognition and emotion. However, determined to investigate the problem further following completion of his graduate research, he concluded the techniques available at the time for studying the neural basis of emotion in humans were too limited and that he would be better off with laboratory methods using rats and other animal subjects. It was a course that eventually led LeDoux to believe, as it has led many other researchers cited here, that there is much about the neural systems of the brain that humans and other animals share. Inspired by Darwin's own comparisons between the emotional expressions of humans and other animal species,[45] he suggests that: 'Rather than trying to figure out what is unique about human emotion, we need to examine how *evolution stubbornly maintains emotional functions across species* [emphasis added] while changing other brain functions and bodily traits'.[46]

Similarly, LeDoux's approach is based on the Darwinian premise that emotions have evolved together with other brain functions by natural selection to ensure the survival of the individual and species. However, sticking with his reductionist perspective and rejecting the idea that the brain as a whole has some kind of overall function, he asserts it is rather 'a collection of systems, sometimes called modules, each with different functions',[47] that have evolved for specific purposes; learning bird songs, memorising the location of food, language skills in humans and so forth. Pursuing the same line of thought, LeDoux treats the functions of the brain as a problem in 'reverse engineering', taking the present product apart and working backwards to figure out how evolution might have operated to put it all together.

Primal fears

Treating emotions themselves as a range of different kinds of responses, LeDoux focuses much of his book on what has been learnt from non-human animals about one particular emotion, fear, which, he argues, tells us, perhaps than any other emotion, more about the way they have evolved across species, including our own. This does not mean, he adds, that specifically human traits like writing poetry are unimportant, but simply that they are *irrelevant* to our response to any unexpected and imminent threat to our existence. Certain basic emotions like fear, he argues, that are essential to survival have been conserved throughout evolution, and while modified over time for different species as needed, the principles remain approximately the same, cutting across bodily and behavioural differences. Such emotions remain the same across species, he explains, because the brain systems responsible for mediating those functions are also fundamentally the same for different species.

Elaborating on the theme, LeDoux argues that while there are areas of the human brain that are not present in other animal brains, brain evolution is *basically conservative* and the structure and function of systems such as those handling fear that have been especially useful for survival, have been essentially preserved intact. Controversially, however, in defining fear as a *subconscious* 'system of defensive behaviour' common to all animals, he rejects the association of fear with *subjective* (conscious) feelings of fear, claiming that, as he deduced from his work with Gazzaniga, emotional behaviours such as fear evolved *independently* of conscious feelings, which, he believes, are only possible with the human capacity for self-consciousness.[48]

In conclusion, LeDoux suggests that understanding how emotions such as fear are generated at unconscious levels, may help, in turn, to unlock the key to the human, self-conscious mind:

> By treating emotions as unconscious processes that can somehow give rise to conscious content, we lift the burden of the mind-body problem from the shoulders of emotion researchers and allow them to get on with the problem of figuring out how the brain does its unconscious emotional business. But we also see how conscious emotional experiences are probably created. They are probably created the same way that other conscious experiences are – by the establishment of a conscious representation of the workings of underlying processing systems.[49]

Self-regulation of emotions

However, whilst LeDoux accepts that other animals have emotions like us, which can teach us much about how they evolved, his explicit rejection of the idea that non-human animals might also experience any actual *feelings* of emotion – because, so he claims, such feelings can only occur in human brains capable of full self-consciousness – suggests an unresolved anthropo-centrism. Crucially, dependent as his claim is upon a strict, either/or logic of self-consciousness, the approach permits no variations of self-awareness or self-agency, such as those described in this and previous chapters. LeDoux's dis-missal of any argument suggesting there is anything more to the brain than its different parts and functions, is also challenged by other neuroscientists cited in these chapters offering a more complex perspective of interconnecting sensory systems and overlapping brain functions, but most of all by emergentists, who point to the general failure of mechanistic and deterministic perspectives to explain how higher levels of development could arise out of lower levels.

Polyvagal theory

Where LeDoux relies exclusively upon his experiments with other animals for his speculations about human behaviour, Stephen Porges[50] approaches the subject of emotions from the human end of the evolutionary spectrum, while also tracing their roots in other mammalian species. Setting out his 'polyvagal theory' of the neurophysiological foundations of emotions, Porges concentrates on the part played by the 'vagus' – a family of neural pathways originating in several areas of the brainstem – in the autonomic nervous system monitoring heart, lungs and skin, or 'peripheral physiology' as it is designated. The vagus, he contends, is the neural key to emotional expression; including, significantly, those emotions involved in *social interaction* as well as fear of danger. Also like LeDoux, Porges' work in this area dates back to the late 1960s, when, as a graduate student doing research on the possible links between heart rates and levels of attention, he noted that *heart rates stabilised* whenever subjects focused their attention on a task; a key discovery he followed up with fur-ther research confirming that reduced heart-rate variability was associated with faster reaction times.

While much else has changed in the 40 years of research Porges writes of since then, heart-rate studies remain an important feature of his laboratory work. However, for Porges, there was always a lot more to it than links to attention spans. While new disciplines have emerged during that period, many scientists, he notes, are still mired in the mind-body dualism trap and current measures of heart-rate variability are mostly described in purely clinical health terms as 'potential biomarkers'. However, the polyvagal theory he has developed since his first discoveries, he asserts, contests this implicit dualism by providing a 'bidirectional brain–body model' linking the autonomic nervous system with emergent behaviours of a *social and defensive nature*. A key concept in the theory is that of 'vagal tone', an idea, he explains, that was first proposed in 1910 by two clinical psychologists, H. Eppinger and L. Hess, to describe individual differences in the autonomic nervous system; their objective being to treat dysfunctions in the system and related neuroses for which there was no known anatomical basis and no effective cure at that time. Though the psychologists' clinical aims differed from Porges' own research interests, the problem they described in their case studies regarding the regulation of autonomic functions, suggested to Porges it might be closely related to the regulation of emotions.

Social sensitivities

What the case studies of Eppinger and Hess showed, Porges argues, was that, not only was the vagal system important in mediating physiological and psychological responses – hence circumventing any mind-body dualism – but individual differences in physiology (i.e., vagal tone) were also related to individual differences in behaviour; including perhaps, other forms of emotional expression beyond the neurotic symptoms of their clinical subjects.

Porges traces the origins of the interrelation between physiological and psychological conditions to the extended period of maturation and dependence upon their adult carers, not only of human infants, but also the offspring of all mammalian species. As the infant develops, he explains, its dependence upon others decreases in parallel with changes in the neural regulation of the autonomic nervous system and it begins to *self-regulate*. Newly formed, higher brain circuits impact upon the neural pathways from the brainstem controlling the autonomic system, so that the infant becomes increasingly capable of *initiating social interactions* with others in answering its physiological needs – making sure it gets fed when it needs to and so forth. As the infant's self-regulatory and social skills develop in unison, it also appears to be more comfortable on its own and is able to rapidly calm down, and moreover, to remain calm after any sudden challenging experiences. In turn, as those combined skills develop further, the central nervous system expands, supporting enhanced cognitive abilities and greater control over those peripheral motor systems controlling facial expressions, hands and other movements with which the maturing infant engages with the human and material world. Putting it all together, Porges writes:

> We propose that the developmental changes in the neural pathways that regulate autonomic state *provide a neural platform to support the expanding abilities of the infant to engage objects and people in a dynamically changing environment* [emphasis added]. Thus the emergent behavioral repertoire and social-interactive needs of the rapidly developing young infant should be studied within the context of the maturational changes in the autonomic nervous system.[51]

Furthermore, he observes, *all* mammalian species are both polyvagal and highly *social* creatures, most especially humans, with a need to maintain social interactions throughout their life span. Failure to do so, for whatever reason and regardless of age, leads to profound disruptions in the individual's ability to self-regulate normal physiological states, undermining physical and mental health.

What may have been previously accepted as common knowledge – social dys-
function affects physical and mental health – is therefore cast in a new light by
Porges as a *breakdown in the normal regulatory function* of the polyvagal system in
mediating psychological and physiological conditions.[52]

Safety first

Searching further for the evolutionary roots of normal as well as abnormal
social behaviours linked to the regulatory functions of the polyvagal system,
Porges argues that the mammalian nervous system has evolved with specific
neural and behavioural features that regulate subconscious, or visceral, feelings
in response to any environmental challenges or interactions with others:

> To survive, mammals must determine friend from foe, evaluate whether the
> environment is safe, and communicate with their social unit. These survival-
> related behaviors are associated with specific neurobehavioral states that
> *limit the extent to which a mammal can be physically approached and whether the*
> *mammal can communicate or establish new coalitions* [emphasis added].[53]

Unlike the reptiles from which mammals are descended, he explains, whose
nervous systems evolved purely for survival in dangerous and life-threatening
situations, mammalian nervous systems have evolved to promote social interaction and bonding in *safe* environments, whilst retaining two more primitive
neural circuits inherited from their reptilian predecessors regulating *defensive*
strategies – such as fight-or-flight. It is important to note, he adds, that the
former social behaviours and feelings are *incompatible* with the neural systems
supporting the latter defensive behaviours. The mammalian nervous system
thus supports *three evolutionarily distinct neural circuits* in a hierarchy of adaptive
responses, the most recent, socially developed, circuit being deployed in the
front line of engagement with others. Should that fail to provide sufficient
safety in the face of any serious challenges to the individual, however, the
older survival-orientated circuits are brought into play. Porges suggests that
the same strategy and its physiological and psychological effects is observable
in human social behaviour with its everyday focus on communication through
facial expressions and speech: 'An important characteristic of these prosocial
behaviors is their low metabolic demand and the rapid "switching" of transitory engagement to transitory disengagement strategies (i.e., speaking then
switching to listening)',[54] the implication being that such strategies relieve the
participants from excess psychological and physiological pressures.

   Similarly, although love and other complex emotions are commonly
associated uniquely with human behaviour, in sharp contrast to LeDoux's dis-
missal of the idea that animals might also experience emotional feelings, Porges
argues that they too may be traced back to the evolutionary requirement of all
mammalian species for stable attachments to others. Thus an *integrated system of*

social behaviour promoting intimacy and providing a secure and stable environment for reproduction and the rearing of offspring has evolved for all mammals,
eventually leading to enduring pair-bonds – a social system mediated by the
same autonomous nervous system of self-regulation he describes – which
governs responses to perceived threats to that security, but is inflected towards
the expression of a different set of emotions.

Chapter 6

The evolving self

Assuming, as the major discoveries described in the previous chapter indicate, that the ability to distinguish between self and non-self is dependent upon neuronal processes operating at a subconscious level, it may be asked at what point or level and by what means do sentient creatures – meaning humans as well as other animals – acquire the higher levels of self-awareness leading to conscious behaviour? If self-consciousness originates not in the development of the individual self *per se*, but in people's dealings with one another, then clearly the level of self-consciousness attained will be heavily dependent upon the nature and *quality* of those social interactions.

The mutual development of self-awareness and social awareness accords with much else that is written in this book on the grounding of the self – and with it the whole self-field in all its manifestations – in the social and cultural milieu in which an individual develops, from the earliest forms of animal group activities to the most complex forms of human society. Such issues test anthropocentric presumptions regarding human versus other animals' capacities for self-awareness, the answer to which, as Darwin also intimated above, may lie, not in any strict lines drawn between species, but in all the *variations in between* – what Kurt Lewin described as the new, Galilean mode of thought and which Darwin's theory of graduated descent helped to usher in.

Metamorphosis

Situated at the primitive end of animal sentience, the seemingly magical case of the metamorphosis of caterpillar into butterfly, for example, defies Aristotelian logic, arousing the curiosity of children as well as scientists. Addressing a question on the matter to 'Curious Kids', an online programme inviting children to send in questions they would like an expert to answer for them, Evan, a five-year-old, wrote in: 'We have caterpillars at home. I would like to know whether they will remember being caterpillars when they are butterflies'.[1]

His question was answered by Michael Braby at the Australian National University, who explained that, while he thought it was doubtful that a butterfly or a moth (which undergoes the same extreme transformation) remembers being a caterpillar, 'it may well remember *some experiences* [emphasis added] it learned as a caterpillar'.[2] Perhaps anticipating Evan's possible disappointment with his answer, he suggested that fact alone is remarkable since, once inside the 'pupa', the hanging sack (chrysalis) where the metamorphosis takes place, 'the body tissues of the caterpillar are completely reorganized to produce the beautiful adult butterfly that emerges from the pupa', actually turning into liquid in the process. He went on to describe a series of tests on moths carried out by a team of American scientists to see whether they did, in fact, remember experiences from their caterpillar past lives. Carefully designing their experiments to eliminate the possibility of a purely sensory transfer of experiences from one body form to the next, they trained the caterpillars to dislike the smell of a particular chemical, ethyl acetate, found in nail polish remover, giving the caterpillars tiny electric shocks every time they smelled the chemical. Soon enough, the caterpillars learned to avoid the smell because it reminded them of the electric shock. Following the caterpillars through into their second lives as moths, each adult moth was tested again for their reactions to the same chemical odour. The result, Braby informed his young questioner, was that most of the moths avoided the odour, indicating they *continued* to associate it with the electric shocks they had experienced in their former lives as caterpillars. Thus, Braby concluded:

> The study showed that memory, and therefore the nervous system, *stays during the complex transformation from the caterpillar to the adult moth* [emphasis added]. So while a moth or butterfly may not remember being a caterpillar, it can remember experiences it learned as a caterpillar.[3]

Evolutionary implications

We are not told if Evan was satisfied with his expert's carefully worded answer, which left the main issue of self-consciousness unresolved. Evan and other followers of the programme might well have thought: 'That's very interesting, but does the butterfly actually *know* it was a caterpillar?' However, viewed from the dynamic perspective outlined earlier of successive or *serial* selves as 'an overlapping chain of experience memories', as Parfit describes them, then the idea of any remembered experiences being carried *intact* through such a drastic metamorphosis as that experienced by caterpillars, acquires an altogether broader evolutionary significance.

Other earlier studies of complete metamorphosis, or 'holometabolism' as it is known, involving every stage in the transformation, support a reassessment of the evolutionary implications. Recounting their own extensive research into caterpillar–moth metamorphosis, Douglas Blackiston et al.[4] address the key question of the survival through the transformation of caterpillar into moth of *associative memory* – memories, like the above trained association of a particular chemical odour with an electric shock, where the organism has *learned* to link one experience or event with another. In view of the radical changes from one life form to another, they ask:

> [...] might it be possible for learned associations formed at the larvae stage to be accessible to the adult? This intriguing and controversial idea challenges our understanding of neuronal fate during metamorphosis in holometabolous insects. If associative behavior is indeed retained across the pupal stage, might it result from the persistence of larvae neurons through metamorphosis and their subsequent integration into the adult nervous system?[5]

Following similar experimental procedures to those described by Braby, the team employed mild electric shock treatment in training the larvae of Lepidoptera, a species of moth, to avoid a gaseous compound. As with the former experiments, the adult moths retained the aversion to the compound acquired by their larvae predecessors. In addition, the team conducted a parallel series of experiments testing the possibility of a similar aversion to chemicals contacted by larvae *directly from their environment* being carried forward into their adult forms. However, no related changes of behaviour could be observed in the adult moths from such sources; from which the team concluded that the duplication in adult moths of behaviour acquired by larvae trained to avoid exposure to the gaseous compound 'represents true associative learning, not chemical legacy, and, as far as we know, provides the first definitive demonstration that *associative memory survives metamorphosis* [emphasis added] in Lepidoptera'.[6]

The implication is that at least *some* of the neural connections responsible for caterpillar memory must have survived the drastic melting down and reorganisation of organic material required to complete the full metamorphosis. And if the butterfly/moth can remember an odour it learnt to avoid in its previous incarnation, then surely, it may be surmised, it must also remember much else from its former life.

Consciousness and memory

It is no great stretch in turn to suggest that caterpillar/butterfly nervous systems may have their own ways of linking all these disparate memories together in a coherent manner – ways that we might ourselves recognise as the primitive foundations of what is called *autobiographical memory* and the foundations of self-awareness. While, for the most part, memory systems of that kind linking together memories formed at different periods in animal lives have generally been associated in the research – like self-consciousness and language – with human development, there have been notable exceptions. Presenting his alternative, 'adaptive model' of memory, Mark Howe,[7] for example, offers much ground for reasoning that humans may not be the only creatures gifted with related memory systems, if in a more basic form, as the resilience of the caterpillar-butterfly memory suggests. As Howe describes it, memory has an explicit Darwinian purpose: 'Memory relevant to "our self" not only helps to define us [...] but also helps us in our quest to adapt to and survive in the world in which we find ourselves'.[8]

Howe traces the origins of the animal memory system back to what is called the 'Cambrian explosion' of around 540–560 million years ago, during which time all the major animal body plans appeared and several neurobiological advances occurred, enabling the preservation of basic associative information of the sort retained through the caterpillar's metamorphosis in stable, long-term memory traces (and generally without such severe physical disruptions). Binding up information this way into associative links, he suggests, allows the animal to recognise significant features in its environment based upon *partial clues* only, for example, detecting the possible presence of hidden predators from their odour or the rustling of long grass concealing them. Furthermore, the preservation of unified associations of this sort allow animals to *anticipate* the future presence and behaviour of other creatures from their previous encounters – associations that, Howe suggests, would offer clear advantages for an animal's chances of survival, both immediately and into the future.

Co-emergence of self and memory

Significantly, he goes further to suggest that the evolution of associative memory may also be at least partially responsible for the emergence of consciousness, and specifically self-consciousness; the reason being that it provides the essential link between an organism's past experiences and their future needs. Similarly, *feelings* and memory are linked together insofar as it was only when a *particular* feeling could be associated with a *particular memorised experience* they could assume their function in sensing hunger or danger, for example. The accumulation of these memorised links between individual feelings and experiences, so it is argued, would have given rise to a subjective or 'first-person' consciousness and a specific sense of selfhood with the capacity, based upon those memorised links, to modulate future behaviour in similar situations.

And if, Howe speculates, there are evolutionary links between associative memory and the appearance of at least a rudimentary self-consciousness, then we should not be surprised at the possibility of similar links between full self-consciousness and a more fully developed autobiographical memory system.[9] Whatever underlies their parallel development, the emergent 'self-memory alliance', as he describes it, equips the individual with a more efficiently organised system of related feelings and experiences it can draw upon – many with 'fitness-relevant' advantages – together with the possibility, at least for humans, for *self-reflection* of the kind that enables us to travel back and forth in time, recapturing (and editing where desired, consciously or not) those memories and feelings.

Constructing the human 'me'

In support of the co-emergence of self and memory in both humans and non-human animals, Howe includes a passing reference to the idea that a shared 'core self' might have evolved that is common to mammalian species, together with an examination of the so-called 'mirror test' for self-recognition, which, until recently, only humans and the great apes were thought to be able to pass – important matters further discussed in later sections of this chapter. However, while he concedes there is increasing neurological and behavioural evidence, including the discovery of von Economo and mirror neurons, to support the idea there are cross-species parallels in complex cognitive and emotional behaviours and social relationships, he draws the line at the capacity for self-reflection, which he maintains remains a uniquely human feature. Just because, Howe argues, some other animals, which now include Asian elephants, pass the mirror test, which involves the subject simply touching a mark placed on its forehead that it perceives in the mirror – thereby recognising the image as 'me' – does not necessarily mean they also possess the same sort of representational self that would enable self-reflection. Human infants, he suggests, who normally achieve the task between 18 and 24 months of age, may draw upon a whole range of other behaviours indicative of emergent self-consciousness that are quite different from those of other animals, such as being able to correctly *name* their mirror image as 'me', or actually using their own name – an achievement usually following mirror recognition at around 22 months of age or thereafter. In addition, emotional expressions of embarrassment (blushing, averting the gaze from the mirror) distress and so forth indicative of a growing awareness of how *others* might be reacting to them, confirm that mirror self-recognition in human infants is associated with growing awareness of a 'referent self', or the 'me' in subjective experience.

For Howe, such developments substantiate the emergence of self-consciousness as the driving force in the co-emergence of autobiographical memory, in that the *awareness of the infant of its own individuality* and involvement in the world about it *requires* the integration of what are previously an assorted collection of disparate memories, but which, via autobiographical memory, attain a unique, *personal signature*. A further key step in the co-emergence of self and early memory, he explains, is the ability to recall whole experiences involving 'the who, what, where, and when of the event',[10] as distinct *episodes* in a series of related personal events, the construction of which carries particular *meanings* for the individual. However, as the child grows and experiences similar events across different situations, it begins to detect *regularities* between experiences and its own role in them and to link them together in new ways that may *change their significance*, reducing the need to retain the details of every similar experience. By such means, Howe concludes, maturing humans are able to actively *construct* a coherent personal history and framework for understanding the world in which they live, and upon which they can build in preparing for a less certain future. For Howe, therefore, as with Parfit, continuity of the emergent self is firmly associated with a linked series of experience-memories: 'Moreover, it is the dynamic interplay between the emerging self-consciousness and memories of the self-in-events that gives rise to the developing sense of identity as well as the apparent *continuity of the self* [emphasis added] across experiences and time'.[11]

Knowing and feeling

Though Howe, like other writers on the subject cited in this book, may therefore be reluctant to give up the idea of a firm cognitive barrier over which only humans so far have jumped, he offers plentiful evidence and support for *lowering* that barrier, to the point where, as Darwin himself counselled, it would be wiser to think of the differences between humans and other animals in terms of gradations rather than absolute differences. Recall, for example, the research on place and grid cells described in the previous chapter and the key role that memory plays in locating spatial landmarks – and quite possibly experienced events within the same framework – and you have, as some researchers suggest, the foundations for higher level spatial behaviour and cognition.

The possibility of a broader evolutionary framework for an emergent self, encompassing the full spectrum from the most primitive to the most advanced manifestations of consciousness, has also preoccupied Antonio Damasio[12] in his search for the neurobiological foundations of the 'feeling self'. Like other thoughtful writers on the subject, Damasio rejects the idea that, beyond body mapping and other neuropsychological functions, there exists a homunculus 'in charge of knowing'. However, rather than taking the lack of any central controller as evidence there is no self which is playing that role, Damasio sees the issue of a self as critical to the explanation of consciousness. Explaining how he had reached that conclusion from his work on the neurophysiology of emotions, he recounts that he had come to understand how different emotions originate in the brain and are 'played out' in the body, the combined signals of which produce the actual *feeling* of emotions. However, he could not understand just how it was that the product of all that brain activity could become *known* to the organism experiencing those emotions:

> What else happens in the organism and especially, what else happens in the brain, when we know that we feel an emotion or feel pain or, for that matter, when we know anything at all? I had come up against the obstacle of consciousness. Specifically, I had come up against the obstacle of self, for something like a *sense of self* [emphasis added] was needed to make the signals that constitute the feeling of emotion known to the organism having the emotion.[13]

Whilst Damasio stresses that understanding the nature of consciousness is not restricted to understanding the self, he links the two problems together as *integrated outcomes* of brain activity, neither of which can be fully understood without the other. First, he explains, there are those brain functions concerned with generating mental images of an object, by which he means everything *external* to an individual that is experienced through the normal sensory channels, which he describes as the 'movie-in-the-brain'. And second, there are those brain activities responsible for identifying the experience of the former images as *belonging* to a particular self, who, in the human case, is an observer and knower as well as a potential actor. In sum, Damasio writes: 'Consciousness, as we commonly think of it, from its basic levels to its most complex, is the unified mental pattern that brings together the object and the self'.[14] Simply put, therefore, consciousness *necessitates* having a self that is the knower.

Reversing the narrative

Similarly, he derides the commonly expressed theory that consciousness only emerged with human language and the ability to freely interpret events and to draw inferences from them – a viewpoint, he comments, that consigns all other creatures to an 'incognizant existence'. In rejecting that view however, Damasio does not deny the importance of language in the emergence of higher levels of human development, or 'extended consciousness' as he describes them. But he contests the idea that the evolution of consciousness can be understood from a 'top-down' approach that takes language and associated cognitive traits as a given. What he proposes instead is a *reversal* of the standard evolutionary narrative of consciousness and to look for its genesis, not at the top end but at the very beginnings of sentient life:

> It requires us to consider early living organisms first, then gradually move across evolutionary history toward current organisms. It requires us to note *incremental modifications* [emphasis added] of nervous systems and link them to the incremental emergence of, respectively, behaviour, mind, and self.[15]

The three-stage self

Retracing those evolutionary steps, Damasio identifies three major stages in the development of full self-consciousness: from its primitive origins in a 'protoself', followed by the 'core self' and lastly the 'autobiographical self', each of which is rooted in a neurological bonding of brain and body. The protoself consists mainly of body mapping structures of the kind described earlier, together with whatever primordial feelings reflect the current state of the body. At this stage, he argues, beyond those primitive manifestations of sentience, the organism exists *below* the level of self-consciousness. The core self, in turn, remains grounded in the protoself but reaches outwards to link the protoself with the external objects it engages with and which affect or modify it in some way. Lastly, the autobiographical self encompasses all aspects of the social persona, which, together with the core self, constructs a *knowing* self, aware of its past history and present state as well as its future intentions.

Drawing upon his knowledge as an accomplished brain scientist, including his own work with schizophrenia patients of the kind described above, Damasio explains the different neurobiological processes involved in each stage of development and their various locations in the brain. However, whilst at the highest level all three selves interact to produce the knowing self, he cautions against looking for a single neurobiological key to unlocking that unity:

> No single mechanism explains consciousness in the brain, no single device, no single region, or feature, or trick, any more than a symphony can be played by one musician or even a few. Many are needed. What each of them contributes does count. But only the ensemble produces the result we seek to explain.[16]

The real key to understanding what unites the ensemble we call a self, he suggests – minus any conductors – requires a different approach to the problem which treats the self as a *process* rather than a thing, a process, moreover, that is active at all times during consciousness.

Homeostatic rules

However, at this point, having offered a glimpse of what a viable solution to the enigma of the self might look like, Damasio's persuasive approach and arguments falter as he falls back upon limited concepts of homeostasis and natural selection to expound what he means by that process. The management of bodily life, he explains, requires that the chemical and biological mechanisms that sustain a healthy organism be maintained within a defined range of parameters, the safe variation of which is usually very small. Like the founders of cybernetics and many others before him Damasio is also drawn to analogies with computers and other machines with homeostatic capabilities. However, aware of the limitations of such analogies, he argues that the difference between such engineered machines and living organisms is that organisms actually *die* if their homeostatic components and systems fail the strict criteria of biological survival, while machines can simply be readjusted or repaired. Furthermore, every component (i.e., single cell) of a living organism is itself an organism similarly equipped with its own homeostatic rules and mechanisms, equally subject to malfunction and death.

The core self across species

Beyond those basic homeostatic processes, however, for which Porges' polyvagal theory of self-regulation described in the previous chapter offers a more cogent explanation, we are left, as so often with research based upon the neurosciences, to wonder just what kind of superordinate process or controller – if certainly not Penfield's homunculus – might be involved in actually *coordinating* all those individual components Damasio alludes to in his orchestral ensemble, to produce the integrated whole we call a human being or other animal. As with the above limitations of Maturana and Varella's homeostatic model of cellular organisation, Damasio's theory of a multi-stage self is hampered by a basically synchronic model, ill-suited to explaining either the emergence of new levels of being or the dynamic forces that govern the changes from one level to another.

That said, the proposed three-stage self has attracted particular attention amongst some neurobiologists and cognitive scientists for what it suggests of potential evolutionary links between the development of full self-consciousness in humans and more basic forms of self-awareness in other animals. Following Damasio's reversal of the conventional 'top-down' perspective, which associates self-consciousness only with the highest levels of human linguistic and cultural achievement, Panksepp and Northoff[17] argue that, while they do not deny those achievements, they are built upon the evolutionary platforms provided by earlier manifestations of an animal self, actively engaged with the environment:

> Consciousness, as one of the most crucial features of human existence, is increasingly becoming a topic of neuroscientific inquiry. This forces us to reconsider what it means for humans to possess a 'self'. Likewise, evolutionary perspectives coax us to entertain such issues in other organisms, for they too may possess such attributes of mentality. *If we have core selves, perhaps they do also* [emphasis added]. This is rather likely since such a basic level of self may allow organisms to become spontaneously *active* organisms, able to relate to the environment soon after birth.[18]

Self-related processing

Elucidating their concept of a 'trans-species core-self', Panksepp and Northoff offer a complex picture of the interactions between self and environment that goes beyond the simple homeostatic model proposed by Damasio, while still building on the latter's concept of linked stages of development. The collection of nervous systems, or 'self-related processing' (SRP) as they call it, underlying the emergence of a core-self describe a 'fundamental process' including, but not limited to, cognition, enabling organisms to experience various 'affective' or emotional states and feelings as they interact with their environment. Furthermore, most of *all* this brain activity – and not just at the most primitive level of the protoself, as Damasio suggests – occurs below the level of full consciousness:

> We assume that self-related information processing does not typically occur on an explicit and consciously aware level – in a cognitively explicit way – even though it may be rich in affective consciousness. Instead, we

assume it to be either *cognitively preconscious or unconscious and thus implicit* [emphasis added].[19]

Guided by the positive and negative effects of those experiences and feelings, organisms may thus progressively learn more about the environment, and how, as organic entities themselves, they relate to it. Drawing similar conclusions to Porges, they affirm that much of the sifting through of external stimuli for further integration in the nervous system is dependent upon the *organism's emotional state*. Accordingly, while each level of the self exhibits its own form of order, like the upper two floors of a three-storey building, each of which is dependent for its stability on the structure of the floor below, both the core-self and the upper reaches of human self-consciousness *remain firmly rooted in the affective nervous systems of the proto-self*. These, Panksepp and Northoff explain, originate in the very oldest, subcortical regions at the rear of the brain linked directly to the spinal cord, which regulate the central nervous system and channel the motor and sensory systems from the rest of the brain through the body.

Critical neural network

The authors' main focus of interest however, is the core-self as both a cross-species concept and the bridge between the primitive level of the proto-self and the higher levels of the self-conscious human self, which they attribute to a central neural processing network called the 'subcortical-cortical midline system':

> At its lowest levels, it is largely instinctual, affective, but deeply embedded within life-supportive environments. At its highest levels it becomes immersed and moulded by individual learning and cognitive functions as well as ecological and cultural issues. In so doing, we begin to articulate a *common psychobiological basis* [emphasis added] for constituting diverse emergent expressions of self across species – a trans-species, neurobiologically based, multi-layered concept of an objective self.[20]

Focusing on studies of instinctual emotional processes as the most promising evidence of a neural foundation for such a core-self, Panksepp and Northrup write that artificial stimulation of specific regions of animal brains not only yields distinct emotional displays but also indicates whether animals respond positively or negatively to such states. Significantly, the same effects have been found in homologous brain regions in all of the different species of mammals studied. Moreover, the fact that human subjects, who can provide verbal self-reports on their responses, have comparable feelings during the tests, along with self-conscious *ownership* of such experiences, validates the cross-species nature of the underlying primal emotional processes. All the basic emotional operating systems also converge on the same primitive brain regions, suggesting that a core-self may be constructed out of the most ancient nervous systems as a 'universal' feature of the mammalian brain. In turn, they point to 'massive interconnectivities' between these ancient brain regions and nervous systems and the higher functions located in the frontal cortex and other more recently evolved parts of the human brain: 'What is coded is thus not each process by itself, in an absolute way and independent of other stimuli, but rather their *dynamic interactions* [emphasis added]'.[21]

Evolutionary continuity

It should by now be apparent from those earlier explanations of advanced cognitive and social skills displayed by some of our primate cousins, that, if there is any remaining cognitive or other barrier between a cross species core-self and human consciousness, then the more we learn about animal behaviour, the lower or more porous that barrier looks. In his challenging work on the subject, the title of which, *Are We Smart Enough to Know How Smart Animals Are?* speaks volumes, Frans de Vaal[22] reports that, while the evolution of animal cognition generally was commonly believed to stop far short of human cognition, an 'avalanche of knowledge' was now available to dispute that claim, which he refutes himself in no uncertain terms:

> The comparison is not between humans and animals but between one animal species – ours – and a vast array of others [...]. We're not comparing two separate categories of intelligence, therefore, but rather are considering variation within a single one. *I look at human cognition as a variety of animal cognition* [emphasis added].[23]

Methodological issues

In support of that approach, de Vaal offers numerous examples of the hitherto unknown, ignored or underestimated cognitive talents and skills of diverse species whose abilities pose the clearest challenges to human exceptionalism. In addition to other commonly found features of animal cognition such as tool use, empathy and cooperative behaviour, like Damasio, de Vaal favours evolutionary continuity over conventional dualisms like 'body and mind' or 'reason and emotion' and finds strong evidence of a sense of self amongst his animal subjects.

Taking a closer look at the mirror test, which, as explained above, supposedly discriminates between human and animal subjects possessing self-awareness and those lacking it, de Vaal points out that the methodology underlying the test, like many others of its kind, is fatally flawed. Since humans are *already* familiar with what mirrors are and do, they are at an advantage over other species that do not normally see their reflection in mirrors at all, let alone frequently like most humans. What are needed instead, he argues, are 'species-specific' tests, which are based on how *the animal sees the world*, not how humans see it. As difficult as that might seem, he describes a successful modification of the mirror test devised by one of his students to suit Asian elephants at the Bronx Zoo in New York. Dispensing with the human-sized mirrors used in previous tests failed by elephants, which offered only partial views of the animals' bodies, his student chose a mirror large enough to suit his large subjects and supported it so they could feel, smell and move *around and behind* the mirror as well as in front of it. After duly exploring the mirror from all sides and studying its reflection, one elephant named Happy rubbed the mark – a white cross on the forehead – repeatedly while standing in front of the mirror, clearly connecting the image with its own body.

Since then numerous similar tests with Asian elephants have been conducted with positive results, from which de Vaal concludes that the challenge is to devise tests suited to the animal subject's particular anatomy, temperament, sensory capabilities and natural interests. Neither, he argues, should self-awareness be tied to any single test or absolute benchmark. Citing research in self-agency of the sort described above, he writes that species that do not demonstrate mirror self-recognition are nevertheless perfectively capable of identifying their own actions from any similar actions by others:

> Every animal needs to set its body apart from its surroundings and to have a sense of agency [...] Self-agency is part of every action that an animal – any animal – undertakes. In addition, some species may possess their own unusual kind of self-recognition, such as bats and dolphins that pick out the echoes of their own vocalizations from among the sounds made by others.[24]

On the overriding issue of consciousness de Vaal quotes from *The Cambridge Declaration on Consciousness* issued in 2012 by a group of prominent scientists: 'The weight of evidence indicates that humans are not unique in possessing the neurological substrates that generate consciousness'.[25] While the carefully worded statement does not imply actual proof of animal consciousness, de Vaal finds it encouraging enough to add: 'I can live with that'. Taking the *Declaration* as a positive sign that science is increasingly leaning towards continuity over discontinuity in the evolution of consciousness, he concludes with a final challenge to entrenched beliefs that take human capacities as the measure of all things: 'What if theory of mind rests not on one big capacity but on an entire set of smaller ones? *What if self-awareness comes in gradations* [emphasis added]?'[26]

Other minds, other bodies

Written in the same provocative spirit as de Vaal's work, in *Other Minds*, Peter Godfrey-Smith,[27] who is a practiced diver as well as a philosopher of science, has made good use of his aquatic skills in opening up the formerly unknown world of the gifted octopus and other cephalopods, who, like de Vaal's animal subjects, challenge anthropocentric notions of consciousness. Cephalopods, Godfrey-Smith writes, 'are an island of complexity in the sea of invertebrate animals [...] an independent experiment in the evolution of large brains and complex behavior'.[28]

However, remarkable as those achievements are, no evolutionary miracles or jumps were involved. Like de Vaal and others cited here, Godfrey-Smith favours evolutionary continuity over any sudden eruptions or breaks with precedent, a process involving a smooth transition from minimal to more elaborate kinds of sensitivity to the world, for which he argues the evolution of intelligent life in the seas – the ultimate source of all life on Earth – has much to teach us. For most of the Earth's history, he reminds us, the only form of life existed as single-celled organisms in the sea. As primitive as they are, however, their ability to *sense and react* to their environment, including other single-celled organisms, provided the evolutionary springboard for *all* sentient life. From there, it was a relatively short but transformative step to multi-cellular life, the success of which depended upon the coordination between cells, internally within the organism and externally with the environment. From such humble but promising beginnings, the nervous systems of all multi-cellular animal species evolved, leading in mammals and other species to the brains – literally the 'headquarters' of animal nervous systems – and complex interconnected branches, subsystems and many functions described by other researchers in this book.

But not all animal species. As Godfrey-Smith explains, the cephalopod family remains an important exception to the accepted norms of animal evolution. The precise origins of that exception are still uncertain but are now thought to predate the Cambrian Explosion. Though otherwise radically different from all those later sea and land-based body forms, the earliest likely cephalopod ancestor shared a universal, *bilateral* body plan – a vital asset for any creature in orientating itself and moving about within its environment, enabling the sea-bound species to develop more complex nervous systems and prosper amongst the competition.[29]

The outcome is the family of extraordinary creatures we know today, who, though, like us, have impressively large brains, have a completely different configuration of nervous systems from us or any other large-brained animal. Vertebrates have a cord of nerves running from a central brain at one end of the body down the backbone. Cephalopods also have a brain located in the front of the main body, but it is only part of a less centralised, or *distributed* nervous system, comprised of many small knots of neurons, or 'ganglia' connected to each other and spread throughout the rest of the body. In the octopus, the star of the family, the majority of neurons – nearly twice as many as in the brain – are located in the eight arms themselves, which have their own sensors and controllers with the capacity for sensing chemicals (odours and tastes) as well as touch.

As smart as they are, however, with the exception of some squid, cephalopods are not known for being sociable creatures, particularly the octopus, the behaviour of which Godfrey- Smith describes as following a life of 'lone idiosyncratic complexity'. Given that, as also suggested by other researchers in this book, advanced cognitive abilities are generally associated with high levels of social interaction, he wonders what it can be that drove evolution to gift the octopus with such a large brain, decentralised as it is. The answer, he suggests, lies in a combination of two important factors, each of which requires high levels of neuronal coordination. The first factor – unique to the species – is the number and highly flexible nature of the octopus's many limbs, the coordinated movement of which, in comparison with stiff-jointed vertebrates like us and countless other animals, requires complex sensory and control systems of their own to manipulate objects as cleverly as they do. The second factor is the characteristic varied behaviour of the octopus in foraging for food, which involves adapting today's menu to the circumstances and opportunities of the moment, together with removing the choice parts of their prey, such as crabs and scallops, from their protective shells and casings – no mean task – while at the same time watching out for possible danger to themselves. Though, as Godfrey-Smith observes, the octopus's interactions with others may not be of the friendly, collaborative sort normally associated with social behaviour, taken altogether, they are none the less complex for that, their engagement with predators or prey requiring that they also be tuned to *their* actions and perspectives if they are to survive.

Perceptual constancies

The implication is that, should observers choose to drop their normal human-centred perspective on the world and look at things – difficult as that may be – from the organism's viewpoint, *intelligent behaviour can be seen to take many forms*, depending upon the specific nature and complexity of the interactions between an organism and the environment to which it is attuned. As a philosopher, however, Godfrey-Smith is especially concerned with the question whether, given their large and unusual brains, cephalopods can tell us something new about the emergence of consciousness and subjective experience as a gradual, rather than a sharp or divisive process separating 'us' from 'them'. Octopuses, he notes: 'have an opportunistic, exploratory style of interaction with the world. They are curious, embracing novelty, protean in behavior as well as in body'[30] – all features that have been associated with human consciousness.

A key part of that capacity for dealing with novelty, he suggests, is due to the fact that, for all the differences in body form and nervous system, like us and other vertebrates, cephalopods are capable of distinguishing perceptual constancies, meaning links between perception and action are created which subconsciously adjust for changes in the size and appearance of objects as the animal approaches or moves away from them – a basic but essential requirement for interpreting, anticipating and adapting to more complex changes in their environment, and which, as suggested above, the bilateral layout of the cephalopod body will certainly have helped.[31] All the while, the individual cephalopod sense of self will have been sharpened through those same interactions with others in its world, not unlike the manner in which the human subjective self evolves out of its interactions with other humans.

Based upon his studies with the cephalopods and other research on animal behaviour of the sort described elsewhere in this book, Godfrey-Smith also disputes speech – meaning human speech composed of words and sentences – as being necessary for higher levels of cognition: 'It has become clear now that very complex things go on inside animals *without the aid of speech* [emphasis added]'.[32] Though many cephalopods can change their colour at will, suggestive of a possible form of cephalopod communication, it turns out the species is in fact colour blind, and that their fast-changing and moving patterns of colour probably evolved from an inherited camouflage function and perhaps now better express what is going on *inside* the animal's distributed brain, rather than being purposefully directed outside to any receiving other.

Subjective experience

What counts, therefore, in Godfrey-Smith's smooth-running version of the evolution of animal intelligence, is not so much self-awareness and consciousness as concepts and processes in themselves, as the *interactions* between conscious and unconscious levels of subjective experience, from which higher levels of self-consciousness might have emerged. The same interactions between different levels of consciousness, he suggests, may also help to explain what it is that really *does* distinguish us from other animals, if only by matters of degree.

Searching further, he points to the concept of 'inner speech' in *Mind and Society* by Lev Vygotsky,[33] the Russian pioneer of developmental psychology, who argued that the acquisition of speech in early childhood involved both *inner and outer* forms of speech, the inner version of which has its own patterns and rhythms and which make higher-level, organised thought and subjective experience possible. For Vygotsky, inner speech has a role in what is now called the 'executive control' functions of the brain, exerting a top-down control over regular, perhaps unwise, habits when needed. It also provides a 'medium of experiment, for putting ideas together to see what comes of their combination'.[34] Yet all of this is going on as a kind of *unconscious or semi-conscious preamble* to any external and more precise communication of thought through actual speech.

Looping the loop

Drawing upon the storehouse of information and imagery housed in personal memory, inner speech, Godfrey-Smith suggests, with all its semi-conscious chatter and half-formed ideas, 'can have huge effects on subjective experience', whether conscious or unconscious. The key to understanding *conscious* subjective experience, however, is that it is *integrated knowledge that can be 'broadcast'* and made available to others as well as to the self:

> Information from several different senses, and from our memory, is brought together to give us a sense of an overall 'scene' that we inhabit and act in [...]. Inner speech does not live in a little box in your brain; inner speech is *a way your brain creates a loop*, intertwining the construction of thoughts and the reception of them.[35]

Spoken language in turn provides the organised structure that allows us to complete the process and to take the final step towards reflective thought, in which it is our *own* thoughts that engage us. However, rather than being *responsible* for subjective experience, as others who equate consciousness with human language have argued, Godfrey-Smith suggests that these higher-level developments are amongst the more sophisticated features of human life that have *reshaped* subjective experience in us. So, while he acknowledges the importance of inner speech in the development of subjective experience, he allows that other animals, not least the intelligent cephalopods, have done pretty well in developing their own inner lives *without* language.

A genuine parting of the ways between human and non-human forms of consciousness arises, however, with the emergence of the *written word*, creating a more precise and concrete expression of one's own thoughts, which, when put down in writing, as in a diary, amounts to a form of *external memory*. Moreover, though the message may not be directed at others, as a higher level form of inner speech, Godfrey-Smith argues there is nevertheless a process of communication going on – only now it is *between a present and future self* for whom the writer is planning and which has become the subject of conscious reflection: 'When we see the human mind as the locus of countless loops of this kind, it gives us a different perspective on our own lives and the lives of other animals'.[36] As impressive as the cephalopods' nervous systems may be, he concludes, lacking in the same feedback loops that go with external forms of memory, they eventually ran into an evolutionary cul-de-sac, leaving the development of a more complicated mind to humans.

The cultural ratchet

Approaching the subject initially from a human perspective, in *The Cultural Origins of Human Cognition*, Michael Tomasello[37] adopts a similar position to Godfrey-Smith on finding major differences from other animals' achievements in the *externalised accumulation* of human knowledge; a position, however, that he was to modify considerably in his later work:

The evidence that human beings do indeed have species-unique modes of cultural transmission is overwhelming. Most importantly, the cultural traditions and artifacts of human beings *accumulate modifications over time* [emphasis added] in a way that other animal species do not – so-called cumulative cultural evolution.[38]

While at this point Tomasello acknowledged that social and cultural transmission amongst animals is a fairly common, time-saving evolutionary process enabling individual organisms to acquire the knowledge they needed to get through life, he argued that it was generally restricted to the young mimicking the tried-and-tested habits and skills of their parents and others of their species. What makes the transmission of human culture truly so different, he explains, is that once a new tool or other innovation has been conceived and adopted as normal practice, subsequent *improvements* are also carefully preserved from generation to generation, producing what he describes as the creative 'ratchet effect' of human culture – something he argues that, for all their other proven talents, is beyond the capacities of other species:

> Perhaps surprisingly, for many animal species it is not the creative component, but rather the stabilizing ratchet component, that is the difficult feat. Thus, many nonhuman primate individuals regularly produce intelligent behavioural innovations and novelties, but then their group mates do not engage in the kinds of social learning that would enable, over time, the cultural ratchet to do its work.[39]

Shared intentionality

Based on the work of Jean Piaget,[40] the French child psychologist and epistemologist, Tomasello identifies those special 'kinds of social learning' as the ability of humans to understand others as *intentional agents* with behavioural goals just like themselves – an ability which manifests itself in the behaviour of children as young as eight to nine months of age but which, at the time of writing *Human Cognition*, he believed to be beyond the capabilities of other species at any age. However, writing in the preface to his more recent work, *A Natural History of Human Thinking*,[41] Tomasello explains that, while vital differences remain between the evolution of human and non-human primate cognition and culture, the ground has shifted since the former book was written and much more is now known about the behaviour of great apes themselves as intentional agents:

> The critical difference now seems to be that humans not only understand others as intentional agents but also put their heads together with others in acts of shared intentionality, including everything from concrete acts of collaborative problem solving to complex cultural institutions.[42]

According to what Tomasello elaborates as his 'shared intentionality hypothesis', while the crucial difference in social learning enabled humans to achieve all that we now freely associate with human culture and civilisation, the roots of that difference are to be found much further back in evolutionary time, when early humans first began to coordinate their individual efforts in the collaborative task of foraging for food. Up until that point, there was not much difference, he suggests, between the individual and group behaviour of humans and that of non-human primates, who understood many aspects of their physical and social worlds in similar ways to humans, including the relational structure of those worlds. Thus *all* primates evolved the goal-orientated cognitive skills required for finding, identifying (categorising) and procuring foods in the spatial and physical world they inhabit, together with the communicative and negotiating skills required to prosper in social groups of their own kind where the competition for food, mates and other resources is paramount.

Primate powers

Following a now well-established trail, Tomasello points to the great apes for evidence of still-closer comparisons between human and non-human primate skills, particularly in the all-important use of tools. Amongst other enlightening experiments, he describes one where chimpanzees were presented with a food extraction problem they had not encountered before, the solution to which necessitated choosing a new tool from a varied selection left for them in a different place from that of the food. In addition to analysing and memorising the food extraction problem well enough to choose a remote but appropriate tool, to succeed while avoiding repetitive trials with different tools the subjects needed to *imagine* using their chosen tool well enough *beforehand* to verify its suitability for the job, before returning to extract the food. Tomasello reports that many animals passed the test – often at the first attempt – some even saving the tool for possible future use.[43]

Great apes have demonstrated similarly high levels of cognition in their social world. A typical experiment in power relationships between great apes involved a dominant male and subordinate female competing for food. One piece of food was left in an open space outside the apes' enclosure that was visible to both, while another morsel was placed on the subordinate's side of a screen placed in between the pair, so that only the subordinate could see it. When the subordinate's door was opened before the dominant ape's door was, despite being given a head start the subordinate chose to take the food on her own side of the screen, leaving the more exposed food to be taken by her neighbour; indicating she *guessed* how he would act according to what he could and could not see: 'This means that nonhuman great apes not only are intentional agents themselves', Tomasello observes, 'but also understand others as intentional agents'.[44]

Underpinning the cognitive sophistication of the great apes across both physical and social realms, he argues, is the ability to *monitor their own actions*. Like humans, for much if not all of the time they are aware of what they are doing and are able to learn from their mistakes and improve their performance. Over and above the more action-based forms of behavioural self-monitoring however, Tomasello points to evidence of higher level *cognitive self-monitoring* in experiments with rhesus monkeys. One experiment involved the monkeys having to memorise or distinguish between several objects. If they failed on the first trial, they got nothing and were compelled to take time out to re-think their approach before the next attempt. However, on each trial they were also offered the chance of opting out of the problem early for a lesser but guaranteed reward, but at the cost of losing valuable time-out before any retrials. The result was that many subjects chose to opt out of those tasks they were most likely to fail, thus evincing a purposeful strategy: 'They seem to know that they do not know or that they do not remember' what they need to know or remember to solve the problem.[45]

Interdependent lifestyles

All of these cognitive traits involving internal representations of things and events, inference and self-monitoring by the great apes qualify for Tomasello as crucial evidence of *individual* intentionality similar to that of humans. However, as important as they are to understanding individual behaviour, he argues they fall short of the *shared* intentionality he maintains sets *Homo sapiens* firmly on the fast track of evolution and which still sets humans apart from all other animals. So, then, what was it that brought about an evolutionary shift of such magnitude that one particular species of primate could henceforth dominate every other living species on the planet?

Tomasello puts the crucial development of shared or 'joint' intentionality as he also calls it, down to a change – probably stimulated, he speculates, by new ways of collaborative foraging by early humans – from the mainly *competitive* social structure of non-human primate groups, to the emergence of *cooperative* patterns of behaviour amongst humans:

> The first and most basic point is that humans began a lifestyle in which individuals could not procure their daily substance alone but instead were *interdependent with others* [emphasis added] in their foraging activities – which meant that individuals needed to develop the skills and motivations to forage collaboratively or else starve. There was thus direct and immediate selective pressure for skills and motivations for joint collaborative activity (joint intentionality). The second point is that as a natural outcome of this interdependence, individuals began to make *evaluative judgments about others* [emphasis added] as potential collaborative partners: they began to be socially selective, since choosing a poor partner meant less food.[46]

Significantly, Tomasello adds, not only were individuals learning to evaluate others as potential collaborators, but they also now had to contend with the knowledge that *they themselves* were subject to being evaluated by others for the same purpose, giving rise to a 'concern for self-image' of the sort other primates are not bothered with. From such beginnings, he posits, to which were added the pressures of competition between social groups and increasing population sizes, early humans developed the sense of group-mindedness and identity upon which all human cultures are based, and from which the cumulative fruits of cultural production stem.

Chapter 7

Tacit nexus

The previous chapter concluded with an explanation by Tomasello of the significance of shared intentionality in human development, which he claims underpins humankind's unique cultural achievements. However, differences between levels of cognition and collaborative behaviour attained by humans and other animals remain a matter of much contention, with contrary writers in the same chapter making the case for evolutionary continuity over radical change.

Researchers of many disciplines now also believe that language and intelligence evolved in tandem with the growing *complexity* of cooperative behaviour from *Homo erectus* onwards – and possibly earlier – culminating in the emergence of symbolic systems and abstract thought in human cultures, and with it, the ability to learn from and to generalise from concrete experience. A fundamental part of that process was the simultaneous development of tools and other artifacts of countless types and forms – achievements that originated in earlier primate skills – the repeatable character of which, along with the recognition and communication of other stable phenomena, went to make up the classification systems common to all languages.

Much, if not the greater part of these developments occurred – and continues to occur – at a *subconscious or tacit level*, normally only rising, as it has been suggested, to levels of greater awareness when regular patterns of behaviour are disturbed by unexpected events. Thus cooperative behaviour, language, artifacts and practical intelligence all evolved together as integral elements of the human self-field, creating a tacit nexus of knowledge and skills supported by a complex web of social and cultural systems, the nature of which has shaped the practice of science as much as any other human activity.

Overlapping brain functions

While neuroscientists have focused in the past on *locating* any neural centres in the brain associated with different cognitive and behavioural functions, cross-disciplinary research by behavioural scientists and neurobiologists now also suggests that the evolutionary foundations of language, behaviour and tool-use lie more in the *overlapping* of the neural circuits controlling those functions than in their separate development. As Kathleen Gibson[1] argues, such research contests long-held beliefs – supported by specialised disciplines – that subjects be treated as separate phenomena requiring separate approaches:

> To understand the evolution of the human mind, we must first confront this fundamental question of whether human behavioral and cognitive domains are separately compartmentalized, as self-contained 'modules', or whether they exist only as *interrelated aspects of a total system* [emphasis added].[2]

The same research supports the theory that increased brain size is a major source of difference between non-human and human evolution and was crucial to the rapid and sustained course of human development.[3] Whilst Gibson acknowledges the communicative abilities as well as the widespread tool-using and making skills of non-human primates, she argues that they still fall far short of human technological and linguistic achievements. For example, in addition to those vocal and gestural forms of communication acquired in the wild, in captivity all species of great apes, but especially chimpanzees, can be taught a basic 'language' of symbols. However, Gibson observes that such skills are limited at best to the syntactic constructions of a three-year old human child and are focused exclusively on simple needs (requests) or objects in the immediate environment. Thus, while none of the differences she describes between the achievements of human and other primates can sensibly be described as absolute, they are nonetheless remarkable for that. Three key factors, she explains, underlie those differences:

> First, humans possess a far greater degree of brain-size-mediated information processing capacity and apply this capacity to their tool use, language and social behavior. Second, human tool use, language and social behavior are mutually interdependent [emphasis added]. Third, tool use and language are so strongly canalized in the human species that they emerge in most mentally normal children by one and a half to two years of age. In contrast, apes exhibit minimal, if any, genetic canalization in these behavioral domains.[4]

Since all these factors depend upon the greater information processing capacities of the enlarged human brain – three to four times the size of the average ape brain – Gibson contends they must have evolved gradually along with the larger brain. Moreover, as they are all interdependent, none of these intellectual capacities could have reached their stellar human levels alone, but were dependent upon the integration of all three. Significantly, some regions of the brain also increased in size more than others, the greatest proportional increase being in the so-called 'neocortical association' or higher-order areas. As Gibson explains, injury to these areas can cause severe deficiencies in language, object manipulation and social behaviour, indicating the same regions of the brain have important 'synthetic functions' in mediating between more specialised functions, combining separately generated sensory perceptions or motor acts into simultaneous or sequential constructs.

Stringing things together

Writing in the same volume of essays as Gibson, William Calvin[5] offers an account of these synthetic functions from a neo-Darwinian perspective:

> It is traditional to talk about language origin in terms of adaptations for verbal communication, to talk about tool making in terms of natural selection shaping up the hand and the motor cortex, to talk about the evolution of intelligence in terms of how useful versatile problem-solving and look ahead would have been to hominids. But might natural selection for one of these improvements serve to haul along the others as well? Indeed, might some fourth function be the seed by which the others grew? What are the chances of coevolving talk, technique and thought?[6]

Following all the shortcomings of the Modern Synthesis recorded in these pages one might wonder at Calvin's unquestioning faith in the powers of natural selection. However, his 'unitary hypothesis', as he calls it, throws light on a more complex picture. In particular, referencing Darwin's important but neglected observation that the *transitions* of organs over time often involved the probability that one function might be converted to another, Calvin's evolutionary focus on novelties and invention fits well with the concerns of the Extended Synthesis. Citing the case of the origin of bird flight and the functional changeover of feathers from simple body cover to providing feathered forelimbs for airborne flight, he asserts Darwinian functional conversion over competing theories of innovation: 'Nature does takes leaps, and such conversions of functions are even faster than those anatomical leaps envisaged by proponents of punctuated equilibria and hopeful monsters'.[7]

The same principle applies to hominid advancements in tool use, language and intelligence. In general, he observes, the brain excels at creating *new uses for old things*. It can do this because the brain's composition and neural mechanisms enable it to compare dissimilar things and to combine sensory schemas and movement programmes in new ways. Specifically, the left hemisphere of the brain is especially good at 'stringing things together'; a process involving a *sequence* of actions that Calvin explains is fundamental to a host of what are normally thought of as evolutionarily distinct functions. Prominent amongst those overlapping functions he lists: tool making and use, for which a novel sequence of movements is required; creating meaningful linguistic sequences out of individually meaningless vocalisations, which enabled humans to progress beyond the limited vocalisations of apes and other creatures; making a new plan of action each step of which, if the plan is to succeed, needs to be mentally rehearsed before execution, and not least, *targeted throwing* of all kinds, which, like executing a novel plan of action, includes a 'get set' phase involving the production of whole chains of nerve impulses running to different muscles in anticipation of the final action.

But what is it, Calvin asks, about the brain that is responsible for these over-lapping functions? Contrary to common assumptions about the mapping of separate brain functions, he explains, while the motor cortex broadly controls the movement of different parts of the body, it is the premotor and prefrontal cortex that is primarily responsible for stringing things together ready for execution, and not the motor cortex, which only comes into full play once things get started.[8] Neuropsychologists have also now found that patients with damaged prefrontal areas have difficulties in planning a sequence of movements. Similarly, overlaps between language disorders and sequential hand movements have been found in patients who have suffered heart strokes, so that, while they could handle each movement involved in say, unlocking a door, turning the handle and opening the door, they could not do it all in one normal smooth sequence.[9]

Rapid sequencing

Different plans, though, require different amounts of neural sequencing power. Most plans of action, Calvin observes, do not need a detailed specification of each step before being implemented since normal feedback systems suffice for guidance along the way. However, 'there are some physical movements which are too rapid for feedback to guide them: they are over and done with by the time the first feedback arrives'.[10] Compared to most modern elec-tronic systems, neural feedback systems are, in fact, quite slow; human reac-tion times normally require hundreds of milliseconds – much too slow for skills like dart throwing.[11] Calvin concluded that, for throwing movements requiring ultra-fast reaction times, feedback from joints and muscles are effect-ively wasted. Such movements require an altogether different strategy – also common amongst non-human primates – involving meticulous advance prep-aration and a memory bank for storing up related muscular instructions ready for enactment:

> You need something like a *serial buffer memory* [emphasis added] in which to load up all the muscle commands in the right order and with the right timing relative to one another – and then you pump them out blindly, without waiting for any feedback.[12]

More than that, Calvin speculates that, since every throwing action will vary, even if only slightly from past similar actions, more than one buffer memory and stored planning track is required to provide a viable set of tried-and-tested actions to choose from, together with a 'best-so-far' candidate. And the more promising candidates available for selection, the better. So buffer memories need to store enough alternative sequences acquired in practising the relevant movements to provide a winner for a particular situation. Calvin invites us to think of a 'railroad marshaling yard [with] many candidate trains vying for the chance to be let loose on the track'.[13] Meantime, muscles are held firmly in check until the best choice sequence is finally released and limb movements all combine to hit their target – everything happening subconsciously in just a few milliseconds, powered by what he describes as the brain's ultra-fast version of the Darwin Machine of natural selection, sifting through all the candidates for the most likely winner.[14]

Speculating further, Calvin offers a 'throwing-based evolutionary scenario' from the development of hominid behavioural skills involving throwing actions – skills that hominids shared with other primates such as throwing rocks to injure prey or scare predators away – to the technically enhanced progression of *Homo* from spear throwing to using bow-and-arrow and crossbow for more distant targets. Beginning with the first hominid improvements in hand throwing, each step, he argues, would have required related large increases in neural power to handle the extra brain work involved in gaining those improvements; increases that, along with an increase in brain size, he suggests might also have been temporarily 'borrowed' from other regions of the brain to supplement those regions more specialised in sequencing. In conclusion, he writes: 'Throwing seems to be a fast track for hominid evolution; whether it is the fastest track to a versatile sequencer and its Darwin Machine secondary uses, can be better judged when a similar analysis is available for language, intelligence, tool making, and other candidates'.[15]

Practical intelligence

Rather than loading responsibility for the accelerated evolution of humans on to any *single* factor, however, it is at least probable if not highly likely, as Gibson suggests, that the remarkable speed of human development is the *combined* outcome of several key cognitive, behavioural and technical elements – including perhaps, all of those alternative factors suggested by Calvin – the interactions of which multiply any 'bootstrapping' effects that any single factor might have on its own.

Research on the early development of language and object manipulation in children offers further insights into just how such a combination of key factors might work together to speed up cognitive development. Andrew Lock[16] describes how, about the age of nine months, infants show pre-verbal evidence of intentional actions using physical gestures developed in imitation of adult models to communicate their needs. Parallel with such gestures, infants develop 'vocal counterparts' with the aim of drawing attention to their gestures, which are also not truly symbolic, but are recognised as *equivalent* to the physical actions. Later, aged around 15–24 months, the manipulation of objects, commonly stimulated in 'naming games' between infant and parent, plays an increasing role in the development of symbolic communication: 'Objects similar in adult eyes can be substituted for each other while requiring the same response, so that sounds are not linked to say, just one picture of a dog, but many different forms of dog; and can be substituted in other game formats'.[17]

After a relatively slow stage accumulating a basic vocabulary – about fifty words is usually regarded as the take-off point – the outcome is a 'naming explosion' in which infants rapidly build up their repertoire of named objects and groups and begin to add words that relate them to specific contexts. Notably, those advances do not replace the cognitive procedures that have gone before, but build upon them, moving from naming things to that of *predication*, which entails not just identifying a ball as a specific object but also *saying something about the ball*. Nevertheless, Lock adds, as the infant reworks its communicative repertoire into a linguistic one, it does not need to articulate *everything* it wants to say during this period:

> At the same time, it should be recognized that this symbolic referential and predicative system, while pre-grammatical, is effective in specifying a range of intentions and meanings. *The infant is able to convey implied meanings of a far greater range and power than it is able to render or control explicitly* [emphasis added].[18]

Technical thinking and linguistic development

Lock's observations on the implicit meanings infants attach to the naming and manipulation of objects, like Godfrey-Smith's observations in the preceding chapter on the importance of inner speech, were strongly influenced by and support what Vygotsky describes in his research as the first demonstrations of practical intelligence by infants. Vygotsky was particularly impressed with the work of K. Buhler, who 'established the developmentally important principle that the beginnings of intelligent speech *are preceded by technical thinking* [emphasis added], and technical thinking comprises the initial phase of cognitive development'.[19] Buhler was a pioneering researcher himself in comparing the early cognitive development of children and that of primates, specifically chimpanzees, well ahead of much of the related research reported here. However, Vygotsky faulted Buhler for arguing that, based on his belief that cognitive development in both apes and children was similar at this early stage but *separate* from linguistic development, 'technical thinking, or thinking in terms of tools',[20] as Buhler expressed it, *remained* independent of conceptual and linguistic development in humans and had less impact on that process in its later stages than other forms of thinking. 'This analysis', Vygotsky asserts, 'postulating the independence of intelligent action from speech runs contrary to our own findings, which reveal the *integration of speech and practical thinking in the course of development* [emphasis added]'.[21]

Neither, for Vygotsky, whose primary concern is with the development of practical intelligence and technical thinking in humans, is that development a simple matter of the mechanical imitation and repetition of adult actions. Vygotsky views all such actions as taking place within a social and cultural milieu, in which the child, through actively reaching out and interacting with its environment, begins to master its surroundings prior to mastering its own behaviour:

> The most significant moment in the course of intellectual development, which gives birth to the purely human forms of practical and abstract intelligence, occurs when speech and practical activity, two previously completely independent lines of development, converge. Although children's use of tools during their preverbal period is comparable with that of apes, as soon as speech and the use of signs are incorporated into any action, the action becomes transformed and organized along entirely new lines. The specifically human use of tools is thus realized, going far beyond the more limited use of tools possible among the higher animals.[22]

Internalised sign systems

In turn, Vygotsky was profoundly influenced in his concept of practical intelligence by Friedrich Engels' concept of human labour and tool use, about which Engels wrote: 'The specialization of the hand – this implies the *tool*, and the tool implies specific human activity, the transforming reaction of man on nature'.[23] And further:

> [...] the animal merely *uses* external nature, and brings about changes in it simply by his presence; man, by his changes, makes it serve his ends, *masters it*. This is the final, essential distinction between man and other animals.[24]

As the editors of *Mind and Society* write, in extending Engels' concept to include the role of signs together with that of tools in mediating human–environment relationships, Vygotsky showed how culturally produced sign systems might be internalised, transforming behaviour and bridging early and later forms of development: 'Thus for Vygotsky, in the tradition of Marx and Engels, the mechanism of individual developmental change is rooted in society and culture'.[25]

Dexterous hands

Affirming what Engels accurately intuited about the same body part, in *The Hand*, Frank Wilson,[26] a neurologist, boldly asserts that the hand is far more than just a useful part of the human anatomy; together with the brain it has always been at the very centre of human development:

> I would argue that any theory of human intelligence which ignores the interdependence of hand and brain function, the historic origins of that relationship, or the impact of that history on developmental dynamics in modern humans, is grossly misleading and sterile.[27]

In a key chapter entitled 'Hand-Thought-Language Nexus', Wilson recounts how the previous work of three leading figures on the evolution of language and intelligence prepared him for that revelation. From Robin Dunbar, a biologist, he learnt that 'brain growth, the evolution of language, and the need for intelligent behaviour were necessary concomitants of the *increasing social complexity of hominid community life* [emphasis added]'.[28] As our hominid ancestors spread out across the Eurasian continent and encountered new and greater environmental challenges, Dunbar explained, so their survival became ever more dependent upon the *group*, and on the development of working relationships and higher levels of social intelligence and communication needed to sustain and strengthen group coherence.

From Merlin Donald, a psychologist, Wilson learned that beginning with the apes, the nature of knowledge itself underwent a major transformation. Donald presents a multi-stage evolutionary picture of the 'cognitive architecture' of the brain, by which the development of the human mind can be traced back through major adaptations of the primate mind, each of which resulted in the emergence of a new representational system. Significantly, however, the emergence of the new system *does not displace previous systems*. Instead, Donald writes: 'Each representational system has remained intact within our current mental architecture, so that the modern mind is a mosaic structure of cognitive vestiges from earlier stages of human emergence'.[29] A vital part of that cognitive picture, Wilson notes, is the importance Donald attaches to the developmental relationship between the primate hand – particularly that of the chimpanzee – and its uses. For the first time in evolution, Donald writes, there was a fusion between visual, tactile and positional feedback systems: 'Hand control may be regarded as the crossing of a biological Rubicon in that a dominant distal sense – vision – comes to control and modulate actions directly'.[30]

Lastly, Wilson presents the work of Henry Plotkin, a professor of psychobiology and the third major influence on his own approach, as a seamless extension of Donald's: 'Plotkin regards the term "knowledge" as signifying more than words or facts in the head. *Knowledge is any state in an organism that bears a relationship to the world* [emphasis added]'.[31] Plotkin describes the genetic accumulation of the knowledge constituted in the biological structure of the human body itself, combined with random mutations as a source of novel variants, as *Homo's* 'primary heuristic'. Alongside this genetic heuristic, he describes the manifestation of intelligence as a 'secondary heuristic' of a quite different character, about which Wilson comments: 'As Plotkin accounts for it, intelligence is one of the true Cinderella stories of evolution; it is the principal adaptation that evolved in primates to meet the "Uncertain Futures Problem."'[32] While the biological inheritance bequeathed to individuals by their genes worked well enough for the purposes of survival in familiar environments, Plotkin argued, something more than group membership alone was required to handle all the new and potentially life-threatening situations our ancestors met with in less familiar worlds.

However, faced in conclusion, as Wilson writes, with the 'Gordian knot, the nexus of knowledge, language and intelligence',[33] Plotkin offers no more than an acknowledgement that, since language is unique to our species, 'we must be genetically disposed to learn, think in and communicate by language'.[34] The central question of the evolutionary origins of language itself is left unanswered – a failure that Plotkin himself, after sifting through Chomskian linguistics and other contenders, concedes: 'What I cannot understand, and neither can anyone else, is exactly what the functional origins of language are'.[35]

Unification of action, thought and language

Returning to his own theory about those origins and the paramount role the development of the hand plays in the story, Wilson writes:

> What I am suggesting is that perhaps we *do* know what the functional origins of language are. It is likely that sometime during its stewardship of the genetic lineage of *Homo*, *erectus* completed the final revisions to evolution's modeling of the hand, opening the door to an enormously augmented range of movements and the possibility of an unprecedented extension of manual activities. As a collateral event, the brain was laying the foundations of cognitive and communicative capacity [...] The handyman's hand was more than just an explorer and discoverer of things in the objective world; it was a divider, a joiner, an enumerator, dissector, and an assembler.[36]

Following Vygotsky, Wilson observes that, though they may have separate, pre-human evolutionary origins, action, thought and language uniquely come together in humans in the very early stages of childhood, 'during which words that were originally object attributes come increasingly to be manipulated and combined, just as *real* objects are manipulated and combined by the child'.[37] At the same time, Wilson adds, the hands themselves are undergoing a transformation, getting ready for a leading role in the performance. Around one year of age, as the child's hands with their independently moving fingers develop their manipulative abilities, the world of objects and the child's knowledge of what can be *done* with those objects in the hand increases rapidly:

> In other words, the thought-language nexus is becoming a hand–thought–language nexus. The child learns with real objects, by trial and error, to make constructions that are inevitably composed as discrete events *unified through a sequence of actions* [emphasis added].[38]

The cognitive foundations for the impressive skills of the trained surgeon, pianist, rock climber, magician and other dexterous cases with which Wilson vividly illustrates his arguments, are therefore all laid together with the development of language in early childhood as a fully integrated process. Concluding his hymn to the hand, Wilson writes:

> The brain does not live inside the head, even though that is its normal habitat. It reaches out to the body, and with the body it reaches out into the world. We can say that the brain 'ends' at the spinal cord, and that the spinal cord 'ends' at the peripheral nerve, and the peripheral nerve 'ends' at the neuromuscular junction, and on and on down to the quarks, but *the brain is hand and hand is brain* [emphasis added], and their interdependence includes everything else right down to the quarks.[39]

Science and praxis

The tacit nexus of knowledge and skills Wilson elucidates, however, is far from limited to activities where manual dexterity is a characteristic feature. While science is not readily associated with practical knowledge and skills, Thomas Kuhn makes a strong case for reassessing the actual praxis of science, which involves many of the cognitive processes described above by Vygotsky and Wilson. Best known for his radical history of science, *The Structure of Scientific Revolutions*[40] and related concept of scientific 'paradigms' – traditions of scientific thought and experiment shared by scientists working on similar problems – Kuhn effectively demolished the idea that all scientists spend their working lives searching for evidence of new phenomena that would explain the unexplained and change the way we look at the world. Not at all, Kuhn argued. Drawing a line between 'normal science' and the rare but true revolutions in scientific knowledge that really *do* change our understanding of the world, Kuhn claimed that, following well established paradigms, the great majority devoted their careers to working out the details and implications of *existing* theories accepted by their peers. Only when presented with mounting and incontrovertible evidence of anomalies in the dominant theory, accompanied by an incompatible but promising rival theory, would scientists reluctantly shift their allegiance to the new camp, in what Kuhn describes as something like a religious conversion.

Normal science as a necessary preparation for new discoveries

However, elaborating in a later and less-familiar work, *The Essential Tension*,[41] on the meaning of normal science and how it functions, Kuhn presents normal and revolutionary science as *complementary* rather than conflicting activities:

> New theories and, to an increasing extent, novel discoveries in the mature sciences are not born *de novo*. On the contrary, they emerge from old theories and within a matrix of old beliefs about the phenomena that the world does *and does not* contain.[42]

Even towering figures like Copernicus, Darwin and Einstein, he suggests, would have acquired basic research skills and professional commitments in the course of working on current paradigms. Thus, whilst scientific revolutions of the order initiated by such figures may indeed be rare events in the history of science, in his revised account Kuhn argues that normal science provides a necessary *preparation* for such events. Moreover, blurring the line he had previously drawn between normal and revolutionary science, he explains that normal science is itself replete with far smaller but 'structurally similar' events:

> Contrary to a prevalent impression, most new discoveries and theories in the sciences are not merely additions to the existing stockpile of scientific knowledge. To assimilate them the scientist must usually *rearrange the intellectual and manipulative equipment* [emphasis added] he has previously relied upon, discarding some elements of his prior belief and practice while finding new significances in and new relationships between many others.[43]

Value of concrete exemplars

Underlying the evolution of scientific knowledge, therefore, is a continuous tug-of-war between convergent and divergent thinking, in which, from time to time, divergent thought triumphs over conventional beliefs and methods, before things settle down again under the new consensus. While acknowledging the necessity of both tradition and change in science Kuhn writes: 'Both my own experience in scientific research and my reading of the history of the sciences lead me to wonder whether flexibility and open-mindedness have not been too exclusively emphasized as the characteristics requisite for basic research'.[44]

Pursuing the argument and offering his 'second thoughts on paradigms',[45] Kuhn describes a paradigm as a 'disciplinary matrix' comprising several elements and levels of thought, involving *both* the conscious and unconscious assimilation of scientific knowledge and methodology. Of the three principle constituents of a disciplinary matrix he describes, symbolic expressions, analogical models and concrete exemplars, he highlights the last of these as being of special importance to the conduct of normal science, and in the long run, also to scientific innovations. Firstly, concrete exemplars as taught to fledging scientists in the form of key experiments in the history of scientific achievements, are crucial to understanding how the first two, more abstract, forms of knowledge correspond with whatever aspect of nature with which they are concerned. Kuhn contends students of science learn how to match symbolic generalisations to particular problems and situations in their field, not so much through any explicit correspondence rules, which he suggests are hard to define anyway, but through *repetition of the actual key experiments themselves.*

Secondly, the same repeated experiments provide vital and continuous sources of knowledge and inspiration to scientists in those periods researching a new problem *preceding* the invention and acceptance of a viable theory, or during those equally uncertain times covering the transition from one dominant theory to another.[46] Analogical models also serve a similar heuristic function in so far as, with the classic examples of magnetic fields or the billiard ball model of the random behaviour of gas molecules and many others, they provide conceptual bridges between abstract theorising and the concrete world.[47]

Hunting for similarities

However, it is the latter pragmatic illustrations of how science is actually *done* upon which, he argues, both novice and experienced scientists rely to provide them with the cognitive training and groundwork for future innovations, as well as the development of current theories. Building up a stockpile of such exemplars not only opens up a wealth of existing knowledge and skills – how reliable experiments are made, data is gathered and interpreted and so forth – but also provides vital experience in the *perception of similarities* between problem solutions, which is a form of analogical reasoning itself, from which scientists are able to draw more general conclusions. The process of cognition, Kuhn suggests, is not unlike the way a child, asked to group a collection of animal figures that includes both familiar and unfamiliar creatures, looks for similarities between the known and unknown figures:

> In the same way, the science student, confronted with a problem, seeks to see it as like one or more of the exemplary problems he has encountered before. Where rules exist to guide him, he, of course, deploys them. But his basic criterion is a *perception of similarity that is both logically and psychologically prior* [emphasis added] to any of the numerous criteria by which that same identification of similarity might have been made.[48]

Artifactual knowledge

Pursuing a similar line of thought to Kuhn's, in *Thing Knowledge*, Davis Baird,[49] also a philosopher of science, explains how scientific instruments themselves, such as the measuring instruments he describes, combine different kinds of knowledge essential to the regular conduct and further development of science. According to Baird's 'instrument epistemology', a device, like a person, can be said to have 'working knowledge' when it performs a function regularly and effectively. 'Model knowledge', however, encompasses the 'field of possibilities' that enable the results of an experiment to be understood within the context of current scientific practice. Lastly, 'encapsulated knowledge', as the term suggests, consists of the *material integration* of the two former kinds of knowledge within the instrument itself and the specific signal it is designed to produce, indicative of its interaction with the phenomena it is measuring. While a device therefore simply reproduces the same functions and results over and over again, scientific instruments of measurement embody *progressive improvements* in the method and precision by which the matters they are designed to measure are accomplished, and thus represent, in instrumental form, a reservoir of scientific knowledge that can be relied upon for further progress.

Encapsulated skills

Taking the example of the development during the 1940s of so-called 'direct-reading' spectrometers - measuring instruments which afford an immediate analysis of a selected spectrum of properties in a substance, such as a concentration of specific chemicals - Baird explains that the success of such instruments depends:

> [...] on the ability of their makers to put in material form the knowledge and skills necessary for reliably making such analytical measurements. In the language of technology studies, these instruments 'de-skill' the job of making these measurements. They do this by *encapsulating in the instrument the skills previously employed by the analyst* [emphasis added] or their functional equivalents.[50]

He goes on to detail the different skills that have to be built into direct readers for them to do their job reliably; a complex task that includes the ability to recognise the chemical properties of interest to the measurer, together with knowledge of the techniques needed to encode and visually display such information in a precise, readable manner. However, repeating the mantra of systems theorists, he adds that, nevertheless, the whole is more than the sum of its parts. Thus a variety of different *forms of knowledge* embracing optics, electronics and spectrochemical analysis, combined with the technical skills needed to *make* the instrument, are materially synthesised within the same artifact.

Gifting knowledge

Baird finds inspiration for a 'materialistic conception of knowledge' in the integration of scientific knowledge in such instruments, the invention of which, like that of the more familiar telescope, often *precedes and creates the conditions for the theoretical as well as the empirical advancement of science.* However, commenting in conclusion on the critical social and cultural impacts of an increasing reliance upon machine-based forms of graded testing for human performance, Baird cautions against the danger of imbuing instruments with an unquestionable objectivity, in contrast to the assumed subjectivity of the human expert – a reliance now driven by marketing forces and what he describes as a 'push-button' culture. Information thus gained, he points out, is not immune from political exploitation and distortion, while human experts, such as those upon whose knowledge and skill the design of such instruments is originally based, are perfectly capable themselves of objective thought.

Drawing upon a distinction made by Lewis Hyde[51] and others between market and 'gift economies', Baird further argues that, unlike the monetary motivation driving market economies, the primary reward for the individual involved in the creation and dissemination of knowledge lies in the satisfaction he or she derives from the production and donation of that knowledge to society. Though their careers are increasingly dependent upon their publications, academics, for example, are not actually *paid* for the individual research papers they contribute to academic journals and books, and to which they devote much of their time. As such, the published articles themselves are intellectual gifts given freely in exchange for the intellectual gifts of others. More generally, he suggests the fundamental difference between gift economies and market economies, in which everything is treated as a commodity for sale, is that:

> Gift economies serve to bind people together. They create and maintain social groups. All the various expectations that govern gift exchange serve this end […]. Seen in a wider social context, gift economies *establish social boundaries* [emphasis added]; one must give to the group and receive the group's gifts in return.[52]

As idealistic as the characterisation of gift economies might appear – academics for sure, in this writer's experience, are not all altruistic angels – Baird might well have included a far larger cross-section of the population who voluntarily elect to work in the many other branches of employment in what are generally bracketed under the *public sector*, and upon which most of the rest of the working population depends. Together with the products of the market economy consumed by workers in both economies, each, until recently, has largely supported the other. That situation, however, along with much else that has shaped the evolution of the modern human self, has undergone radical changes in recent times, the examination of which the following part of this book on 'the self in the world' is focused.

Part III

The self in the world

To characterize properly the psychological field, one has to take into account such *specific* items as particular goals, stimuli, needs, social relations, as well as such more *general* characteristics of the field as the *atmosphere* (for instance, the friendly, tense, or hostile atmosphere) or the amount of freedom. These characteristics of the *field as a whole* are as important in psychology as, for instance, the field of gravity for the explanation of events in classical physics.

Kurt Lewin, 1951[1]

Chapter 8

Technically extended selves

Just as other vital aspects of the human self have evolved out of more primitive animal states, so has the technically extended human self evolved out of construction and tool-making behaviours common to other species, often, if not mostly at subconscious levels, as described in the previous chapter. Moreover, contrary to claims that the historical accumulation of knowledge and skills is unique to human cultures, further evidence presented in this chapter suggests that the cultures and technological knowledge of at least some other species also have *cumulative features,* including the transmission of knowledge embodied in the artifacts themselves.

Such are the far-reaching impacts of technology on human development and culture, however, that some writers on the subject argue that, rather than natural selection, it is *artificial selection* driven by technology that is responsible for the course of human evolution, a course in which technology has taken on a virtual life of its own, pulling human development along with it. A final section, 'Promethean gifts',[1] questions how difficult it now is, given modern technology's momentum, for human individuals and societies to exert any real choice in the form of technological beings we might like to be, let alone change the destructive direction of human development – vital issues to be taken up again in later chapters.

Nature's home builders

For much of the last century, architecture, as with tool use and manufacture, was generally regarded by archaeologists, cultural historians and architects themselves as an exclusively human preoccupation, mostly restricted to advanced, urban cultures. Breaking ranks, in 1977 the architect and author Bernard Rudofsky published *The Prodigious Builders,*[2] in which he dared to compare the nests, burrows and other homes built by animals with those of humans, an idea which, aside from passing analogies, had never before taken hold. Like his earlier seminal work, *Architecture Without Architects,*[3] published in 1964, the main contents of the later book are devoted to persuading architects weaned on what he calls 'pedigreed architecture' – that is, architecture with a firm date and historical lineage attached – to learn from the much neglected but vast 'storehouse of human experience' available from the constructions societies and individuals have created for themselves, guided only by local building and cultural traditions. Introducing the earlier book, he writes:

> Architecture without architects, as I call the topic in hand, is not just a jumble of building types traditionally slighted or altogether ignored, but the silent testimonial to ways of life that are heavy on acute insight, albeit light on progress. It goes to the roots of human experience and is thus of more than technical and aesthetic interest. Moreover, it is architecture without a dogma.[4]

Naturalist's approach

Where the first book, however, is focused more on what is now variously described as 'vernacular', 'indigenous' or 'self-built' architecture, the latter work offers both a broader scope from prehistoric times onwards and a naturalist's, rather than an historian's approach, covering a range of constructions by other species along with copious examples of human creativity.[5] Rudofsky's inclusion of animal constructions together with those of humans in the later publication is all the more noteworthy for its timing. Animal tool use had only been discovered in the previous decade and the constructions of other species were then still a long way off from being accorded the attention they are now by researchers of animal behaviour or niche construction theorists. Drawing upon the available knowledge of his time, Rudofsky nevertheless found much to admire in both lines of production, including the aesthetic as well as the technical qualities of animal structures such as the tunnels and wells dug by moles, which he enthusiastically describes as 'stylish underground dwellings'. More generally, he writes:

> Many beasts have an uncanny talent for engineering; not only did they invent all sorts of tricky walls and roofs, they sometimes skipped – as did the termites – our cumbersome building techniques and went right on to mastering highly sophisticated modern building methods.[6]

Amongst the many other examples of 'advanced design' by animals worthy of comparison with human constructions – and indeed, in Rudofsky's view, even surpassing human efforts – he points to the precise hexagonal geometry of the honeycomb, quoting Darwin's own observation that bees 'have made their cells of the proper shape to hold the greatest possible amount of honey, with the least possible consumption of precious wax in their construction'.[7] About which Rudofsky adds: 'Would to God that our architects had that much bee sense and obeyed similar principles of economy!'[8]

It is doubtful that, in shaping their underground dwellings, moles are motivated by the same aesthetic sensibilities as Rudofsky's, any more than the precise geometrical creations of the honey bee are the invention of a bee mathematician.[9] For all that, the achievements of some species, such as the complex constructions of termites, whose towering mounds Rudofsky likens – proportionate to the size of the insects themselves – to modern skyscrapers, call out for such comparisons. Built with comparable methods, starting with a skeleton framework which is then filled in, the same durable constructions with their labyrinthine interior passageways and chambers, Rudofsky writes, impressed eighteenth- and nineteenth-century biologists 'so much they assumed without question that the creatures that built them must be highly intelligent and their society comparable in almost every way with human society'.[10]

Insect cities

Rudofsky's insights have since been amply supported by more recent and detailed research into all forms of animal architecture, of which Mike Hansell's study, *Built by Animals*,[11] offers an extensive account. However, while he is also drawn to making occasional analogies with human constructions – usually, like Rudofsky, in the animals' favour – Hansell, a natural historian himself, is more conscious of the dangers of anthropocentrism and has a deeper agenda. Following the publication in 1976 of Donald Griffin's *The Question of Animal Awareness*,[12] he relates how he chose to learn what he could of 'the nature of animal minds' from the homes they build and the methods they employed.[13] Accordingly, Hansell takes the view that no questions of animal thought and feeling should be treated as being beyond the scope of scientific enquiry – an ambitious project, which, he concedes, is constrained by the limitations of our present knowledge of animal builders, but which he enlivens with numerous examples suggestive of how that knowledge might be extended.

Amongst nest builders, the so-called 'social insects' such as the industrious honey bees and termites which fascinated Darwin and the Victorian naturalists whom Rudofsky quotes, are of particular interest to Hansell since their nests are made to house a whole colony, with all its attendant organisational complexities and supportive activities. A honey bee nest, with its extraordinarily precise construction of hexagonal cells, is the outcome of a collaborative effort by as many as 10,000 adult bees, the purpose of which is the storage of honey and the rearing of their offspring during their maggot-like larval stages – a construction that Hansell describes as 'an extraordinary development of social living that has no equal among vertebrate animals other than us'.[14]

Like Rudofsky, Hansell also revels in the scale of some constructions relative to the size of their builders. The subterranean labyrinths of leaf-cutter ants, for example, which extend as much as six metres underground, house as many as 8 million adults, plus two or three million larval stages and eggs all within the same structure – population numbers equivalent to large human cities. It is, however, not only the comparative scale of such constructions that impresses Hansell, but also the highly efficient systems of natural ventilation and food production the ants have developed to sustain their underground life styles. The fresh cuts of grass leaves harvested by the insects from which they get their name, are not actually eaten directly but are instead chewed to a pulp, producing a compost for the purpose-made fungus gardens the ants have built underground to grow the colony's food. The whole underground complex with its passages, chambers and domestic and horticultural areas must be well ventilated, for which the structure also incorporates a novel system of its own. Soil excavated from below is reused on the surface of the nest to form a shallow mound pierced by numerous entrance holes, each topped by a small earthen turret. Similar to the 'induced flow' of air across the wings which aircraft designers use to help lift the heavy vehicle, the passage of wind over the surface of the mound is enough to create differential air pressures between the lowest and highest parts, thus drawing the air out from passages below to be vented through the towers on the uppermost part.[15]

No need for big brains

Neither is the principle governing the leaf-cutter ants' ingenious ventilation system unique to that species, but is also employed by some termite species in the construction of their own mounds, together with some burrowing rodents.[16] How is it, Hansell ponders, that such sophisticated technologies of construction could have been developed by such supposedly primitive creatures as insects and other animal species for their own purposes?

For one thing, he suggests, generally speaking animals don't have to have big brains to be good builders. While brain size, as others in this book argue, certainly counts for a lot in human development, Hansell hypothesises that other factors matter far more in non-human technological development. First, he suggests that natural selection favours building methods that involve a *limited range of repetitive*, tried-and-tested animal behaviours. Secondly, animals tend to use *standardised materials*, their properties and use being more predictable and therefore conducive to repetitive building routines. Thirdly, preceding the development of any other tools – either for building or any other purpose – animals were entirely reliant upon the strengths and special capacities with which their own bodies endowed them, from which Hansell deduces that 'building behavior evolved from behavior that was originally nothing to do with building'.[17]

In itself, he argues, there is nothing remarkable about that, since everything in nature evolves out of a modification of something that previously worked a little differently. However, barring any building equipment other than the builder's own body, it suggests a fundamental symmetry between the specialised evolution of the builders' anatomies and that of their dwellings: 'There are only a limited number of bits of the body of any organism – human, fish or spider – which are suitable for modification as building equipment, and only a limited number of ways that they can be effectively modified'.[18] Thus, channelled by anatomical constraints and the limitations of easily learnt, repetitive building methods and materials, the complex forms of animal architecture are generated, Hansell suggests, without the need for large brains, the drawback being that, compared to the human product, innovation was relatively restricted – not altogether a bad thing, Rudofsky might have argued – given the different environmental outcomes.

Emergent properties

Nor, as far as some social insects like the mound-building termites are concerned, was there any apparent need for much overt communication between individual insects in the process of construction. Like other social insects, termites have evolved an efficient division of labour,[19] amongst whom the specialised building workers have developed their own ways of exploiting the knowledge embodied in the building itself. Just as the scientists Baird describes in the previous chapter tap into the scientific knowledge embodied in their instruments, so do the termite builders tap into the artifactual knowledge secreted in the materials and complex structures and spaces of their mounds. Comparing their stealth-like building methods to those of human architects and their coordinated teams of engineers and other building experts, Hansell, whose theoretical perspective may be counted amongst emergentist schools of thought, maintains the organisation of nest building by social insects differs radically from our own methods of construction:

> No individual or individuals can be said to be 'in charge'; there is no hierarchical structure or line management. Where there is a sequence of activities to be completed, individuals are stimulated to become active or inactive through very simple signals from other colony members or *by the nest itself* [emphasis added].[20]

He describes an experiment conducted in the 1980s by Pierre-Paul Grasse, a pioneer researcher in termite behaviour, who demonstrated that, when worker termites were removed from the nest and placed in a fresh space together with some nest material, they initially placed drops of the material around the space at random. Little by little, however, as they continued to deposit new drops of material or move some of those they had already placed at random, larger, evenly spaced blobs of material mysteriously appeared. These 'attracted' fresh material which other termites added on top of the blobs, creating small pillars. Adjacent pillars in turn grew towards each other with the addition of more material to form arches.

The mystifying process of attraction, Grass found, was explained by the inclusion by each termite of a chemical signal, or pheromone, of their own in small pellets of the building material, which attracted other termites to set their loads down on the same spot. Initially, all locations appear equally attractive, but as soon as one point garners even slightly more material than others, a process of positive feedback is initiated, leading to the accumulation of yet more material in ever-more complex shapes, each step in the process serving to guide the next: 'Such a building process', Hansell surmises, 'would demand very little of the termites in terms of understanding or decision-making, it does not even require any direct communication between the members of the workforce'.[21]

Based upon Grass's experiments, a computer model simulating the construction of a queen's chamber was subsequently developed incorporating only the workers' responses to the queen's own pheromone template and the attraction of other workers' chemical signals left in the building material. What such models of emergent properties demonstrate, Hansell argues, is that complex architectural forms 'can be generated using very simple rules, in particular rules that don't require members of the workforce to pay any attention to each other but just to *converse with the emerging architecture* [emphasis added]'.[22]

Animal tool use

In addition to the impressive animal record of durable home building, a growing body of evidence suggests that animal tool use and manufacture for foraging and other transient goals is also a common if not *normal characteristic* of animal behaviour across vastly different species, the full extent of which can only be guessed at. Expanding on Benjamin Beck's 1980 work, *Animal Tool Behavior*,[23] the first comprehensive survey of the field, Shumaker et al.[24] document the various actions and behavioural patterns associated with each form of tool use and manufacture, species by species: from invertebrates, fish, amphibians, reptiles, birds and non-primate mammals, through prosimians ('pre-monkeys' like lemurs) and monkeys and, finally, apes. As difficult as it might seem, after considering all the alternative definitions of animal tool use that have been offered since their first discovery, sticking close to Beck's original definition they offer a revised, if still long-winded, version covering *all* of these cases:

> The external employment of an unattached or *manipulable attached* environmental object to alter more efficiently the form, position, or condition of another object, another organism, or the user itself, when the user holds *and directly manipulates* the tool during or *prior* to use and is responsible for the proper and effective orientation of the tool.[25]

Modes of animal tool use and manufacture

Most of their study, however, is given over to a meticulous cataloguing of all the different techniques or modes of tool use and manufacture employed by each of the species covered in the book, listing a maximum of twenty-two possible modes of use and four of manufacture.[26] However, aside from acknowledging that, as *Homo sapiens'* closest ancestors and the most talented animal tool users, chimpanzees have attracted by far the greatest interest amongst other species, Shumaker et al. make no explicit effort to relate their findings directly to human tool use; their research being entirely focused on the non-human animal world. Nor, other than their reference to the use and manufacture of more than one tool to complete more complex jobs, or 'associative tool use' as it is called, do they include larger and fixed constructions like beaver dams and nests within their definition of a tool, since they specifically exclude any final product that cannot itself be manipulated and which may have other than temporary environmental impacts – a disputable restriction as the authors themselves concede.

The value of their encyclopaedic work rests more on the incontrovertible evidence they provide of the true *scale* and variety of tool use and manufacture across the animal world, far exceeding previous expectations. Equally important, in establishing a common framework and terminology for the field, they facilitate comparative studies between different species, thereby directly or indirectly facilitating comparisons between human and non-human tool use.

Knowledge in common

Approaching the subject from an epistemological viewpoint, in *Animal Constructions and Technological Knowledge*, Ashley Shew[27] deals with the issue of comparative human and non-human achievements in more direct terms:

> Typically, we think of things as 'technological' only when they are made, designed, employed, or implemented by human beings, and, in fact, the idea of technological knowledge – knowledge of how things work, of how to work things, and how to create devices – had generally been discussed by historians, anthropologists, and philosophers of technology and of engineering in terms of *human* agency [...] This assignment of technological know-how to humans alone, however, neglects the technological knowledge and know-how implemented by non-human animals.[28]

Shew's aim in questioning the long-held and still common belief that technology is an exclusively human provenance – what she describes as 'the human clause' – is to free the related terminology of 'artifacts', 'tools', 'technology' and 'knowledge' from their anthropocentric associations, so we can see both human and non-human tool-using behaviour as existing along the same *spectrum* of technology: 'There is no *à priori* reason', she asserts, 'to bar non-human animals from the category of creators and users of technology'.[29]

Knowing how and knowing that

Sorting through various interpretations of technological knowledge, Shew references a much-quoted distinction by the philosopher Gilbert Ryle between 'knowing how' and 'knowing that'.[30] The former refers to the knowledge involved in performing a task while the latter, more abstract or intellectual level of thought involves what a person *believes* to be true or not.[31] In addition, drawing upon Baird's materialistic philosophy of 'thing knowledge' discussed above, Shew also suggests that, much like the scientific instruments Baird describes, the physical tools used by other animals as well as by humans encapsulate and transmit technological knowledge in themselves.

In addition to these two principal forms of technological knowledge, Shew raises the difficult question as to whether or not there might be evidence of *design* in non-human animal tool behaviour: 'Figuring out whether a tool-making animal has an idea of some end or object in mind may be tricky, but we can watch for and identify behavior that indicates prior consideration or planning'.[32] Amongst other sources, Shew cites the work of Walter Vincenti[33] on the design process in human engineering, who distinguishes between 'normal' and 'radical design': 'normal' design referring to cases where there is *existing* knowledge of how a device works and how it should be used, while 'radical' design occurs in situations where no such relevant knowledge or precedents exist, requiring *new* solutions to fill the gap. While Vincenti himself, whose research focuses mostly on aeronautical engineering, does not address the possibility that other animals might be possessed of such knowledge, he promotes a biological model of the growth of engineering knowledge over time as an adaptive and *iterative process* based on neo-Darwinian concepts of variation and selection, which, Shew suggests, affords comparisons with biological cases. Aside from a common use of terms like 'design' and 'function' in biology as well as engineering, she argues that, 'in those cases where we can see evidence of *intentional* design on the part of some animals, we might talk about the design process and the transformations of knowledge that take place in very much the same terms as Vincenti uses to describe human aeronautical engineers' processes and learning'.[34]

As an unambiguous demonstration of intentionality and forward planning, Shew cites the amusing and well publicised case of a bonobo chimpanzee named Santino at a Swedish zoo, who became famous for hoarding piles of stones to throw at visitors gathered across the water from its island enclosure. Some of the missiles were collected from the shoreline but others were *specifically manufactured* by Santino for the purpose by breaking off chunks of concrete from artificial rocks on the island, suggestive of advanced consciousness and cognitive abilities not normally accredited to non-human animals.

Comparable tool-making skills

The tool-making skills of Kanzi, another male bonobo chimpanzee, are also of special interest as the research involved an explicit comparison with the archeologically recorded skills of hominids in making cutting tools from stone. To see whether apes could learn to use and manufacture the *same kinds of tools* as those of early humans, the researchers chose Oldowan stone-cutting tools from over 2 million years ago. First discovered in the 1930s by Louis and Mary Leakey in a valley in Tanzania (after which the tools are named), they are made by chipping off flakes from their stone cores to form sharp edges – the oldest known tool industry. Showing Kanzi how useful such tools could be, the team used similar tools made by themselves to cut the cords around some boxes containing some of the ape's favourite delicacies. Following their example, on the first day Kanzi used the stone tools the researchers had made to perform the same task. Thereafter, he rapidly took matters into his own hands. The next day he was already deciding for himself which of the tools he was offered had the sharpest cutting edge. After a few demonstrations by the researchers Kanzi also began experimenting with making his own tools and within a month was making flakes by striking rocks with 'hard-hammer percussion'. After several more months, Kanzi had devised his own method of making new tools by throwing a stone down onto the hard floor of his enclosure, splintering it into flakes for cutting.

Noting that Kanzi had not shown any specific interest in throwing things before, the researchers, Shew reports, treated the action as an innovation, suggesting that the ape had discovered for itself the relation between the force of throwing and successful flaking. Thereafter, Kanzi's hammer-like actions became more forceful with increasingly successful results, producing – so the researchers claim – objects comparable with the original flakes found by archaeologists.

Cumulative technology

However, while acknowledging the importance of primates as our closest animal precedents in the use of technology, Shew's goal 'is not simply to change the human clause to "the human and chimpanzee clause"',[35] but to 'blow it up' altogether, for which she points to numerous other species' capacities for tool use. Similar to, but far shorter and more theoretically focused than Beck et al.'s extensive list, they include some unfamiliar and surprising examples like the so-called 'sponging' tactics of a group of bottlenose dolphins in Western Australia's Shark Bay – surprising because, while dolphins are famous for their social intelligence and communicative skills, their streamline body shapes do not lend themselves as readily to tool use as those of other creatures. The tactic entails the dolphin breaking off a piece of marine sponge, placing it over its nose and then using it to probe the seafloor for hidden fish. While other dolphins in the area, who have been under observation since 1984, employ a variety of non-tool using foraging behaviours, the relatively small and recently discovered sponging group, which consists entirely of female dolphins and their daughters, are the only dolphins to use the technique, leading the researchers to believe it is 'highly likely that sponging is *culturally transmitted* [emphasis added] mainly within a matriline, i.e., daughters learn this behavior from their mothers'.[36]

Crow craft

Shew also cites evidence of learned behaviour in the more advanced tool-making skills of New Caledonian (NC) Crows. First observed in the wild by Gavin Hunt,[37] a well-established researcher of the species, the crows employ two types of hook – tools they manufacture from twigs and leaves – to dig prey out from their hiding places, demonstrating a high degree of standardisation in tool shaping of the kind acquired by early humans for their cutting tools. The hooked-twig tools are made by first stripping the leaves and bark from the twig, the end of which the crows then carve into the shape of a hook with their beaks. Similarly, the stepped-cut tools are cut from the edges of pandanus leaves (similar to palm leaves), forming a sharp and firm taper, the uncut edges of which consistently face upwards from the narrow ends. The observed actions of the crows using the tools to capture their prey were likewise deliberate, indicating to Hunt they fully understood the functionality of their creations.[38]

More important still, Shew reports that recent research of NC crow tool-making behaviour in the wild by Hunt and his colleague Russell Gray[39] provides, as the two researchers describe it, 'the first indication that a non-human species may have evolved rudimentary cumulative technology'.[40] Based on their analysis of well over 5,000 pandanus tools found at 21 sites, amongst which they found three distinct tool types, 'wide', 'narrow' and 'stepped', Hunt and Gray identify three primary processes involved in the cumulative evolution of the tools: 'diversification of design; cumulative changes to tool lineages, and a faithful transmission of design through social processes'.[41] Furthermore, they conclude that the three types of tool, which are all made from the same material, are most likely the outcome of variations of the same original tool rather than having been developed separately. The fact that all the stepped tools were well made (as evidenced by the initial cuts to the leaves) also suggests individual tool makers were either tutored by or had imitated more experienced crows, indicative of the social transmission of skills, the cumulative outcome of which amounts to an *evolutionary history* of crow tool development.

Artificial versus natural selection

So where, if at all, does human technology and its uses differ significantly from the technologies employed by our evolutionary predecessors? In their study of early human tool use, archaeologists Kathy Schick and Nicholas Toth[42] focused on the Stone Age and the appearance of the Oldowan stone tools described above as the period in which tool use and manufacture by our predecessors surpassed anything that had been achieved by non-human animals, defining us as 'profoundly technological creatures'. From a Darwinian perspective, they suggest, as primitive as they might seem to us now, such technologies bestowed our predecessors with significant adaptive advantages in the competition for survival, shaping the course thereafter of human evolution: 'Genetically, anatomically, behaviorally, and socially, we have been shaped by natural selection into tool makers and users'.[43]

Significantly, they argue, the manufacture and use of the Oldowan tools coincided with the emergence of *Homo habilis*, first in the *Homo* line, followed by the much larger-brained *Homo erectus* and our own species, indicative of a mutual influence between tool use and brain size. In addition, the level of skilled work that went into manufacturing the sharp and purposefully shaped tools qualifies them specifically as early *human* artifacts, distinct from the stone tools used by other animals. Recall that Kanzai, the chimpanzee who learnt how to make similar cutting tools, was first *shown* how they were made by the ape's human instructors, and only *later* refined his own manufacturing skills. Whatever other primates might or might not have achieved in that way by themselves, the authors maintain that tool manufacture and use was never as *central* to other primate lives in the way they became central to our own ways of life and behaviour – a reasonable, if disputable, claim given the importance of many, if not most, animal tools used for foraging for food, which is as central to life as it gets.

Stepping back in tool-making time

Understanding what all that involved, however, requires more than just sticking names and dates on artifacts. As graduate students in the late 1970s at the University of California, Berkeley, Schick and Toth participated in a programme of so-called 'experimental archaeology' conducted in northern Kenya by Glynn Isaac, intended to *duplicate* the tool-making techniques of our ancestors to find out just what is involved in the process. The method requires that researchers approach the problem of first finding and then shaping the right materials just as our tool-making ancestors did – stepping back in time and putting themselves in their ancestors' place, so to speak – the success of the exercise being measured by the quality of the researchers' products compared to some original samples.

What these and other experiments showed was that finding the material (quartz being the preferred stone) for the hammers used to produce the hand axes and other stone tools of the period, and then using those hammers to produce the final artifacts, involved much planning and other patterns of behaviour indicative of levels of cognition beyond anything achieved by our closest primate relatives. Commenting on Kanzi's otherwise impressive performance as a stone tool maker, for example, the authors observe that, for all his skills, he never grasped the same understanding of the importance of the *angles* at which the stone flakes were cut that Oldowan hominids had. Rather than applying the kind of highly controlled, forceful strikes that can be seen in the original Stone

Age artifacts, Kanzi simply bashed the edges of cores with his hammer stone. The authors conclude:

> Although the products of Oldowan technology are quite simple, the processes required in the hominid mind to produce these forms show a degree of complexity and sophistication: in other words, *skill*. We feel that these early stone tool-making hominids had evolved, by 2.4 to 1.5 million years ago, to an important new level of intelligence and cognitive operations not present in earlier hominids or in modern non-human primates, including the highly intelligent apes.[44]

What eventually mattered more, however, than the tool-making skills hominids might have inherited from other primates, Schick and Toth argue, is the emergence of *animal culture*. The manner, for example, in which the stone tools used by chimpanzees for breaking nuts are begged, borrowed and even stolen by individuals within the group, could, they speculate, have generated pressures for regulating social behaviour in favour of sharing *personal possessions*. The creation of a level of *shared learned behaviour* of this kind by our predecessors – not unlike, it may be added, the kind of cooperative patterns of behaviour described by Tomasello above – allows us to see what the primeval stages of culture may have been like in the human evolutionary past. However, although culture, in the ethological sense of learned behaviour being passed on to other individuals, is relatively widespread amongst non-human animals, they point out that it does not *automatically* generate tool use or other forms of technology. Only in the human lineage, they maintain, do we find 'that *culture and technology are coupled* [emphasis added] and fundamental to our existence'.[45] Citing Lumsden and Wilson's work on gene-culture coevolution, they suggest that the interaction between the two factors was crucial to the further development of technology, with all its other impacts on human evolution:

> A critical aspect of this reverberating effect between genes and culture, particularly in its early phases, would have been technology. This likely included not just making tools, but conceptualizing possible needs for them, anticipating more concrete possible times and places they might be needed, creating and maintaining more complex mental maps of stone tool and food resources in their environment, and amplifying this new conceptual realm by using tools to make other tools.[46]

Thus, the invention and development of tools, they maintain, would have played a vital role in *accelerating the pace* of human evolution, not just for what they did in transforming the lives of early humans, but for the importance they placed upon cognitive and cultural development in the sharing of information and, not least, in planning for an uncertain future.

Evolutionary turning point

In his radical reworking of evolutionary theory, *The Artificial Ape*,[47] Timothy Taylor, also an archaeologist and prehistorian, goes further still in making the case for technology shaping human evolution. However, contrary to the Darwinist story of natural selection underpinning Schick and Toth's account, culminating in *Homo sapiens* and all its achievements – a story that, as we have seen, has come under fire from many quarters – Taylor argues that, from the earliest use of tools onward, technology essentially *displaced natural selection* to become *the* primary force driving human evolution:

> My idea is simple. Instead of thinking that human beings evolved from apes to a point where they were intelligent enough to be able to make chipped stone tools and all the other objects we surround ourselves with, I think that *these objects created us* [emphasis added].[48]

Furthermore, Taylor identifies what he believes to be the precise moment of invention in early human history when technology took over from natural selection. From that moment on, it was the forces of *artificial selection* – selection led by technological innovation and development - that made us what we are. That moment came, he contends, with the simple but epochal invention, not of stone tools, but of a different kind of artifact, the baby sling:

> It was a moment seized by a female as, for the very first time, she turned to technology to protect her child. In that moment, everything that we were going to become was made not just possible but inevitable.[49]

In supporting his argument, Taylor cannot produce any physical remains of the first baby sling the way that other archeologists have dug up their stone and metal artifacts, though he would doubtless very much like to. The first baby slings, he speculates, would almost certainly have been made from animal skins or some other natural material which, unlike stone tools and their kind, would not have survived intact over the following millennia. Nevertheless, Taylor is convinced that something similar to the baby slings still in use by women all over the world, was essential to the continued survival of the physically weak human animal compared with its far stronger competitors. The biological problem for which the baby sling was the artificial solution, he explains, was the growing size of the infant human brain and protracted length of early develop-ment, in comparison with the much smaller brains and rapid development of other primate infants, who are up and about within days of their birth.[50]

Physiological changes

However, there was a hitch to any further development, and that was the limitations to the growth of brain size imposed by the physiological changes involved in gaining upright posture – changes boosted by a new diet of cooked meat. While the same diet provided the vital source of extra energy needed for any further growth of brain size, the reduction in intestinal length required for the more easily digested food, together with the change of posture led, in turn, to a shrinkage of the large pelvic girdle characteristic of *Homo's* female predecessors. That made giving birth to an infant with a larger-than-normal ape-size skull a difficult and even life-threatening procedure, which modern women still have to cope with. In addition, there was the difficulty of carrying a helpless infant around, which unlike other infant apes, could not simply ride on its mother's back clinging to her body hair while she moved around on all four limbs, but had to be supported by one arm of its upright, relatively hairless mother for long periods, thus rendering that arm useless for anything else – not a good thing in a world fraught with daily dangers.

Perhaps one such tired mother, Taylor surmises, suddenly had the bright idea of reducing her burden with a makeshift baby sling, probably improvised from a spare animal skin cut to shape with a stone tool, and, finding it did the job well enough, stuck with it, improving it over time. And why not, we may ask? If the apes and monkeys described in Chapter 2 were capable of novel behaviour, why not *Homo habilis*? And why not a talented female, moreover, just like the female Japanese monkey showing her clan the way to clean the sweet potatoes left for them on the beach? Having set the example, why should the actions of the unknown inventor of the baby sling not also be quickly imitated by other females in the group, creating a new and very useful tradition? Once discovered, as Taylor explains, there was a huge incentive to continue using the device from the individual energy savings thus gained; more than enough to encourage others to follow suit.[51]

Certainly the associated energy savings would have spurred its widespread adoption, whether by imitation or independent discovery. It was not the only turning point in human evolution, Taylor writes, but a very special one nevertheless, removing the anatomical limits to bipedal expansion: 'Increased intelligence, in turn, allowed the development of a more complex techno-cultural system, the evolution of a fully and habitually two-legged stance, and the possibility of colonizing all the continents of the world'.[52]

Self-producing technologies

In *The Nature of Technology*,[53] Brian Arthur presents a still-more-radical theory of technology as an evolutionary force of its own applicable to *all forms of artifacts*, which is to say, both the tools themselves and the products of those tools, whether transient, mobile or fixed in place.[54] Though his examples are all taken from human technologies and their products, Arthur's theory of 'combinatorial evolution', as he calls it, is equally applicable to both human and non-human animal technologies. Similar to the theories of self-producing systems expounded by Maturana and Varella and others in this book, as an engineer, economist and 'theorist by profession and nature' wanting to better understand his work, Arthur arrived at his theory independently. He recalls that, compared to the many detailed studies of the invention and history of specific technologies and their impact on human society, he discovered 'there was no overall theory of how technology comes into being, no deep understanding of what "innovation" consists of, and *no theory of evolution for technology* [emphasis added]'.[55]

How technological innovation works

Seeking to fill that gap, like Vincenti, Arthur first looked to Darwinian evolutionary theory but found that, while something like the descent of species might account for the variations over time of specific technologies as they are adapted for different uses, it could not account for technological innovation and the emergence of what, on the face of it at least, appear as entirely *new* forms of technology. Also familiar with aeronautical engineering, Arthur draws upon his knowledge of innovations in that field as well as many other forms of technology. For example, echoing the frustrations of biological evolutionists themselves with the limitations of Darwinian theory when it comes to explaining its novelties, Arthur observes that a radically new technology such as the jet engine is unlike the internal combustion engine or any of its predecessors, so cannot be explained as a variation of those technologies.

While such abrupt and radical novelties are familiar enough to emergentists in other fields, Arthur has his own explanation for their occurrence in the technological world. To understand how technological innovation works, he reasons, you have to 'look inside technologies' and check the *origins* of their components, each of which comprises a technology in itself. To take the example of the jet engine again, Arthur points out that major components like compressors, turbines and combustion systems can all be found in other, previously existing technologies; which *also* include components inherited from yet-still-other technologies, from which he concludes: 'Novel technologies must somehow arise by *combination of existing technologies*' [emphasis added].[56]

The components of a major technology like the jet engine are consequently all *similar* in that they comprise technologies in themselves. *Recursiveness*, Arthur asserts, is therefore an integral feature of any evolving technology, great or small. However, linking novel technologies back to pre-existing ones still does not provide us with a full sense of how the *whole of technology* builds up from what has been invented before. For that, he argues, we have to include the *progressive accumulation* over time of all these different combinations:

> If new technologies are indeed combinations of previous ones, then the stock of existing technologies must somehow provide the parts for combination. So the very cumulation of earlier technologies begets further cumulation [...] Early technologies form using existing primitive

technologies as components. These new technologies in time become possible components – building blocks – for the construction of further new technologies. Some of these in turn go on to become possible building blocks for the creation of yet newer technologies.[57]

Each new technology thus provides the resources and impetus for the next innovation, the cumulative effect of which bootstraps the overall collection of technologies upwards, creating ever-more-numerous and complex forms in a self-producing process.

Natural phenomena and technological domains

In addition to combination and recursiveness, Arthur identifies two further key features in the evolution of human technologies: the capture of natural phenomena and the emergence of 'domains' of similar or interacting technologies. For the first, he writes: 'Technology builds out not just from a combination of what exists already but from the constant capturing and harnessing of natural phenomena'.[58] By phenomena, he refers to everything from the heat of fire and the momentum of stone in motion exploited by early humans for cooking and tool use, to the oscillation of pendulums or quartz crystals upon which the accurate functioning of modern clocks depends. Phenomena, therefore, are basically *natural effects* existing independently of humans, which have to be captured and turned to human use by the development and refinement of appropriate technologies.

A domain is likewise defined as a collection or *assemblage* of related technologies, which may focus around particular clusters of phenomena or a central technology, the development of which is measured in decades rather than years. Invoking the common definition of complex systems, Arthur writes that domains are nevertheless more than the sum of their component technologies:

> They are coherent wholes, families of devices, methods, and practices, whose coming into being and development have a character that differs from that of individual technologies. They are not invented; they emerge, crystallizing around a set of phenomena or a novel enabling technology, and building organically from these.[59]

Neither are domains developed by a single practitioner or small groups, but by wide numbers of committed parties, the combined impact of which can affect economies far more than individual technologies. For example, while the introduction of the railway locomotive in the early nineteenth century did not affect economies much at the beginning, the cumulative impact of cross-country railway systems carrying freight as well as people had a significant economic effect, changing activities, industries, and organisational structures. Moreover, domains – which Arthur also describes as technological 'fields' – also go through distinct cycles of life, from youth, through adulthood to old age much like organisms, though not always as smoothly as that might suggest. Some, especially the domain of information technology and computation, change their character or 'morph' every few years, as Arthur puts it, usually when the domain's principle areas of application have changed; the availability of large frame computers in the 1960s, for example, first attracted commercial interests, followed in the 1980s by the common use of personal computers, and in the 1990s by the advent of the Internet. Each stage, in turn, transformed human society and culture at large, as well as whole economies, culminating in the current development of what Arthur calls 'network intelligence' systems, with all their controversial uses – a subject we shall return to in chapters to follow.

Technology as a form of life

Concluding his analysis of the mechanisms and processes of technological evolution, Arthur offers one last challenging thought. Given that, as he describes it, technology is 'self-creating', he asks whether we can say that it is in some sense literally alive? He goes on to argue that, while there is no formal definition of 'life', we generally judge whether something is 'alive' or not by asking whether it meets certain criteria, a question he addresses in the language of self-organising and autopoietic systems: are there simple rules by which technology puts itself together, and are such entities self-producing? The answer to which, Arthur holds – in so far as technology as a *collective entity* is concerned – is affirmative:

> By these criteria technology is indeed a living organism. But it is living only in the sense that a coral reef is living. At least at this stage of its development – and I for one am thankful for this – it still requires human agency for its buildout and reproduction.[60]

Promethean gifts

It may be, however, that rather than technology somehow breaking away from human development to forge ahead under its own steam, as Arthur suggests, it will be increasingly difficult to draw any kind of line between the two, such is the complexity of their interrelations. Contemplating an extreme but all-too-plausible human state of hybrid, biotechnological life, in *Natural-Born Cyborgs*, Andy Clark,[61] for example, writes that:

> We shall be cyborgs not in the merely superficial sense of combining flesh and wires but in the more profound sense of being human–technology symbionts; thinking and reasoning systems whose minds and selves are spread across biological brain and nonbiological circuitry.[62]

But then again, he argues, to the extent that human evolution has been largely inseparable from and dependent upon technological advances in one form or another, it was always thus. In so far as the subtle merging of biological and technical elements in that evolution are concerned, the mechanistic, intimidating image we have of cyborgs as portrayed in science fiction movies is therefore misleading – an error Clark sets out to address in his book. Exploring a wide range of research covering what he describes as the little-understood relationship between biology, nature, culture and technology, he urges us to accept a new, more concrete concept of a hybrid self as deeply embedded in the material and technological world:

> In embracing our hybrid natures, we give up the mind and the self as a kind of wafer-thin essence, dramatically distinct from all its physical trappings. In place of this elusive essence, the human person emerges as a shifting matrix of biological and non-biological parts.[63]

Whilst acknowledging the dangers of a further merging of technology and self – dangers he outlines in a concluding chapter on 'bad borgs', including inequality, intrusion, uncontrollability, overload and alienation – he argues that, only by accepting ourselves for the hybrid beings 'we truly are', will we be able to ensure that any future biotechnological unions will be positive ones.

As laudable as those sentiments might be, they suffer from the same anthropocentric faith in human rationality and the ability to change course at will that continues to undermine any more effective efforts to *really* see ourselves for the conflicted beings we actually are. For all its complexities, uncertainties and dangers, the future course of human biotechnological evolution, Clark implies, rests with us. As far as any problems of controllability are concerned, 'the kind of control that we, both as individuals and as society, look likely to retain is *precisely the kind we always had: no more, no less*'.[64]

However, contrary to the equanimity with which Clark views the issue of human control over the Promethean gifts bestowed upon our species, as the remainder of this book lays bare, technology's accelerating momentum as a dynamic force of its own, supported by mostly complicit individuals and societies, has already gone far beyond any previous state in the human–technological contract than even perceptive analysts of that contract like Taylor and Arthur imagined was possible.

Chapter 9

Self-images

As distillations of major elements comprising the self-field, whether of a tacit or explicit nature, self-images provide a vital bridge between the public and private realms of personal experience. As such they shape our lives, not in any deterministic manner, but in the symbolic sense of *giving form to our lives* in ways that can be readily communicated to others and which, in a self-conscious state of mind, we may contemplate and modify as circumstances require.

In giving that form, self-images also delineate the visible boundaries of the self-field. Whether through the affirmation of those boundaries that an individual receives from his or her interactions with others, or through those personal things we accumulate through life which have a tangible material and spatial dimension, they create a picture of *who we are* and of our *place* in the world. The interaction with others may involve individuals with whom we have particularly strong personal relationships, as with family members, partners and close friends, or with social groups we identify with most – the subject of the next chapter. Other sources and expressions of self-images may involve anything from the homes and places we live in to the special attachments we have to objects like treasured ornaments and mementos, favourite clothes or private automobiles – the latter's popularity having repercussions far beyond personal use. The precise ingredients and composition of these images will also certainly change along with related changes in how and with whom we spend our lives, but their purpose will remain more or less the same, which is to provide a mirror to ourselves and a guide in our relationships with others as we navigate those changes.

Throughout all of these developments and what follows in the remaining chapters, the part played by material culture and modern technologies of production and communication in shaping the human self-field – and which often shape the form of research itself – is crucial to understanding the evolution of the modern self and the social and cultural values we have, in turn, knowingly or not, helped to create and abide by.

Good impressions

In *The Presentation of Self in Everyday Life*,[1] Irving Goffman's insightful perspective on self-images, the sociologist argues that we are all highly conscious of what others think of us and are constantly striving to make a good impression on them. Likening our performance to that of an actor, he presents a *dramaturgical model* in which individuals act out the characters expected of them by the other characters sharing the same 'stage'.[2]

Published in 1959, Goffman's dramaturgical principles, which he maintains can be applied to any 'concrete social establishment', point towards many of the principles of social interaction later posited by Pierre Bourdieu. A social performance of this kind, Goffman explains, involves both conscious and unconscious elements: 'When an individual plays a part he *implicitly requests his observers to take seriously* [emphasis added] the impression that is fostered before them',[3] a requirement demanding a minimal level of commitment on both sides to their mutual roles. In much the same way a professional actor *identifies with the character* he plays on stage or screen, so, therefore, does each person acting out their part identify with their chosen character. Similarly, the individuals at whom the performance is directed – who, like any theatre or movie audience, must willingly suspend their disbelief in what is going on before them – also commit themselves to their own roles. Much as Bourdieu describes the tacit social contract underlying the relationships between organisation and agents, so too is there an implicit agreement amongst Goffman's actors to accept the character each plays in their daily drama. The extent of that commitment may nevertheless vary greatly between actors, from those who genuinely identify with their given roles and social functions, and those more 'cynical' performers Goffman describes who are selfishly motivated in guiding their audience as a means to their own ends. Such individuals, he suggests, care little for what others think of them or the situation they are in and may derive personal satisfaction instead from being able to play with matters their audience take more seriously than they.

Seen and unseen audiences

In formulating and improving on their performance, individuals may also tend to conform to what they understand to be a shared *idealisation* of the character and behaviour their social role requires of them, involving, for example, what Bourdieu might also describe as the preparation of 'proper' behaviour expected of someone aspiring to a higher level of social status.[4] However, Goffman argues that an individual performance should not only be interpreted in personal terms, but is also often aimed at expressing the characteristics of the *task or job* that is being performed, rather than the characteristics of the performer. Moreover, such performances may involve the close cooperation of other participants, or what Goffman calls a 'performance team'. In such cases, each member of the team will be reliant upon the good conduct and behaviour of the other members who, in turn, are compelled to rely upon each member in reciprocal bonds of dependence, cutting across differences in rank or status.

Just as individual performers in more private situations may act out a social role as though to an *unseen audience*, incorporating whatever moral or behavioural standards they deem appropriate to those situations,[5] so may a performance team also conform with certain moral or behavioural standards required of its function. However, *the larger the team,* the more the reality espoused by the team may change. Thus, in the same way Bourdieu's organisations trim realities to suit their own purposes, Goffman suggests that, instead of a rich definition of the actual situation in which the team is working, 'reality may become *reduced to a thin party-line* [emphasis added], for one may expect the line to be unequally congenial to the members of the team'.[6]

Bodily idioms

In a later work, Goffman[7] applies his dramaturgical model to individual behaviour in public places and gatherings, which present a larger but visibly demanding audience. In such situations where spoken language is not called for, bodily appearance and comportment, involving all manner of silent but meaningful personal behaviour, from dress and physical bearing and gestures to whatever emotional expressions suit the occasion, count for everything:

> Half-aware that a certain aspect of his activity is available for all present to perceive, the individual tends to modify this activity, employing it with its public character in mind. Sometimes, in fact, he may employ these signs solely because they can be witnessed.[8]

Even if those in the audience are not fully conscious of any tacit communications between them, they would quickly sense if there was anything unfitting in any individual's comportment. Taken altogether, such behaviours and gestures, Goffman argues, constitute a 'body symbolism' or idiom of individual acts requiring acceptance by both individual actors and public audience, those others in this case being drawn from – and only drawn from – those who are actually present at the same time in the same place. It is also in the special character of these public situations that, unlike other personally directed performances, bodily idioms cannot be so easily focussed or shielded, and are mostly accessible to practically everyone in sight who is involved in the same situation. Nevertheless, while being relatively imprecise compared to speech, Goffman suggests such idioms function perfectly well in handling matters of social propriety in the public places and situations where such performances are played out.[9]

Social class and eating habits

It was Bourdieu, however, expanding on his field theory of the habitus and the importance of class and socially accepted forms of behaviour – especially eating habits – influencing body images and idioms, who has provided the most controversial thoughts on these matters. Unlike Goffman's focus on bodily idioms in public situations involving non-verbal forms of communication, Bourdieu's attention to eating habits necessarily includes both private and public dining locations involving mixed forms of communication. According to Bourdieu, however, *social class* is the principle force shaping perceptions of the human body, overriding variations of location and communication, just as it is the principal force shaping all other aspects of the habitus. Food tastes, he explains, depend upon how each class perceives the body and the effects of their eating habits on its strength and health as well as its beauty, together with the categories used to judge those effects, which may vary in importance from one class to another and which each class may rank in different ways to other classes.

Whereas the male working classes, he argues, generally pay more attention to bodily *strength* than shape, and prefer food that is both cheap and nutritious, the professional classes, being more mindful of their appearance, prefer food that is not only tasty, but also healthy and non-fattening: 'Taste, a class culture turned into nature, that is, *embodied*, helps to shape the class body'.[10] As a basic principle of classification incorporated into the body and everything assimilated by, ingested by and associated with it, physiologically and psychologically, the body, Bourdieu asserts, is the clearest materialisation there is of class taste. Taken all together, the multiple effects of that classification principle, which is to say, the impact of the class system upon the body, from its shape and dimensions, to all the different ways of feeding and caring for it, reveal 'the deepest manifestations of the habitus'.[11] Similar oppositional traits and the overriding idea of the male body as a source of power, Bourdieu contends, in contrast to perceptions of the weaker, female body, underlie differences of eating and drinking habits between the sexes. It suits a man, for example, to eat and drink more than a woman – and to eat and drink stronger stuff – while the women have to be content with the tit-bits and occasional sip of aperitif. Thus, he argues:

> [...] one can begin to map out a universe of class bodies, which (biological accidents apart) tends to reproduce in its specific logic the universe of the social structure. It is no accident that bodily properties are perceived through social systems of classification which are not independent of the distribution of these properties among the social classes.[12]

Reciprocal perspectives

Two influential American and British psychologists, George Kelly[13] and R. D. Laing,[14] whose respective key works on personal construct theory and interpersonal perception were both published in the 1960s, also throw much light on the psychological and social processes involved in understanding others. Kelly, for example, argued that construing others in oppositional terms, as Bourdieu's subjects do, whether in terms of class or sex, is just the kind of thing people *normally* do in making sense of the world they live in. Against the then prevalent, passive model of human beings promoted by behaviourist psychologists like B. F. Skinner,[15] Kelly posited an active, rational model of 'man the scientist', predicting events, putting his predictions to the test of experience and changing them as the evidence from that experience required – a more positive if idealistic viewpoint of human behaviour. Thus, according to his 'fundamental postulate', Kelly writes: 'A person's processes are psychologically channelized by the ways in which he anticipates events'.[16] Furthermore, elaborating on his postulate in a series of theoretical corollaries, he argued that every individual interprets his or her world and anticipates events through a particular range or *personal system of bipolar constructs*, which he elicited from individuals using a methodology he designed for the purpose called the 'repertory grid test'.[17]

Addressing the social dimension of personal construct theory, in his 'sociality corollary' Kelly also states: 'To the extent that one person construes the construction processes of another, he may play a role in a social process involving that person'.[18] Similarly, Kelly asserts that, instead of looking at social and cultural behaviour from a top-down viewpoint, which offers few insights into how such behaviour might be construed or misconstrued by individuals themselves, social psychology should be a psychology of *interpersonal* understandings, not just commonly held understandings. Moreover, stressing the dynamics of social interaction at the personal level, Kelly writes:

> If we can predict accurately what others will do, we can adjust ourselves to their behavior [...] Understanding does not have to be a one-way proposition; it can be mutual.[19]

Similarly, in *Self and Others*, Laing argues that interpersonal communication is properly understood as a *mutually reflective* process:

> No one acts or experiences in a vacuum. The person whom we describe, and over whom we theorize, *is not the only agent in his 'world'*. How he perceives and acts towards the others, how they perceive and act towards him, how he perceives them as perceiving him, how they perceive him as perceiving them, are all aspects of 'the situation'. They are all pertinent to understanding one person's participation in it.[20]

In the same way, while the identities of other individuals involved in personal relationships can differ in many ways, they may serve a *complementary* function in which others fulfil or complete the self, a function he suggests, like Goffman, that is often described in terms of social roles and which can vary in its significance at different periods in life: 'All "identities" require an other: some other in and through a relationship with whom self-identity is actualized'.[21]

Also important in *confirming* or *disconfirming* the personal qualities and capacities of individuals in such roles, confirmation is rarely an either/or process but is always *measured by degrees* according to the nature of the relationship. Thus, confirmation may range from the slightest recognition by another that one simply *exists* in his or her world, to a mutual reliance of one upon the other, as in long-term social and professional relationships. Laing also argues there are different *levels* of confirmation or disconfirmation, in which an action may be confirmed at one level in a relationship but disconfirmed at another – an idea he later formalised in a hierarchical structure of interpersonal perception called 'the spiral of reciprocal perspectives',[22] comprising several levels of increasing complexity. Thus, each level of the exchange upwards from the basic level of 'my view of myself' through the upper 'meta-levels' of interpersonal perception (my view of your view of me, and so forth), incorporates the lower levels.

Experimental simulation of interpersonal dialogues

A similar structure to Laing's, together with Kelly's theory and methodology was incorporated into a computer-based research and training program aimed at improving interpersonal communication and understanding in professional relationships. Developed in collaboration with Nicholas Negroponte and his Architecture Machine Group at MIT (the forerunner to the Media Lab) over the winter semester of 1973–1974, the program was designed by your author during that period as a Visiting Scholar from the UK, to simulate interpersonal dialogues between architects and their clients.[23]

As pioneers in the application of theories and techniques of artificial intelligence to computer-aided design, a principal goal of Negroponte's group was the creation of hardware and software systems capable of recognising and responding to the personal attributes of individual users, the ultimate aim of which was the creation of 'intelligent' buildings and environments.[24] The outcome from those intensive months of collaborative work was ARCHITRAINER, an interactive, computer-based program simulating a dialogue between an architecture student and a hypothetical prospective client, the focus of which was a photographic display of residential buildings of various styles. Designed like a computer game to engage participants, the program is based on the principle that, whether the future 'architect' is a real person or an artificial intelligence it would be better if he, she, or 'it' better understand their clients' own architectural perspectives and values.

Following Laing's spiral structure, ARCHITRAINER embodies three levels of interaction between 'architect' and 'client', each of which incorporates the lessons learnt from the level preceding it. On one side of the exchange, the role of the architect in the program was played by a real architecture student sitting at a computer console studying the display of building designs above the console. Given a few helpful clues to start with, the student's task in each exercise is to learn how the client interpreted those same examples – essentially putting himself or herself in the client's shoes. Sitting inside the computer, so to speak, the client, in turn, was represented by a psychological model of an individual's construct system obtained in a prior interview with another real person using Kelly's repertory grid methodology and the same collection of photographs.[25]

Combining Kelly's construct theory and methodology with Laing's structure of interpersonal perspectives, ARCHITRAINER leads the student architect through a sequence of increasingly challenging exercises designed to teach students how to examine house designs or some other architectural project from the client's perspective, each step of which is monitored by the program's online analysis of results.[26] While the original data on the client's construct system does not change during the course of the dialogue, the teaching system built into ARCHITRAINER effectively provides the opposite meta-perspectives to the student's own that a real client in such a dialogue would normally engage in, adjusting each exercise according to the student's success or failure. In the same manner, the student progresses from an initially straightforward exchange of architectural perspectives to increasingly complex meta-levels of mutual comprehension, mimicking, if not in detail, the interpersonal features of a real-life dialogue.[27]

However, while Kelly's personal construct theory represents a considerable advance over behaviourist theories of the period, it was recognised that his model of rational thought allowed insufficient recognition of any psychological or social constraints on interpersonal understanding. Subsequent research conducted in the UK into the cognitive structures underlying personal construct systems, was therefore specifically designed to elucidate any more specific factors governing their development and perception as integrated wholes, which might affect individual capacities for understanding other persons.[28] Following the related work in construct theory by D. N. Hinkel[29] on *resistance to change* and James Bieri[30] on *cognitive complexity*, a series of studies were carried out with architecture students and professional subjects aimed at testing the ability of individuals to predict the behaviour of others, relative to the *structural organisation* of their own construct systems. The tentative results, graphically represented in the form of 'cognitive profiles' comparing the organisation of individual construct systems,[31] suggests that *more general* systemic properties, such as the degree to which a person's construct system is hierarchically or more flexibly (heterarchically) organised, may have marked effects on an individual's interpersonal skills and their capacity to comprehend the viewpoints of others – developmental factors that accord with much else that has been written in this book about the underlying systemic resistance to change.

Home-making as self-actualisation

The centrality of the home in personal life and its modes of self-expression was also of special concern to Gaston Bachelard, author of *The Poetics of Space*,[32] whose classic work has been influential for many of those seeking a new approach to such issues. As a French philosopher of science, Bachelard had grown dissatisfied with the prevailing line of contemporary scientific thought, which he felt no longer sufficed as an explanation of human behaviour, particularly those spontaneous expressions of the human imagination that poetry and other forms of art ignite in people. In place of that line of thought, he advocated a 'phenomenology of the imagination' that would unlock those vital aspects of human experience overlooked by science.

Originally inspired in his quest for a new approach by the poetic imagination aroused by the written word, in *The Poetics of Space* he chose to apply it instead to the universal idea of the individual home and its personal meanings: 'On whatever theoretical horizon we examine it, the house image would appear to have become the topography of our intimate being'.[33] Neither is Bachelard concerned only with the more general meaning of home. Analysing the archetypal home from 'cellar to garret' and the role its different spaces play in our memories and imaginations, he also takes in those smaller but no less psychologically potent items of furniture like drawers, chests and wardrobes that serve as the repositories of the personal items individuals collect and wear, and the memories they too carry with them. Moreover, he finds in the 'primal images' of animal nests and shells – 'images that bring out the primitiveness in us'[34] – the source of those basic emotions a person feels for whom the home is no less a shelter and refuge from the world outside than nests and shells are for other creatures.

Psychosocial approach

Bachelard's work was avidly read by architects sensitive to the deeper services expected of them, as well as by philosophers and others open to rethinking the ordinary domestic spaces they had taken for granted. Yet, until recently, the subject of the home as a more intimate form of self-expression has been generally overlooked by academic researchers. With few exceptions, research on the idea of home has instead tended to focus on its wider social and cultural meanings from across a wide range of scales from the domestic to the geographical,[35] rather than what individual occupants might actually be doing *inside* all those residential buildings to turn them into real *homes*.

In *House as a Mirror of Self*,[36] Clare Cooper Marcus, a leading author in what might be called the psychosocial approach to the home, turns the mirror around, so to speak, to focus *inward* on the subject possessing it: 'Unable to comprehend all that is encapsulated in the psyche, we need to place it "out there" for us to contemplate, just as we need to view our physical body in a mirror'.[37] Accordingly, Marcus treats the home and related self-images more as an *internal process* of self-actualisation rather than a form of expression aimed at others, though she includes that as well in her analysis. A home, she writes, fulfils many *emotional* as well as functional needs, including: 'a place of self-expression, a vessel of memories, a refuge from the outside world, a cocoon where we can feel nurtured and let down our guard'.[38]

Originally inspired by Carl Jung's reflections on what building his own house revealed to him of his unconscious mind,[39] the research in Marcus's book covers a twenty-year programme of personal interviews she conducted with over sixty individuals, most of whom lived in the San Francisco Bay Area where the author lives and works. Rejecting the idea of conducting any controlled experiments with her subjects, which she believed might fail to reveal their deeper feelings about what their various homes and related associations meant to them, Marcus employed a technique she was trained in by a Gestalt therapist.[40] The free-wheeling method allows subjects to 'play out' their personal thoughts and feelings – such as talking to a former home as though it was another person with whom they had had a close relationship, and now missed – encouraged by Marcus at various points in the dialogue. Though each subject subsequently had a different story to tell about their home-making experiences, a constant theme running through their stories, she explains:

> [...] is the notion that we are all – throughout our lives – striving *toward a state of wholeness* [emphasis added], of being wholly ourselves. Whether we are conscious of it or not, every relationship, event, mishap, or good fortune in our lives can be perceived as a 'teaching', guiding us toward being more and more fully who we are.[41]

While she concedes that much has been written along similar lines about the psychological lives of individuals – especially by Jungians – what her book adds to the debate, she argues, is the idea that the places we live in not only reflect that process but also have a powerful effect themselves in our personal quest for wholeness. In addition to the individual home itself, the significant places described in the autobiographical stories related by Marcus's subjects range from the hiding places and shelters in the home or garden that children create for themselves in establishing their own identity – 'learning to do without our parents' as she describes it – to the actual *location* of the home in town or country.

In a chapter titled 'Self-image and location', drawing upon related studies by other researchers as well as the personal stories of her own subjects, Marcus follows earlier critics of suburban life in highlighting the tensions that can arise between working husbands and their 'stay at home' wives, who may have conflicting emotional and social needs. There are also accounts of conflicts of values regarding life in the city versus the country, where personal identity with a particular form of location and associated way of life can be so strong as to compel changes in relationships with a partner.

Attachments to things

Marcus fills in this spectrum of childhood hiding place to neighbourhood location with other tales of personal struggles for self-expression, sometimes supported by others, and often haunted by memories of parental homes, which she maintains, has a lasting influence on an individual's later experiences. Significantly, however, it is not the actual building that generally exerts such a hold upon its occupants, but the *personal things* they bring with them or accumulate during the time they spend in their homes:

> The key seems to be in the *personalization of space* [emphasis added]. More and more, I found in the stories I heard that it is the moveable objects in the home, rather than the physical fabric itself, that are the symbols of self.[42]

In relating such stories, Marcus is not suggesting that the acquisition of such personal items or changes to the interior of a home can of *themselves* be responsible for any changes in their owners' personalities, but rather that they *support and express* an evolving self. As such, her approach aligns with a burgeoning research literature on the importance people attach to things, together with a wider interest in the nature and impact of material culture on human development. Amongst the different disciplines involved in this research, anthropologists have been especially prominent. However, while anthropology has traditionally been more concerned with what the pattern and order of material objects reveals of the underlying social and cultural order, increasing attention is paid now to the more personal and idiosyncratic relationships between individuals and their homes.[43] Moreover, it is not only the close relationships between objects and owners that is stimulating anthropological interest, but also how those material relationships dovetail with any close relationships of their owners with other persons, particularly those with whom they may share their homes – not so different, perhaps, from Marcus's concerns.

Role of objects in personal relationships

Much of the anthropological literature in this field covers individuals living in widely different regions and cultures.[44] Like Marcus, however, in *The Comfort of Things*, Daniel Miller,[45] a British anthropologist, focuses his research on the inhabitants of a specific area, in this case a single street, Stuart Street, in South London. His book, which explores 'the role of objects in our relationships, both to each other and to ourselves', is based on interviews conducted by Miller and his research assistant of thirty people, selected from 100 individual and household studies conducted in the same street. Contrary to assumptions that the material accumulation of 'ever more stuff' comes at the price of paying less attention to personal relationships, Miller discovered that, 'in many ways, the opposite is true; that possessions often remain profound and usually the closer our relationships are with objects, the closer our relationships are with people'.[46]

Miller describes his approach as unusually 'holistic' compared to mainstream anthropology, though like more conventional research in that discipline he finds an overall logic or 'aesthetic', as he calls it, in the pattern of relationships between people and things, analogous with anthropologists' typical quest for an overarching sense of order in their wider social and cultural investigations. Treating each case, whether it involves one or more persons, as an individual 'portrait', Miller relates the Kafkaesque story of a man, who, having spent his entire adult life living in hostels and working as a humble clerk in a large company (before being pushed into early retirement), found himself, at the age of seventy-five, living alone in a barely furnished apartment of his own for the first time, the rooms of which were almost completely devoid of personal possessions and character – a situation sadly reflected in the interviews in a personal life hardly lived, equally empty of supportive relationships or a substantive interest in anything else.

By contrast, he relates the example of an elderly couple, Mr and Mrs Clarke, interviewed in their home prior to Christmas, painting an idealistic picture of a contented pair who seemingly spend much of their time in between Christmases preparing for the next one, which, as always, will involve much celebrating with close family members and their many friends. The numerous Christmas decorations which festoon the lounge and drawing-room include Chinese lanterns and other specially crafted items collected over the years and lovingly assembled for the occasion, the focal point, of course, being a splendid tree, for which hundreds of ornaments had been collected. In the midst of all this Mr Clarke sits at his desk in the drawing-room, creating, repairing and carefully putting together the last strings of ornaments and lights to be hung up.

Much of that craftsman-like care and attention to detail, Miller explains, derives from Mr Clark's initial training as a chemist and, more generally, his engineering background. Above and beyond those professional sources, however, Miller detects a deeper source derived from the moral satisfaction of a job well done. Moreover, he suggests, both the extreme care taken over the Clarke's collections of things and their caring relationships with the family and friends with whom they share those collections – for Mrs Clarke, their numerous children and grandchildren constitute her own special collection – are driven by the same moral principles. Significantly, from what Miller gathers from his interviews, those principles have also been taken up by family members in conducting their own lives, filling in, he notes, for the apparent absence of any wider support:

> For the street as a whole, what is shocking is *how few households have any relationship to a wider community* [emphasis added], let alone giving service to one. So continuity, to this degree of altruistic commitment, is very clearly something inter-generational. It is the Clarkes' children who, in

turn, become school governors, serve their time on the committees of gym clubs or wine societies, keep an eye on neighbors' pets and children and generally give of their labour and time, and not just out of their pocket, to the service of the wider community.[47]

Following these two polar opposite cases, Miller presents a more varied series of portraits of individuals coping with life as best they can, sometimes successfully, sometimes less so, but who all, one way or another, find comfort and outlets for personal expression in the possessions and mementos they have accumulated in their lives and which now populate their homes. They include mostly familiar objects, like record collections, treasured furnishings and art works and many framed photographs of children, pets and lost or distant relatives and friends – the latter collections being especially prominent in the homes of Miller's immigrant subjects, along with ornaments and other objects connecting their owners with their origins. Less than a quarter of the people living in Stuart Street were born in London, he points out, reflecting the diversity of that city's population. Some, Miller explains, are still not sure if they will stay or return to what they still regard as their homeland, and for whom those objects connecting them with their former homes have a special significance, bridging as they do different worlds and cultures.

Material culture matters

Throughout these sensitively drawn portraits, Miller stresses what all his interviews revealed about the close relations between the character and pattern of objects and the lives of their owners. But it is in the epilogue to the book where Miller draws the most important lessons from all the different personal stories. Returning to the parallels he describes at the beginning of the book between the search for order by his subjects and the wider patterns of order studied by anthropologists, Miller suggests that, minus a strong community life – exemplified in the 'shocking' absence of such bonds between the inhabitants of Stuart Street – typical of modern cities, individuals were in effect creating their *own* orderly and supportive universe *within their homes*.

As an anthropologist, though, Miller's research aims to uncover another set of relationships which, he suggests, his subjects would probably not have mentioned directly were it not for the questions he and his assistant chose to ask them: their personal relationships with material objects. Couching his professional approach in dialectical terms, Miller explains that objects are customarily interpreted by anthropologists as an integral aspect of all personal and social relationships and are inseparable from people's daily lives: 'People exist for us in and through their material presence'.[48] The advantage of this approach, he argues, is that what might first appear as mute forms may, on closer examination, reveal more about the nature of the relationships that bind people together than the people involved themselves might reveal.

In support of his approach Miller points to Bourdieu, who identified an underlying, systemic order in the use of everyday things in his anthropological studies of Berber communities in North Africa.[49] However, while Bourdieu could apply the same perspective in his studies of French secular society of the 1960s, Miller argues that, at least as far as the diverse and multi-cultural inhabitants of London in the new millennium are concerned, that kind of social homogeneity no longer exists. Instead, he suggests that, apart from those state-supported services that keep the country running, what homogeneity remains is provided at the level of the *personal household*, in the networks of relationships he uncovered between people and objects as well as between individual occupants. So, while people may not be wholly shaped by any single culture or society, neither are they free agents who choose their own destiny; instead, they are subject to various influences at different times in their lives, out of which emerges the characteristic traits and lifestyles which Miller describes as a personal aesthetic – a miniature social and material cosmology of its own, analogous to the cosmologies anthropologists find in traditional societies, now reproduced in modern cities on the tiniest personal scale.

Fashion conscious

Within that personal cosmology, which, while much reduced in respect of the traditional forms of social integration Miller alludes to, how a person dresses will also invariably figure high in any chosen modes of self-expression, modes that now include a vastly expanded range of media reaching far beyond the spatial confines of the home – the focus of later chapters below. Like so many other facets of the self-field covered in this book, however, what different authors make of fashion largely depends upon the particular perspective and knowledge they bring to bear upon it. The French semiotician Roland Barthes,[50] for example, differentiated between the history and sociology of clothing, with its dominant themes of protection, modesty and ornamentation, and the modern fashion industry, which he determined required a different approach. Turning in the 1960s to the structural linguistics of Ferdinand de Sausurre,[51] he found ample material for analysis of what he called 'the Fashion System' in popular women's magazines such as 'Elle'. Barthes candidly explains his approach in terms of what linguists describe as the 'pertinence principle', which entails that everything not directly related to the chosen viewpoint, is discarded:

> [...] confronted with fashion clothing we have chosen, from the outset, an 'homogenous level of description', to which we have tried to hold as rigorously as possible; the pertinence chosen is that of semantics; we have decided to look at contemporary Fashion clothing *from the point of view of the meanings that society attributes to it*, to the exclusion of all other points of view.[52]

However, Barthes admits the approach comes at the apparent cost of ignoring many economic, sociological and historical factors that would seem to be essential to understanding the *totality* of fashion. The paradox is, he suggests, that any attempt in turn to examine a complex subject in all its totality invariably falls back upon a more restricted theoretical viewpoint, whether socioeconomic, phenomenological, psychoanalytical or some other approach: 'So it is better then, not to set totality directly in opposition to the pertinence principle and to let this principle develop freely with all these consequences'.[53]

According to Barthes, therefore, other than deciding which of any current trends being promoted in the magazines that an individual believes might suit her best, the strict and well-publicised rules of the fashion industry would seem to exclude any genuine form of personalisation in the manner of dress. Except, perhaps, for that most personal of items: jewellery. In an essay written when he was still formulating his new approach, Barthes implies that, against the historical reverence of gems and jewellery for their own sake, there is much room in modern societies for improvisation in what counts as good taste:

> No matter how little it costs, the piece of jewellery must be thought about in relation to the whole outfit it accompanies, it must be subjected to that essentially functional value which is that of style. What is new, if you like, is that the piece of jewellery is no longer on its own; it is one term in a set of links which goes from the body to clothing, to the accessory and includes the circumstances for which the whole outfit is being worn; *it is part of an ensemble* [emphasis added]; and this ensemble is no longer necessarily ceremonial: taste can be everywhere, at work, in the country, in the morning, in winter, and the piece of jewellery follows suit.[54]

Dressed bodies

Since Barthes made fashion a legitimate subject for serious research there has been a small industry in fashion studies across different cultures as well as in the West, much of it also involving cross-disciplinary approaches. Though mostly focused on the social aspects of fashion, they also encompass personal matters of the body and ambiguities of identity – subjects often ignored in sociological perspectives. For example, Joanne Entwistle,[55] adopting a more personal approach closer to that of Marcus and Miller, writes that, while human beings, like all animals, have bodies, the social world of humans is distinctive for being a world of *dressed* bodies:

> The individual and very personal act of getting dressed is an act of preparing the body for the social world, making it appropriate, acceptable, indeed respectable and possibly desirable too [...] Dress is the way in which individuals learn to live in their bodies and feel at home in them.[56]

However, while the need to dress appropriately for whatever occasion is required underlines its relation to a social order at some level or other, Entwistle points out that, wherever the significance of dress is acknowledged in cultural studies or other disciplines, it invariably omits any significant relation with the body. Finding inspiration elsewhere in Merleau-Ponty's fusion of mind, body and situation in human experience, she suggests his approach offers some useful guidelines for analysing dress as a form of situated bodily practice:

> Dress in everyday life is always located spatially and temporarily: when getting dressed one orientates oneself to the situation, acting in particular ways upon the body. However, one does not act upon the body as if it were an inert object but *as the envelope of the self* [emphasis added].[57]

Likewise, she finds in Bourdieu's concept of the habitus a framework for establishing fashion studies and dress within the context of everyday behaviour. Hinting at the shortcomings of Barthes' approach, she observes that personal habits of dress in everyday life cannot be understood by analysing the fashion industry and magazines alone: 'Choices over dress are always defined *within a particular context* [emphasis added]: the fashion system provides the "raw material" of our choices but these are adapted within the context of the lived experience of the woman, her class, race, age, occupation and so on'.[58]

Habitual wear

In her analysis of blue denim jeans as both a global fashion phenomenon and a highly personal garment, Sophie Woodward[59] offers a good example of one particular item that defies all the normal categories of fashion and dress. As a fashionable item in its own right around the world, aside from a few minor changes of detail, the product has changed little in its long life. Unlike other fashionable items, which are mostly worn sporadically depending upon the occasion and the wearer, it is also one that is *habitually* worn – in the home, at work and at leisure – by its users. Yet, as Woodward observes, not much is said about them. She puts this down to a tendency for people to mostly talk about items of 'special' clothing they rarely wear: 'This inability to speak about clothes that are worn almost all the time, and as a consequence are the most important to people *as an embodied material practice* [emphasis added], is encapsulated with the phrase the "humble blue jean"',[60] popular with fashion journalists focused upon more exclusive and ephemeral products of the industry. However, reinterpreted through a more profound perspective on material culture, Woodward suggests the phrase acquires an altogether different meaning as one of those many things we may be consciously *unaware* of, but which help to frame our personal and social worlds.

Addressing the global scope of fashion and its more intimate aspects together, Woodward argues, presents methodological challenges requiring a multi-disciplinary approach embracing the multiple domains of fashion, including, she suggests, ethnographic studies of women's personal wardrobes. Following Miller's example, she describes a series of searching personal interviews she conducted with women about the contents of their wardrobes, going through each item in turn, encouraging them to describe how they got it, how long ago, what they wore it with and coaxing out any special memories they had of it – building up an intimate picture of the relationship between person and garment. In a manner similar to the explanations of innovation in combinatorial terms repeated elsewhere in this book, Woodward also describes these personal wardrobes as potentially *creative assemblages*, ready for recombination in fresh ways as the occasion and mood demands:

> By combining items of clothing in outfits, clothing practices are by definition *practices of assemblage* [emphasis added]. When new items are combined with old ones, then the collection of clothing in the wardrobe is a possible resource through which 'new' looks and fashions can be created, by reactivating old items or making new combinations.

In conclusion, she urges scholars of fashion not to rely upon what people just tell us about clothing, or what we are consciously aware of, but to pay more attention to matters that may be less accessible but which may ultimately yield a great deal of more significance.

Automania

Of those personal possessions symbolising the paradoxes of the modern era, however, the private automobile best encapsulates both the dream and cold reality of a material and technological culture over which individuals now have little, if any control, but in which they strive for self-expression. Celebrating the French Citroën D.S. 19, or 'Deese' model in his collection of essays on popular culture, *Mythologies*,[61] written in the post-war years before he turned his attention to fashion, Barthes captures the fascination these shining products of the First Machine Age held, and still hold for most people:

> I think that cars today are almost the exact equivalent of the great Gothic cathedrals: I mean the supreme creation of an era, conceived with passion by unknown artists, and consumed in image if not in usage by a whole population which appropriates them as a purely magical object.[62]

While, compared to the average American citizen then enjoying a more prosperous economy, actual ownership of one of these 'magical' objects in the post-war years was still considered a luxury by most Europeans, that did not restrict the promise they held out to people of better times and fortunes ahead. Neither did it restrict Barthes' evident enthusiasm for the new breed of machine represented by the new Citroën, which he suggests 'marks a change in the mythology of cars'. Up until that point, he argues, the ultimate models 'belonged rather to the bestiary of power', whereas the D.S. 19 appears altogether 'more *homely*', with a dashboard that looked 'more like the working surface of a modern kitchen than the control room of a factory'.[63] Other details suggest attention to the *comfort* of the driver rather than performance alone – novel themes to which, Barthes divines, the public positively responded.

Seductive advertisements

Barthes also wrote his celebration of the automobile before he had fully developed his semiological approach and limited his sources of analysis to the printed media. If he had applied his new approach to the contemporary automobile industry as well as fashion he might well have looked to the industry's seductive advertisements, especially in America. There, as Heon Stevenson[64] writes in his history of the media, as befitting the world's most advanced consumer culture, automobile advertisements were developed into an impressive art form as well as an effective tool of persuasion:

> The aspirations of an era are captured vividly in its advertising, which is the focus of a multitude of human concerns and ambitions. At its best, advertising displays the finest fruits of engineering and the graphic arts. By their nature ephemeral, advertisements are compelling freeze-frames of the times that give them meaning.[65]

In contrast to Europe, where new cars only came onto the market whenever they were ready, the automobile market in America was rejuvenated every year by a flood of new models by all the major manufacturers, generating a regular source of public excitement in anticipation of the new features, the first glimpse of which was provided in the manufacturers' beguiling advertisements:

> An advertisement is, and always has been, evangelical. It must cajole, bully, and entice its reader to spend on the strength of its promise, to partake of the enchanted life that the product will bring.[66]

Accordingly, each new model was promoted for its styling and performance, convenience and comfort, depending upon which was the model's strongest selling point. But, as Stevenson explains, underlying all these annual modifications was a calculated campaign by the automobile companies encouraging consumers to *personally identify* with their products. By the 1950s car ownership was no longer the novelty it once was and other psychological messages feeding fantasies of freedom, escape and adventure were employed, with copywriters offering 'the consumer a chance to construct a self-image that was more appealing than the reality'.[67]

Such messages, reinforced by subliminal fears of being 'left behind', proved to be highly effective – as indeed they still are, as the perpetual TV ads of happy drivers roaming magically empty roads and open countryside show – if only for the time needed to get customers into the showrooms. Yet, as Jean Baudrillard[68] bluntly reminds us, so far as the actual vehicle itself is concerned, the possibilities for personalisation were (and are) strictly limited: 'A car cannot be personalized in its essence as a technical object, *but only in its inessential aspects* [emphasis added]'.[69] While he allows that choices *between* models, such as those between luxury cars and basic – but much-loved – models like the Citroën 2CV, are significant in themselves, updated model lines offer mostly the *appearance* of choice. In reality, whether it is a matter of choosing between models we can or cannot afford, or incremental modifications of the models themselves, the choices offered have already been determined for us:

> Our freedom to choose causes us to participate in a cultural system willy-nilly. It follows that the choice in question is a specious one: to experience it as a freedom is simply to be less sensible of the fact that it is imposed upon us as such, and that through it society as a whole is likewise imposed upon us.[70]

Promise of freedom

There was a time earlier in the story, however, when there was a good deal less 'choice' and the automobile's promise of freedom was indeed a reality for a sizeable section of the population. In particular, as Ruth Brandon[71] explains, Henry Ford's affordable Model T revolutionised farmers' lives: 'Suddenly, into those overworked, isolated existences burst the prospect of freedom'. And not just the freedom of mobility either, as the Model T's engine could be 'hooked up to power anything from a saw to a washing machine'.[72] The change in women's lives went far beyond washing day, however. Hitherto restricted to the five-mile radius of the farmer's 'team haul', the growth of car ownership, which was fastest in the rural states of America, integrated those isolated homesteads into the surrounding community, so they became part of a local township, and beyond that a county, a state and ultimately the American nation and culture itself.

Then there were the vacations – also something previously restricted to the privileged few – now available to any family with a Model T they could just jump into and drive off somewhere – anywhere at all – even if they could not afford a hotel; why, they brought one with them, didn't they? Such was the growing bond between American families and their new possession that, when faced during the Depression in the 1930s with the hard choice between selling the car or the home, Brandon writes, many families opted to keep the car: 'As long as you had a car, you had both a home and the mobility to look for work. While there were wheels, there was hope'.[73]

It is out of such stories that mythologies are born, and while automobile advertising has certainly evolved since those formative years, the methods and messages it has since developed to entice consumers build upon the foundational myths of freedom created in those first decades, when the automobile really *did* deliver on its promises. While Baudrillard may therefore be perfectly correct in pointing out the limitations to consumer choice imposed from above, the methods since practised by automobile manufacturers and their advertisers would likely not be anywhere near as effective were it not for those underlying myths.

Human costs

As strong as those mythologies were, however, they could not conceal the brutal fact that the attractions of the automobile bore a punitive cost in human life. As Rudi Volti[74] recounts, in 1965 there were 49,163 deaths from automobile accidents in the US, and while the figure actually represents an *improvement* over the previous decades' figures,[75] it is still a larger sum than the *total* US losses in Vietnam from that year onward until the end of the war. However, safety issues were virtually ignored by most automobile companies until the 1960s, when growing numbers of critics assailed the industry for the deaths and injuries on the roads, and the slower but no less deadly effects of the increasingly polluted air of American cities. More worrying still, however, as Volti explains, is the apparent *indifference* of consumers at large to their own safety during that period – except presumably those who had been directly affected by death or injury. Firmly convinced from the outset that 'safety doesn't sell', the leaders of the industry interpreted the lacklustre response by consumers to the Ford company's proclaimed new safety features in their 1956 model line, as evidence they were right all along.

That dam was breached in 1965 with the publication of Ralph Nader's *Unsafe at Any Speed*.[76] Though it was met with little interest at first, Volti relates, the clumsy efforts by General Motors, which produced half of all American automobiles at the time, to investigate Nader's private life in search of anything that might undermine his public standing – for which Nader successfully sued the company – aroused public anger, and a great deal more interest in his book. Following the National Traffic and Safety Act passed by Congress in 1966 empowering the federal government to set safety-related standards and recall any defective vehicles – the first of its kind – a series of new performance criteria were established for brakes, lights, and tyres, together with changes to the interior of cars to reduce injuries to drivers and passengers thrown about by collisions. Despite a requirement in 1968 that all new models also be fitted with seat belts, getting drivers and passengers to actually use them proved to be a much more difficult task; a problem reflected by similar trials in other countries, which has only been resolved by electronic warnings and the threat of fines – still often ignored – in those countries where they have been implemented.

Whilst there have been steady improvements in safety and other measures to reduce harmful emissions from car engines, they are set against a background of continued resistance and deceptive advertising practices by the industry.[77] It would seem that, for a large part of the general population at least, such has been the grip of the automobile upon their owners' lives and imaginations that many are prepared to risk those lives daily rather than have anything or anyone come between them and their experience, no matter what efforts are made to persuade them to change their behaviour. Whatever progress has been achieved has also been overtaken by the steep rise in car ownership in India and China and other fast-developing countries, as the people of those regions aspire to the same dream of freedom, but find themselves trapped in a far darker and more dangerous world of polluted cities and crowded roads.

Self and group identity

In the previous chapter, we looked at the formation of self-image from several viewpoints, from body image and what we learn about ourselves from others, to the self-image we project through our attachment to our homes and personal possessions, including simple objects, clothing and automobiles. More generally speaking, self-image is profoundly influenced by whichever social group or groups we identify with most. Whether they involve membership of a social class, a particular political or religious group, or the sense of purpose and personal identity that comes with spending many years with other workers in the same occupation and workplace, self-image is more often *sensed* rather than thought out, and is generally governed by common human emotions as much as by any self-conscious calculation of personal interests.

No less important, as we shall see in this and the following chapter, advances in the technologies of production and consumption have also had the most profound effects on the historical evolution of group identities and the modern self-field, and are now threatening deeply held values and perceptions of what it is to have a fully functioning self.

Tribal ties

From being born into a family onwards, we quickly learn, just as our primate ancestors did before us, that membership of any group also carries *obligations* as well as the advantages of a home base and protection from the world beyond, including other groups. What is not always acknowledged or fully understood, however, is that group identity is defined – especially within class as well as political, religious and racial groups – as much by the perception of *differences* between groups as by what the members of any one group have in common. Though we may be reluctant to admit it, like most of our predecessors we are basically 'tribal animals'[1] and are profoundly influenced in our beliefs and trust or distrust in others by whatever group or groups we belong to, which, in the case of modern humans, may be as many and diverse as can be tolerated by the society in which we live.

The dilemma has an ancient history in the West. In *The Righteous Mind*,[2] Jonathan Haidt's analysis of how group mindedness can divide as well as unite individuals and societies, the author records a passage from Plato's *The Republic*,[3] in which Plato's brother Glaucon 'challenges Socrates to prove that justice itself – and not merely the reputation for justice – leads to happiness',[4] the implication being that people only behave well because they fear the damage that any misbehaviour might do to their reputations. In response, the philosopher likens justice in a man to justice in a *polis* or city-state. In the just city, Socrates explains, everyone works for the common good, while in the unjust city, group is pitted against group, the 'powerful exploit the weak, and the city is divided against itself'. Since only philosophers care about 'what is truly good, not just what is good for themselves', he argues, then only rule by philosophers can prevent the *polis* from descending into 'the chaos of ruthless self-interest'. The same conditions, Socrates claims, apply to the happy individual, for 'if philosophers must rule the happy city, then reason must rule the happy person'.[5] And since a reasoning person genuinely cares about the general good, he concludes, they will not be solely concerned about appearances.

In relating the dialogue, Plato sought to support his own arguments, as a former student of Socrates and champion of reason, for the ideal city-state governed by philosophers for the general good of all. However, the problem with the ancient philosopher's line of thought, Haidt writes, is that 'the assumed psychology is just plain wrong'. In Haidt's view, 'Glaucon was right: people care a great deal more about appearance and reputation than about reality',[6] a claim he supports with numerous examples of the psychological and social pressures, whether of a religious, political or other nature, that groups exert on individual members. Moreover, he argues, the moral judgements individuals make are generally made on the basis of *intuition* rather than reason and are most often governed by the values and interests of their own political or religious group.

Instinctive bias in favour of people like themselves

While such views go against the grain of liberal beliefs, Haidt is not alone in his assessment of the psychological effects that belonging to a particular social group can have on individual members. In his prologue to *Against Empathy*, Paul Bloom[7] takes issue with the uncritical view of empathy as a psychological and social power for good, the benefits of which are supposedly shared by all the parties concerned:

> Empathy has its merits. It can be a great source of pleasure, involved in art and fiction and sports, and it can be a valuable aspect of intimate relationships. And it can sometimes spark us to do good. *But on the whole, it's a poor moral guide* [emphasis added]. It grounds foolish judgements and often motivates indifference and cruelty.[8]

As critical as Bloom's opening salvo on empathy seems, he hastens to add that he is not encouraging people to be selfish or immoral. On the contrary, he suggests, 'if we really want to live in a better world, then we should do without empathy'. The problem is that for most people, feeling what they think other people are feeling and experiencing, only really applies to other people who are *like themselves*. The result, he argues, is an *instinctive bias* in favour of the views and values of whatever group it is that we mostly identify with, as neatly encapsulated in a toast Bloom learned as a child from a relative: 'Here's to those who wish us well. All the rest can go to hell'.[9]

Bloom's work follows the similar case made by Haidt for the powerful influence of the collective over the individual mind when it comes to making moral judgements or defending the interests of one's own group. Other writers on the socio-political sphere such as Cass Sunstein[10] and co-authors Christopher Achen and Larry Bartels,[11] also warn us not to rely too much on people working things out for themselves based upon the available evidence on the issues concerned. Most individuals, they argue, tend to vote with and support whichever political leaders or party their own social group identifies with and *who confirm their own beliefs*, rather than by any more rational process of thought or debate. Thus Sunstein writes: 'people are motivated to accept accounts that fit with their pre-existing conceptions; acceptance of those accounts makes them feel better, and acceptance of competing accounts makes them feel worse'.[12]

Discomfort with inconsistent beliefs

In turn, all the above researchers owe much to Leon Festinger's[13] original theory of 'cognitive dissonance', the name he gave to the *psychological discomfort* that people acquiring inconsistent beliefs feel. The theory, Festinger explains, rests upon two basic hypotheses. Firstly: 'The existence of dissonance, being psychologically uncomfortable, will motivate the person to try to reduce the dissonance and achieve consonance'. Secondly: 'When dissonance is present, in addition to trying to reduce it, the person will actively avoid situations and information which would likely increase this dissonance'.[14]

In clarifying the nature of dissonance itself, which he likens to feelings of hunger, frustration or disequilibrium caused by the existence of *conflicting relations between opinions or beliefs* held by an individual, Festinger stresses that cognitive dissonance is a motivating factor in itself, aimed at resolving such conflicts. And, just like hunger, dissonance leads to activities aimed at reducing the problem. It may be a very different kind of motivation, he concedes, from that which psychologists are accustomed to dealing with. However – and subsequent developments have surely proven him to be right enough – it is just as powerful as any other. It is also a motivating factor, he stresses, which operates in everyday life in a wide variety of different contexts. Wherever opinions are formed or decisions taken, some level of dissonance may be *unavoidably* created between what a person believes and acts upon and those *contrary opinions* pointing in a different direction.

Only rarely, however, if ever, he suggests, does the individual concerned accept such conflicts as inconsistencies in his or her beliefs, preferring instead to *rationalise* them one way or another, the way a chain smoker might deny health warnings as being exaggerated, leading inevitably to psychological discomfort. In many such cases, the dissonance may persist and remain unresolved, even when actions are taken to reduce its sources, as when the chain smoker finds consolation and justification in sticking to his habit in what might now be described, to borrow a phrase, as 'alternative facts', or perhaps just the similar habits of friends. If those tactics do not succeed however, then, Festinger asserts, '*his efforts to reduce the dissonance will not cease* [emphasis added]'.[15]

Influence of groups

Festinger was also notably interested in the influence of groups on cognitive dissonance. A series of experiments he describes recorded the effects that discussions of personal opinions and beliefs with groups of other persons had in swaying viewpoints one way or another. Small groups of individuals were instructed in such a way as to make them either more or less attractive to the members of the group, who were then asked to write down their opinions on some chosen topic, such as a labour-management dispute. The written opinions were then circulated amongst the group members, who, having read those opinions, were asked to comment further on the topic in question, again in writing, so that any changes of viewpoints were all recorded. Significantly, it was found that the *relative attractiveness of the group to its members* had a marked effect, individual members being more likely to move their own opinion *closer* to that of other members – that is, to reduce any dissonances – or else to try to persuade others to agree with their own positions if they were attracted to a group, than if they were *not* so attracted.

Festinger concluded from these and similar experiments that, given any unacceptable differences of opinion between members of a group to which they were attracted, they might adopt one of several strategies to reduce the dissonance. One way would be for a member to simply *change* his or her own opinion so that it corresponded more closely to that of the other members. A second way would be for a member to try to persuade any others who disagreed with his or her own opinion to change *theirs*. Taken together, both these methods, Festinger suggests, 'represent the usual sort of influence process which results in *movement toward uniformity in groups* [emphasis added] in the presence of disagreement'.[16] A third and more controversial way of reducing dissonance, Festinger argues, is to point to attributed differences in characteristics or motivations between oneself and others, so as to suggest they cannot be truly compared with oneself or one's own beliefs – or in an extreme case, to simply reject and derogate the other(s). While clearly the last strategy, if applied by a group member to other members of his or her own group is unlikely to win over those members, if aimed, however, at *other* groups perceived to be hostile to one's own group, it is far more likely to succeed in cementing internal membership.

Self and the out-group other

All three of the strategies that Festinger describes to reduce cognitive dissonance within groups involve issues of empathy and identifying with the minds of others, whether it means one person moving closer to what another person thinks, or pointing to perceived or exaggerated differences with other groups to strengthen one's own group identity.

The problem with Festinger's theory, however, as with its variations, is the tautology of the basic argument, which is that views and values that do not conform with an individual's assumptive views and values cause feelings of discomfort, which, in turn, cause that person to suppress or avoid those feelings by one strategy or another – strategies which, in fact, simply *confirm the original problem* of cognitive dissonance.

What Bloom brings to the discussion of the influences and pressures upon personal beliefs, is a fresh look at what has hitherto been taken for granted as the correctness and fundamental virtues of empathy as a social process of cognition and mutual understanding – in short, the belief in empathy as 'an absolute good'.[17] Whilst he acknowledges the importance of empathy in human behaviour, he likens it to a narrowly focused spotlight, in that it only works well when directed by one person at other specific individuals:

> Further, spotlights only illuminate what they are pointed at, so *empathy reflects our biases* [emphasis added]. Although we might intellectually believe that the suffering of our neighbour is just as awful as the suffering of someone living in another country, it's far easier to empathize with those who are close to us, those who are similar to us, and those we see as more attractive or vulnerable and less scary [...] In this regard, *empathy distorts our moral judgements in pretty much the same way that prejudice does* [emphasis added]'.[18]

In short, empathy, as with cognitive dissonance, essentially *reinforces* an existing bias toward those persons who *already* share an individual's own outlook. Sunstein goes still further to argue that, when the members of any group with a political, religious, environmental or other social cause talk together, encouraged by hearing their views and values echoed by other members of the group, their attitudes towards the issues in question invariably *harden and shift toward ever more extreme positions*, in which 'outsiders' who do not share the same views and values are regarded with increasing enmity. Similarly, Achen and Bartels suggest that, far from facilitating reasoned and responsible government, the electoral politics of democracy actually encourage the *exploitation* of group-mindedness by the propagation of whatever policies appeal most to targeted group identities – what is now generally called the 'politics of identity'.[19]

Collective emotions

Whilst acknowledging his position is an 'unfashionable' one, Bloom's response to such problems is to urge us to resist the easy attraction of own-group empathy, which only *exaggerates* the differences in beliefs and behaviour with other groups, and turns instead to reason and compassion when making any moral judgements about those differences. In other words, he writes, 'we should strive to use our heads rather than our hearts'.[20]

As much as any liberal-minded person educated in the virtues of reason might sympathise with such arguments, as Haidt and others cited here suggest, things work out differently in real life, and self-image – 'appearance and reputation' as Haidt describes it – generally counts for more than reasoned argument in maintaining a personal course in society. Moreover, Gunter Gebauer[21] argues, matters of this kind are largely governed by *emotional factors* and what a person *feels* is right for himself or herself rather than by any process of conscious and deliberative thought. Such feelings may also be reinforced by the *collective* emotions we experience in groups, particularly in mass gatherings. While large events of this sort are often – and not without justification – assumed to involve the absorption of the individual self by the mass, Gebauer contends that this represents only one side of the experience. There is another, equally important side we need to appreciate if we are going to understand the individual as a 'feeling and sensing' self, and that is when the individual experiences a sense of *belonging* to a group, as when the individual's feelings are *typical* of the group's feelings.

Feelings of this nature, he suggests, need not make a person any less of an individual, but they clearly indicate when they feel at home and when they do not: 'We are almost never aware of these feelings of belonging until they have *negative* effects'.[22] Accordingly, in belonging to one group, a person may also be viewed by people in other groups as 'bad' or just someone to be avoided. Belonging to a specific group, Gebauer writes, therefore has *social and ethical* implications: 'Its negative impact arises from social processes, from the *boundaries between social groups* [emphasis added], with their practices of demarcation and differentiation and their images of themselves and the others'.[23]

Group dynamics

All these studies address different aspects of what Gordon Allport describes in his timeless work, *The Nature of Prejudice*,[24] as the dynamic between in-groups and out-groups:

Every line, fence, or boundary marks off an inside from an outside. Therefore, in strict logic, an in-group always implies the existence of some corresponding out-group. But this logical statement by itself is of little significance. What we need to know is whether one's loyalty to the in-group automatically implies disloyalty, or hostility, or other forms of negativism, toward out-groups.[25]

Addressing the question of whether it is possible for an in-group to exist *without* an out-group, he lists familiar examples of the Machiavellian tactic of creating a common enemy in order to bind an in-group more closely together. Such cases, he suggests, are so numerous as to tempt one to accept the doctrine. However, while agreeing that a potentially threatening out-group can drive an in-group closer together, he cautions against rushing to judgement:

> The situation, it seems, can best be stated as follows: although we could not perceive our own in-groups excepting as they contrast to out-groups, still the in-groups are *psychologically primary* [emphasis added]. We live in them, by them, and, sometimes, for them. Hostility toward out-groups helps strengthen our sense of belonging, but it is not required.[26]

The key factor determining the members of one group's attitude toward out-groups, Allport argues, is more likely to be the level of personal *familiarity* involved, with the familiar invariably being *preferred* over the unfamiliar, out-group other. For example, he notes that if a child is asked which children are better, the children in the same town or those in another town, it will invariably state a preference for the children in its home town, because it does not *know* the children in the other town: 'What is alien is regarded as somehow inferior, less "good," but there is not necessarily hostility against it'.[27] Whilst there is a natural inclination to favour one's own group, Allport concludes, the response to other groups may therefore vary widely from characterising an out-group as the common enemy to be defeated at all costs, to one of tolerance and appreciation for its members' diversity, and anywhere in between.

Lasting effects of ritual gatherings

While research of this nature on groups might seem remote from more personal matters of the individual self, it shows just how deeply personal self-images are bound up with group identities and the feelings of belonging that go with group membership, whether formal or informal. This applies – and sometimes especially so – at the broadest level of identification with national groups as well as with smaller and more local groups. Contradicting Gebauer's view that mass events need not diminish a person's individuality, Manuela Beyer[28] and her co-authors, for example, contend that collective emotions associated with ritual gatherings of national groups *last well beyond* any specific event and influence intergroup relations in the long as well as the short term, affecting perceived borders and demarcation lines between groups. In particular, national flags and other potent symbols play a large part in stirring up collective emotions and affirming group membership and values, all of which, dependent on the intensity of identification with the in-group, can have lasting effects on individual as well as group attitudes and behaviour toward other groups.

Sectarian conflict

There are few better places to view those effects than in the Northern Ireland capital of Belfast, a city divided by British colonial history and a legacy of decades of sectarian conflict between Catholic and Protestant populations – otherwise known euphemistically as 'The Troubles' – as graphically recorded in the city's famous wall murals.[29] A constant visual reminder of the history and self-images which drove the conflict, the divisions illustrated in those vivid murals are, however, far from over. Despite a dogged peace process and the ensuing power sharing under the 'Good Friday Agreement' of 1998, the fundamental social and political issues which fuelled the conflict remain largely unresolved. Once an industrial powerhouse of the British Empire and a major shipbuilding centre – the famed products of which included the Titanic – like other major regional cities in the UK, Belfast lost most of its industrial strength in the post-war years to new competitors in the Far East and elsewhere.

A fragile peace

What it retained, as local historians David McKittrick and David McVea[30] explain, were the vestiges of an unbalanced colonial economy and social system in which 'the Protestant settler community enjoyed political and economic ascendency'[31] over the indigenous Catholic population.[32] In 1969 tensions between the two populations in Northern Ireland, aggravated by a declining economy, finally exploded into open and violent conflict, stoked by political and paramilitary forces on both sides of the border with the Republic – a border quickly closed down to prevent the smuggling of arms and fighters up from the south. By the time the Good Friday Agreement was signed off almost thirty years later, the conflict had cost a total of 3,644 lives across the state, of which well over half were civilians from both sides, the rest being paramilitary, police officers and members of the British army.

The Agreement and establishment a year later of a new devolved government, which included a 'battery of safeguards' written into the new constitution to ensure adherence to its power-sharing principles and to counteract discrimination, was quickly followed by a dramatic fall in fatal attacks. However, contrary to widespread assumptions that the fall in numbers signalled an end to the conflict, As Peter Shirlow and Brendan Murtagh[33] argue in their disturbing analysis of segregation and violence in the city, it simply served to hide a transformation in the form of violence deployed: 'the nature of violence shifted away from paramilitary and state assaults towards a more sectarianised and repetitive violence of interface rioting and attacks upon the symbols of tradition'.[34]

While a whole new generation has now grown up in Northern Ireland in relatively peaceful circumstances, in many ways relationships between the two sides, particularly in Belfast itself, but also around the province, have accordingly become more polarised than ever. In addition to the prominent wall murals and displays of the British flag, the Union Jack, in public places, amongst the major 'symbols of tradition' referred to above, the annual parades held across the province in celebration of Protestant victories over Catholics in 1689–1690 at the siege of Derry and the decisive Battle of the Boyne, are a continuing source of disturbance and frequent riots. Mostly orchestrated by the Orange Order, a Protestant settler organisation founded in 1795, the purpose of the parades, many of which run through streets historically located in areas whose populations have since changed from Protestant to Catholic, creating potential points of conflict, was described in one official report on similar riots in the nineteenth century as a deliberate provocation: 'The celebration of that (Orange July) festival is plainly and unmistakeably the originating cause of these riots'. The report pointedly adds that the event was used 'to remind one party of the triumph of their ancestors over those of the other, and to inculcate the feelings of Protestant superiority over their Roman Catholic neighbours'.[35]

Effects of spatial segregation

No less damaging than the annual parades in its lasting effects, the spatial segregation between the two populations in the towns and cities of Northern Ireland, especially in the inner residential areas, also serves to entrench and reinforce individual and group prejudices. In Belfast, while the commercial centre of the city affords relatively neutral ground to its citizens, the segregation of Catholic and Protestant residential areas in other parts of the city is stark. Compared with its famous Berlin counterpart, the construction of a series of high walls slicing through large areas of Belfast separating Catholic from Protestant homes may seem insignificant from a global viewpoint, but is none the less brutal for its impact on life in the city.[36] Constructed during the height of The Troubles, the walls still exist. At points where they run close to the houses either side, they are topped by high fences to protect homes from missiles launched from the other side. Most shocking of all, at several other key points, high metal gates in the walls are closed every night to be only opened in the morning – a virtual overnight curfew.

While some might argue that, given the continued strife the walls and gates are still needed, the problem, as Shirlow and Murtagh explain, is that the places they create either side of those walls also serve to further cement differences and discontents, as well as to fortify group identity:

> Segregated places are the sites of social exclusion, fatalism and economic truncation. They are also the places within which resistance against economic, social and cultural 'others' is commonplace.[37]

A result of such concentrated grievance, they observe, is that the negative effects have been self-reinforcing, confirming deeply held group beliefs and prejudices: 'Sectarianism, for some, endures like a comfort blanket'.[38] Consequently, despite legislative efforts to promote equity in the labour market and other areas, they have done little to change positions and viewpoints on either side. In the meantime, the authors observe, the middle-class residents of both sides, who might have done more to bridge sectarian divisions in the city, have decamped to the shared spaces of suburbia, where they are relatively free to enjoy the benefits of social and spatial mobility.

In conclusion, pinpointing problems in the democratic process itself, Shirlow and Murtagh argue that the continuing strife between the two populations comes down to a failure of their leaders and the more extreme members of both communities, who are all too willing to *exploit* prejudices rather than attempt to overcome them:

> In effect, sectarianism is not merely a repressive relationship between communities but also *within them* [emphasis added], given that highly vocal sectarians undermine the capacity or desire to publicly articulate a shared intracommunity future.[39]

Chapter 11

Occupational identity

There has probably been no greater factor shaping adult minds in modern times than the form and place of work. Until recently, belonging to a specific social group has largely meant sharing the same occupation and workplace, with profound impacts upon the evolution of the human self-field which are inextricably tied to that of social class. However, the social and economic gains that followed the growth and power of the modern workforce have since been eroded in America and other countries by a warped political and economic system that favours a now tiny but powerful minority.[1] The result is that growing numbers of the population in some of the wealthiest nations in the world have been deprived of a secure livelihood while an ever-larger share of that wealth has been funnelled toward the richest individuals, creating severe social inequalities in income and access to affordable housing and health care.

Such issues do not fall readily within the scope of the research psychologist's conventional focus on personality traits and cognitive indexes. However, like the proverbial 'elephant in the room', whose presence is huge but goes purposefully unnoticed by the room's distracted human occupants, those issues can no longer be ignored, however uncomfortably they may fit within specialised disciplines. Any serious field theory of the self in particular must necessarily acknowledge the impact of those deprivations upon the minds and lives of those affected – sufficient at the very least to set those effects within the broader context of the self-field. Similarly, only by knowing how the form and place of work has shaped lives in modern history, with all their previous gains and losses, is it possible to appreciate the full extent and meaning of current developments, and the technological and economic factors that now threaten to deprive a great many more individuals of the means to achieve a full and satisfactory life.

Creation of a modern workforce

As Joshua Freeman[2] describes in his history of the modern factory, the creation of the modern workforce involved the invention and spectacular growth – in sheer size as well as importance – of an entirely new building type, which affected the lives of workers and society at large in fundamental ways:

> Unlike many older types of buildings – the church, mosque, palace, or fortress, the theatre, bathhouse, dormitory or lecture hall, the courtroom, prison, or city hall – the factory is strictly a creature of the modern world, *a world it helped to create* [emphasis added].[3]

While most of the current debate on the subject in America as in other countries in the West, has focused on the *closure* of factories and their economic and social impacts, Freeman points out that, worldwide, manufacturing is on the rise. Though a mere 8 per cent of Americans now work in factories, manufacturing jobs as a proportion of the global workforce are still growing, up from 22 per cent in 1994, to almost 29 per cent in 2010, down just 1 per cent from the (2008) pre-recession level. In 2015, China alone – commonly described as the 'world's factory' – employed 43 per cent of its workforce in industry.[4] Similarly, at this very time, the largest factories in history – employing between 100,000 and 200,000 workers or more – are currently in operation, turning out products like smartphones, laptops and clothing made by popular brand-names, which for billions of eager customers around the world define what it means to be modern.

Factory prototypes

Factories were not always so large, however, nor were they mostly located in China. Beginning in the eighteenth century with the Lombes' Derby Silk Mill in England – the prototype for the cotton mills that drove the Industrial Revolution – the earliest factories were all powered by waterwheels and had to be located next to rivers, setting in train the movement of workers from farms and other places of work to new locations, with far-reaching consequences. From the latter part of the eighteenth century onwards, the increasing use of slave labour on the cotton plantations in the Americas also made available unlimited supplies of raw material for the textile industry, an irony not lost on Freeman: 'Thus, the rise of the factory system, with its association of modernity, was utterly dependant on the spread of slave labor'.[5]

   Eventually, machinery powered by waterwheels gave way to steam-powered machinery, enabling factories to be located in the urban centres of population, accessing a bountiful source of local labour and obviating the need to provide workers' housing in remote riverside locations. The knock-on effects of using steam engines, which required coal-fired boilers, were huge, leading to a rapid expansion of the coal industry – a further driving force of the Industrial Revolution – and an equally rapid degradation of the now heavily polluted towns and cities where the new and much larger factories were located. Conditions in the factories themselves were also generally grim and severe exploitation of the young and mostly female workforce, including children – preferred by employers since they could be paid less – was the norm.

However, whilst conditions in the smaller cotton mills of North America were generally better than in their English counterparts, by the time of the American Civil War a critical awareness of an emergent system of class differences embodied in the factory system was brewing on both sides of the Atlantic. Until then, most American mills were powered by water and were therefore dispersed in the smaller riverside towns and cities – attractive locations for the workforce, which, as in the English mills, was mostly young and female. Their impact on women's lives, not unlike the later impact of the first affordable automobiles on women's' lives in rural America described in Chapter 9 was transformative. The cotton mills, Freeman observes:

> […] provided an escape from families, rural life, boredom, and isolation, a chance to experience a new, more cosmopolitan world of independent living, consumer goods, and intense sociability. Earning their own living gave women a sense of independence and relieved their parents of a burden.[6]

Class division and unionisation

By the middle of the nineteenth century, however, the young women of America had grown tired of the cotton mills, with their low pay, long hours and heavy workload, and were finding alternative forms of employment in the cities and other parts of the country opened up by the railroads. Fortunately for the mill owners, they were rapidly replaced by a new and virtually endless source of cheap labour resulting from the mass immigration of poor families from Europe, and especially from famine-plagued Ireland, throwing class differences between owners, managers and workers into stark relief. Men, women and children alike accepted the same low pay and conditions of work as whole families struggled to support themselves, while their employers – no longer needing to offer free housing and other inducements to attract workers – profited from what, Freeman writes, Alexis de Tocqueville astutely discerned as a growing class division in America, based on the factory system and its methods of operation:

> The efficiencies of large factory production, [de Tocqueville] predicted, would enrich manufacturers to the extent that they would become a new aristocracy, threatening democracy, while workers were physically and mentally disadvantaged by the narrow, repetitive nature of factory tasks.[7]

By 1900, half of all the large factories in America were either in the textile or iron and steel industries. It was in the latter industry, however, dominated by Andrew Carnegie's US Steel – 'the largest corporation ever created' – rather than the relatively fragmented textile industry, where class warfare was most intense. Technologically more complex than the production of cloth, Freeman explains, steel production required coordinated activity by *teams* of workers. Compelled, like the employees in the cotton mills, to work long hours – twelve hours a day, seven days a week, eventually reduced to six days – for low rates of pay in harsh conditions, the same necessity for teamwork created the social bedrock for what, after many struggles, became a successful trade union movement. Between 1917 and 1920, union membership in the US increased by nearly 70 per cent, reaching just over 5 million, with one out of every six non-agricultural workers signed up. Hereon, sharing the same occupational identity meant, at least for large sections of the working population, not only sharing the same form of work and workplace, but also membership of a highly organised group whose duty it was to protect and advance their interests, and which, in return, required and expected support and loyalty from its members.

Fordism

Compared with the mostly repetitive tasks required of workers in the cotton mills, steel production, just as it had been with iron, largely involved the finishing of relatively small batches of components for a growing variety of purposes, from structural steel of all kinds and sizes to pipes, wires, bars and tinplate. In turn, the process required skilled and experienced workers operating the adjustable machinery needed to meet the different specifications, whose personal and collective value the unions could deploy in bargaining with their employers. Some steel mills, like Carnegie's Homestead plant in Pennsylvania, which was also the most technologically advanced of its time, were also gigantic, employing many thousands of workers in the same place, which further empowered the unions to strive for better conditions.

However, another, very different, model of factory production emerged in the early twentieth century with the invention by Henry Ford of the mass-production line. Immortalised in Charlie Chaplin's silent movie, *Modern Times*, with its hapless hero unable to keep up with the line – literally swallowed by the machinery – Ford's production lines have generally been, with good reason, interpreted as the sublimation of the individual worker to the machine. However, as Freeman explains, there was also much more to what is called 'Fordism' than that simple, grim picture might suggest. On a technological level, while he is credited with the invention of the mass-production line, all the major technologies and manufacturing processes of Ford's new system for the mass production of automobiles were already in use, in some form or another, in different industries. It was Ford's particular genius, however, to gather all these pre-existing technologies and processes together into one continuously operating production line – a perfect example of what Arthur describes in this book as the 'combinatorial evolution' of new technologies. Previously, the interchangeability of parts and standardisation of tolerances required for the production and assembly of complex products like guns and clocks was already well established in the United States. However, the specialised machinery needed was expensive, involving a heavy investment in both machines and the skilled workers needed to build and maintain them, which all needed to be set off by the production of large numbers of goods.

Continuous flow

Alternatively, Ford deduced, less-skilled workers could be used to operate the machines and assemble the parts, which is where the idea of 'continuous flow' comes in – a concept already well established in oil refining, brewing and other industries involving the processing of liquid products. It was, however, Freeman notes, the meat-packing process which most influenced Ford, in which whole carcasses of slaughtered animals hung on overhead conveyors are moved along from worker to worker, each of whom cuts or removes a particular part, from the largest to the smallest, ready for further processing. The secret to continuous flow, therefore, was a sharp *division of labour*, with each worker performing just one or a small number of operations on whatever was being moved from worker to worker along the automated line.

The combination of standardisation and continuous flow production epitomised in the Model T, changed ideas about manufacturing and factories for the next half century, and what it meant to be a 'worker' in a modern industry. Before the Model T, teams of workers assembled an entire automobile together in a *collaborative process*, responsible for and sharing the satisfaction of seeing the outcome of their joint efforts taking shape as they worked. With the advent of the continuous production line, however, each stationary worker – hence the term 'work station' – completed an endlessly repeated operation, as the body of the vehicle itself, just like the carcasses in the meatpacking factories, was mechanically conveyed from one work station to the next, except that, in this case, the bodies were being *put together* rather than being taken apart.

The Five-dollar Day

As radical as the change in production systems was, it was not Ford's only innovation. The repetitive and debilitating nature of the work – which carried none of the occupational rewards skilled workers valued – created numerous labour problems for Ford. Turnover rates skyrocketed, along with the speed of production and size of the factories. By 1924, Ford's Highland Park plant averaged 42,000 workers, with workers crammed as closely as possible together along production lines to minimise the time 'lost' between work stations. The overwhelming majority of the Ford workforce was also comprised of newly arrived immigrant workers from Europe, many of whom spoke little English, presenting further problems of communication. Not least, 'the introduction of the assembly line coincided with a national surge of labor militancy', affecting other automakers as well as Ford. The short strikes organised by the major unions achieved only modest gains, but the spectre of longer and more costly strikes haunted employers. Ford's response was a well-calculated programme of higher pay and shorter hours, dubbed the 'The Five-dollar Day', doubling the current rate of below $2.50 and shortening the working day from nine to eight hours for a six-day week. Just as Ford intended, the dramatic increase in wages not only helped to retain his workers, but also enabled them to purchase the Model Ts they were helping to build.[8]

Automation

Nevertheless, as self-serving as it was to Ford's commercial interests, the Five-dollar Day was widely greeted as a milestone in modern history:

> Just as the 'factory system' of early nineteenth-century England captured the interest and imagination of journalists, political activists, writers and artists, so, too, did the 'Ford system' of the twentieth century. Once again, it seemed like a new world was aborning. Part of what made Fordism so transfixing was the promise of a wholesale rise in the standard of living and amelioration of the class conflict that had been shaking the United States.[9]

Amongst those whose imaginations were similarly captured, Ford's doctrine of mass-production was eagerly taken up by pioneering modernist architects and planners, in a manner which was to dramatically affect the way people lived together in cities for generations ahead. For the Swiss-French architect Le Corbusier, who, like most leaders of the modern movement in architecture and design, had little if any personal experience of how things were actually made in factories,[10] the twin themes of standardisation and mass-production were more of an *ideology* than practical technologies, as vividly expressed in his 1927 manifesto, *Towards a New Architecture*.[11] Also discarded in the same messianic declaration are any 'dead concepts' of houses, which is to say, personal homes:

> If we eliminate from our hearts and minds all dead concepts in regard to the houses and look at the question from a critical and objective viewpoint, we shall arrive at the 'House-Machine', the mass-production house, healthy (and morally so too) and beautiful in the same way that the working tools and instruments which accompany our existence are beautiful.[12]

Thus it was that 'standardization' in modernist minds and projects came to mean the standard *forms and shapes* of prefabricated building components, invariably produced by large construction companies with little regard for quality of manufacture, or any understanding of the actual processes of controlled factory production underpinning more seasoned industries.[13] The outcome, still visible in myriad soulless apartment blocks around the world, was the needless destruction of whole urban districts – invariably in the poorer quarters of cities – and with them, the dispersal and destruction of entire communities.

Also hampered, like their modernist predecessors, by a personal lack of knowledge of mass-production fundamentals, later projects in the 1960s by avant-garde groups in Japan and the UK envisioned a mass-consumerist urban future of 'Plug-in Cities', where individual homes not only *looked* like automobiles, but were also purposefully designed to be disposed of and replaced as soon as they were outdated by new models.[14] As with the consumers of real automobiles, the choice of homes in these mechanistic visions, where cities themselves look like gigantic machines, is sublimated to the machinery of production, with personalisation and self-expression governed by the cycles of planned obsolescence.

Flexible manufacturing systems

Unbeknownst to these groups or to anyone else similarly seduced by the imagery rather than the less-visible technicalities of mass production, an alternative and truly revolutionary concept of factory production was already taking shape in the early 1960s in a factory in East London owned by the Molins Machine Company, a manufacturer specialising in producing metal components for factory machinery. 'System 24', as it was called, was the world's first, fully computer-controlled, 'flexible manufacturing system', and could turn out small batches of customised components as readily as thousands of identical parts in continuous streams, 24 hours a day non-stop – hence the name.[15] The attraction of the new system for manufacturers was that it offered the prospect of both variable and mass-production in the same continuously operated line. More than that, it afforded the first concrete example of what Stafford Beer[16] envisioned in a landmark 1962 paper as the future 'cybernetic factory'. Designed to operate like a complex and sensitive organism and adapt to a fast-changing environment of consumer needs, Beer's visionary factory reverses the previous history of mass-production and the subservient relation of consumers to production systems.[17]

The vanishing workplace

Conceived ahead of its time, however, it was left to other advanced industries, led by the automobile and aircraft sectors, to take up the challenge of customised automation embodied in System 24 and to put the essential supporting hardware and software systems required into practice. For the most part, the building industry, as conservative as ever, remained split between the small-scale, on-site production of housing and the continued production of large-scale, industrialised building systems. Crudely designed and manufactured but increasingly popular with government planners and construction companies, they were widely adopted for projects in both the developing and the developed worlds. It was not until the 1980s that a handful of more adventurous and technologically competent architects and engineers in Europe, supported by equally forward-looking clients and construction companies, began employing computer-based design and manufacturing systems similar to those in the automobile and aircraft industries.[18]

There was, however, another side to computer-based automation, which, like Fordism before it, was to change forever the very nature of the workplace, not only for factory workers, but also for future office workers and professionals too. As humbling and stressful as the repetitive work was for employees, Ford's model of factory mass-production continued to provide both employment and rising standards of living for large sections of the working population for many years, together with the personal and group identity which came with having an actual place of work and membership of a specific social group. Compared to the now-familiar, fully automated assembly lines of modern automobile factories manned by rows of industrial robots, Ford's semi-automated assembly lines crowded with human workers might well seem like a labour union's dream.

Pandora's box

Theoretically speaking, things were not supposed to work out like that. Small numbers of industrial robots programmed to perform repeatable operations have been in use in factories since the 1960s; usually, like the contemporary NC machines, as part of a larger process of production involving both human workers and other machines spread out over the factory shop floor, rather than in any automated sequence.[19] Ideally, further advances in flexible manufacturing systems and robotics would have been confined to relieving humans of tedious or dangerous forms of work, leaving them to work together with computer-controlled machines in flexible and creative combinations in a new era of craft manufacture[20] – not unlike the mixture of human and automated production methods involved in earlier forms of batch production, which can still be found in many factories around the world producing high-quality goods for specialised markets.

Instead, computerisation has opened a Pandora's box of new and ever-higher levels of automation reaching into virtually every corner of modern economies, often with the compliance of the general population – if not the actual individuals losing their jobs – in the belief that most people will ultimately benefit from the process. In *The Glass Cage*, Nicholas Carr's[21] examination of the human consequences of automation, he observes that the problem with automation is that it often gives us the things we could do without (i.e., too many consumer goods) at the price of the jobs we really do need. Citing what Mihaly Csikszentmihalyi describes as 'the paradox of work', which the latter discovered in the 1980s whilst researching subjects' psychological attitudes to work and leisure, Carr writes that the results of the research were surprising:

People were happier, felt more fulfilled by what they were doing, while they were at work than during their leisure hours. In their free time, they tended to be bored and anxious. And yet they didn't like to be at work. When they were on the job, they expressed a strong desire to be off the job, and when they were off the job, the last thing they wanted was to go back to work.[22]

What the research reveals, Carr suggests, is that people are extremely *bad* at understanding which activities give them satisfaction and which don't. Moreover, 'people allow themselves to be guided by social conventions – in this case, the deep-seated idea that being "at leisure" is more desirable, and carries more status, than being "at work" – rather than by their true feelings'.[23] The explanation for this conundrum, Carr argues, is that while many jobs may feel tedious and unfulfilling in the actual execution of the work, they impose a structure on our world that we miss when left with time on our hands. Even though we may not be aware of it, we are 'happiest when we're absorbed in a difficult task that has clear goals and that challenges us not only to exercise our talents but to stretch them'.[24] In short, jobs – preferably challenging ones but also any jobs involving workers' continuous focus on well-defined tasks – provide a vital *sense of purpose and direction* that is missing in leisure time.

The encroachment of AI

Unfortunately, modern technologies, especially technologies embedded in modern systems of communication, tend to acquire, as we have seen, a life and momentum of their own, aided and abetted by their owners and users – often with scant regard for the human consequences. So it has been with the progression of automation from the relatively simple, reprogrammable robots and NC machines based in factories, to the infinitely wider penetration of artificial intelligence (AI) into every form and place of work; though with varying degrees according to the nature of the work involved, about which there is much argument. A much-quoted 2013 study by Carl Frey and Michael Osborne,[25] for example, estimated that as much as 47 per cent of current US jobs were at risk from the encroachment of AI. However, a more recent review of the research by Andrey Kurenkov et al.[26] suggests that the impact of AI on jobs is unlikely to be 'significantly more disruptive than the impact of automation in the past'.[27]

It all depends on the extent to which the nature of the work is amenable to computerisation, and on the *level* of the AI involved. While the kind of fully autonomous AI systems capable of rivalling human capacities for learning and innovation may yet be a long way off – if indeed they will ever fully materialise – the kind of AI systems now being deployed in offices and commercial enterprises of every sort involve *task-specific*, algorithmic procedures designed and monitored by humans.[28] As with earlier forms of automation, jobs involving relatively simple tasks that can be precisely specified are most at risk. The major hurdle for researchers in extending AI systems any further into the workplace, Carr explains, lies in the difference between what Polanyi originally distinguished as *tacit* and *explicit* forms of knowledge;[29] the latter being relatively easy to pin down and inscribe in algorithmic form. The former, however, as other writers in this book confirm, involves far more complex processes of cognition, much of which occurs at a subconscious level:

> Tacit knowledge, which is also sometimes called procedural knowledge, refers to all the stuff we do *without thinking about it* [emphasis added]: riding a bike, snagging a fly ball, reading a book, driving a car. These aren't innate skills − we have to learn them, and some people are better at them than others − but they can't be expressed as a simple recipe.[30]

What AI can and cannot do (yet)

However, elaborating on the current state of the art in AI and automation, Carr suggests that, while the psychological distinction between tacit and explicit knowledge remains perfectly valid as far as human behaviour and skills are concerned, it no longer provides a firm guide to current discussions of advanced stages of automation. He adds that does not mean computers will soon be able to think and do everything else the way humans do: 'Artificial intelligence is not human intelligence. People are mindful; computers are mindless'.[31] Nevertheless, AI has made significant inroads into many of those activities dependent .upon tacit knowledge which were previously thought to be beyond the reach of automation, of which the rapid development of self-drive technology by Google and other companies, is leading the way. The secret of their success so far, Carr explains, lies in the exponential *speed and data handling capacities* of modern computers, enabling them to apply explicit forms of knowledge in performing many complex tasks we normally do using tacit knowledge. Thus, while viewed as a semi-conscious and smoothly operating totality, tacit knowledge and skills may appear to be beyond the reach of AI, when broken down into many simpler and specifiable cognitive steps and procedures and reassembled as an integrated programme, for all practicable purposes − at least as far as driving and other repetitive skills are concerned − it may soon be hard to tell the difference between what humans and machines can do.[32]

Moreover, given the deadly global toll on the road from accidents − now running at shocking levels of around 1.35 million deaths per year with 20–50 million more people suffering non-fatal injuries[33] − self-drive technology may well be one encroachment of AI into 'normal life' to be warmly welcomed. But it doesn't stop there, Carr warns, as many of the clever things professionals do don't actually need a living brain to carry them out. So, while doctors, lawyers, architects and teachers may not be in actual danger of losing their jobs, they are becoming increasingly reliant upon computers to carry out important parts of their work – generally, it may be added, in *support* of those tasks.[34]

Social groups most affected

What is also generally agreed, however, is that just how much individual employment prospects will be affected by AI and automation in the future depends largely on a person's level of education: the higher the level and the more complex and creative the work is, the safer the job. The most vulnerable groups being the lesser educated or trained individuals engaged in relatively unskilled work.

And therein lies the main problem with the future penetration of automation into the workplace: the social groups likely to be most affected are the same lower-income groups already struggling with insecure jobs and rising living costs, and who, without massive investment in retraining programmes, are unlikely to find future employment in a shrinking job market. In the UK, for example, a recent study by the Office for National Statistics (ONS)[35] estimates that around 1.5 million workers are at high risk of losing their jobs to automation of this kind, with supermarket checkout assistants amongst the most vulnerable, having already lost over 25 per cent of jobs between 2011 and 2017. Some retail outlets are even experimenting with 'Shop Smart' technologies requiring no checkout assistants at all, which track and bill customers as they take what they want from the shelves. Other jobs similarly affected include laundry and farm workers, who have lost 15 per cent or more jobs over the same period.

The ONS also reports that women are more likely to lose out from automation than men, with a higher proportion of roles currently filled by women being at risk. In 2017, 70.2 per cent of high-risk jobs were held by women. Other groups most affected include young adults on entry-level and insecure jobs which can be easily computerised, and anyone whose education falls short of the higher levels. By contrast, higher levels of education generally protect workers from automation, with only 1.2 per cent of jobs in the UK held by those who had been through higher education or university being at risk, against 39 per cent of those jobs held by people with lower education levels.

Whilst the figures suggest something less than the total wipe-out of jobs by automation across the working spectrum anticipated by some, there remains, therefore, a no-less-troubling picture of already vulnerable people threatened with losing whatever tenuous position in the economy they retain; and more than that, as Carr writes, losing a vital part of their being along with it:

The choices we make, or fail to make, about which tasks we hand off to computers and which we keep for ourselves are not just practical or economic choices. *They're ethical choices* [emphasis added]. They shape the substance of our lives and the place we make for ourselves in the world. Automation confronts us with the most important question of all: What does *human being* mean?[36]

Chapter 12

Selves online

Together with the other two major, computer-based technologies of the era – automation and AI – the Internet completes a technological triumvirate, the combined personal, social and cultural impacts of which are reshaping the modern self-field. Reaching into all areas of public and private life, the latter technology in particular has been undergoing a sharp reappraisal lately concerning the possibilities of new forms of social organisation and individual participation in the democratic process that unrestricted access to the Net once held out – and still does for many users around the world. Post the non-materialisation of the promised democratic revolution, however, plus the revelations detailing the theft and exploitation of personal data by corrupt and powerful interests to purposefully *subvert* the democratic process, and we enter a whole new and far more dangerous world in which the individual human self now struggles for survival.

The following three chapters examine the transformative impacts of the Net on its users and society at large, and what they bode for the future evolution of the self-field. While the growth of the Net, like its other two computer-based partners, has a momentum of its own, the narcissistic tendencies and other negative psychosocial symptoms fuelled by social media, also have their roots in a wider failure of modern societies to provide for and sustain a secure and fulfilling social and cultural milieu, in which the human self can grow and prosper. Similarly, what has now been exposed – contrary to former hopes for the new media – as a *concentration* of corporate and political power within the Net, would not have been possible were it not for the historical accumulation of power by previous similar groups and interests, and which is now driven by computerised economic and financial systems that even the most powerful groups themselves can no longer control.

Cultivating the narcissistic personality

In the same period that Marshall McLuhan[1] issued his proclamation of the cultural impact of mass-media in the new epoch, other social critics of American culture took the growing signs of personal narcissism amongst the population as proof of the post-war collapse of community life in the face of rampant individualism, but saw no direct connection between the two phenomena.

Christopher Lasch, however, author of *The Culture of Narcissism*,[2] saw things differently. Pointing the finger instead at the contemporary 'awareness movement' in America, Lasch interprets the same development as a reverse process of increasing *dependency* of the individual on bureaucratic and therapeutic systems of support – a situation encouraged and ripe for exploitation by organised political and economic forces. In actual fact, he writes: 'the cult of intimacy originates not in the assertion of personality *but in its collapse* [emphasis added]'.[3] Accordingly, he argues that, for many people, the therapy industry, as it may be called, has displaced religion and former systems of belief in the provision of psychic support:

> The contemporary climate is therapeutic, not religious. People today hunger not for personal salvation, let alone for the restoration of an earlier golden age, but for the feeling, the momentary illusion, of personal well-being, health, and psychic security.[4]

Quoting Susan Stern's memoir of her experience with the militant Weathermen group in America, Lasch contends that, for many individuals like Stern, the radical politics of the 1960s served mainly as a vehicle for filling 'empty lives' and providing an otherwise missing sense of purpose. Describing her reaction to the demonstrations at the 1968 Democratic National Convention in Chicago, Stern wrote not about the purpose of the demonstrations themselves nor about the political implications of the city's oppressive and violent response, but only about her personal feelings: 'I felt real', and 'I felt I was part of a vast network of intense, exciting and brilliant people',[5] and so forth. Unlike the genuine political activist committed to social change, Lasch argues, Stern's trivialisation of political conflict and dependence upon others for a sense of selfhood, typifies the void at the heart of American society: 'She needed to *establish an identity* [emphasis added], not to submerge her identity in a larger cause'.[6] Moreover, while the Weathermen may have suited Stern's personal needs at the time, Lasch suggests the group, with its own preoccupations with drugs, sex and violence and general moral and psychic confusion, was also just as much a product of those uncertain times as Stern herself. Far from the revolutionary movement it purported to be, it offered no constructive response at all to America's social and political ills.[7]

Lasch's analysis of the narcissistic personality is significant, not only for what it tells us of the condition of American culture in the turbulent 1960s and 1970s, but also for what it reveals to us of the social and psychological origins of the self-absorbed personality in the age of the Internet.[8] As deep as the effects the Net has since had upon individual lives, the prevailing culture in America (and other countries in the West), as Lasch describes it, provided fertile ground for the technological nourishment of those same social and psychological disorders he diagnosed. Like McLuhan, who understood before anyone else the potential impact the mass-media of the 'electric age' could have upon established ways of life and thought, Lasch perceived in 'the mechanical reproduction of culture' in his own time, ample breeding grounds for the budding narcissist:

> Modern life is so thoroughly mediated by electronic images that we cannot help responding to others as if their actions – and our own – were being recorded and reproduced by means of photography, motion pictures, television, and sophisticated recording devices.[9]

Bidirectional media

However, as Nicholas Carr[10] points out, there is one very important, if obvious, difference between the electronic mass-media McLuhan and Lasch wrote about, which could only be *received* by their consumers, and the later Internet, which is *bidirectional*, transforming the nature and possible extent of personal engagement:

> The ability to exchange information online, to upload as well as download, has turned the Net into a thoroughfare for business and commerce [...] But the Net doesn't just connect us with businesses; it connects us with one another. *It's a personal broadcast system as well as a commercial one* [emphasis added].[11]

What even the earliest and most perceptive media analysts could not foresee, though, was the extent to which the two functions or aspects of the Internet – the commercial and the personal – would quickly merge, to the point where they are now virtually indistinguishable, the social and political consequences of which are only now being grasped. Inspired by McLuhan's dictum, 'the medium is the message', in her 1984 pioneering study, *Mind and Media*,[12] Patricia Greenfield presents a broadly optimistic study of how television, video games and personal computers can be employed to promote cognitive skills and social growth, punctuated by reports of possible negative influences and effects, amongst which the thorny issue of the aggressive themes of most games is only briefly covered. For Greenfield, the primary appeal of video games, the violent content of which she argued was 'certainly not a necessary feature', lay in the possibilities for *personal interaction* with the media and the challenge of forms of cognitive complexity not available with conventional games.

Reviewing the original work in her introduction to the 2014 edition, Greenfield claims her arguments for the cognitive benefits of video games have since been vindicated by further research and the widespread use of such games in training programmes. She concedes, however, that far greater attention has also since been given by researchers to the *social effects* of gaming over the cognitive effects. This she attributes largely 'to the influence of television research, where violence and aggression (the dangers) have always garnered much more attention than cognitive skills (benefits)'.[13] Affirming the value of her original research, she writes that, for all the technological advances and increases in the complexity of games since those early years: 'the issues concerning cognitive and social development have not changed'.[14] Greenfield and her colleagues have also since moved on themselves and focus their attention now on the newer social media, where she observes that things are more problematic:

> Our most recent research in this domain has revealed a social cost to the astronomical rise is screen use and screen-based communication. We have found that only in-person interaction – not electronic communication – can maximize the development of social skills and the experience of bonding with friends.[15]

Hooked on the Internet

However, while acknowledging the aggressive content of video games and more recent issues of the excessive time spent on social media against actual personal contact, Greenfield makes no mention at all in her introduction to the new edition of the growing problem of video game *addiction*. Contrary to Greenfield's claim that the developmental issues concerning video games 'have not changed', the subject now commands the attention of researchers and mental health organisations around the world.[16]

The problem – a form of *behavioural* addiction distinct from those involving drugs or other substances – is important, both for the sheer scale of the problem itself and for the fact that, like the AI industry it closely parallels, computer-based gaming is supported by a technologically advanced and rapidly growing global industry, the human cost of which has been grossly underestimated. Mark Griffiths et al.[17] recount that, while the first commercial video games were released in the early 1970s, it was another decade before the first article specifically referring to 'video game addiction' was published – just a year before Greenfield's book. Since then, however, there has been a steady flow of studies and articles on the subject, the content and methodology of which has changed significantly along with the growing popularity and sophistication of the games, as the technological media upon which they are played has evolved. Where the earliest studies were all focused on 'pay-to-play' video arcade games and were mostly based on a mixture of researchers' and players' own observations of their behaviour, the 1990s saw researchers switch to game playing on home consoles and PCs and the use of self-reporting methods adapted from studies of pathological gambling. The difficulty with that approach, Griffith et al argue, is that, while 'there are clearly many similarities between gambling and video gaming, they are different behaviors and specific video game screening instruments should have been developed'.[18]

The availability of the Internet and the possibilities it offered for online gaming between many players was accompanied, in the 2000s, by a sharp rise in the number of studies of gaming addiction, many of which were carried out in the UK and focused on 'Massively Multiplayer Online Role-playing Games', or MMOROGs, the awkward name given to games involving networks of players spread across the Net. The development saw an equally sharp change in the way research data was collected, much of which was obtained directly online.[19] However, as wide ranging as these studies are, their findings are far from conclusive. Unsurprisingly, given the aggressive content of so many games, the literature indicates that adolescent males and young male adults are at greater risk of addictive symptoms than females or other groups – especially male university students who, as well as enjoying flexible timetables, have unlimited access to high-speed broadband.[20]

Psychosocial consequences

While the full extent of addiction amongst different groups of the population is unclear, a large number of studies referenced by the authors confirm the negative effects of excessive video game playing amongst identified sufferers can be severe, covering a frightening range of psychosocial consequences, including:

> […] sacrificing work, education, hobbies, socializing, time with partner/ family, and sleep, increased stress, an absence of real-life relationships, lower psychosocial well-being and loneliness, poorer social skills, decreased academic achievement, increased inattention, aggressive/oppositional behavior and hostility, maladaptive coping, decreases in verbal memory performance, maladaptive cognitions, and suicidal ideation.[21]

Other studies link video game addiction to specific *personality traits*, amongst which Griffith et al. also list: neuroticism; aggression and hostility; avoidant and schizoid interpersonal tendencies; loneliness and introversion; anxiety, social inhibition, and last, but not least, narcissism. While few if any of the symptoms in these lists are exclusive to video game addicts – many would certainly be shared by gambling addicts and a good sample of the listed physical effects are suffered by countless sedentary office workers – the association of so many harmful symptoms with a specific and increasingly popular activity around the world is cause for alarm.

Games designed to keep players playing

A follow-up review of the research on gaming addiction by Daria Kuss,[22] a co-author of the former review, spotlights those forms of addiction specifically involving MMOROGs, which he distinguishes from other Massively Multiplayer Online games (MMOs) that do not involve role-playing.[23]

According to Kuss, in 2012, over a billion individuals around the world played computer games of one kind or another on the Net, powering an 8 per cent growth in the computer gaming industry over the same year, of which by far the most popular and studied of games by researchers are the MMOROGs. They are the most popular of games – as many as 46 per cent of all online gamers play MMOROGs – and potentially the most addictive, he argues, because they offer a wider range of incentives to play than other games do, and, most importantly, incentives to *keep on playing*. MMOROGs like the highly successful *World of Warcraft* (WoW), are 'game universes' played by thousands of online players at the same time, unrestricted by spatial or temporal boundaries. The ability of individual players to tailor their online personas and roles to the game through their *avatars* – essentially virtual selves, the physical as well as behavioural characteristics of which players can manipulate according to taste[24] – is also a major part of their attraction. WoW, for example, creates a 'fantasy world of Azeroth' populated by members (players in their virtual guises) of the opposing factions of the 'Alliance' and the 'Horde'. In 2013, Kuss notes, as many as eight million players immersed themselves in the Azeroth world and its warring factions, proving the game's mass appeal.

Gaming motivations

Such games satisfy various motivations, headed by a sense of *achievement*, participation in an online *social environment*, and the satisfaction that comes from personal *immersion* in a challenging task. Each of these primary motivations, Kuss explains, covers a number of other motivating factors, which together offer a variety of different ways individual players may gain satisfaction. The sense of achievement, for example, includes progressing in the game via different levels of play, the acquisition of power and status from competing with others, plus the bonus of the reputation and admiration that gravitates to successful players from the gaming community itself. The latter factor could also be described under the second, social motivation, along with chatting online and forming new friendships and other relationships in the game, together with the satisfaction of working in a team. All of which, the research suggests, creates an especially important motivation for gamers, not least for the way such factors *blur the boundaries* between *real* and *virtual* social networks. The third kind of motivation, the experience of immersion, is driven by a desire to explore new worlds and roles through players' customised avatars – often radically different from their real-life personas – which might appear to be positive factors, but which may also involve forms of *escapism*, effectively playing, consciously or not, to avoid real life (see below).

Taken altogether, Kuss observes, the mass appeal of MMORPGs rests on their versatility because they are tailored to gamers young and old, male and female, who have different game preferences. The same factors, he suggests, may be at least partially responsible for the accumulating research suggesting that

MMORPGs are more addictive than any other types of games, either online or offline, because of the way players are *regularly rewarded* during the course of play, encouraging them to continue playing.[25]

Escapist motivations

The simulated environment of the game itself also creates its own context which can influence whether an individual's excessive gaming habits can tip over into genuine addiction. In one of his own studies into what playing a popular game like WoW can tell us about gaming addiction, Kuss interviewed eleven WoW players, the majority of whom were typically young adult males. Significantly, Kuss found that potential gaming addiction was associated with escapist motivations, in turn suggesting that, dependent upon personal circumstances and the structure and contents of the chosen game, *online playing fulfilled a 'narcotic' function*, similar to other forms of addiction. In one case, some particular features of WoW held a special attraction for the player, enabling him to 'enact heroic tales' through his avatar and membership of the Horde, the highlight of which was his participation in killing the king of the opposing Alliance, an experience that the player said he would remember for the rest of his life. Moreover, having recently 'physically migrated' to another country, where he continued playing the game, the social structure of WoW enabled him to mentally return to a familiar environment still inhabited by his original fellow countrymen. In this way, Kuss observes, the structure and provisions of the game, which encourage a sense of *belonging to a community* – both the simulated one within the game and the community of players themselves – left the player feeling *dependent* upon his alternative life on the Net.

Similarly, at the *cultural level* of online game playing, where researchers investigate what games like WoW offer players in the formation of communities and cultures, the individual's potentially addictive game playing is examined within an anthropological framework of players' shared beliefs and practices. One such study, Kuss reports, suggests problematic and addictive gaming can occur when players' success in gaming serves to compensate for a *lack of success* in real life, and in which online social relationships via players' avatars acquire increasing significance over offline relationships – a potentially dangerous situation, he writes, 'because association of the self with the game and the avatar could lead to dissociation' from social life in the real world.[26]

Specific methods designers use

Such studies present a disturbing picture of the emergence of a new therapeutic industry in the age of the Net, the personal and social impacts of which make earlier versions of the sort Lasch describes look relatively harmless. Nor is it any accident that online games, especially MMORPGs, exert such a hold over their players. As Ciaran O'Connor,[27] a psychotherapist who has worked with game designers themselves as well as problem gamers writes: 'Games are designed to be fun and engaging; it should be no surprise that they have particular methods for achieving this'.[28] Like Kuss, O'Connor identifies online role-playing games like WoW as being the most 'likely to spark addiction in a gamer', closely followed by online 'shooters' like 'Call of Duty' and 'real-time strategy' games such as the 'Command and Conquer' series, all of which embody the crucial – and potentially addictive – social dimensions of shared digital worlds and communities of like-minded enthusiasts. However, unlike Kuss and other academic researchers on the subject who focus their attention exclusively on the players, O'Connor's personal experience in the gaming industry as well as being a counsellor for problem players, enables him to offer a more critical perspective on the industry's own responsibilities in these matters:

> There are in my experience as a game designer, plenty of freemium development studios out there that don't give due consideration to addiction and, generally unwittingly but sometimes very deliberately, many studios that actually aim to twist the lives of their users until every waking hour and every dollar they earn is poured into the game.[29]

Moreover, O'Connor's insider's knowledge of the industry enables him to go further than other researchers in pinpointing the specific methods used to keep gamers in their seats. He identifies three particular design features of successful online games '*that unfairly angle games* [emphasis added] towards addicting their players',[30] which players should be wary of: firstly, games that rely upon *rewarding* players as their main method of entertainment; secondly, games that require players' attention for *more than an hour* at a time, and thirdly, games that have *no definite end*. For the first, O'Connor suggests that if a player finds he or she is more attracted by the *gratification* that comes with being rewarded than by the nature of the actual rewards themselves – whether of a material or other kind – then they are in danger of falling into 'a notoriously addictive trap' and should look for games with other attractions. For the second, he advises players to beware of online games with built-in *social commitments* that compel players to keep playing for long hours - for fear of letting the team down if they quit the game early, for example - before the task or quest is successfully completed. Lastly, he warns that 'nearly every game that has been played addictively' is of the 'endless' type, ideally – from the designer's viewpoint – where players compete against or alongside other players with minimal need for new resources. It is for this reason, O'Connor observes, that online social games, where the main incentives to keep playing are provided by *other players*, 'are so much more addictive than offline ones'.[31]

To be fair, in addition to advising players on how to avoid games with addictive features, he also advises game designers on how to create less potentially harmful games, naming a few examples of such games on the market. There can be little doubt though, from the repeated observations by O'Connor and other researchers, that addictive gaming is a *social* as well as an individual problem, which often involves individual players' attempted escape from a difficult and painful life into a virtual world, where they find, if only temporarily, the support and affirmation they fail to find in the real world. As O'Connor writes in the concluding chapter to his perceptive and compassionate work:

> When a soul perceives a threat to its essence, such as lasting pain, the dread of depression or the sense of being useless or unlovable, it will often turn to a pleasurable, affirming or engulfing behavior in order to feel safe.[32]

The networked self

As widespread and potentially harmful as online gaming is, it is only one aspect of many now well documented uses and abuses of the Net, amounting to a digital tsunami threatening to overwhelm the integrity and stability of the modern self-field, together with the democratic culture that until now has supported and maintained that field. In the prologue to his 1996 work, *The Rise of the Network Society*, Manuel Castells[33] asserts the paramount importance of the ongoing technological revolution in reshaping the material basis of modern society, the outcome of which, he writes, is a desperate human search for identity: 'In a world of global flows of wealth, power, and images, the search for identity, collective or individual, ascribed or constructed, becomes the fundamental source of social meaning'.[34] While the significance of identity – especially ethnic and religious identity – has always been a basic feature of human society, he argues that the current disintegration of historically based human organisations and institutions, together with the weakening of formerly strong social movements – an evolution in which the Net has played a major, if not an exclusive role – has meant that people increasingly shape the meaning of their lives, not around *what they do*, but along other lines, based upon what *kind of person* they are, 'or believe they are'. The net result is that: '*Our societies are increasingly structured around a bipolar opposition between the Net and the Self*'.[35]

Growth of social media

However, it was not until the advent of founder Tim Berners-Lee's Web 2.0 shortly after the turn of the millennium, that the Net evolved into a fully fledged, two-way interactive medium for social networking. Up until that point, as the historian of social media, Jose van Dijck,[36] recounts, the Net offered mostly services that people could either just utilise themselves or employ to build their own social or commercial groups of users, but the service itself did not automatically connect users with anyone else. That all changed with Web 2.0 and the graduation to full, automated connectivity, spawning a host of now familiar, purpose-designed social media, the major names of which, like

Facebook, Twitter and YouTube rapidly overtook gaming as the most popular online activity, and, as van Dijck writes, as a vital factor influencing the self-field: 'Social media platforms have unquestionably altered the nature of private and public communication'.[37]

Initially, though, things looked different. Like the telephone and other new communications technologies and infrastructures that have generated their own social and cultural practices, the new online services were perceived optimistically as offering fresh and seemingly unlimited possibilities for personal and social interaction anywhere in the world: 'a vast unexplored territory, where boundaries between different mediated activities had yet to be demarcated'.[38] Accepting those possibilities at face value, the same counterculture Lasch describes above welcomed the Net for what it promised of new forms of direct action and self-government free of control from other powers. The dream, however, was short-lived:

> The period when users purportedly helped construct a new public space, outside corporate control, only lasted a few years, however. Commercial developers like Google, AOL, and Amazon, at the turn of the millennium, incorporated the Web 1.0 and, virtually overnight, replaced dot.com-munism by dot.commercialism.[39]

As Web 2.0 developed as a *functional* infrastructure, offering programmed services with specific objectives, the character and purpose of the Internet also changed radically, which Dijck likens to changing from water delivered via pipes to selling bottled water. Rather than simply channelling casual social activities, the new social media platforms operated more like *applied services*, each with its own rules and communicative techniques for formalising and structuring social interaction. All of this makes using the Net *easier* while at the same time *reducing the control* individuals have over their communications, and ultimately, their accessibility and value in the public domain – a development, as Castells anticipated, with far-reaching consequences for the integrity of the self.

Promoting the self

As the best-known example of how social media platforms have evolved along these lines, Facebook offers a classic example of the growth and power of social media in shaping human relationships. A key feature of Facebook's strategy, van Dijck argues, is 'promoting the self as the center of an extensive network of friends'.[40] As good as it sounds, the description is misleading. As Facebook has grown, the very definition of 'friendship' has undergone a concomitant, Orwellian development, where both strong social ties – meaning those based on real life friendships - and weak ties, which are not, are all counted together indiscriminately. 'Friending', as it is called – or building up as many online 'friends' as possible – has thus become *the* primary measure of popularity for the so-called 'selfie' generation, who, it would seem, have generally leapt at the chance of sharing as much of their personal daily lives with as many others as they possibly can. Beginning with ad hoc collections of text, photos and videos, 'Likes' and other personal responses to online posts, the introduction by Facebook in 2011 of their new compulsory format 'Timeline', Dijk explains, marked a major transformation in how all this personal data was structured. Once opened, every single piece of data that a user had already uploaded onto Facebook was *automatically* transferred onto Timeline's format, which organises an individual's records *in sequence* according to the date the item was added. As well as reorganising existing personal data, Timeline prompts users to add *more* personal photographs and other records from their past to enhance the biographical character of their page. In so doing, Dijk observes, Facebook's new format *changes the meaning* of those records, from a fragmented collection of personal events and souvenirs, to the creation of a *virtual narrative* of an individual life.

While many users welcomed the further memories and associated feelings that came with the new structure – much as we do when we peruse old photo albums – others were more doubtful about making so much personal information available online. And with good reason. Prior to the advent of Timeline, Facebook users had been free to choose between making their personal data available to 'friends only', or to go 'public'. However, in switching to the new format, Dijck writes; 'every formerly inserted piece of data *was set by default to "public"* [emphasis added] even if you had previously set it to "friends only"'.[41] Users had a mere *seven days* grace to decide whether or not to reset the privacy settings for any particular item for accessibility by friends, a wider circle or by the general public – a laborious process he suggests a large number of users were unlikely to be bothered with, delivering a bonanza of additional personal data to Facebook to make use of for whatever purposes its owners chose. 'With the introduction of Timeline', Dijk writes, 'Facebook has crept deeper into the texture of life, its narrative principles imitating proven conventions of story telling, thus binding users even more tightly to the fabric that keeps it connected'.[42]

Chapter 13

Transformations

What the exponential rise in the use of social media described in the previous chapter amounts to, as van Dijck and other writers cited in this book reveal, is not so much a reinforcement or even a meaningful extension of the self, but a *transformation* of the social relationships upon which a person depends for affirmation of their worth. Just as the cultivation of the narcissistic personality in Lasch's America represented a *weakness* rather than a strength of the individual's position in society, so does the new social media expose the fragility of the self in the age of the Internet, dependent more than ever upon technology's props for survival in an artificial and precarious world.

Over and above the disproportionate amount of time individuals of all ages now spend online relative to direct personal and social contact, there is a growing concern about the diminution and possible loss of the *reading culture* that has nourished the critical and imaginative minds vital to modern democracies in an interconnected world of different cultures and mindsets. In its place, personal and immediate access to multiple sources of information all at the same time has led to a drastic shortening of attention spans and the addictive use of social media and search engines as severe as any such behaviours associated with online gaming. Concerned observers warn of a severe deterioration of social skills and relationships and a general 'dumbing down' of modern life and thought, and even of a reconfiguration of the human brain itself – a situation ripe for exploitation by any individuals or organisations mindful only of pursuing their own interests, at whatever cost to anyone else's.

Turning points

It is a condition that Sherry Turkle, a prominent clinical psychologist and researcher at MIT, describes in her book, *Alone Together,*[1] as one of the many human costs people pay for spending so much of their time on the Net, at the price of deeper, face-to-face relationships. As the author of two earlier and influential studies of the impact of computer-based technologies on personal and social behaviour,[2] Turkle had previously documented what she interprets as significant turning points in their development and human effects – developments she finds have taken another, and worsening turn:

> I feel witness for a third time to a turning point in our expectations of technology and ourselves. We bend to the inanimate with new solicitude. We fear the risks and disappointments of relationships with our fellow humans. We expect more from technology and less from each other.[3]

Nomadic cyborgs

The scene that Turkle paints is of a majority of the population in her country *permanently* linked – or 'tethered' as she describes it – to the Net, unable, even if they wanted to, to detach themselves from what has become as much a part of themselves as any normal body part. Taking a markedly more critical view than Clark on the subject as discussed above, she describes how, in 1996, a group of young researchers at MIT proudly presented themselves as nascent 'cyborgs', bedecked with portable computers, radio transmitters and keyboards stuffed into backpacks and pockets, plus such technological exotica of the time as digital displays clipped onto eyeglass frames – mostly devices, in fact, that smartphones and a globally accessible Net were soon to make redundant.

While faculty supporters generally interpreted the group's adoption of their cyborg personas as no more than an accommodation to an increasingly complex information environment in which they now lived, Turkle heard a story of a different kind from the group's members, summed up by: 'They felt like new selves'. Proud of his hi-tech kit, one normally shy but reborn individual boasted that he now felt 'invincible, sociable, better prepared. I am naked without it. With it, *I'm a better person* [emphasis added]'.[4] Together with the would-be cyborgs' sense of empowerment, however, Turkle detected nomadic feelings of diffusion; of a 'wandering in and out' of the physically real, for what was tangibly real was now only part of their daily experience:

> The multiplicity of worlds before them set them apart; they could be with you, but they were always somewhere else as well. Within a decade, what had seemed alien was close to becoming everyone's way of life [...] This is the experience of living full-time on the Net, newly free in some ways, newly yoked in others. We are all cyborgs now.[5]

Perpetual connectivity

Based upon her extensive field research and clinical studies, as well as her personal observations, Turkle provides fresh insights into the different experiences individuals of all ages have in their exchanges with the digital and automated world, from the seductive interactions of adults and children with so-called 'sociable robots', to which she devotes the first half of her book, to compulsive texters and Net users. For example, every student in a 2008 American public high school study cited by Turkle, regardless of cultural and economic background, possessed a cell phone supporting texting, while most students also had smartphones they could use to access the Net. Another 2010 American study she quotes reports that, on average, teenagers send over 3,000 text messages each a month. What she documents in her book, Turkle observes, is no less than 'the future unfolding'.

Turkle is nevertheless quick to stress that, for the most part we have all been willing participants in what – on the surface at least – was both presented and broadly accepted as a liberating development. Parents and children alike feel more secure in being able to keep in touch at all times, while they have transformed the way business, education, scholarship, medicine, travel and even dating are done. Not least, global connectivity can turn the most isolated place into a focus of learning or economic activity.

For the young, in particular, she writes, connectivity offers new possibilities for experimenting with their identity and exploring new social spaces, an exploration they can continue through their adult life via the Net. However, it is also in just such matters that, psychologically and socially, things get more complicated:

> When part of your life is lived in virtual spaces […] a vexed relationship develops between what is true and what is 'true here,' true in simulation. In games where we expect to play an avatar, we end up being ourselves in the most revealing ways; on social-networking sites such as Facebook, we think we will be presenting ourselves, but our profile ends up as someone else – often the fantasy of who we want to be. Distinctions blur. *Virtual spaces offer connection with uncertain claims to commitment* [emphasis added].[6]

We might all be sharing cyberspace, Turkle suggests, but not much else. Social network users would not expect, for example, their 'cyberfriends' to drop by to celebrate their children's successes or to help them through the death of their parents, or any other truly personal event. Everyone knows this, yet the emotional commitment to cyberspace is high and never ending. People are constantly checking their emails, whether alone or in the company of others, as though searching for something or somebody that their lives have thus far failed to deliver.

Disconnection from surroundings

Not only does all this obsessive activity on the Net reduce the actual time spent in direct, 'messy' engagement with others, but it can *disconnect* people from whatever concrete spatial and social surroundings they may be in when they are on their phones: 'A "place" used to comprise a physical space and the people within it. What is a place if those who are physically present have their attention on the absent?'[7]

Of more concern still – at least to those like Turkle (and your author), who grew up in and fondly recall a different time when travelling to new places actually *meant* leaving one's familiar abode and personal circle behind, at least temporarily, to focus on the new place and its people – current travellers she divines, never really leave their networked habitats behind them. Nor do they wish to. She recalls the time she took her daughter Rebecca for a holiday in Paris and noted she was frequently talking on her mobile phone to her friends back in Boston, where they lived. Concerned that Rebecca was not getting the most from her holiday abroad in one of the world's great cities, Turkle gently suggested that she might get more out of her experience of Paris if she was not being constantly reminded of her life in Boston. Not appearing to understand her mother's point, her daughter simply replied that she *liked* being in touch with her friends back home.

Treating people as objects

The generational difference in a mother and daughter's experience of the same city, though not altogether unexpected as generational differences go, served to focus Turkle's mind, not only on how often the colleagues she worked with, whether glued to their phones at board meetings or conferences, 'were elsewhere as well', but also how many people out on the streets of Boston were seemingly oblivious to everything else around them except their phones. While the phenomenon is now widespread amongst all ages, the obsessive need for constant contact with someone – anyone it seems, so long as they are somewhere *else* – is most apparent in the behaviour of the young. Turkle describes the case of Ricki, a fifteen-year-old student at a private school for girls in New York, who treats her contact list on her phone 'like a list of "spare parts" for her fragile adolescent self'.[8] In answer to Turkle's query as to what she means when she says 'get it' if a contact is slow in answering her call, Ricki explained it meant not only 'pick up', but 'get me' – a response suggestive to Turkle of more of a narcissistic *dependency* on her contacts to validate her thoughts and feelings of the moment, than simple teenage impatience.

However, like Lasch and the researchers into online gaming addiction discussed above, who describe the weakness of personalities dependent upon imagined sources of support they fail to find elsewhere in their lives, Turkle argues that narcissism is not so much about people who love themselves, as about fragile personalities in need of constant affirmation, but who cannot handle the complex demands made upon them by real-life, difficult individuals. Consequently, they choose instead to keep their 'friends' at a safe distance, where they can pick and choose who or what they need at any moment and feel comfortable with:

So, the narcissistic self gets on with others by dealing only with their made-to-measure representations. These representations (some analytic traditions refer to them as 'part objects', others as 'self-objects') are all that the fragile self can handle [...] In a life of texting and messaging, those on that contact list can be made to appear almost on demand. You can take what you need and move on. And if not gratified, you can try someone else.[9]

Filling in the gaps

In explanation of the apparent willingness of so many people to suspend any disbelief in the artificial worlds and relationships they give themselves up to, Turkle recalls her own experience in the mid-1970s as one of a number of students at MIT using ELIZA, a program designed by the AI pioneer Joseph Weizenbaum to simulate a dialogue with a psychotherapist – her first encounter with a program that 'offered companionship'. Students would type in a thought expressing some anxiety or other about their relationships with family or friends, to which the program would respond 'sympathetically', requiring clarification of the problem. Turkle points out that Weizenbaum's students clearly *knew* the program did *not* in fact understand them, but nevertheless pursued the dialogue, eager for a response:

> More than this, they wanted to be alone with it. They wanted to tell it their secrets. Faced with a program that makes the smallest gesture suggesting it can empathize, people want to say something else.[10]

In their eagerness to be understood, even by a limited off-line program like ELIZA, Turkle deduced that, by willingly 'filling in the blanks' left by the program's inadequacies, *the students were themselves complicit* in the deception – a factor she underestimated at the time, but now perceives as an existential threat to the human self: 'We seem determined to give human qualities to objects and content to treat each other as things'.[11]

Cultural shift

Like Turkle, Maryanne Wolf, a celebrated cognitive neuroscientist and author of two books on the evolution of the reading brain, is deeply concerned about the negative impacts of digital technologies on a former bedrock of human society and culture. While reading books might not, at first, seem connected with the problems of understanding others in real life, Wolf contends they are intimately related activities and skills. Describing the transformative power of the written word in the first of her books, *Proust and the Squid*,[12] Wolf adopts the writer Marcel Proust's metaphor for reading as an 'intellectual sanctuary' and doorway onto countless other real or imagined worlds the reader might not otherwise experience. The very act of readers yielding themselves up into those other worlds and realities, Wolf argues, involves a personal process of empathy with the characters in the book they are reading and their perspectives – the kind of *real* empathy that requires the acceptance of other possible worlds and views – without which readers can have little or no understanding of what is going on within the pages.

Similarly, Wolf finds analogies between what neuroscientists first learned from the remarkable squid in the 1950s about the way neurons fire and connect with each other and their 'clever ways of adapting when things go wrong',[13] as well as current investigations into how various cognitive processes work in the brain. Amongst those investigations, research on the process of reading 'offers an example par excellence of a recently acquired cultural invention that requires *something new from existing structures in the brain* [emphasis added]'.[14] Outlining the research in terms similar to those employed by other writers quoted in this book on combinatorial processes of innovation and neural plasticity, Wolf explains that:

> Underlying the brain's ability to learn reading lies its protean capacity to make *new* connections among structures and circuits originally devoted to other more basic brain processes that have enjoyed a longer existence in human evolution, such as vision and spoken language. We now know that groups of neurons create *new connections and pathways* [emphasis added] amongst themselves every time we acquire a new skill.[15]

Learning to read a new language, for example Chinese, involves using a different set of neuronal connections than those used in reading English, and vice versa. When Chinese readers first try reading in English, their brains automatically attempt to use the same neuronal pathways they acquired in learning their own, very different language script, before they adapted to the new language: 'The act of learning to read Chinese characters has literally shaped the Chinese reading brain'.[16]

From oral to writing cultures

Pursuing the same story of intellectual and biological development, Wolf traces the history of writing and the reading brain from early pictographic writing systems, the characters of which built upon the visual system's *pre-existing ability* to recognise the objects they represented, through the evolution of more abstract symbols which directly convey concepts formulated in spoken language. So, instead of visual objects, written words increasingly came to mimic *sounds* – a further cognitive evolution which Wolf speculates would have necessitated a 'criss-crossing' of neural circuits located in different parts of the brain dealing with the formerly separate, but now integrated, visual, oral and linguistic functions involved.

The development and consequent spread of the Greek alphabet and the economical writing systems we know today, which require only a minimum number of signs (twenty-six letters in many alphabets) to represent the whole repertoire of sounds in a given language, marked a decisive shift from oral culture to writing culture and left its own neural traces in a further restructuring of the reading brain.[17] Where the efficiency of the alphabet really scores, Wolf suggests, is in stimulating *novel thought*. All writing systems, even the earliest, she argues, lift the burden of *collective memory* from oral traditions, thus greatly extending the boundaries of what could be thought and recorded through time by many more people: 'By taking a meta-view of this entire history, we can see that what promotes the development of intellectual thought in human history is not the first alphabet or even the first iteration of an alphabet, *but writing itself* [emphasis added]'.[18] Citing Vygotsky on the creative act of putting unspoken thoughts as well as spoken words into writing, she observes that the process both releases and 'changes the thoughts themselves'. The more people learned to use written language and to communicate their thoughts with greater precision, the more the human capacity for abstract and novel thinking accelerated. While the alphabet is therefore not unique in its role in the development of abstract and novel thought, Wolf contends that the increased cognitive efficiency and creative potential that comes with using such an economical and easy-to-learn system – of which the Greek alphabet is a prime example – made it possible for ever more people to engage in novel thought at earlier stages of the novice reader's development:

> This then, marks the revolution in our intellectual history: the beginning of the democratization of the young reading brain. Within such a broadened context, there can be no surprise that one of the most profound and prolific periods of writing, art, philosophy, theatre, and science in all of previous recorded history accompanied the spread of the Greek alphabet.[19]

The threat to critical thinking

Much to Wolf's consternation, however, by the time she completed her history of the reading brain and its significance in the evolution of human thought and culture, she came to realise that the literate society and culture she eulogised was under threat from a new and rapidly growing culture based on the Internet. Her response was her second book, *Reader, Come Home*,[20] published a decade after the first, in which she observes that during the seven years it took her to explain the 6,000-year evolution of the reading brain, the entire literacy-based culture that nourished it was already being displaced by a wholly different, digitally based culture.

Written as a series of personal letters to her readers, in her new book she appeals to them not to forget or take for granted the profound gift of reading that literate culture offers them. Literacy, she reminds us, is an 'unnatural' product of *cultural origin* and there is no genetically based programme to ensure that young readers will always develop the neural circuits required for reading.

The remarkable plasticity of the human brain that has enabled it to adapt to and make room for learning and reading quite different languages like English and Chinese, may also, she suggests, eventually reshape the brain to accommodate entirely new systems of communication and media – and may already be doing so as the young give more of their time over to digital media and less to reading books.

Defending the transformative effects that reading bestows upon the minds of readers against what she perceives as the mounting dangers of dilution and displacement by the new media, Wolf argues that 'deep reading', as she calls it, involves forms of thought and feelings that digital media does not – or at least, not of the same level or intensity or in such rich mixtures of the kind that are stimulated when reading an engaging book. A key factor distinguishing the two forms of media and the way they are used, she explains, is the differences in what she describes as the nature or 'quality of attention' involved, a challenge, she writes, that society is only just beginning to acknowledge: 'Will the quality of our attention change as we read on mediums that advantage immediacy, dart-quick task switching, and continuous monitoring of distraction, as opposed to the more deliberative focusing of our attention?'[21]

At stake, she argues, are critical thinking and other dimensions of thought that reading more demanding texts have nourished over centuries of literary culture. Expanding on Proust's original metaphor, amongst those other dimensions she includes: the capacity to *form images* in our minds as we read evocative words and passages; *empathising* with the thoughts and feelings of the characters in a book, by which we learn to see the world as others do; the accumulation over time of the *background knowledge* we need to evaluate new information for ourselves in whatever medium it is received, and *analogical thinking and inference*, by which we are able to build upon our pre-existing knowledge in dealing with what we cannot at first understand or predict. All of which, she suggests, supports the development of critical thought one way or another, and it is just the possible loss of that vital, *integrative function* of deep reading that Wolf believes most threatens the foundations of modern society and culture.

Wolf finds support for her concerns in quoting the literary scholar Mark Edmundson's explanation of critical thinking as including the power to examine and to potentially reject *one's own* personal convictions: 'What good is this power of critical thought if you do not yourself believe something and are not open to having these beliefs modified?'[22] Edmundson warns of the threat to critical thought that comes from any powerful system of belief that is impervious to change or criticism, but sees opposite and equal dangers in the total *absence* of any strongly held beliefs amongst many young people today, who are either insufficiently informed about past systems of thought or who simply can't be bothered to learn from them. Either way, Wolf writes: 'Intellectual rudderlessness and adherence to a way of thought that allows no questions are threats to critical thinking in us all'.[23]

Rewiring the brain

Other writers have voiced similar warnings about the dangers of losing a literary culture upon which much of modern society has hitherto been built. Such warnings, as the research on neural plasticity described in the first part of this book confirms, underline the importance of *repeated practice* in retaining specific skills and modes of thought acquired in the course of life – the simple message of which boils down to, 'use it or lose it'. Carr,[24] who has followed the effects of the Net on personal and social lives as closely as he has tracked the automation of work, notes with some concern what he feels to be changes in the pattern of his own thoughts. He notices it most clearly when he is reading, of which he has done a great deal in the course of his profession. Where before he would find it easy to immerse himself in a book or lengthy article, he now finds his attention drifting after only a couple of pages: 'The deep reading that used to come naturally has become a struggle'.[25]

Carr believes he understands the problem. For well over the previous decade – his book was published in 2010 – like most other writers he took full advantage of the possibilities for online research that came with the Net as well as doing all the other things like banking, keeping up with friends and events, etc., that now come so easily to regular users. As a writer, he describes the Net as a 'godsend', saving him countless hours – though no doubt formerly pleasurable ones – hunting through libraries full of actual books and journals. The advantages are real enough, he writes, but, as McLuhan first warned us, media not only 'supply the stuff of thought, but they also *shape the process of thought* [emphasis added]'.[26]

What Carr believes the Net is doing is steadily *reducing his capacity for concentration and contemplation*, a worrying observation he finds repeated by both friends and some of the bloggers he follows. One such blogger, a former literature major and 'voracious book reader', is convinced that there is more to the Net than a simple change of content or reading style – the way he actually *thinks* has changed since becoming a regular user. Like Wolf, Carr points to the neural plasticity of the brain, the purpose of which was first thought to be confined to repairing injuries to its functions and sensory systems, but which, as noted elsewhere this book, has since been accepted as a vital property of a normal functioning brain and healthy being, enabling it to adapt to changing conditions throughout life. And if the brain can adapt so readily to other, lesser behavioural and cultural changes, it may be asked, why should it not adapt to as pervasive a technological and cultural phenomenon as the Net, though not, perhaps, in directions that we might always be happy about, or even fully conscious of?

Differences between biological and computer memory

Moreover, Carr suggests that memory – that other precious faculty we learnt about above that is such a vital element in the autobiographical development of the self – is also threatened by the very same changes in the way we think online. Quoting the work of neurobiologists on the consolidation of human memory, he attacks the whole idea of 'outsourcing' memory to the Web, suggesting that its supporters have overlooked a fundamental difference between biological and computer memory: 'Biological memory is alive. Computer memory is not'.[27] Computer memory consists of essentially static bits and pieces of information that, while they can be moved around and stored in different places, *always stay the same*. Biological memory, by contrast, is an *integral part of the developing self* and is in a constant state of renewal, changing over time even as the brain–body complex itself changes. Long-term memories that have been safely tucked away in the brain undergo an automatic process of consolidation and reassessment when recalled into short-term memory, gaining whole new sets of connections as they are 'updated' to fit in with current experience and streams of thought.

Also contrary to what is commonly thought, when comparisons are made between human and computer memory systems, while the human capacity for short-term, or 'working memory' is limited, Carr explains, such is the brain's plasticity there is virtually no limit to its ability to make room for *new* memories. The more we build up our personal stock of memories, too, the easier it becomes to learn new ideas and skills: 'We don't constrain our mental powers when we store new long-term memories. We strengthen them'.[28] Human intelligence grows along with each expansion of memory, and it is out of such continual growth that we all build up our personal stock of shared knowledge and culture, along with more personal memories, most of which remain stored away at unconscious levels in long-term memory until called forth by current events and needs. None of which, Carr argues, is replicated at all when we use the Web, which may be useful as a supplement to short-term personal memory, but offers no equivalent process of consolidation and renewal for the infinitely larger and deeper stock of memories out of which a living, cultured self is created:

> The offloading of memory to external data banks doesn't just threaten the depth and distinctiveness of the self. It threatens the depth and distinctiveness of the culture we all share.[29]

Augmented reality

Susan Greenfield, a leading British neuroscientist who has also previously documented her concerns about the effect of the new media on personal identities and social relations,[30] confirms her fears for the future well-being of the self in her more recent book, *Mind Change*.[31] Citing Goffman's work on self-images, she writes that social media like Facebook and Twitter not only now offer the widest possible opportunities for promoting the most positive images – they also now allow for distortions and exaggerations of personality of a kind individuals could never get away with so easily in direct exchanges with others. A likely outcome of those opportunities, she suggests, could be a narcissistic obsession with the self, for which social networking sites provide an ideal platform. One study she cites of over 14,000 college students, for example, found that, even before the advent of Facebook, twenty-first century students rated significantly higher on tests for narcissism when compared to students from twenty years previously. Narcissism itself, she concedes, is a complex phenomenon covering a whole range of characteristics, from exhibitionism to feelings of superiority and self-sufficiency. Nevertheless:

> The basic fact remains across different age groups and irrespective of the particular characteristics that predominate; *enthusiastic use of social networking sites is linked strongly to narcissism* [emphasis added]. Of course, human beings have always been vain, self-centred and prone to bragging, but now social networking provides the opportunity to indulge in this behaviour unabated, around the clock.[32]

However, like both Wolf and Carr, Greenfield reserves her worst fears for the progressive weakening and possible loss of critical thought previously supported by stronger literary and social cultures. Also, like Wolf, she praises novels in particular for transporting readers into other worlds peopled with unfamiliar characters we learn to understand, the key to which is the author's skilful *narrative* linking worlds and characters together in ways we can make sense of, which, in turn, helps us to make sense of our own lives and trajectories. However, minus the intellectual background of a literary, critical culture, significant parts of the human brain, she argues, are effectively being 'rewired' to better suit a fragmented and transitory digital environment, leaving individual minds ever more exposed to factual distortions and manipulation:

> Without a personalized conceptual framework that enables us to use the Internet to frame and think about open-ended and difficult questions, we run the risk of being passively driven by isolated facts as we lurch from one disconnected but amazing screen experience to another.[33]

Stepping warily into the digital future, she contemplates a continuous state of 'augmented reality' where, thanks to devices like Google Glass – a normal looking pair of spectacles which both records and presents information to the wearer via the eyeglass itself – we will all be able to summon up anything we want from the Net by a simple voice call, thus staying virtually connected every waking moment of our lives. As Greenfield notes, studies suggest the majority of smartphone users are already 'emotionally attached' to their phones, are easily 'panicked' when they misplace them and *dread* losing them – a condition that even has its own name: 'nomophobia'. Imagine, she writes, 'the type of emotional attachment we might have to intensively integrated devices that

provide more entertainment, faster answers and even more sanitised socializa-
tion, all seamlessly'.[34]

Given the common attachments to material objects noted elsewhere in this
book, that might not be as troubling to many phone users as it might appear to
more detached observers. According to Greenfield, however, users' emotional
attachment to their phones is by no means the whole story, and inventions such
as Google Glass could sound the death knell for personal privacy. In the words
of Andrew Keen, author of *Digital Vertigo*, whom Greenfield quotes in support
of her apocalyptic vision:

> *Google Glass* opens up an entirely new front in the digital war against
> privacy. These spectacles, which have been specifically designed to record
> everything we see, represent a developmental leap in the history of data
> that is comparable to moving from the bicycle to the automobile. It is
> the sort of radical transformation that may actually end up completely
> destroying our individual privacy in the digital 21st century. When we put
> on these surveillance devices, we all become spies, or scrooglers, of every-
> thing and everyone around us.[35]

Chapter 14

Loss of the private self

When Christopher Lasch, writing in his prescient work on narcissism, warned below of the growing dangers to personal privacy by unnamed but powerful 'forces', he could not have known just how far into the private self those forces might reach, aided by technologies of communication and data analysis that were then barely conceived of, let alone operating across the world:

> The socialization of the young reproduces political domination at the level of personal experience. In our own time, this invasion of private life by the forces of organized domination has become so pervasive that personal life has almost ceased to exist.[1]

However, while the technological battlefront has greatly expanded since the publication of that work and some of those forces now have familiar names like Facebook and Google, Lasch's unblinking dissection of the social and political malaise underlying the deterioration of the modern self, is as valid now in the age of the 'selfie' as it was then, in the heyday of the awareness movement and its false promises of personal intimacy.

Lasch's analysis of the social and political forces undermining the private self has also now been updated and fortified by Shoshana Zuboff, who has given the name 'surveillance capitalism' to those forces, coupled with 'Big Other' – her name for the computational infrastructure based on the Internet 'that renders, monitors, computes, and modifies human behavior',[2] with its suggestions of George Orwell's 'Big Brother'.[3] Zuboff's compelling study verifies what a shocked world first learnt in 2013 from Edward Snowden[4] – but still struggles to comprehend – that US and British intelligence agencies have full access to the personal communications and details of countless Google and social media users. More recently, the revelations by other whistleblowers of the exploitation by Cambridge Analytica, the UK-based data analytics company, of personal information obtained from millions of Facebook users' files, shows just how such information can be manipulated for specific political ends unbeknown to the individuals concerned – a disturbing story of our time to which the first half of this penultimate chapter is devoted.

A cautionary tale of the digital age

While there have been ample previous warnings cited in these pages of the dangers to the private self of overexposure on the Internet, the Cambridge Analytica case in particular, involving as it does the use of psychologists' knowledge of personality traits as well as AI techniques, casts a new and troubling light on the full extent of those dangers. Beginning in 2015 with a report in *The Guardian* newspaper that the company was using personal data 'harvested' from Facebook's American users to influence voters, the scandal exploded in March 2018 with the detailed exposé by Christopher Wylie, a Canadian-born, former key employee at Cambridge Analytica. Published simultaneously by *The Guardian* and *The New York Times* and broadcast on *Channel 4 News* in the UK, Wylie confirmed that the personal data of over 50 million Facebook users (actually many more, as it transpired) had been secretly misused explicitly for political purposes – including swaying both UK and American voters respectively in the 'Brexit' referendum on EU membership and the US Presidential election in 2016. Up until that point Facebook itself had maintained a studious silence, saying only that they were conducting their own internal investigation into the matter.

Since Wylie dropped his bombshell, however, not only has Facebook been compelled to defend its performance before British as well as American official inquiries, the scandal – a cautionary tale in itself of the digital age – focused public attention on the real or potential misuse of personal information on the Net for political or commercial purposes. More serious still is what Wylie's own published account of the Cambridge Analytica story, appropriately if crudely titled *Mindf*ck*,[5] reveals of the apparent ease with which victims' minds and decisions were manipulated, and just how vulnerable the online self now is to such forces. Recounting his testimony to the US congressional committee investigating the scandal, he writes: 'Facebook is no longer just a company, I told them. It's a doorway into the minds of the American people'.[6]

Tools of persuasion

Plainly, there have always been individuals and groups ready to exploit any weaknesses in society's safeguards to their own advantage. The vital difference in our own time is the sophistication of the technical and informational tools of persuasion now available to companies like Cambridge Analytica and their customers, which can readily access formerly private domains of the self in ways that make the fictional world of Orwell's Big Brother alluded to by Zuboff look like child's play.

In particular, Wylie shows just how effective those tools can be in the political arena, where the outcome of elections and referenda that can determine the fate of nations for years to come, often rests upon the uncertain decisions of a very small minority of voters. His story is also important for what it reveals of the lesser-known background to the public exposures, and of the motives and modus operandi of the organisations involved, which included the use of *psychological* as well as technical expertise. Significantly, as Wylie explains, albeit the most notorious case to date of its kind, Cambridge Analytica was also far from being the first organisation to exploit the Internet and social media to target and recruit individual voters.

Having mixed freely with hacker communities as a skilled teenage programmer, Wylie writes: 'as a hacker, I learned that every system has weaknesses waiting to be exploited'.[7] It was an insight, he quickly learnt, which applied to political as well as IT systems. Hired as a political and technical assistant by the Liberal Party of Canada (LPC), along with several others Wylie was sent by the party to the US to observe Barack Obama's campaign in the Democratic primaries and to bring back whatever he learned that could be used in their own campaigns. While Obama's opponents were still relying upon standard recorded advertisements, his campaign team were re-writing the rule book on election campaigns and tapping into local organisations through the Net to help get out the votes. Underlying Obama's grassroots revolution and shrewd use of the Net and social networks, however, the team had developed a far more powerful set of AI-supported campaign tools for 'microtargeting' individual voters. Aimed in particular at *swing voters* who might be persuaded to decide in their favour, they entailed searching through voter's personal data to determine how best to pitch their campaign. As Wylie recalls, the team's leader Ken Strasma was crystal clear about their goals and methods for achieving them:

> *Everything we do*, he said, *is predicated on understanding exactly who we need to talk to, and on which issues.* In other words, the backbone of the Obama campaign was data. And the most important work Strasma's team produced was the modelling they used to analyse and understand that data, which allowed them to translate it into an applied fit – to determine a real-world communications strategy through artificial intelligence.[8]

Mining the data

The secret of the Obama team's success, Wylie learnt, was a data processing infrastructure and stockpile of personal information on voters created by a company in Boston called Voter Activation Network (VAN). By the end of the 2008 campaign, the team had amassed *ten times* more personal data than they had in the primaries. Contrary, therefore, to the familiar story told in the press of Cambridge Analytica opening up a Pandora's box of informational tools for targeting individual voters, as important as their part was in the whole saga, as Wylie observes, that box had already been opened many years previous to Analytica's own actions: 'By directly communicating select messages to select voters, the microtargeting of the Obama campaign had started a journey toward the *privatisation of public discourse in America* [emphasis added]'.[9]

Psychological warfare

Having learnt all he could from the Obama campaign and successfully demonstrated a VAN-based Canadian version of that campaign to the LPC's headquarters, the party leaders nevertheless decided, for reasons Wiley does not explain, not to continue with the programme.[10]

It was a chastening experience he was soon to repeat. Having moved to London to pursue his studies at the London School of Economics and Political Science, he had been invited to work as a data analyst with the Liberal Democratic Party (LDP), who had heard of his work for the LPC through the party grape-vine, but eventually also failed to follow his recommendations. Henceforth, Wiley would work only for private companies, who, he determined, valued his talents more.

Wiley's own involvement with Cambridge Analytica began in the same period. Better known by its two American directors, Robert Mercer, the billionaire owner of a computer engineering company 'turned social engineer', and Steve Bannon, a former editor of a far-right website and future campaign director and adviser to Donald Trump, Cambridge Analytica was originally created as an off-shoot of a British company in London, Strategic Communication Laboratories, latterly called the SCL Group. By the time Mercer and Bannon arrived on the scene, however, Wiley himself had already been working for a year with SCL as a data analyst. Disappointed with his experiences with political parties, he had been happy to accept an invitation from Alexander Nix, a director at SCL, who was impressed enough with his record to give him free rein to do whatever he felt was necessary to improve the operations of the company. As Wiley quickly learnt, those operations included working for military and intelligence agencies conducting propaganda operations around the world – essentially psychological warfare, as he describes it.

Up until the formation of Cambridge Analytica, Wylie had been engaged on numerous foreign projects for SCL, whose former clients had included branches of both the British and US governments.[11] In the process, he came to think of his new work as a further development of the psychological and behavioural research he had undertaken earlier whilst trying to understand voters' behaviour, only this time he was dealing with quite different peoples and cultures. Over the same period, the rapid spread of social media around the world had transformed the whole process of data collecting, offering trails of detailed personal information that would have previously taken many months of careful observation to obtain.

Engineering social change

Whilst Wiley was working for the Lib Dems in London he also had trouble identifying the party's voters as a *group*. Compared with the other major British parties, they 'were an odd eclectic mix' and seemed to come from all levels and corners of society. Seeking help on the problem, he was put in touch with Brent Clickard, a PhD student of experimental psychology at Cambridge University, who suggested he should look into *personality traits* as factors in voting behaviour, for which he recommended the well-established, five-factor model described in the opening chapter of this book. As Wiley read the research, the approach came to him as a revelation: 'I finally realized something. Maybe the Lib Dems didn't have a geographic or demographic base; maybe they were a product of a *psychological base*'.[12]

Seeking help again in his new work for SCL, Wiley persuaded his new employers to hire Clickard as a consultant for the company. Thus, aided by Clickard and several others, Wiley tapped into the Net and local telecom companies for information on targeted individuals wherever they could. By the time he came to present their work at SCL in November 2013 to Mercer and Bannon as the company's prospective new backers, he was already running several successful projects in foreign countries on different continents. He had also had a preliminary meeting with Bannon some weeks earlier in Cambridge – a city much admired by Bannon, who subsequently named the new company after it[13] – and ran a short, 'proof of concept' study with his team in Virginia during the state-wide elections there; all of which satisfied Bannon enough to suggest that Mercer might be interested in putting serious money into their work.

Though each American, Wylie suggests, had different conceptions of what radical social change ultimately entailed – Mercer was mainly focused on controlling elections while Bannon pursued a broader cultural revolution – both recognised the potential use of SCL's work for engineering social change. Following the November meeting, a new plan of operation was agreed with SCL, backed with Mercer's money.[14] However, although Cambridge Analytica was put together with SCL as a business, as Wylie later learned, making money was never the goal of its wealthy owner, nor of Bannon, who both had other ideas:

> The firm's sole purpose was to cannibalise the Republican Party and *remould American culture* [emphasis added]. When CA launched, the Democrats were far ahead of the Republicans in using data effectively. For years, they had maintained a central data system in VAN, which any Democratic campaign in the country could tap into. The Republicans had nothing comparable. CA would close that gap.[15]

Psychological expertise

Prior to the creation of Cambridge Analytica, Clickard, who divided his time between Wylie's team at SCL and his own research in psychology at the University of Cambridge, had introduced him to Dr Aleksandr Kogan at the University's Psychometrics Centre. Kogan and his colleagues, who specialised in the computational modelling of psychological traits, had published several papers for academic journals using data from social media to piece together psychological profiles of individual users; research supported at that time by Facebook, which hoped to profit from such knowledge in increased sales of online advertising.

Following Analytica's addition to SCL's corporate armoury, by building on the research and psychological expertise of Kogan and his colleagues at Cambridge, Wylie and his team were able to short-circuit much of the ground-work they needed to do in prosecuting their own agenda: 'What Cambridge Analytica eventually became depended in large part on the academic research published at the University it was named after'.[16] The key factor, as always, was having a large enough cache of personal data to sift through in search of which individuals they should target, whether it was voters or anyone else they needed to persuade, for which Facebook had conveniently provided access to Kogan and his team for their academic work. Now Wylie and his team were about to access that knowledge too.

The variation of the original research app that Kogan eventually offered to SCL/Analytica for their use, was 'even better' than Wylie and his team had hoped for. Kogan's new app worked in concert with a survey platform or 'micro-task site' originally developed by Amazon for getting people – who were each paid a small fee for the task – to identify the content of photographs so they could develop algorithms for that special purpose. However, having acquired large lists of willing subjects, Amazon, aware of their market value, subsequently sold their lists to any other researchers also in need of large numbers of people to com-plete similar tasks, including psychologists and university researchers like Kogan and his colleagues, who used them to recruit subjects for their personality tests. Deployed together, app and paid survey platform unlocked the personal data of any Facebook users completing Analytica's own personality test, which Wylie's team devised for the purpose. As Wylie explains, it worked like this:

> A person would agree to take a test in exchange for a small payment. But in order to get paid, they would have to download Kogan's app on Facebook and input a special code. The app, in turn, would take all the responses from the survey and put those onto one table. It would then pull all of the user's Facebook data and put it into a second table. And then it would pull all the data for all the person's Facebook friends and put that onto another table.[17]

The key to the success of Kogan's app thus involved a *two-stage process for mining personal data*, part of which individual subjects were fully aware of and were paid for, albeit not much, and part of which – the access to the data held in both Facebook's members' files and that of all their online friends – they were not aware of at all: 'Using Kogan's app', Wylie writes, 'we would not only get a training set that gave us the ability to create a really good algorithm – because the data was so rich, dense and meaningful – but we also got the extra benefit of hundreds of additional friend profiles'.[18] Launched in the US in June 2014 in time for the midterm elections, Bannon watched with amazement as a demonstration of the app at SCL's London office showed the full extent of the detailed personal information the team had garnered. Picking out one American lady in Nebraska at random, they went through all their records of her data, including state bureau, US Census and commercial data they had purchased, in addition to all her Facebook data: 'We had recreated her life in our computer. She had no idea'[19] boasted Wylie.

Target groups

At the time of the demonstration Analytica had already garnered tens of millions of similar individual profiles. Just two months later, according to Wylie, they had collected the complete Facebook accounts of more than 87 million users; more than enough cases for their new algorithms to sift through and target individuals for persuasion. Flush with Mercer's funds, SCL added numerous other specialist staff, including more psychologists, data scientists, researchers and managers to work on Analytica's programs, crowding Wylie out of the main action.[20]

Under Bannon's direction as vice president, Analytica identified a substantial group of white, mostly male, individuals concerned about the growing minority vote in America, but who were wary of expressing their views openly in a country led by a President of mixed race, and were uncertain what to do about it. As a way of encouraging what was to be Analytica's main target group to express their true opinions about such matters, the firm developed 'fake pages on Facebook and other platforms that looked like real forums, groups and news sources'.[21] Operating at a local level, the fake pages on Facebook would be given titles appealing to right-wing groups, like 'I Love My Country', which Facebook's own recommendation algorithm would then pass on to any of its users who had already indicated they liked such content. Once they had joined Analytica's fake online groups, they would be showered with videos and articles, stoking further discussion and expressions of discontent, often of an extreme nature. In addition to the online fakery, Analytica also organised small but effective *real* meetings in local venues between like-minded malcontents, reinforcing their sense of *belonging to a group* that shared their grievances: 'Now CA had users who (1) self-identified as part of an extreme group, (2) were a captive audience, and (3) could be manipulated with data'.[22]

Winning tactics

By that time, however, it had dawned upon Wylie, who had started out working in politics for parties with liberal agendas, that he was involved in something altogether more threatening. Shown a 'master document of research questions' by a psychologist on the team that Analytica was now using in America, the penny finally dropped:

> We were testing how to use cognitive biases as a gateway to move people's perceptions of racial out-groups [...] In our invasion of America, we were purposefully activating the worst in people, from paranoia to racism.[23]

It was too much for Wylie, who had previously convinced himself, like others he had worked with and personally recruited in London, that the same technologies and technical skills could be put to use for the greater good. Faced with the reality of Analytica's work – work he and his team at SCL had been instrumental in making possible – in December 2014, less than a year after Bannon took over, he left the firm. Shortly before he left, Analytica also hired Brittany Kaiser, an American who had worked in London with the legal team of Julian Assange of WikiLeaks. Later appointed the firm's director of operations in the successful Brexit campaign, Leave.EU, Kaiser would, in due course, also follow Wylie's example in turning whistleblower on the company, recounting how she went on to use the same tactics and tools in that and other campaigns that Wylie and his team had so assiduously developed over the previous years with SCL.[24]

Even now, for all the revelations, it remains uncertain that Analytica's secretive operations had a decisive impact on either the US elections or the Brexit referendum in 2016. What is beyond dispute, however, is that in both cases the victors won by extremely *narrow* margins: the Democrats won the national popular vote but lost in the state caucuses, which determine the final outcome, while the Brexiters won just 52 per cent of the total UK vote, both Scotland and Northern Ireland having voted to remain by substantial majorities. While much of the reporting on the Cambridge Analytica story suggests the company targeted everyone in their campaigns, Wylie also explains that 'not that many people were targeted at all'. On the contrary, they didn't need to do more, 'because most elections are zero-sum games: if you get one more vote than the other guy or girl, you win the election'.[25] Analytica only needed to implant their own finely targeted narrative in a narrow segment of the voting population, and then sit back and watch it do its work.

As Fintan O'Toole writes in his scornful account of the Brexit referendum, *Heroic Failure*,[26] the whole argument for withdrawal was in any case based on a persistent myth. The problem the UK had with the EU was never really a British problem at all – it was always an *English* problem driven by a powerful, if misplaced, sense of national identity, fuelled in turn over previous decades by a relentless campaign of disinformation by the mostly anti-EU British press about the actual control over their lives by the EU, or 'Brussels', as they called it: 'People who identified primarily as English had a grossly exaggerated, camped up sense of the extent to which they were being governed from Brussels'.[27] And it was from this deep well of smouldering resentment, focused in particular upon fears of future tidal waves of uncontrolled immigration from other EU countries,[28] that Cambridge Analytica drew upon in its support for the Brexiters.

Selves for sale

Well before the Leave.EU and Trump election campaigns, however, the techno-logical and social culture in which Analytica spread its corrosive messages was already well established in the minds and habits of regular Net users; many of them, like Sherry Turkle's pioneering young cyborgs at MIT, happily iden-tifying with it as *their* culture. The informational framework and sources of personal data were thus already in place – if not the legal safeguards against their misuse – and ripe for exploitation by individuals and groups both skilful and ruthless enough to do so. As Joseph Turow writes in his revealing study of con-sumer profiling and advertising, *The Daily You*,[29] the same invasive techniques and strategies for psychological profiling that Wylie helped to create and use for political aims, are also regularly used on a far wider scale by media firms to help marketers of goods and services target likely customers on a daily basis with their advertisements:

> Advertisers in the digital space expect all media firms to deliver to them particular types of individuals – and, increasingly, *particular* individuals – by leveraging a detailed knowledge about them and their behaviors that was unheard of even a few years ago.[30]

While much of the new business was handled by specialist media firms, it really took off, Turow explains, with the rapid growth of Google's search engine. Unlike other so-called 'publishers',[31] which charge advertisers a fee for displaying an ad, Google only charged a fee if a person using their search engine *actually clicks on an ad* next to their search results, the logic being that the *act* of clicking on the ad is a significant indicator of that consumer's personal interests and therefore has a cash value in itself – a logic that marketers quickly accepted, enabling the company to amass over half of the money they spend on online advertising. Combined with the ubiquitous 'cookies' planted in most online services, which permit publishers and marketers to recognise a specific computer or user they have previous interacted with – and much else besides, including storing information about users' movements across other websites – any organisation in the business of selling something online was well on the way to having 'measurable ways to know, target, and consider the impact of commercial messages on audiences as never before'.[32]

The competition for the rest of the advertising business online subsequently spawned new forms of organisation, including ad networks, data providers and data exchanges, all busy gathering as much information as possible from any available source, about which individual customers advertisers could most profitably target. It is now common practice, Turow notes, for marketers to use such databases to categorise American consumers individually as 'targets' or 'waste':

> Those considered waste are ignored or shunted to other products the marketers deem more relevant to their tastes and/or income. Those considered targets are further evaluated in the light of the information that companies store and trade about their demographic profiles, beliefs and lifestyles. The targets receive different messages and possibly discounts on those profiles.[33]

Though the American companies involved generally take care to follow the letter, if not the spirit, of privacy laws, Turow observes, the direction in which the new commerce is headed is clear enough: 'Wide-ranging data points indicating the social backgrounds, locations, activities, and social relationships of hundreds of millions of individuals *are becoming the fundamental coins of exchange in the online world* [emphasis added]'.[34]

Concentration of market power

For Rana Foroohar, author of *Don't Be Evil*,[35] a forensic investigation of the 'Big Tech' companies in America whose wealth and power is based upon harnessing and dispensing information via the Net – 'the new "oil" of our economy', as she describes it – aside from the questionable nature of the information-gathering methods involved in targeting consumers, it is the overwhelming concentration of market power in a handful of the largest companies that concerns her most. The bare facts of that concentration of power, as Foroohar rolls them out in the opening pages of her book, are convincing enough in themselves, with ominous implications for the dwindling powers and privacy of individual consumers, as well as for the public institutions charged with their protection:

> The tech industry provides the starkest illustration of the rise in monopolistic power in the world today. 90 percent of the searches conducted everywhere on the planet are performed on a single search engine: Google. 95 percent of all Internet-using adults under the age of thirty are on Facebook (and/or Instagram, which Facebook acquired in 2012). Millennials spend twice as much time on YouTube as they do on all other video streaming services combined. Google and Facebook together receive around 90 percent of the world's new ad spending, and Google's and Apple's operating systems run on all but 1 percent of all cellphones globally. Apple and Microsoft supply 95 percent of the world's desktop operating systems. Amazon takes half of all U.S. e-commerce sales. The list goes on and on. Everything in Big Tech goes big or it doesn't go at all – and the bigger it gets, the more likely it is to go bigger still.[36]

Like Turow, Foroohar pinpoints the symbiotic relationship between the growth of these companies and the new advertising industry, the potential corruptive power of which was clearly understood by Google's founders, Sergey Brin and Larry Page, even as they were working as researchers at Stanford University on the first algorithms that would drive their nascent search engine. At that time, however, while embracing the idea of data mining as a method for analysing future trends and patterns, the two future masters of the largest combined data analysis and advertising machine in the world shunned the idea of allowing advertisers on Google. Adding a cryptic appendix to their first academic report on their work published in 1998, they wrote:

> Currently, the predominant business model for commercial search engines is advertising [...] We expect that advertising funded search engines *will be inherently biased towards the advertisers and away from the needs of consumers* [emphasis added]. Since it is very difficult even for experts to evaluate search engines, search engine bias is particularly insidious.[37]

It was a principle that, once out onto the commercial battlefield, the two ambitious entrepreneurs evidently chose to forget. As Google and other digital giants have grown in tandem with the online advertising industry, Foroohar argues, the rest of the economy has, in turn, suffered as more traditional companies and their employees lost out to the labour-saving technologies and ruthless methods of Big Tech. The consequent social and economic effects have been catastrophic: on job losses, with over half of all public firms in the US closing down over the last two decades; smaller entrepreneurs beaten out of the game (and sometimes getting their ideas stolen in the process), and consumers denied access to financial and other services because of a poor rating by providers' algorithms. Meantime much of the accumulated wealth of Big Tech has been secreted away in offshore tax havens, out of reach of the US government as well as the governments of other countries in which they make their fortunes. The irony, Foroohar adds, is that the digital entrepreneurs that gave Silicon Valley its name, grew rich on the back of research and innovations seeded with US government money (i.e., taxpayer funds) much of which, including the Internet itself, was supported by the Department of Defense, and only later commercialised. Unlike other countries with free market economies such as Finland, which ensures the country gets a fair share of the profits from such enterprises, thanks to the creativity of US company tax consultants, 'the US taxpayer does not reap a penny of the profits these innovations yield'.[38]

Thrown to the wolves

It needs to be remembered, however, that free market capitalism in the US was not always like this. Comparing the machinations of surveillance capitalism with its historical predecessor, Shoshana Zuboff quotes Henry Ford's embrace of consumer needs as an indispensable part of a modern economy: 'Mass production begins in the perception of a public need',[39] to which he responded, as told above by Joshua Freeman, with the Model T, the world's first affordable automobile and, moreover, sufficient wages for his own workers to buy them for *their* individual needs. Elaborating on what she identifies as *two distinct phases* of the modern era in the evolution of consumer markets, Zuboff argues that, while earlier market economies and their leaders were by no means perfect and were often scarred by violence between bosses and workers, their populations of 'newly modernizing individuals' were *valued as essential sources* of both customers and employees – dependencies that were eventually acknowledged in institutionalised form. The availability of affordable goods and services was thus regulated 'by democratic measures and methods of oversight that asserted and protected the rights and safety of workers and consumers'. In addition, the production and marketing of those goods and services afforded 'durable employment systems, career ladders, and steady increases in wages and benefits'.[40] For all its faults, therefore, Zuboff suggests that, compared to what has happened over the past few decades during which this form of market economy was 'systematically deconstructed' and its consumers thrown to the wolves by Big Other, the reciprocity between the preceding market and social order 'appears to have been one of its most salient features'.[41]

Zuboff is most eloquent, however, in describing the impact that tearing down the institutional walls protecting workers and consumers from commercial abuse has had on their 'right to sanctuary', by which she means not only individual privacy and the protection afforded by society's framework of laws, but also the fundamental need for *personal shelter* of a kind as common to other animals as it is for humans. Inspired by Bachelard's poetic ruminations on the sanctity of home, she writes:

> Home is our school of intimacy, where we first learn to be human. Its corners and nooks conceal the sweetness of solitude; its rooms frame our experience of relationship. Its shelter, stability, and security work to concentrate our inner sense of self, an identity that imbues our day dreams and night dreams forever.

All this, however, is now threatened by the penetration and destruction of these private spaces and worlds by the 'instrumentarian power' of Big Other, by which the complexities of human behaviour and experience are reduced to technically measurable data points in the service of behavioural control:

> According to Big Other's architects, these walls must come down. There can be no refuge. The primal yen for nests and shells is kicked aside like so much detritus from a fusty human time. With Big Other, the universe takes up residence in our walls, no longer the sentinels of sanctuary. Now they are simply the coordinates for 'smart' thermostats, security cameras,

speakers and light switches that extract and render our experience in order to actuate our behavior.[42]

The fightback

Such is the precarious situation that large sections of the populations of even some of the richest countries in the world now find themselves, that they have been given a name as a new social class-in-the-making. In *The Precariat*,[43] Guy Standing warns of rising social unrest as individuals and groups driven to the brink by the loss of any vestiges of security that once came with stable incomes and homes, vent their frustrations:

> The first stage of any social movement is emergence of a sense of common identity. And the energies unleashed in the city squares, streets, cafés and other public spaces have generated a precariate identity that is becoming a social force.[44]

Standing follows the emergence of this increasingly angry class of individuals as they have struggled in different countries to make their grievances heard by the powers that be – as yet though, with negligible effect upon the globalisation juggernaut he holds responsible for their loss of work and insecurity. Rather than returning to old-style, 'paternalistic' job and employment systems, however, Standing advocates a more open and flexible approach, which recognises the value of *all forms of work*, whether involving formal employment or not. Financial stability and security would instead be provided in the form of a state guaranteed 'basic income', a radical and controversial concept currently under trail in Finland – again a model of liberal values – and elsewhere. While he acknowledges critics' claims that any unconditional payments of that kind could be subject to abuse by recipients and used as propaganda by populist politicians, he argues that such a system would be a lot more efficient and productive than the current system of multiple state benefits built up by previous governments in the UK and other countries. Significantly, he suggests, it would also provide an efficient channel for *redistributing the financial capital* at present horded by an ever-smaller and richer segment of the population, which is responsible for growing inequalities around the world.[45]

Taming Big Other

In a chapter titled, 'The right to sanctuary', Zuboff also searches hopefully – but with a realistic eye on the difficulties involved – for indications that the tide might at last be turning: 'If sanctuary is to be preserved, synthetic declarations are required: alternative pathways that lead to a human future'.[46] She finds, for example, positive signs that at least some parts of the world might be waking up to Big Other's threat, in the new body of regulation passed by the EU in

May 2018, called the General Data Protection Regulation (GDPR). Unlike the relatively unrestricted approach to digital commerce in the US, which has left companies effectively free to operate as they chose unless challenged, the EU's approach places the onus of good behaviour firmly on the data companies, who must justify their activities within the GDPR's regulatory framework. Thus, for example, companies are *legally required* to notify individuals when their personal data has been breached; must obtain clear and unambiguous consent from individuals to prevent any misuse of such data; and are banned from making personal information public by default – all measures intended to strictly control or exclude precisely those freedoms of operation that Facebook and other companies have previously taken for granted and have been accused of abusing. Backed by substantial fines for any violations – up to 4 per cent of an offending company's *global* revenue – significantly, the GDPR also allows for class-action lawsuits in which individual users can combine to assert their privacy and data protection rights. While it remains to be seen how effective the GDPR will be in taming Big Other in actual practice – whether it does, in fact, signify radical change or whether it, too, will succumb to more conservative pressures – of one thing Zuboff is absolutely certain:

> Individuals each wrestling with the myriad complexities of their own data protection will be no match for surveillance capitalism's staggering asymmetries of knowledge and power. If the past two decades have taught us anything, it is that the individual alone cannot bear the burden of this fight at the new frontier of power.[47]

Charting a new course

Adding further weight to the critiques offered by Zuboff, Turow and others cited above, Amnesty International's damning report on the business model of Google and Facebook, *Surveillance Giants*,[48] quotes from Andy Rubin, the co-founder of Android – the smartphone platform owned by Google – who neatly captures the company's approach: 'We don't monetize the things we create … we monetize users'.[49] Laying out the threats to privacy, concentration of power and history of failed promises and abuses of the Net, including a brief summary of the Cambridge Analytica scandal, the report states: 'Ultimately, it is now evident that the era of self-regulation in the tech sector is coming to an end: further state-based regulation will be necessary, but it is vital that whatever form future regulation of the technology sector takes, governments follow a human–rights based approach'.[50]

Pursuing that approach, they point out that existing human rights law, as established by the Human Rights Council in 2016, already requires governments 'to adopt, implement and, where necessary, reform laws, regulations, policies and other measures concerning personal data and privacy protection online'.[51] Offering Amnesty International's own recommendations for action by States and companies, the majority of which are aimed at States – who ultimately bear the responsibility for ensuring companies adhere to the law – the report urges governments to build upon and enforce existing legislation 'to guarantee people a right "not to be tracked" by advertisers and other third parties'.[52] In turn, they call upon Google, Facebook and other technology companies to 'find ways to transition to a rights-respecting business model', beginning by addressing 'the systemic and widespread human rights impacts of their business models as a whole'. In addition, companies should refrain from lobbying governments to dilute data protection and privacy law, and remedy 'any human rights abuses which they have caused or contributed to through their business operations'. In fairness to Google and Facebook, Amnesty International also invited both companies to respond to their report, which concludes with a six-page letter in reply from Facebook. Google apparently did not respond.

Similarly, the proposed *Contract for the Web*,[53] launched by the Web Foundation thirty years after its founder, Tim Berners-Lee first created the World Wide Web, outlines nine principles aimed at three primary groups, 'governments', 'companies' and 'citizens', each of which are allocated three key principles of their own:

Governments will:

1. Ensure everyone can connect to the internet; so that anyone, no matter who they are or where they live, can participate actively online.
2. Keep all of the internet available, all of the time; so that no one is denied their right to full internet access.
3. Respect and protect people's fundamental online privacy and data rights; so everyone can use the internet freely, safely, and without fear.

Companies will:

4. Make the internet affordable and accessible to everyone; so that no one is excluded from using and shaping the Web.
5. Respect and protect people's privacy and personal data to build online trust; so people are in control of their lives online, empowered with clear and meaningful choices around their data and privacy.
6. Develop technologies that support the best in humanity and challenge the worst; so the Web really is a public good that puts people first.

Citizens will:

7. Be creators and collaborators on the Web; so the Web has rich and relevant content for everyone.
8. Build strong communities that respect civil discourse and human dignity; so that everyone feels safe and welcome online.
9. Fight for the Web; so the Web remains open and a global public resource for people everywhere, now and in the future.

As important as these principles are, however, as with Amnesty International's recommendations, the contract has no legal teeth whatsoever. Unless and until it acquires the kind of legal backing and stringent measures for enforcement of those principles – particularly at the governmental and international level – as set out in the EU's new legislation, it remains no more than a declaration of intent, dependent, as all such statements of principle are, upon the goodwill, honesty and energies of the signatories for their actual implementation. Given the previous record of Google and Facebook in exploiting the personal data of their users, however, it would seem unlikely that they would change their business model unless compelled to do so by international as well as national law. Notably, while Facebook was amongst the many organisations to sign up, Google failed to endorse the contract, just as they had failed to reply to Amnesty International's invitation to respond to their report.[54] That said, as Zuboff has written, such declarations setting out alternative pathways to a better human future are essential if we are ever to find our way out of the present impasse:

> What life is left to us if taming fails? Without protection from surveillance capitalism and its instrumentarian power – their behavioral aims and societal goals – we are trapped in a condition of 'no exit,' where the only walls are made of glass.[55]

Part IV

Summation

To encompass in research the process of a given thing's development in all its phases and changes – from birth to death – fundamentally means to discover its nature, its essence.

L. S. Vygotsky, 1978[1]

Chapter 15

Instinctive and fuzzy selves

This book was written with the simple but firm conviction that only a radically new approach embracing both human and non-human animal life can explain the true nature and evolution of the self for what it is: a self-organising system of its own; how it functions in a changing environment, and what the major factors in its development have been, and are now. All the other propositions I listed in Chapter 4 and their subsequent elaboration stem from this position. Only by also recognising our own species for the fallible, instinctive creatures we generally are, rather than the self-conscious, rational beings we prefer to *believe* we are, is it possible to resolve the dilemma posed by philosopher John Gray: 'This may be the era of the Anthropocene – the geological epoch in which human action is transforming the planet. But it is also the one in which the human animal is less than ever in charge'.[1]

Resistance to change

Why indeed, it may be asked, as clever as we claim to be, are we now 'less than ever in charge' of events, to the extent that *Homo sapiens*, together with countless other species on this planet, is threatened, if not with total extinction, then with catastrophic losses of life and the natural resources that have sustained us this far – a fate that humanity has patently brought upon itself?[2]

Underlying that ecological failure to take early and effective action to avoid impending disaster, I have argued, is a failure to understand and acknowledge the *conservative nature of a largely unconscious self* – overtly expressed in a stubborn *resistance* to any changes that might present a threat to that self, the roots of which lie deep in our animal past. Tracking those roots through the book, the same tensions between existential identities and pressures for change drive the evolution of the self at all levels of development, from the earliest and most basic manifestations of animal self-awareness to the highest levels of human behaviour.

Following a background overview of changing theoretical and research approaches, the main body of the book set out two distinct but mutually supportive paths of thought and research, from the metatheoretical in the second part to the socially and culturally grounded expressions of 'the self in the world' covered in the third part. At the highest level, the metatheoretical framework I advanced – a fusion of cybernetic theories of self-organisation and field theory – provides the foundation for my theory of the self-field as a self-organising system of extended cognition, the fundamentals of which are common to animal life.

Within that metatheoretical framework, the various levels of research covered, from the social and behavioural levels down to the genetic and neuronal levels of analysis and their interactions, involve a rich mixture of perspectives and methodologies. Given, for example, so many different interpretations by emergentists as to how new levels of organisation arise spontaneously out of lower levels, it was suggested by one researcher that the phenomenon is simply best accepted as a 'brute fact' of evolution. Likewise, other writers advocate acceptance of a *pluralistic epistemology* appropriate to the many disciplines and levels of analysis involved in evolutionary theory. Both arguments offer pragmatic solutions to dealing with what are plainly complex issues. However, they leave the most important question raised by these discussions unresolved: if natural selection alone is not responsible for pushing evolution along and integrating all these diverse phenomena, as Evo–Devo critics of the Modern Synthesis maintain, then what else is?

In answer to that question I argued that, seen from the field view of self-organisation, emergentists have got the whole process back to front. Theories of emergence generally portray higher levels of organisation arising out of entities that were, in some sense, previously *less organised*. However, according to Goodwin's definition of self-organisation, as previously quoted: 'The organism is not so much a self-organising system that generates an ordered state from more or less disordered parts; it is more a self-organised entity that can undergo transformations *preserving this state* [emphasis added]'. In other words, forms of life, from single-celled organisms to individual humans, do not evolve from *less* organised entities to *more* organised wholes – they *begin from their very inception as organised wholes*, the *conservation* of which, under pressure of change from internal or external sources (upward and downward pressures) is steadfastly maintained throughout the lifespan, or as much as it normally can be.

Similarly, describing living beings above as the product of 'operational principles subordinated to a centre of individuality', it was Polanyi who first pinpointed the *identity of the organism*, as an individual and member of a particular species, as the key to what governs its development as a whole, no matter what form that might take. Maturana and Varella also propounded the same fundamental principle with their circular organisation of self-producing (autopoietic) systems; a concept, however, which failed to accommodate emergent phenomena of the sort that Polanyi enunciated. Over longer periods, as Polanyi and other pioneering theorists have consistently argued, there is undoubtedly an evolutionary trend in living systems towards ever-higher levels of *complexity*, or a hierarchical 'strata of realities' as he describes it, but that should not be taken to mean that simpler forms of life are in some sense *incomplete* in their organisation and function. Rather, emergence is more accurately conceived as a series of developmental steps or *plateaus* in the self-organisation of an organism, *each of which is complete in itself* and tuned to its environment, but, should conditions change, as Goodwin suggests, undergoes whatever transformations required to retain the organism's integrity as a whole and thus continue prospering.

Serial selves

Confusions also colour the arguments about whether there is such a thing as a coherent self, whether human or non-human – arguments I rejected for being based on a misguided and fruitless search for an *essential substance* comparable to a physical body, rather than the invisible, self-organising 'field of being' I maintain it is. Based upon the respective psychological and social field theories of Lewin and Bourdieu, I proposed that what Lewin describes as a mode of thought expressed in terms of *serial concepts and gradations* between states, rather than separate concepts, applies equally well to understanding the evolution of the self as a *graded process* of development running through all forms of animal life, human and non-human. Similarly, following the proposal by Parfit that personal identity depends more upon an 'overlapping chain of experience-memories' than any physical sameness or Cartesian logic, I posited a diachronic concept of *serial selves* of varying levels of consciousness held together by the same self-organising pressures.

However, there is a catch to this orderly picture of sequential adjustment of forms of life to changing environmental conditions – a problem from which other animals are not immune, but to which humans are especially prone – the difficulty being that the success of the whole process depends upon just *how sensitive* individuals and species are to those changing circumstances encountered during development, and how *realistic* and effective their responses are. The research presented in this book generally supports the idea that all living systems, whether individual organisms or social organisations, involve some form of *organisational closure*, upon which their continued identity depends. Not the frozen organisation and fixed boundaries originally described in autopoietic theory, however, but a more complex system of what is described in 'second-order' cybernetics and systems theory as *double closure*. At the same time as organisms explore and expand into their environments, faced with being overwhelmed by new information or distractions from their main purpose and functions, they may be motivated to *ignore* any environmental complexities not deemed to be of consequence to the present well-being of the individual or group concerned.

Living systems at all levels of development may therefore consciously or unconsciously *shut out* or *reduce* warning signals of potentially harmful environmental factors that could threaten their ultimate survival. Similarly, what may also appear on the behavioural surface as cognitive dissonance or confirmation bias, are the *symptoms* of a deeply rooted and *instinctive* resistance to any changes to ingrained habits of thought and behaviour that might threaten the identity of the individual concerned.

Playing our part in the game

What also makes such problems so difficult to resolve is that those potentially harmful ingrained habits are often mixed up with perfectly *normal* aspects of social life acquired in the playing out of our respective roles – what Goffman describes metaphorically as life's daily drama and Bourdieu as the *habitus*, or the 'space of life-styles'. For Goffman, self-images are not so much created by individuals of their own volition but are mostly generated *subconsciously* in the process of fulfilling our social obligations: doing the job we have chosen to do or participating in other specific social activities; a habitual performance requiring a minimum level of *personal identification* with the assigned roles we play in those activities. Likewise, other players on the same stage act out their own parts in a tacitly accepted process of social engagement. Moreover, where closer teamwork is required, the obligation to conform with the moral and behavioural standards required of the team's function may impose further constraints on individual players. And the larger the team, the more the values the team promotes may change, with the danger, as Goffman writes, that reality may be 'reduced to a thin party-line'.

Similarly, the social fields and institutions Bourdieu describes, with all their customary rituals and rewards, create the settings for a 'common, meaningful world', in which individuals may, in the process of finding their place in that world, acquire their *own* identity. In so doing, however, like Goffman's actors, they may also find themselves caught up in a larger and trickier game of identity formation, fraught with its own dangers as well as rewards, in which the greater the *autonomy* of the organisation and field it is engaged in, the more the perception of realities is *trimmed to suit the logic and interests of the organisation they serve*. Highly significant too, are the observations presented by several researchers that, not only does the influence of groups often result in a movement towards *uniformity* of thought and behaviour within groups, but, as Sunstein suggests, hearing other members of a group voice the same opinions can *harden attitudes*, moving group members towards increasingly *extreme positions* and hostility towards any others not sharing those views – a key factor successfully exploited by Cambridge Analytica in their subversive campaigns.

In dealing with such pressures, which, as others have written in this book, are common to most forms of group activity, individual selves may struggle to maintain an independent identity. Fortunately, as difficult as it may be to balance them all effectively, most of us play out *several* complementary roles during the course of the day and week, let alone in the lifetime of a developing self, involving other individuals we relate to at home and elsewhere in our social lives – a diversity of roles that, theoretically at least, if not always in practice, affords the opportunity of viewing any one of those roles from a different and more self-conscious angle.

Not just a collection of neurons

Keeping all those different daily and weekly selves in rein, I propose, is the same self-organising system of cognition I have described which manages the sequence of individual selves over the longer term, and which we refer to as the 'I' in common language. The self, therefore, and the conservation of its individual identity through the day as well as through the lifetime, I maintain, provides the vital *integrative dynamic* missing from other theories and factors offered in this book purporting to shape human development.

As much as the research at the neurobiological level described in Chapter 5 and elsewhere in these pages has enlarged our understanding of the brain–body complex, many of the findings on body mapping and related neuropsychological disorders reported here nevertheless provide only a *partial view* of the holistic phenomena of life actually encompassed by the self-field – a window onto the self, if you like – but like all windows, they offer only a glimpse of the wider world beyond.[3]

Recent discoveries across a range of complex phenomena from peripersonal space and canonical neurons to VENs and mirror neurons, however, often supported by researchers from other disciplines,[4] show a movement towards focusing on *overlapping* rather than separate brain functions. Contrary to Maturana and Varella's refutation of any possibility that, *independently* of human observers, the nervous systems of organisms themselves might be capable of *internally* representing their environmental interactions, such research suggests that *some* form of internal representation, no matter how primitive, is fundamental to the evolution of self-awareness in all sentient creatures. Taken together, the research yields a more complex picture of interacting neurological and sensory subsystems functioning at different levels of cognition, most of which are shared between humans and other animals and which originate in the evolution of earlier species. Significantly, such research also confirms the extent to which humans and other animals generally operate at *subconscious* levels of being. The boundary conditions of the self-field prove to be largely governed by deep-seated fears of actual or potential threats to survival – not necessarily of the physical self, but of the psychic identity of the individual self – the intimations of which we first *feel* as *emotions*, rather than conscious thoughts.[5]

Toward a cross-species self

Amongst the most promising ideas to straddle different levels of thought and investigation is the concept advanced by Damasio and others of an evolutionary *three-stage self*, each phase involving a neurological fusion of brain and body: from a primitive, sensory-based *protoself*, through an outward-reaching *core self* and, finally, to the reflective, *autobiographical self* commonly associated with full human self-consciousness. A key point in the three-stage schema is that, while each level marks a significant further evolution of the self, each new self also remains grounded in and builds upon the preceding stage, so that, at the highest level, all three selves work together as an integrated ensemble.

When it comes to the key question, however, of what actually ensures that all the different factors involved work together in harmony, Damasio resorts to a description of *homeostatic systems* similar to those governing autonomic bodily functions or the design of homeostatic machines – all basically *synchronic* systems, none of which explain what actually generates or controls the transition from one primary stage to another, or indeed, any levels in between. For Damasio, as in the research by other neuroscientists described in this book, organisms operate as *collections* of neurobiological sub-systems functioning at different levels, which somehow all work together as an ensemble, the systemic reason for which, however, remains unexplained. Appeals to Darwinian natural selection for support which, as Evo–Devo researchers have argued in these pages, provides no answers at all to nature's innovations, are equally fruitless. Similarly, any suggestion that, at the highest level, such a process is synonymous with full consciousness does not stand up against the evidence offered time and again by other researchers cited here, that there are forms of self-awareness that operate for the most part *below* the level of consciousness, not just at earlier stages of the animal self's evolution, but also at the human level.

An alternative concept of a *trans-species core self* was presented by Panksepp and Northoff based upon a collection of self-related processing systems typically operating at *preconscious or implicit* levels, but which are rich in 'affective consciousness', meaning the *emotional states and feelings* aroused as organisms interact with their environment. Neurobiological evidence of the activation of specific regions of animal brains in various species, traceable back to the primitive nervous systems of the protoself, has also been found. A core self is therefore common not only to different animal species, including our own, but, crucially, also links both lower and higher selves through a central neural processing network connecting the brain with parts of the nervous system *that evolved much earlier* – findings that match other quoted observations above that 'the modern mind is a mosaic structure of cognitive vestiges from earlier stages of human emergence'.

Relations of degree

Together, the idea of an evolutionary three-stage self and a trans-species core-self go some way, not only to explaining the common basis for an animal self, but also the *continuing influence* of the most primitive forms of self-awareness on human behaviour including, perhaps, those instinctive feelings of discomfort described above which an affected person automatically attempts to reduce, just as other animals may sense some as yet unseen danger to their own being and take avoiding action.

However, serious questions remain as to what actually links all the different stages together or drives the whole transitional process. Is there a sudden evolutionary leap, for example, from protoself to core self and then again from core to autobiographical self, with no significant levels in between? Or, as I have argued, the evolution of the self, whether within a single lifespan or the life of a whole species, proceeds as a *sequential process* of self-organisation best described by what Parfit calls 'relations of degree' between states, and Lewin as the logic of 'serial concepts' and gradations, the consistent aim of which is the creation and conservation of a coherent identity.

Roots of self-awareness

Such an approach suggests the origins of self-awareness lie much further back in evolutionary time than has been generally assumed. Recent research on animal metamorphosis, for example, confirms that *associative memory* – upon which autobiographical memory and self-awareness depend – may, in some species, survive even extreme metamorphosis This raises some intriguing questions: For example, does a butterfly *know* in some sense that it had a previous and very different life as a caterpillar? Similarly, research in *self-agency*, such as the ability of the cricket to distinguish between its own noisy actions and those of other members of the same troupe, points to the evolutionary roots of self-awareness and, as some argue, the fundamental ability to distinguish between self and other at the human level, the failure of which is recognised as a common form of schizophrenia.

Numerous other studies of non-human animal behaviour and cognition recounted here, from cooperative behaviour and social learning to diverse tool-making and using skills, and even the ability to anticipate and respond to the behaviour of other members of a species, also support the idea of *evolutionary continuity* between species rather than any sudden, magical appearance of full self-consciousness, as has been associated with the birth of human language. On the contrary, it was argued that human intelligence and language have evolved together with the development of tools and other artifacts in a tacit nexus involving a similar overlapping of brain functions as that described above, in which the evolution of the hand, from ape to the more dextrous human model, also plays a major role.

Such discoveries highlight related questions raised above as to whether the strict logic of precisely defined classes of phenomena is at all appropriate to understanding the characteristically flexible boundaries of an evolving self. However, an alternative and more suitable 'fuzzy logic' invented by Lotfi Zadeh[6] for dealing with such ambiguities has been available since the 1970s. Virtually ignored until recently by psychologists, Zadeh, like Parfit and Lewin, questioned the inviolable assumption of classical logic that a statement must be either *true or false*, with no room for equivocation. Based on fuzzy set theory, a related branch of mathematics he helped to develop in the 1960s, which covers classes with approximate *grades of membership*, Zadeh perceived that many classes of biological species and other objects in the 'real physical world', as he describes it, have an ill-defined status: 'Yet the fact remains that such imprecisely defined 'classes' play an important role in human thinking'.[7]

From the outset, therefore, Zadeh's motivation was to create methods of representing and dealing with classes of objects that are *not* precisely defined – an approach now recognised by psychologists as opening up 'new and potentially useful ways of looking at human cognition, reasoning, communication, decision making, and the like'.[8] Similarly, it may be hoped that hard-to-pin-down but vital features of the self-field detailed here, that have so far eluded full recognition for a previous lack of more precise tools of expression, may now lie within the scope of such tools.

Techno-cultural coevolution

The third part of the book examined the diverse expressions of the self in the experienced world and the growing extent to which those expressions are mediated by technology, the uncontrolled – and possibly uncontrollable – consequences of which we now wrestle with. Progressing from those forms, such as home building and tool use that are common to both human and other animal species, through to those more advanced levels where humans have outstripped all other forms of life, each chapter presents a picture of the self in a world increasingly shaped by technology, affecting both group and individual behaviour.

Chapter 8 on the technical extensions of the self, commenced with Rudofsky's pioneering treatment of animal constructions on an equivalent level to human self-build traditions, or what he calls 'architecture without architects' – a view strongly supported by more recent and extensive research on 'animal architecture', as the manifold creations of other creatures are now called. Other authors contend that the possession and development of *technological knowledge*, whether acquired directly from other members of the same species by learning or embodied in the tools or constructions themselves, is a common feature of animal behaviour, rather than being exclusive to the *Homo* line.

The reliance upon technology by so many animal species as well as by humans has also prompted some writers to argue that *technology itself* and not natural selection, has been the true engine of animal evolution. Most clearly, perhaps, as Taylor asserts, in the case of our own species, beginning with the invention of the baby sling and the possibility it afforded for infant, pre-human brains to grow larger outside the womb. Explaining his *combinatorial theory* of technological innovation, Arthur goes further still in speculating that modern technologies effectively have a life of their own, not unlike Maturana and Varella's self-producing organisms, the potential future outcomes of which he clearly fears. Not so Clark, who, in accepting a near-future human race of cyborgs ever more dependent upon technology – not the semi-mechanical cyborgs of movie fame but the ever more blurred line between the human mind and AI – observes that humans have *always* enjoyed an intimate relationship with technology. As long as we acknowledge that relationship, he suggests, we will be able to pick and choose our future bio-technological selves at will.

Social creatures

However, as Gray bluntly points out at the head of this chapter, controlling our own futures is proving a great deal more difficult than Clark suggests it might. Over and above being supremely technological creatures, like most other animal selves – the independent-minded octopus excepted – the human self, as the research on the self and group identity in Chapter 10 confirms, is also fundamentally a *social creature*, just as much dependent upon the cooperation and affirmation of others to get through life as any other social species. Distinct from the long-term effects of gene-culture coevolution, the effects upon the self-field of techno-cultural coevolution at both the personal and group levels, which can be observed over much *shorter* historical time-spans, show few substantial signs, if any, of being brought under control, but which must also be accounted for.

Some of those coevolutionary effects are also clearly observable in the achievements of other technologically endowed creatures, as well as those of humans. It is surely no coincidence, for example, that the most impressive non-human animal constructions, such as the 'insect cities' described in Chapter 8, are the *collective creation* of socially dependent insects. Similarly, it has been repeatedly observed by researchers quoted in this book that the invention of new tools and techniques by our ancestors is invariably accompanied by new or more intensive forms of collaborative behaviour, whether searching for the right materials to make those tools or hunting together with new weapons also made together. All activities, as Tomasello argues, that entail what he describes as *shared intentionality*, and with it, the ability of individuals to not only make evaluative judgments about others engaged in joint enterprises, but also to be aware they may, in turn, be subject to judgment by those same others – an awareness generating a new concern, he suggests, with *self-image* and fitting in with the group.

Loss of critical culture

Given what has been explained above about the evolutionary roots of self-awareness, whether those higher levels of cognition and growing concerns with self-image mark a genuinely decisive step beyond any stage of development yet

reached by any other species, as Tomasello holds, remains a matter of contention.[9] What began, however, as a more or less natural outcome of a direct process of communication and role playing between individuals – as formalised by
Goffman, Kelly and Laing in their respective psychological and social models
and explored in my own related experiments at MIT – has undergone dramatic changes over the last half-century, transforming the techno-cultural basis
of self-images, and with it, our engagement with the world at large. As Wolf
explains in her history of writing, the human reading brain, with its capacity
to imagine alternative worlds and perspectives, has been both the product and
mainstay of a literary and critical culture underpinning democratic societies. As
far as any truly significant difference between the evolutionary achievements of
humans and other animals is concerned, rather than the more common claims
made for human language, it is also the *written* word, not spoken language,
together with the invention of easy-to-learn alphabets, which Wolf argues was
vital to the exponential development of human knowledge and culture. It is a
viewpoint endorsed by Gray, who asserts: 'What is distinctively human is not
the capacity for language. It is the *crystallization of language in writing* [emphasis
added]'.[10] In turn, it is inconceivable that, beyond shared intentionality, the
cultural 'ratchet effect' described by Tomasello could have worked so well for
humans, without the invention of writing to record and pass on the memories
and achievements of individuals and nations for future generations to reflect
upon, and sometimes even, to learn from and to criticize.

No more it seems. Against the benefits of the Internet for unlimited personal
communication across the globe, as Wolf and other concerned observers like
Turkle warn us, the growing amount of time individuals – especially the
young – spend on the new social media and other Net platforms now threatens
that culture, and with it, the much-needed further development of the knowledgeable and critically aware self it previously nourished. As much as, if not
more than, the loss of the deep reading culture Wolf laments, are the corrosive personal and social effects of time lost that was formerly spent in direct
exchanges with other real, engaging minds, and, moreover, with emotionally
expressive faces;[11] as distant a model of social engagement as there can be from
Facebook's idea of collecting as many 'friends' as possible – never mind the
quality, feel the quantity, so to speak.

The profligate species

Taken all together, the impact of the shift of human attention towards the Net
upon personal and cultural life, reach far beyond anything McLuhan anticipated.
Symptoms include a marked degradation in the *quality* of social relationships,
accompanied by narcissistic levels of obsession with endless 'selfies' and other
self-images – actively encouraged by the major social platforms – together with
shortened attention spans and other diminished cognitive faculties. All formerly
nourished by time spent both in direct social interaction and immersion in

written texts and the other worlds described by Wolf. Deprived of previously accessible doorways into other minds provided by close personal contact or deep reading, together with the exposure of one's *own* thoughts and beliefs to those of others, tech-savvy modern humans now cast wildly about on the Net searching for quick and easy substitutes.

We are the product now

That, however, is only half the story. The increase in the *numerical quantity* and *speed* of information and social interaction the new media facilitates at the expense of *depth*, feeds into and is actively exploited by commercial and political interests, both public and clandestine, with devastating effects upon the private self and whatever fragile powers of choice and expression individuals formerly exercised. Thus, depending upon social class and economic means, while self-image and material culture, whether expressed through the clothes individuals choose, the homes and places they live in, the personal objects they collect or the private automobiles they drive, have always counted in modern societies, the advent of the Net and the power of so-called Big Tech companies like Google have transformed the technological mediation of those choices.

While in the past, advertisers of automobiles and other products have also been equally astute in pressing the right psychological and social buttons to sell their goods, their methods were an open book compared with the secretive methods of targeting individual buyers now employed across the Net, where data on personal tastes mined from social media has a cash value all of its own. As Foroohar writes of the commercial alliance between Big Tech and advertisers: 'We think we are the consumers. In fact, we are the product'.[12]

Similarly, related advances in computer-based technologies and AI are impacting on employment, displacing large sections of the human workforce with automated methods of production and operation. The crippling outcome has not only been the loss of secure incomes but also the loss of a major source of personal identity, along with the bargaining power once-powerful unions exercised in improving working conditions and social status. Faced with shrinking opportunities for a full life in the real world, millions have turned to online gaming and avatars – especially addictive role-playing games involving large groups of other players – affording some escape from the difficult realities of life and providing alternative, if unreal, opportunities for acting out dreams of personal success players may have failed to find elsewhere.

Fatal weakness

The combined personal and social effects of these developments have left individuals and groups vulnerable to political manipulation by organisations like Cambridge Analytica using the same data mining and psychological techniques to subvert the democratic process, further weakening any possibility of implementing the kind of radical social and cultural reforms environmentalists and writers like Zuboff have called for.[13] While other species described here have made good use of technology in successfully modifying their environments to better ensure their survival and prosperity, for all their remarkable technical skills – with the notable exception perhaps of the much-travelled termite – their efforts have been both technically and geographically limited to relatively small areas of habitation.

Not so our own prolific species. Indications of psychological denial similar to those described above were already apparent in the failure of previous, geographically limited human civilisations that, for all their monumental technical and cultural achievements, ignored warning signs they were exhausting the natural resources upon which their survival depended.[14] No such geographical limitations have restricted later civilisations, however, who, ever since Queen Elizabeth I of England granted The East India Company their charter – the world's first shareholder-financed, multi-national corporation and the model for all modern multi-nationals[15] – have reached out across the oceans, siphoning off both natural and human resources as they went, taking the first momentous steps toward globalisation.

Self-preserving selves

While they may be newly empowered by the Net and AI in extending their reach ever deeper into the lives and minds of consumers, the digitally based corporations of our time, it could be said, are only doing what comes naturally to them. Just as the loyal 'servants' of the East India Company identified with and supported their employer wherever they were posted, so, too, do the employees and directors of modern corporations– and for much the same psychological and social reasons, as Bourdieu explains, that hold all modern organisations together.

Similarly, I submit that, in cases where an organisation's activities involve sensitive environmental and social issues, comparable, deep-seated psychological motivations drive the aggressive response to criticism and denial of wrong doing by corporate leaders, whose personal identities are no less bound up with the organisations they serve, and whose interests they may have spent much of their adult lives promoting and defending. The effect – a closing of the ranks and shutting out of unwelcome views and information – is a visible sign of the double closure common to all self-organising systems described here, except that, in this case, due to the lack of adequate constraints, both environmental and human, they can and do have destructive and even self-destructive consequences. As irrational as such expressions of climate change denial are – there has been a near total scientific consensus on the human causes of climate change for many years[16] – they also need to be understood as an extreme form of a far more widespread reaction in America and other parts of the world, supported by a biased media, neo-liberal thinktanks and other organisations, to what is interpreted as a threat to a whole way of life. Which, given the dire consequences of a heating climate for future life on this Earth, is close to the truth, if not quite as the deniers see it.[17]

Existential crisis

A similar evolutionary mixture of expansion and closure of human organisations that characterises modern social organisations, it may be speculated, also accompanied the emergence of the first human institutions, ensuring further order and stability in a rapidly changing and increasingly complex social and cultural world.[18] However, the evident failure of modern governments and state institutions everywhere to get to grips with the debilitating personal effects of unequally weighted and insecure social and economic structures – let alone deal with climate change – is evidence enough they are no longer fit for purpose. We are accustomed to calling a state that cannot provide its citizens with adequate employment, public services and secure homes, a 'failed state'; but a civilisation that does not provide the conditions for its own survival, let alone the survival of much of the rest of life on this planet, is no less a *failed civilisation*.

Tragically, the unparalleled technological and communicative powers accumulated by our species has enabled humankind thus far to ignore nature's own early warning signs of overreach, by simply expanding yet further and faster into her territory, devouring her resources and scorning the protests of anyone standing in the way. Led by a tiny but powerful minority who, fearful for their personal survival, have effectively *created their own illusional reality*, large sections of the global population – equally fearful of true or imagined threats to their way of life and encouraged by like-minded individuals in their own social circles – have in turn passively accepted the more comforting realities daily presented to them by their leaders, supported by a digital media industry in 'fake news' and 'alternative facts'.

Final confrontation with reality

However, though deniers may continue to refute the existence of climate change, it is unlikely they will be able to avoid a final, brutal confrontation with the reality of a decaying world they cannot control. Though there have been ample signs of approaching bioclimatic catastrophe for decades now, 2019 must surely go down as an historical turning point to dwarf all others in recent times, if not a final wakeup call. We have been repeatedly warned by scientists about potential 'tipping points' as supposedly safe limits to greenhouse gas emissions are breached, or soon will be, after which global warming is effectively *irreversible*, but which have been mostly played down, even by scientists themselves, due to a lack of more precise data. Nonetheless, progress in analysing vital signs of *concurrent trends* in the impacts of climate change, together with a recent and dramatic *acceleration* of those trends and their disastrous effects across the globe, have compelled scientists to drop their reservations and confront the predicament of a possibly endless cycle of climate change with calamitous consequences for life on the planet.[19] In a late 2019 report by a group of scientists concerned with the lack of progress in dealing with that predicament, they write:

> Despite 40 years of global climate negotiations, with few exceptions, we have generally conducted business as usual and have largely failed to address this predicament. The climate crisis has arrived and is accelerating faster than most scientists expected. *It is more severe than anticipated, threatening natural ecosystems and the fate of humanity* [emphasis added].[20]

Neither will appeals to reason alone, which have thus far proven to be ineffective, be sufficient, nor will any radical plans unless they gain the active support of a hitherto lax majority, who would rather look the other way than confront the harsh realities they now face. Meanwhile the voracious destruction of what remains of the natural environment continues unabated while the civilisation celebrated for its technological achievements is imploding, driven by its own relentless momentum – not without, however, some unforeseen and ironic consequences for those who have, thus far, profited from that destruction. Having replaced major sections of the human workforce by machines, 'intelligent' or otherwise, corporations have not only successfully reduced their labour costs and what remains of the power of any troublesome unions, but they have also deprived themselves of the loyalty and support of the salaried men and women who used to work for them, and who – as Ford understood so well – provide the consumers they need to buy the products they are now so efficiently producing without their help.

Nothing to lose from change; everything to gain

Without that personal support and purchasing power of a human workforce, therefore, despite all that is being done by Big Tech and their psychological and AI helpers to pacify the population, it may possibly dawn upon those who have been thrown aside, that they owe nothing at all to present society; indeed, they have nothing to lose from changing it – and just possibly, everything to gain. Most likely, therefore, if anything is going to save us from the existential crisis now facing humanity, like all innovations, it will involve a reworking and creative combination of known, ecologically sensitive models of development and related technologies based upon renewable sources of energy, but which have never before been applied together on a truly global scale, supported by the social and economic structures required for a more equitable society.[21]

Whatever happens now, it is clear that, such is the level of greenhouse gas production already in the pipeline, no matter what is done now to ameliorate the situation, the planetary climate will most probably surpass the artificial benchmark of 2 degrees centigrade above pre-industrial levels presently agreed upon internationally – but yet to be enforced – bringing the fearsome prospect of runaway global warming ever closer. As bad as things look, however, what would be truly inexcusable would be to do nothing about it. As Bill McKibben[22] has written, there is no one else to blame but us, and now, virtually alone on this planet, only we can put things right again:

> We have deprived nature of its independence, and that is fatal to its meaning. Nature's independence *is* its meaning; without it there is nothing but us.[23]

Pandemic postscript

Call it what you want: faith in human rationality and ingenuity or just plain faith, unjustified optimism is a dangerous state of mind. As we have now seen with the laggardly responses everywhere to both the climate crisis and the Covid-19 pandemic, it encourages people at all levels of society to think matters are not as urgent as they really are, so they avoid taking the hard decisions and effective actions they desperately need to do. As I write this brief postscript before this book goes to press, there is nothing that I have seen or learned since Covid-19 went global, that has caused me to revise my analysis of the deeply embedded resistance to change in the human psyche and its evolutionary roots; nor, unfortunately, my assessment of the potentially fatal effects for humanity of that resistance.

However, it is not just the world's political leaders who have failed so abysmally to protect their populations from these dangers that we should worry about, but *the reasons why people vote for them*. It would appear that a significant proportion of the population, if not the majority in democratic countries as well as other parts of the world, are all too easily misled into believing whatever doctrine or message offers the least challenge to their present convictions and way of life, whatever the contrary facts might be, and who find it easier to blame others for what has gone wrong. As the British philosopher Bertrand Russell, who had no illusions about human fallibility, once famously lamented: 'Most people would sooner die than think; in fact, they do so' – a tragic observation for which there has been no shortage of supporting evidence during the current pandemic.

Doubtless some readers may dismiss such views as being unduly pessimistic. On the contrary, I believe Russell was simply expressing a much-needed *realism* of the sort I have advocated throughout this book, and which has guided me towards my own theory of what leads the human self to instinctively reject unwelcome facts, even, as now, when confronted by the most severe threat to their survival. As reported here and elsewhere, social engineering exploiting those same psychological factors is now being practised by political and commercial powers with a technical efficiency and on a scale that behaviourists like B. F. Skinner would have envied. And while optimistic thinkers see opportunities in the present pandemic crisis to reconfigure human society and resolve the environmental crisis all in one go, the same political and commercial leaders and forces who continue to deny the latter, will most surely use the pandemic to justify *increasing* the surveillance techniques they have deployed so effectively until now in their own interests. While there may indeed be a case for using smartphones, for example, to help track persons who may have been contaminated, there can be no justification for any systemic or permanent intrusions, such as are already in place in China and the US. Though Net libertarians might argue that, in a period when much of the world's population is confined to their homes, bothersome issues of privacy no longer count, I would argue the situation calls for *more*, not less, vigilance if we are to preserve what is left of the private self and whatever precious sanctuary the home still offers.

Similarly, despite the most obvious links between the causes of climate change and the speed with which the pandemic has spread, from mass air travel to the respiratory problems caused by the polluted air of our cities, it would be foolish to think that either producers or consumers of the services and vehicles generating that vicious cycle will give them up and change their businesses and ways of life easily. Though the skies over city streets temporarily devoid of vehicles may be wonderfully clear for now, we have only to look at the many careless individuals disregarding the strict advice of medical experts and the safety of others to break their confinement – fortunately a minority for now in those countries imposing a strict lockdown – to realise just how difficult it is going to be to implement all the social and economic reforms required to prevent another pandemic, let alone reverse global warming.

What cannot be denied is that, compared with the continued inability of the world's governments to agree on an effective and enforceable global plan of action to deal with the climate crisis, for all their initial failures, the response of most governments to the pandemic has been lightening swift, grounding planes and people, and, in many countries, offering economic support to those individuals and commercial enterprises most affected. The comparison has led some observers to wonder why similar decisive steps have not been taken to mitigate the most severe effects of climate change, which ultimately present a far *worse* threat to humankind. The plain answer is that, while the global toll in human life from the effects of a warming planet is steadily rising, it is not yet on the same scale nor has the same psychological immediacy as the deaths from the pandemic, together with all its other palpable impacts on daily life.

In addition, while we now know that we are perilously close to overriding the physical and geographical tipping points of climate change reported in my summation, we do not yet know where the psychological, social and cultural tipping points might be that could provide the final push needed to goad humanity into effective action to resolve these crises. Probably, as with the mounting evidence of concurrent trends in the effects of global warming, the accumulating evidence of links between both emergencies, whether it be industrialised agriculture and the loss of biodiversity or our polluted cities, may finally convince enough people it really *is* time to change. Most important of all, after watching so many dedicated and exhausted doctors and nurses struggling to save lives with insufficient equipment – the direct result of previous governments' reduced support for public services in many countries – they may finally reject the destructive free market ideology which has brought the world to this dire state.

For researchers concerned with understanding the psychological responses to these crises, it may also be a good time to reconsider their approach to problems of cognitive bias as though they can be separated from the social and political circumstances in which they arise – what I described as the 'elephant in the room'. Certainly, no field theory of the self of the kind I have proposed in this book can ignore the influence of group mindedness and related pressures – of which many examples are cited in these pages – on political choices. The issue, as we have seen, is especially important when it comes to voting habits and their potential manipulation by corrupt powers, particularly in flawed electoral systems where disunited opposition parties find it difficult to break the grip on power held by malfunctioning but more united parties. Given the higher levels of strategic planning – and yes, rational thought – that tactical voting entails it is no surprise it remains an unpopular method with both ordinary voters and professional politicians; a failure that has permitted the passing of ill-considered programmes and the election of some of the least-qualified leaders in the world. It may be too much to expect any swift resolution of such problems, but an ancient system of government born of a small polis that cannot be better adapted to deal with the dangers as well as the opportunities presented by mass communication and data systems, is likely to perish along with the civilisation it has hitherto supported.

Notes and references

Preface

1   Abel, C. (2015). *The Extended Self: Architecture, Memes and Minds.* Manchester University Press, Manchester.
2   Abel, C. (2013). 'The extended self: tacit knowing and place identity'. In *Rethinking Aesthetics: The Role of Body in Design* (Bhatt, R. ed.), pp. 100–139, Routledge, New York,.
3   Abel, C. (2013), p. 128.
4   See Abel, C. (2015), p. 54.
5   I am aware that, while the research by neuroscientists and others described in this book supports my case that the human animal is not alone in possessing a self, some readers may be critical of the methods used in those investigations, which often involve conducting live experiments with other species as well as human subjects – a morally difficult and, for many, no doubt sensitive topic for which, given the valuable knowledge such research has yielded about the capabilities of nature's creatures, there are no easy answers. For a comprehensive review of the debate, see Newton, D. E. (2013). *The Animal Experimentation Debate: A Reference Handbook.* ABC-CLIO, Santa Barbara.
6   Abel, C. (2017, 3rd edn). *Architecture and Identity: Responses to Cultural and Technological Change.* Routledge, Abingdon.

Introduction

1   See Diamond, J. (2005). *Collapse: How Societies Choose to Fail or Survive.* Allen Lane, London.
2   If that was not clear enough before, then it must surely be now. From climate change denial to the current rise in the most aggressive forms of group expression in Europe and the United States, as well as in other parts of the world, the apparent willingness of individuals to suspend any critical faculties they might otherwise possess and to blindly follow whatever leaders or groups they identify with most, can no longer be ignored. Nor is the problem solely one of insufficient education or social deprivation, though both have been exploited by leaders of all stripes. The still unfolding story, for example, of the withdrawal of the United Kingdom from the

European Union, or 'Brexit' as it is called, shows all too clearly a widespread refusal by British 'Leavers' to confront the very real and problematic consequences of that withdrawal, which cuts across all social and educational levels.

3 See Polanyi, M. (1958). *Personal Knowledge: Towards a Post-critical Philosophy.* University of Chicago Press, Chicago, IL. Also Polanyi, M. (1967). *The Tacit Dimension.* Anchor Books, New York. Also Polanyi, M. (1969). *Knowing and Being.* University of Chicago Press, Chicago.
4 Beginning with, for example, Abel, C. (1981). 'The function of tacit knowing in learning design'. *Design Studies,* Vol. 2, October, pp. 209–214. For later discussions of Polanyi's thought, see Abel, C. (2013). 'The extended self: tacit knowing and place identity'. In *Rethinking Aesthetics: The Role of Body in Design* (Bhatt, R., ed.), pp. 100–139, Routledge, New York. Also Abel, C. (2015).
5 Lewin, K. (1935; 2013). *A Dynamic Theory of Personality: Selected Papers.* Read Books, Milton Keynes. Also Lewin, K. (1951; 1964). *Field Theory in Social Science: Selected Theoretical Papers.* Harper & Row, New York.
6 Kuhn, T. (1962). *The Structure of Scientific Revolutions.* University of Chicago Press, Chicago, IL.
7 Stiegler, B. (1998). *Technics and Time, I: The Fault of Epimetheus.* Trans. Richard Beardsworth and George Collins. Stanford University Press, Stanford, CA.
8 See Abel, C. (2015) Especially Chapters 7 and 8.
9 Lewis, S. L. and Maslin, M. A. (2018). *The Human Planet: How We Created the Anthropocene.* Pelican Books, London.
10 See Polanyi, M. (1967).
11 See Polanyi, M. (1958), p. 300.

PART I The background

1 Mead, G. H. (1934; 1962). *Mind, Self, & Society: From the Standpoint of a Social Behaviorist, Vol. 1.* The University of Chicago Press, Chicago, p. 140.

Chapter I The nature–nurture debate

1 Darwin, C. (1972; 1859, 1st edn). *On the Origin of Species: A Facsimile of the First Edition.* Antheum, New York.
2 Tomasello, M. (1999). *The Cultural Origins of Human Cognition.* Harvard University Press, Cambridge, MA.
3 Tomasello, M. (1999), p. 49.
4 Bouchard Jr T. J. (1999). 'Genes, environment and personality'. In *The Nature-Nurture Debate: The Essential Readings* (Ceci, S. J. and Williams, W. M. eds), pp. 98–103, Oxford, Blackwell.
5 Bouchard Jr. T. J. (1999), p. 101.
6 Bouchard Jr. T. J. (1999), p. 102.
7 See Adam, D. (2018). *The Genius Within: Smart Pills, Brain Hacks and Adventures in Intelligence.* Picador, London.
8 Plomin, R. and John C. Defries (1999). 'The genetics of cognitive abilities and disabilities'. In *The Nature-Nurture Debate* (Ceci, S. J. and Williams, W. M. eds), pp. 178–195.
9 Plomin, R. and John C. Defries (1999), pp. 178–179.

10 Identical and fraternal twins are both born from the same pregnancy. However identical (monozygotic) twins have the same father whereas fraternal (dizygotic) twins have different fathers. Identical twins also share 100% of their genes while fraternal twins generally share 50%; about the same as any other siblings.

11 Plomin, R. and Defries, J. C. (1999), p. 183.

12 Plomin, R. and Defries, J. C. (1999), p. 186.

13 Keller, E. F. (2000). *The Century of the Gene*. Harvard University Press, Cambridge, MA.

14 Hubbard, R. and Elijah, W. (2000). *Exploding the Gene Myth: How Genetic Information is Produced and Manipulated by Scientists, Physicians, Employers, Insurance Companies, Educators, and Law Enforcers*. Beacon Press, Boston.

15 Ceci, S. J. and Williams, W. M. (1999), p. 7.

16 Carey, N. (2012). *The Epigenetics Revolution: How Modern Biology is Rewriting Our Understanding of Genetics, Disease and Inheritance*. Icon Books, London.

17 As the name implies, epigenetics ('epi' is the Greek derivative for 'upon', 'over' or 'beside') is tasked with explaining those personal inherited characteristics that cannot be explained by the genetic code and its direct effects on the characteristic form (phenotype) of the organism alone, or by mutations and natural selection.

18 Carey, N. (2012), p. 2.

19 Pursuing the theatrical analogy, Carey likens the process to two modern film versions of Shakespeare's *Romeo and Juliet* separated by sixty years, each of which presents a radically different interpretation of the same original play, involving different directors and leading actors, reflecting the changing cultural times. See also Ridley, M. (2003). *Nature via Nurture: Genes, Experience and What Makes Us Human*. Fourth Estate, London. Offering a similar interpretation to Carey's analogy, Ridley writes: 'Genes are not puppet masters, nor blueprints. Nor are they just the carriers of heredity. They are active during life; they switch each other on or off; *they respond to the environment* [emphasis added]. They may direct the construction of the body and brain in the womb, but they set about dismantling and rebuilding what they have made almost at once in response to experience. They are both cause and consequence of our actions'. Ibid, p. 6.

20 See also Diamond, J. (1999). 'War Babies'. In *The Nature-Nurture Debate: The Essential Readings* (Ceci, S. J. and Williams, W. M. eds), pp. 14–22, Blackwell, Oxford.

21 In the case of the mothers' malnutrition occurring in the late months of pregnancy, despite having as much food as they wished during their lifetime, 'the babies who were born small stayed small all their lives, with lower obesity rates than the general popula-tion'. Carey, N. (2012), p. 3. Contrarily, if the malnutrition occurred during early preg-nancy, though the children were born with normal body weights, they suffered later from higher than normal rates of obesity and diabetes as well as mental health problems.

22 Carey, N. (2012), p. 7.

23 Carey, N. (2012), p. 104.

24 Carey, N. (2012), p. 112.

Similar studies were carried out by a different group of scientists with mice as their subjects, the males being fed an abnormally low protein diet with an increased level of sugar to compensate for the energy loss. As with the former experiment, the males were mated to females fed on a normal diet. Focusing on the liver function and looking for any subsequent abnormalities in the mouse pups they found genetic mis-regulations similar to the former study with rats, together with other epigenetic changes in the pups' livers, supporting Carey's conclusion.

25 Francis, R. C. (2011). *Epigenetics: How Environment Shapes Our Genes*. W. W. Norton & Co., New York.

26 Francis, R. C. (2011), p. 5.

27 Francis, R. C. (2011), pp. 28–29.

28 Carson, R. (1962; 2000). *Silent Spring*. Penguin Books, London.

29 Carey, N. (2012), p. 114.

30 Not everyone involved in the debate agrees with that conclusion, however. See, for example, Plomin, R. (2018). *Blueprint: How DNA Makes Us Who We Are*. Allen Lane, London.

31 Rose, H. and Rose, S. (2012). *Genes, Cells and Brains: The Promethean Promises of the New Biology*. Verso, London.

32 Rose, H. and Rose, S. (2012), p. 73.

33 Rose, H. and Rose, S. (2012), p. 74.

34 Kosslyn, S. M. (2002). *Neural Plasticity: The Effects of Environment on the Development of the Cerebral Cortex*. Harvard University Press, Cambridge, MA.

35 Kosslyn, S. M. (2002), p. 1.

36 See also Huttenlocher, P. R. (2002). *Neural Plasticity: The Effects of Environment on the Development of the Cerebral Cortex*. Harvard University Press, Cambridge, MA.

37 Kosslyn, S. M. (2002), p. 5.

38 Kosslyn, S. M. (2002), p. 170. See also Denes, G. (2016). *Neural Plasticity Across the Lifespan: How the Brain Can Change*. Routledge, London.

39 Kosslyn, S. M. (2002), p. 7.

40 Kosslyn, S. M. (2002), p. 203.

41 Overton, W. F. (2004). 'Embodied Development: Ending the Nativism-Empiricism Debate'. In *Nature and Nurture: The Complex Interplay of Genetic and Environmental Influences on Human Behaviour and Development* (Coll, C. G., Bearer, E. L. and Lerner, R. M. eds), pp. 201–223, New York: Psychology Press.

42 See Merleau-Ponty, M. (1962). *Phenomenology of Perception*. Trans. C. Smith. Routledge and Kegan Paul, London.

43 Overton, W. F. (2004), p. 202.

44 Overton, W. F. (2004), p. 204.

45 Lerner, R. M. (2012). 'Genes and the Promotion of Positive Human Development: Hereditarian Versus Developmental Perspective'. In *Nature and Nurture: The Complex Interplay of Genetic and Environmental Influences on Human Behaviour and Development* (Coll, C. G., Bearer, E. L. and Lerner, R. M. eds), pp. 1–33, New York: Psychology Press.

46 Lerner, R. M. (2012), p. 11.

47 Lerner, R. M. (2012), p. 12.

Chapter 2   Inheritance systems

1 Darwin, C. (1972; 1859, 1st edn). *On the Origin of Species: A Facsimile of the First Edition*. Antheum, New York.

2 Pigliucci, M. and Muller, G. B. (2010). 'Elements of an Extended Evolutionary Synthesis'. In *Evolution – The Extended Thesis* (Pigliucci, M. and Muller, G. B. eds), pp. 3–17, The MIT Press, Cambridge, MA.

3 Pigliucci, M. and Muller, G. B. (2010), p. 7.

4 Tomasello, M. (1999). *The Cultural Origins of Human Cognition*. Harvard University Press, Cambridge, MA, p. 78.

5 Kirshner, M. W. and Gerhart, J. C. (2010). 'Facilitated Variation'. In *Evolution – The Extended Thesis* (Pigliucci, M. and Muller, G. B. eds), pp. 253–280, The MIT Press, Cambridge, MA.

6 Kirshner, M. W. and Gerhart, J. C. (2010), p. 253. Summarising their theory of 'facilitated variation', the authors liken evolutionary theory to a three-legged stool based on natural selection, genetic variation and phenotypic variation; the first being covered by Darwin and the second by the Modern Synthesis, leaving the third to be finally explored by evolutionary biologists like themselves.

7 Kirshner, M. W. and Gerhart, J. C. (2010), p. 277.

8 Muller, G. B. (2010). 'Epigenetic innovation'. In *Evolution – The Extended Synthesis* (Pigliucci, M. and Muller, G. B. eds), pp. 307–332, The MIT Press, Cambridge, MA.

9 Muller, G. B. (2010), p. 309.

10 Muller, G. B. (2010), p. 310. In accordance with current classifications of morphological novelty, Muller identifies three distinct types: Type I novelties refer to the primary anatomical architectures of body plans; Type II novelties are discrete new elements added to an existing body plan, and Type III novelties involve major character changes to existing body plans.

11 Muller, G. B. (2010), p. 322. In addition, rather than employing terms suggestive of the teleological character of natural selection, Muller repeatedly presents phenotypic innovation in terms of *emergence*, a concept that allows for *internally generated* developments as well as those stimulated by environmental factors. Thus phenotypic innovation is 'rooted in the *emergent effects* [added emphasis] of interacting levels of biological organization' Ibid, p. 313. Or again, summarising the core principles of epigenetic innovation theory, Muller writes: 'In this scenario, novelties *emerge as side effects* [emphasis added] of evolutionary modifications to developmental systems'. Ibid, p. 313. For more on emergence, see Chapter 3.

12 Muller, G. B. (2010), p. 323.

13 Wagner, G. P. (2014). *Homology, Genes, and Evolutionary Innovation*. Princeton University Press, Princeton, NJ. Wagner defines homology as 'the existence of the same body parts in different and often distantly related organisms – aka homologs'. Ibid., p. 8.

14 Wagner, G. P. (2014), p. 2.

15 Employing similar epigenetic and systemic terms to those used by other Evo–Devo researchers, Wagner explains that individual body parts are generated by gene regulatory networks, or Character Identity Networks (ChINs), as they are called, 'that *enable the expression of different developmental programs* in different parts of the body'. Wagner, G. P. (2014), p. 3. Maintained by positive feedback loops between genes, cell types and 'transcription factor complexes' (see below), ChINs have been found to be evolutionarily more stable than other elements of an organism's developmental programme 'and are often rigidly associated with the identity of the character that they enable'. Ibid, p. 4. Moreover, Wagner observes, the genes responsible for determining character identity 'vary much less between species than those responsible for *positional information*' [emphasis added]. Ibid, p. 6.

16 Wagner, G. P. (2014), p. 425.

17 Odling-Smee, J. (2010). 'Niche inheritance'. In *Evolution – The Extended Thesis* (Pigliucci, M. and Muller, G. B. eds), pp. 175–207, The MIT Press, Cambridge, MA.

18 Originally proposed in 1959 by C. H. Waddington, a developmental geneticist, and subsequently by a population geneticist, R. C. Lewontin, the concept of niche

construction has been theoretically elaborated by Odling-Smee at the level of animal construction, and more recently, at the level of human activity.

19 Odling-Smee, J. (2010), p. 176.

20 Odling-Smee, J. (2010), p. 182. For example, where maternal conditions can result in physiological states – poor health, obesity and so forth – being passed on to the mothers' offspring and even subsequent generations.

21 Dawkins, R. (1982; 1999). *The Extended Phenotype: The Long Reach of the Gene.* Oxford University Press, Oxford.

22 Odling-Smee, J. (2010), p. 190.

23 Odling-Smee, J. (2010), p. 194.

24 Odling-Smee, F. J., Laland, K. N. and Feldman, M. W. (2003). *Niche Construction – The Neglected Process in Evolution.* Princeton University Press, Princeton, NJ.

25 Odling-Smee, F. J. et al. (2003), pp. 47–48.

26 Laland, K. N. (2017). *Darwin's Unfinished Symphony: How Culture Made the Human Mind.* Princeton University Press, Princeton, NJ.

27 Laland, K. N. (2017), p. 3.

28 Laland, K. N. (2017), p. 7.

29 Research and development of the game itself proceeded in two stages. The first stage was conducted as an open international tournament in which the participants were invited to try out the three 'moves' in response to a varied and changing set of environmental scenarios and resources provided to them by Laland and his team. The amount of time devoted to each strategy was also recorded. In the second part of the game's development the recorded strategies and outcomes of each player's performance were converted into digital formats as components of the completed computer-based game. Finally, the whole range of submitted strategies and outcomes were played off against each other in search of the most effective combinations in coping with complex and changing environmental pressures.

30 The available resources for each scenario, which included hunting and fishing opportunities as well as sowing crops for food supplies, also evolved during the game, presenting further adaptive challenges. Subsequent computer simulations played off the players' best choice strategies against each other, the outcomes of which were closely analysed for the strengths and weaknesses of each strategy. Finally, the winning strategy was identified as making the most efficient use of time, energy and resources in the evolutionary game of survival.

31 Laland, K. N. (2017), p. 67.

32 Laland, K. N. (2017), p. 72.

33 Laland, K. N. (2017), p. 72. However, Laland's conclusions invite a note of caution. As with any artificial experiment simulating highly complex, real-world behaviour, the results will inevitably be influenced by the goals, structure and rules of the experiment established by its designers. Above all, while the game's outcomes, as Laland describes them, purport to throw light on habits of social behaviour common to both animals and humans, it should not be forgotten that the principal agents in the game were not simple organisms surviving in a natural Darwinian world, nor even the smart, tool-using chimpanzees Laland describes, but educated human beings. Most were academic researchers like the game's designers themselves, some of whom also used highly sophisticated techniques, such as looking into the future as well as back into the past when working out their best-choice strategies; a sophisticated form of learning that Laland concedes would be beyond

the capability of most, if not all, animals, but is common in human cognition. Given the general direction of evolution from simpler to more complex forms of life, if the aim of the game is to trace the evolutionary origins of human social learning in animal social behaviour, then players cannot logically employ any methods of learning exclusive to humans within the game, since in evolutionary history they would only follow *later* from simpler forms of learning. Even time-travelling agents might find that one paradox too many.

34 Key, C. A. and Aiello, L. C. (1999). 'The evolution of social organization'. In *The Evolution of Culture: An Interdisciplinary View* (Dunbar, R., Knight, C. and Power, C. eds), pp. 15–33, Edinburgh University Press, Edinburgh.

35 Key, C. A. and Aiello, L. C. (1999), p. 16.

36 Key, C. A. and Aiello, L. C. (1999), p. 17.

37 Key, C. A. and Aiello, L. C. (1999), pp. 18–19. The authors define the energetic cost of reproduction as 'the sum of the energetic costs of every single activity that contributes to the production of a single surviving offspring'. Ibid.

38 Key, C. A. and Aiello, L. C. (1999), p. 21.

39 Key, C. A. and Aiello, L. C. (1999), p. 27.

40 Lumsden, C. J. and Wilson, E. O. (1983). *Promethean Fire: Reflections on the Origin of Mind*. Harvard University Press, Cambridge, MA. Specialised researchers may also wish to see the authors' previous work, Lumsden, C. J. and Wilson, E. O. (1981). *Genes, Mind, and Culture: The Coevolutionary Process*. Harvard University Press, Cambridge, MA.

41 Lumsden, C. J. and Wilson, E. O. (1983), p. 2. In advancing their theory of the evolution of mind, the authors clearly equate their idea of mind with full self-consciousness and the emergence of human language and culture, a common anthropocentric approach. However, as interpreted by the metatheory set out in these pages, while having a mind *presupposes* having a self and a related identity, *having a self does not presuppose having a mind*; at least not a reflective, fully self-consciousness one – merely, as all animals have, a self with the capacity to *distinguish between self and other*. Evolutionarily speaking, the emergence of the animal self therefore *precedes* the emergence of mind and provides the foundations for its eventual full development in humans.

42 Lumsden, C. J. and Wilson, E. O. (1983), p. 19.

43 Lumsden, C. J. and Wilson, E. O. (1983), p. 20.

44 Durham, W. H. (1991). *Coevolution: Genes, Culture, and Human Diversity*. Stanford University Press, Stanford, CA.

45 Durham, W. H. (1991), pp. 8–9.

46 Durham, W. H. (1991), p. 9.

47 Durham, W. H. (1991), pp. 242–243.

48 Odling-Smee, F. J. et al. (2003), p. 250.

49 Jablonka, E. and Lamb, M. J. (2005). *Evolution in Four Dimensions: Genetic, Epigenetic, Behavioral, and Symbolic Variation in the History of Life*. The MIT Press, Cambridge, MA. Also critical of the narrow focus of the MS on genetic inheritance procedures, the two authors trace the interactions between genes and all three other dimensions, from genes and epigenetic systems, through genes and behaviour, to genes and language, identifying each of the main factors affecting the transfer of variations from one to the other level along the way.

50 Jablonka, E. and Lamb, M. J. (2005), p. 341.

51 Jablonka, E. and Lamb, M. J. (2005), p. 194.

52 See Cassirer, E. (1955). *The Philosophy of Symbolic forms: Vol I, Language*. Yale University Press, New Haven, CT. Also Cassirer, E. (1962). *An Essay on Man*. Yale University Press, New Haven, CT.

53 Jablonka, E. and Lamb, M. J. (2005), p. 201.

54 See Dawkins, R. (1989, 2nd edn). *The Selfish Gene*. Oxford University Press, Oxford.

55 Jablonka, E. and Lamb, M. J. (2005), p. 55.

56 See also Sperber, D. (2000). 'An objection to the memetic approach to culture'. In *Darwinizing Culture: The Status of Memetics as a Science* (Aunger, R. ed.), pp. 163–173, Oxford University Press, Oxford. Like Jablonka and Lamb, Sperber, who is a psychologist, argues that memes are not so much simply copied, as reconstructed by inference, a complex process of cognition involving the attribution of intentionality as well as learning skills. For a related critical evaluation of Dawkins' concept of the meme and an alternative interpretation, see Abel, C. (2015), especially Chapters 6 and 8.

57 Jablonka, E. and Lamb, M. J. (2005), p. 220.

58 Jablonka, E. and Lamb, M. J. (2005), p. 221.

59 Bonduriansky, R. and Day, T. (2018). *Extended Heredity: A New Understanding of Inheritance and Evolution*. Princeton University Press, NJ.

60 Bonduriansky, R. and Day, T. (2018), p. xii.

61 Bonduriansky, R. and Day, T. (2018), p. 82.

62 Bonduriansky, R. and Day, T. (2018), p. 82.

PART II   The metatheory

1 Darwin, C. (1871; 2009). *The Descent of Man, and Selection in Relation to Sex, Vol. 1*. Cambridge University Press, New York, pp. 104–105.

Chapter 3   Self-organisation

1 See, for example, Koestler, A. and Smythies, J. R. eds (1971). *Beyond Reductionism: New Perspectives in the Life Sciences*. Macmillan, London. Also Harre, R. (1972). *The Philosophies of Science*. Oxford University Press, Oxford.

2 Bertalanffy, L. von. (1950). 'The theory of open systems in physics and biology'. *Science*, 13 January, Vol. 111, pp. 23–29. See also Bertalanffy, L. von. (1968). *General System Theory: Foundations, Development, Applications*. George Braziller, New York.

3 Polanyi, M. (1958). *Personal Knowledge: Towards a Post-critical Philosophy*. University of Chicago Press, Chicago, IL.

4 Polanyi, M. (1958), p. 383.

5 Polanyi, M. (1958), p. 389.

6 Prigogine, I. and Stengers, I. (1985). *Order Out of Chaos: Man's New Dialogue With Nature*. Flamingo, London.

7 Prigogine, I. and Stengers, I. (1985), p. 292.

8 For a general introduction, see Lewin, R. (1993). *Complexity: Life on the Edge of Chaos*. Phoenix, London.

9 Coveny, P. and Highfield, R. (1995). *Frontiers of Complexity: The Search for Order in a Chaotic World*. Faber and Faber, London.

10 Coveny, P. and Highfield, R. (1995), p. 7.

11 Dupre, J. (1993). *The Disorder of Things: Metaphysical Foundations of the Disunity of Science*. Harvard University Press, Cambridge, MA.

12 Dupre, J. (1993), p. 1.

13 Feyerabend, P. (1975). *Against Method*. New Left Books, London. However, while advocating a competitive approach to scientific theory, contrary to some postmodernists' suggestion that, consequently, 'anything goes', at no point did Feyerabend question the need for verifiable evidence, without which scientific enquiry would have no meaning. Rather, his philosophy is better described as a form of what I call 'critical relativism', in which each theory or concept is subject to critical examination by an alternative theory – an approach I based on Wittgenstein's 'language games'. For a discussion, see Abel, C. (1979). 'The language analogy in architectural theory and criticism: Some remarks in the light of Wittgenstein's linguistic relativism'. *Architectural Association Quarterly*, Vol. 12, December, pp. 39–47. For a related discussion of Feyerabend's philosophy with relevance to research methods in design and environmental psychology, see Abel, C. (1982b). 'The case for anarchy in design research'. In *Changing Design* (Evans, B., Powell, J. A. and Talbot, R. J. eds), pp. 295–302, Chichester, John Wiley & Sons.

14 Dupre, J. (1993), p. 242.

15 Clarke, B. and Hansen, M. B. N., eds. (2009). *Emergence and Embodiment: New Essays in Second-order Systems Theory*. London: Duke University Press.

16 Clarke, B. and Hansen, M. B. N. (2009). 'Introduction: Neocybernetic emergence'. In *Emergence and Embodiment: New Essays in Second-order Systems Theory* (Clarke, B. and Hansen, M. B. N., eds), p. 6, Duke University Press, London.

17 Clarke, B. and Hansen, M. B. N. (2009), pp. 7–10.

18 In stressing the need for semi-autonomous systems to reduce the general level of environmental complexity to manageable levels, the concept of double closure suggests a refinement of the British cybernetician Ross Ashby's original 'law of requisite variety'. Broadly speaking, the law states that adaptation will proceed most efficiently if there is a match between the organisational level of any living system and that of its environment. See Ashby, W. R. (1962). 'Principles of the self-organizing system'. In *Principles of Self-organization* (Von Foester, H. and Zopf, Jr., G. W. eds), pp. 255–278, Pergamon Press, London. However, by filtering out excessive or irrelevant information, systems with double closure employ a further, proactive strategy aimed at reducing levels of environmental complexity to better accord with the system's *own* responsive capacities.

19 Polanyi, M. (1969), p. 144.

20 Polanyi, M. (1967), p. 34. The two forms of cognition, 'proximal' and 'distal', together stress the *spatial dynamic* underlying Polanyi's theory of tacit knowledge and its relationship to the human body. The first refers to cognitions we feel that are somehow *close* to us, while the second refers to the point of focal awareness (i.e., the task our attention is focused upon) which is felt as something more *distant* from us – aspects that acquire special significance in the light of the research on 'peripersonal' and 'extrapersonal' space described below in Chapter 5. For more on tacit knowing, See Abel, C. (2015), pp. 33–37.

21 Polanyi, M. (1967), p. 35.

22 Polanyi, M. (1967), p. 45. For more on Polanyi's theory of tacit knowing with specific reference to the education and practice of design, see Abel, C. (1981).

23 Gould, S. J. (1987). 'Is a new and general theory of evolution emerging?' In *Self-Organizing Systems: The Emergence of Order* (Yates, F. E. ed.), pp. 113–130, Plenum Press, New York.

24 Gould, S. J. (1987), p. 115.

25 Gould, S. J. (1987), p. 116.

26 See, for example, Koestler, A. (1964). *The Act of Creation*. Macmillan, New York. Also Leatherdale, W. H. (1974). *The Role of Analogy, Model and Metaphor in Science*. North Holland/American Elsevier, Amsterdam and New York.

27 Gould, S. J. (1987), p. 122.

28 Gould, S. J. (1987), p. 127.

29 For a critique of neo-Darwinism, see Kaufmann, S. A. (1993). *The Origins of Order: Self-organization and Selection in Evolution*. Oxford University Press, New York. Kaufmann writes: 'Darwin's answer to the sources of order we see all around us is overwhelmingly an appeal to a single singular force: natural selection. It is this single-force view which I believe to be inadequate, for it fails to notice, fails to stress, fails to incorporate the possibility that simple and complex systems exhibit order spontaneously'. Ibid, p. xiii. For related developments in language studies, see MacWhinney, B. ed. (2008). *The Emergence of Language*. Psychology Press, Hove. Also Tomasello, M. and Slobin, D. I. eds (2015). *Beyond Nature and Nurture: Essays in Honor of Elizabeth Bates*. Psychology Press, Hove.

30 Corradini, A. and O'Connor, T. eds (2010). *Emergence in Science and Philosophy*. Routledge, New York.

31 Corradini, A. and O'Connor, T. eds (2010), p. xi.

32 Corradini, A. and O'Connor, T. eds (2010), p. xi.

33 Gillet, C. (2010). 'On the implications of scientific composition and completeness: Or, the troubles, and *troubles*, of non-reductive physicalism'. In *Emergence in Science and Philosophy* (Corradini, A. and O'Connor, T. eds), pp. 25–45, Routledge, New York.

34 Gillet, C. (2010), p. 29.

35 Gillet, C. (2010), p. 30.

36 Quoted in Gillet, C. (2010), p. 32.

37 Quoted in Gillet, C. (2010), p. 32.

38 Gillet, C. (2010), p. 37.

39 Francesco, M. Di (2010). 'Two varieties of causal emergentism'. In *Emergence in Science and Philosophy* (Corradini, A. and O'Connor, T. eds), pp. 64–77, Routledge, New York.

40 Francesco, M. Di (2010), p. 73.

41 Francesco, M. Di (2010), p. 67.

42 It may also be noted from the work of MacKinnon and Laughlin quoted by Gill above, that, although firm empirical evidence was found by both eminent scientists of the *existence* of emergent properties in the subjects of their research, Gill is not able to offer a clear and unambiguous explanation of the actual *process* of emergence itself, other than that it involves a form of 'non-causal determination' for which he coined the term 'machresis'.

43 Quoted in Francesco, M. Di (2010), p. 73.

44 Francesco, M. Di (2010), p. 74.

45 Andersen, P. B., Emmeche C., Finnemann, N. O. and Christiansen, P. V. eds (2000). *Downward Causation: Minds, Bodies and Matter*. Aarhus University Press, Arrhus.

46 Pattee, H. H. (2000). 'Causation, control, and the evolution of complexity'. In *Downward Causation: Minds, Bodies and Matter* (Andersen, P. B., Emmeche C., Finnemann, N. O. and Christiansen, P. V. eds), pp. 63–77, Aarhus University Press, Arrhus.

47 Pattee, H. H. (2000), p. 66.

48 A pioneer of quantum theory, Bohr chose the inscription, 'opposites are complementary', for his personal coat of arms upon being awarded a knighthood by the Danish king, and included the Chinese symbol of *t'ai-chi* in the centre of the design, illustrating the archetypal male and female poles, *yin* and *yang*, making up a complete circle, or unity.

49 Pattee, H. H. (2000), p. 67.

50 Pattee, H. H. (2000), p. 70.

51 Pattee, H. H. (2000), p. 72

52 Maturana, H. R. and Varela, F. J. (1980). *Autopoiesis and Cognition: The Realization of the Living.* Kluwer, Boston. See also Maturana, H. R. and Varela, F. J. (1987; 1998). *The Tree of Knowledge: The Biological Roots of Human Understanding.* Shambala, Boston. For a general introduction to the theory and its many interpretations, see Mingers, J. (1995). *Self-producing Systems: Implications and Applications of Autopoiesis.* Plenum Press, New York.

53 Maturana, H. R. and Varela, F. J. (1980), p. 5.

54 Maturana, H. R. and Varela, F. J. (1980), p. 13.

55 Maturana, H. R. and Varela, F. J. (1980), p. 5.

56 Maturana, H. R. and Varela, F. J. (1980), p. 6.

57 Although relatively simple in comparison with multi-cellular organisms, since there are single-cell organisms that survive by themselves, they also qualify as examples of individual living systems of sufficient complexity. Mingers offers his own concise description of the individual living cell: 'a cell consists of a cell membrane or boundary enclosing various structures such as the nucleus, mitochondria and lysosomes, as well as many (and often complex) molecules produced from within. These structures are in constant chemical interplay both with each other and, in the case of the membrane, with their external medium. It is a dynamic, integrated chemical network of incredible sophistication'. Mingers, J. (1995), p. 11.

58 Maturana, H. R. and Varela, F. J. (1980), p. 9.

59 Maturana, H. R. and Varela, F. J. (1980), p. 9.

60 Maturana, H. R. and Varela, F. J. (1980), p. 66.

61 Maturana, H. R. and Varela, F. J. (1980), p. 99.

62 Maturana, H. R. and Varela, F. J. (1980), p. 99.

63 Maturana, H. R. and Varela, F. J. (1980), p. 102.

64 Proveti, J. (2009). 'Beyond autopoiesis: Inflections of emergence and politics in Francisco Varela'. In *Emergence and Embodiment: New Essays in Second-order Systems Theory* (Clarke, B. and Hansen, M. B. N. eds), pp. 95–112, Duke University Press, London.

65 Proveti, J. (2009), p. 94.

66 Proveti, J. (2009), p. 101.

67 Proveti, J. (2009), p. 95.

68 Varela, F. J., Thompson, E. and Rosch, E. (1993). *The Embodied Mind: Cognitive Science and Human Experience.* The MIT Press, Cambridge, MA.

69 Proveti, J. (2009), p. 103.

70 Proveti, J. (2009), p. 104.

71 Proveti, J. (2009), p. 104.

72 Proveti, J. (2009), p. 107.

73 See also Moreno, A. and Umerez, J. (2000). 'Downward causation at the core of living organization'. In *Downward Causation: Minds, Bodies and Matter* (Andersen, P. B., Emmeche, C., Finnemann, N. O. and Christiansen, P. V. eds), pp. 99–117, Aarhus University Press, Arrhus.

74 See, for example, Hensel, M., Menges, A. and Weinstock, M. eds (2004). *Emergence: Morphogenic Design Strategies*. Wiley Academy, Chichester. For a critique, see Abel, C. (2007). 'Virtual evolution: A memetic critique of genetic algorithms in design'. In *Techniques and Technologies: Transfer and Transformation. Proceedings of the 4th International Conference of the Association of Architectural Schools of Australia, 2007* (Orr, K, and Kaji-O'Grady, S. eds). University of Technology, Sydney. Re-published under the title, 'Genetic Designs' in Abel, C. (2017 3rd edn), pp. 98–109. See also Wise, C. (2004). 'Drunk in an orgy of technology'. In *Emergence: Morphogenetic Design Strategies* (Hensel, M., Menges, A. and Weinstock, M. eds), pp. 54–57, Wiley, Chichester.

75 Weinstock, M. (2010). *The Architecture of Emergence: The Evolution of Form in Nature and Civilization*. Wiley, Chichester.

76 See Wohlleben P. (2015). *The Hidden Life of Trees*. Trans. Jane Billinghurst, William Collins, London.

77 Weinstock, M. (2010), p. 269.

78 For a related discussion on complementary modes of thought in both Eastern and Western cultures, see Abel, C. (1991). 'The essential tension'. *Architecture and Urbanism*, July, 1991. Republished in Abel, C. (2017 3rd edn). *Architecture and Identity: Responses to Cultural and Technological Change*. Routledge, Abingdon, pp. 196–213.

Chapter 4   The invisible self

1 See Metzinger, T. (2009). *The Ego Tunnel: The Science of the Mind and the Myth of the Self*. Basic Books, New York. Also Hood, B. (2011). *The Self Illusion: Who do You Think You Are?* Constable, London.

2 Dennett, D. C. (1991). *Consciousness Explained*. Penguin Books, London.

3 Blackmore, S. (1999) *The Meme Machine*. Oxford University Press, Oxford.

4 Dupre, J. (1993), p. 6. Note the logical terminology, 'necessary and sufficient'.

5 Dupre, J. (1993), p. 5.

6 Dupre, J. (1993), p. 19.

7 Varela, F. J. et al. (1993), p. 150.

8 Varela, F. J. et al. (1993), p. 59.

9 Varela, F. J. et al. (1993), pp. xv–xvi.

10 Similar essentialist arguments, which stem from Aristotle's original, logically defined concept of natural species, have dogged the science of speciation. However, as John Wilkins explains, most biologists and naturalists reject the essentialist approach as unworkable and accept the more open Darwinian interpretation, which allows for the development of knowledge, and is not so different from that used in everyday language and experience. See Wilkins, J. S. ((2009). *Species: A History of the Idea*. University of California Press, Berkeley.

11 Parfit, D. (1979). 'Personal Identity'. In *Philosophy As It Is* (Honderich, T. and Burnyeat, M. eds), pp. 186–211, Penguin Books, Harmondsworth.

12 Parfit, D. (1984). *Reasons and Persons*. Oxford University Press, Oxford.

13 Parfit, D. (1979), p. 186.

14 See Parfit, D. (1984), pp. 285–289. In the so-called 'Branch Line' version of the experiment, Parfit asks us to imagine that the reassembled body is actually just a *replica* of the original person that has been transported, leaving the original behind to die a few days later, bemoaning his fate. In that case, in what sense, Parfit enquires, could the two bodies be said to be the same person, since for a short time at least they would inhabit different worlds and lead divergent lives? Setting aside the technological questions involved, particularly the lack of a similar machine at the other end of the process ready to do the reassembling part, it is Parfit's use of the experiment to question our assumptions about the nature of personal identity that is important here.

15 Parfit, D. (1979), p. 193.

16 Parfit, D. (1984), p. 209.

17 Parfit, D. (1979), p. 205.

18 Parfit, D. (1979), p. 205. Quoted from Proust, M. (1945). *Within a Budding Grove*. London, p. 226.

19 Yates, G. B. (1987). 'Differentiation, morphogenesis, and death of organisms'. In *Self-Organizing Systems: The Emergence of Order* (Yates, F. E. ed.), pp. 131–132, Plenum Press, New York.

20 Except in my own work. See my preface for previous references to the concept.

21 See Capra, F. (1975). *The Tao of Physics*. Fontana/Collins, London.

22 Goodwin, B. C. (1987). 'Developing organisms as self-organizing fields'. In *Self-Organizing Systems: The Emergence of Order* (Yates, F. E. ed.), pp. 167–180, Plenum Press, New York.

23 Goodwin, B. C. (1987), p. 170.

24 Goodwin, B. C. (1987), p. 169.

25 Goodwin, B. C. (1987), p. 170.

26 Goodwin, B. C. (1987), p. 171.

27 Goodwin, B. C. (1987), p. 176.

28 Goodwin, B. C. (1987), p. 176.

29 Lewin, K. (1951; 1964). Also Mey, H. (1972; 2015). *Field Theory: A Study of its Application in the Social Sciences*. Transl. Douglas Scott, Routledge, London. Explaining the sources of Lewin's theory, Mey points to both the gestalt psychology of Lewin's time, and, equally important, to field-theoretic developments in the physical sciences then revolutionising scientific thought, from which Lewin quotes Albert Einstein's definition of a field: 'a totality of coexisting facts, which are conceived as mutually dependent, is a *field*'. Mey, H. (1972; 2015), p. 22. Lewin was particularly drawn, Mey explains, to the idea that the space *in between* physical objects, as in a magnetic field, can possess energetic properties, not just the physical objects themselves.

30 Lewin, K. (1935; 2013). *A Dynamic Theory of Personality: Selected Papers*. Read Books, Milton Keynes.

31 A belief, as described in Chapter 2, that persists until this day.

32 Lewin, K. (1935; 2013), p. 40.

33 Lewin, K. (1935; 2013), p. 23.

34 Lewin, K. (1935; 2013), p. 45. For a further discussion of the metatheoretical status of field theory, see Gold, M. (1992). 'Metatheory and field theory in social psychology: relevance or elegance?' *Journal of Social Issues*, Vol. 48, No. 2, pp. 67–78.

35 Lewin, K. (1935; 2013), p. 64.

36 Lewin, K. (1935; 2013), p. 168.

37 Lewin, K. (1935; 2013), p. 169.

38 Lewin, K. (1935; 2013), p. 172. Meaning that the destruction or theft of valued objects can be felt as an intrusion or diminution of the nascent self, perhaps just as much as the abrupt termination by an adult of one child's growing friendship with another.

39 Lewin, K. (1951; 1964). *Field Theory in Social Science: Selected Theoretical Papers.* Harper Torchbooks, New York.

40 Lewin, K. (1951; 1964), p. 25.

41 Lewin (1935; 2013), p. 301.

42 Lewin, K. (1951; 1964), p. 45.

43 In his review of Lewin's work, James Shellenberg, for example, observes that, though Lewin acknowledged that the life space was in constant flux, he 'saw no need to include past events in [his] analysis except insofar as they were a part of the present psychological field'. Shellenberg, J. A. (1978). *Masters of Social Psychology: Freud, Mead, Lewin, and Skinner.* Oxford University Press, New York, p. 72.

44 Lewin, K. (1951; 1964), p. 53. Defining the life space in his foreword to the *Field Theory* essays, the editor, Dorwin Cartwright, also stresses Lewin's focus on the past and future as seen exclusively from the individual's personal concerns: 'This life space consists of the person and the psychological environment *as it exists for him*' [added emphasis]. Lewin, K. (1935; 2013), p. xi.

45 Lewin, K. (1951; 1964), p. 59.

46 Lewin, K. (1951; 1964), p. 130.

47 Lewin, K. (1951; 1964), p. 132.

48 Lewin was also drawn to this period as he detected a significant movement in the approach of psychologists to adolescence, from one which focused primarily on the psychological impact of the biological changes involved, to one which emphasised its social aspects, pointing to 'the fact that the behavior typical of this age is rather different in different societies'. Lewin, K. (1951; 1964), p. 135.

49 For Bourdieu's key writings, see Bourdieu, P. (1984; 2010). *Distinction: A Social Critique of the Judgement of Taste.* Transl. Richard Nice. Routledge, London. Also Bourdieu, P. (1990). *In Other Words: Essays Towards a Reflexive Sociology.* Trans. M. Adamson, Stanford University Press, Stanford CA. By his own account, Bourdieu was also strongly influenced by the thoughts of both Ernst Cassirer and Ludwig Wittgenstein on the semi-autonomous character of what Cassirer described as 'culture-forms' and which Wittgenstein called the 'forms of life' embedded in the practical use of language. For an explication of the latter, see Wittgenstein, L (1953, 3rd edn). *Philosophical Investigations.* Transl. G. E. M. Anscombe, Macmillan, New York. Also Winch, P. (1958). *The Idea of a Social Science and its Relation to Philosophy.* Routledge & Kegan Paul, London.

50 Bourdieu, P. (1990), p. 192.

51 Hilgers M. and Mangez, E. eds. (2015). *Bourdieu's Theory of Social Fields: Concepts and Applications.* Routledge, Abingdon.

52 Hilgers M. and Mangez, E. (2015). 'Introduction to Pierre Bourdieu's theory of social fields'. In *Bourdieu's Theory of Social Fields: Concepts and Applications* (Hilgers

M. and Mangez, E. eds), pp. 4–5, Routledge, Abingdon. However, while Hilgers and Mangez identify significant commonalities between field theories, the latter quali-fying sentence excludes the double meaning often attached to the field concept, as in Goodwin's 'self-organised entity', Lewin's 'life-space' and, not least, Bourdieu's own specialised 'social fields', in which the field designates *both* a specific biological, psychological or social entity *and* the self-organising system which produces and maintains it. The ambiguity, which arises from the analogical origins of the concept, is important in so far as it allows for both general and specific interpretations.

53 Bourdieu, P. (1984, 2010), p. 470.

54 Bourdieu, P. (1984, 2010), p. 165. As Bourdieu describes it, the circular logic of the habitus has the same character as the self-organising systems described above: 'the principle of division into logical classes which organizes the perception of the social world is itself the product of internalization of the division into social classes'. Ibid, p. 166.

55 Bourdieu, P. (1984, 2010), p. 470.

56 Bourdieu, P. (1990), p. 195. There are strong allusions in this passage to Wittgenstein's theory of 'language games'. See n 49 above for references to Wittgenstein's thought. For an application to architectural theory and criticism, see Abel, C. (1979).

57 Hilgers, M. and Mangez, E. eds (2015), p. 7.

58 Hilgers, M. and Mangez, E. eds (2015), p. 7.

59 See also Harre, R. (1974). 'Some remarks on "rule" as a scientific concept'. In *Understanding Other Persons* (Mischel, T. ed.), pp. 143–184, Basil Blackford, Oxford. Harre writes: 'Full self-monitoring and awareness of the archetypal cognitive pro-cess involved in social action occurs *only when there is some doubt about how to proceed* [added emphasis], sometimes through uncertainty as to the definition of the situ-ation, sometimes through uncertainty as to the rules for proceeding in a situation whose definition has to be understood'. Ibid., p. 159.

60 Wells, S. (2010). *Pandora's Seed: The Unforeseen Cost of Civilization*. Allen Lane, London.

61 It needs to be remembered that, even before the first evidence of climate change was made public in the 1980s, far-sighted individuals were already warning of the negative impacts of human development on the planetary ecosystem. See, for example, Carson, R. (1962; 2000). Also Ward, B. and Dubos, R. (1972). *Only One Earth: The Care and Maintenance of a Small Planet*. Pelican Books, Harmondsworth.

62 In a postscript to the republication of his original 1971 essay, Parfit wrote that he had changed his mind about the idea of successive selves, suggesting that it was 'only a *façon de parler*' (i.e., a figure of speech) and that 'taken as anything more it can be misleading'. See Parfit, D. (1979), p. 210. However, figures of speech, especially those with metaphorical significance as Parfit's concept has, can and should be taken ser-iously for what they suggest of new ways of thinking. So I have ignored his advice and instead adapted the concept to better suit the purposes of this book.

Chapter 5   Mapping the field

1 For a general account, see Blakeslee, S. and Blakeslee, M. (2007). *The Body Has a Mind of Its Own*. Random House, New York.

2 Fortunately, while the brain receives signals from pain sensors elsewhere in the body, it has none of its own, so a local anaesthetic suffices.

3 To better communicate his findings, in addition to his graphical representations, Penfield also created a literal, three-dimensional model of the homunculus as the 'little man in the brain', with greatly enlarged hands and mouth to match the equivalent surface area in the brain.

4 Ramachandran, V. S. and Blakeslee, S. (2005). *Phantoms in the Brain: Human Nature and the Architecture of the Mind*. Harper Perennial, London. 2005.

5 Ramachandran, V. S. and Blakeslee, S. (2005), p. 84.

6 Ramachandran, V. S. and Blakeslee, S. (2005), p. 29.

7 Moreover, Ramachandran claims the experiments provided the 'first direct demonstration that such large-scale changes in the organization of the brain could occur in adult humans'. Ramachandran, V. S. and Blakeslee, S. (2005), p. 31.

8 Pelligrino, G. di, and Ladavas, E. (2015). 'Peripersonal space in the brain'. *Neuropsychologia*, Vol. 66. January, pp. 126–133. See also Holmes, N. P., and Spence, C. (2004). 'The body schema and the multisensory representation(s) of peripersonal Space'. *Cognitive Process*, Vol. 5, June, pp. 94–105. Also Graziano, M. S. A., and Gross, C. G. (1994). 'The representation of extrapersonal space: a possible role for bimodal, visual-tactile neurons'. In *The Cognitive Neurosciences* (M. Gazzaniga, ed.), pp. 1021–1034, The MIT Press, Cambridge, MA.

9 Pelligrino, G. di, and Ladavas, E. (2015) , p. 126.

10 See also Holmes, N. P., and Spence, C. (2004), pp. 94–105. Introducing their own review of the research on peripersonal space, the authors write: 'The effective "piloting" of the body to avoid or manipulate objects *in pursuit of behavioral goals* [added emphasis], requires an integrated neural representation of the body (the body "schema") and of the space around the body'. Ibid, p. 94.

11 Pelligrino, G. di, and Ladavas, E. (2015) p. 127.

12 Notably, in their earlier research with primates Graziano and Gross employ *both* terms to denote the same brain–body processes: 'We propose that in the primate, the visual space near the body – extrapersonal space or peripersonal space – is encoded by a system of interconnected brain areas'. Graziano, M. S. A., and Gross, C. G. (1994), p. 1021.

13 Pelligrino, G. di, and Ladavas, E. (2015) , p. 131.

14 Pelligrino, G. di, and Ladavas, E. (2015) p. 128. See also Brozzoli, C., Gentile, G., Bergoulgan, L., and Ehrsson, H. H. (2013). 'A shared representation of the space near oneself and others in the human premotor cortex'. *Current Biology*, Vol. 23, September, pp. 1764–1768. It should be noted that, in contrast to some of the more controversial behavioural and cultural claims made for mirror neurons, the implied condition Pelligrino and Ladavas point to for matching representations of body parts between individuals, is that there are significant similarities between the *existing* body schema of one individual and that of another's to provide for an effective neural simulation of the other's actions.

15 Pelligrino, G. di and Ladavas, E. (2015), p. 128.

16 Pelligrino, G. di and Ladavas, E. (2015), p. 129.

17 Moser, E. I., Kropff, E. and Moser, M. B. (2008). 'Place Cells, grid cells, and the brain's spatial representation system'. *Annual Review of Neuroscience*, Vol. 31, pp. 69–89.

18 Moser, E. I., Kropff, E. and Moser, M. B. (2008), p. 70.

19 Moser, E. I., Kropff, E. and Moser, M. B. (2008), p. 71.

20 Marozzi, E. and Jeffrey, K. J. (2012). 'Place, space and memory cells'. *Current Biology*, Vol. 22, November, pp. R939–R942.

21 Marozzi, E. and Jeffrey, K. J. (2012), p. R942.

22 Ferretti, G. and Alai, M. (2016). 'Enactivism, representations and canonical neurons'. *Argumenta*, Issue 2, pp. 195–217.

23 Ferretti, G. and Alai, M. (2016), p. 200.

24 Ferretti, G. and Alai, M. (2016), p. 206.

25 Chen, I. (2009). 'Brain Cells for Socializing'. *Smithsonian Magazine*, June. Saved November 2018 from www.smithsonianmag.com/science-nature/The-Social-Brain.html?c=y&story=fullstory For a more detailed account, see Allman, J. M., Tetreault, N. A., Hakeem, A. Y. and Park, S. (2010). 'The von Economo neurons in apes and humans'. *American Journal of Human Biology*, Vol. 23, pp. 5–21.

26 Chen, I. (2009), p. 2.

27 Chen, I. (2009), p. 4.

28 Ananthaswamy, A. (2015). *The Man Who Wasn't There: Tales From the Edge of the Self*. Dutton, New York.

29 Ananthaswamy, A. (2015), p. 10.

30 Citing William James, Ananthaswamy writes that the first includes 'everything I consider as me or mine'; the second 'my interactions with others', and the last being what James describes as 'a man's inner or subjective being, his psychic faculties or dispositions'. Ananthaswamy, A. (2015), p. 22.

31 Ananthaswamy, A. (2015), pp. 23–24. In addition to schizophrenia and body integrity disorders of the kind described by Ramachandran, Ananthaswamy lists: studies of Alzheimer's, the neurodegenerative disorder resulting in a debilitating loss of memory, and with it, entire personal histories; 'out-of-body' experiences which involve an unsettling, if only temporary disconnection from the bodily self; 'depersonalisation disorder', which deprives a person of the emotions involved in creating a sense of self; autism, which affects a person's interactions with others, thus limiting a vital source of self-awareness, and ecstatic epilepsy, with its transcendental sense of oneness, which appears to offer, if only temporarily, a glimpse of the 'essence of the self'. Ibid, p. 26.

32 Ananthaswamy, A. (2015), p. 25. See also Frith, C. D. (2015). *The Cognitive Neuropsychology of Schizophrenia*. Psychology Press, Hove. Also Ramachandran, V. S. and Blakeslee, S. (2005). While the latter authors seldom use the term schizophrenia in their case studies, many of the neuropsychological conditions they describe fall within that category. Also Zahavi, D. ed. (2000). *Exploring the Self: Advances in Consciousness Research*. John Benjamins Publishing Company, Amsterdam. Parts II and III in the latter work include several essays on the effects of schizophrenia on the self. For a discussion of its particular impacts on self-agency, see Gallagher, S. (2000). 'Self-reference and schizophrenia: a cognitive model of immunity to error through misidentification'. In *Exploring the Self* (Zahavi, D. (2000[BIB-330] ed.), pp. 203–239.

33 Ananthaswamy, A. (2015), p. 111.

34 Ananthaswamy, A. (2015), p. 113.

35 Keysers, C. (2011). *The Empathic Brain*. Social Brain Press.

36 Keysers, C. (2011), p. 48.

37 Borrowing a definition of 'true imitation' from William Thorpe, Keysers stresses the importance of imitation involving the learning of *novel* concepts and skills from others, rather than those the observer will already be mostly familiar with.

38 Keysers, C. (2011), p. 60.

39　Hickok, G. (2014). *The Myth of Mirror Neurons: The Real Science of Communication and Cognition*. W.W. Norton, New York.

40　Hickok, G. (2014), p. 35.

41　Hickok, G. (2014), p. 227.

42　LeDoux, J. (1998). *The Emotional Brain: The Mysterious Underpinnings of Emotional Life*. Phoenix, London.

43　See Gazzaniga, M. S. (1970). *The Bisected Brain*. Appleton-Century-Crofts, New York.

44　LeDoux, J. (1998), p. 11.

45　Darwin, C. (1872; 1965). *The Expression of Emotions in Man and the Animals*. University of Chicago Press, Chicago.

46　LeDoux, J. (1998), p. 107.

47　LeDoux, J. (1998), p. 105.

48　In support of his theory, LeDoux describes a series of laboratory experiments he carried out with rats, called 'fear conditioning', to identify the specific brain processes involved. A variation of the well-known experiments by the Russian physiologist Ivan Pavlov, the procedure devised by LeDoux involves the pairing of a sound with a mild shock given to the feet of the rat shortly afterwards. When repeated a few more times, the sound alone elicits the same reaction to the shock by the rat, which immediately adopts a freezing posture, accompanied by other measurable responses like increased blood pressure and heart rates, together with the release of stress hormones into the blood. The freezing behaviour and related responses of the rats themselves, however, LeDoux points out, are not learned: 'Freezing is something that rats do naturally when they are exposed to danger'. In other words, they are *innate* defensive responses that can be set off by 'either *natural or learned triggers*' covering a wide range of environmental or imagined dangers. Ibid, p. 143. In sum, LeDoux writes: 'Fear conditioning may not tell us everything we need to know about fear, but it has been an excellent way to get started'. Ibid, p. 148. It can be used to show how animal brains process conditioned fear stimuli and controls-related defensive behaviours and, moreover, affords insights into the processes by which emotional memories are established, stored and retrieved.

49　LeDoux, J. (1998), p. 269.

50　Porges, S. W. (2011). *The Polyvagal Theory: Neurophysiological Foundations of Emotions, Attachment, Communication, Self-Regulation*. W. W. Norton, New York.

51　Porges, S. W. (2011), 118.

52　Amongst other possible causes of such breakdowns, Porges cites studies of the disastrous effects that various levels of social abandonment can have on child development, including the well-reported cases of maltreated Romanian orphans. Even after being adopted by caring foster parents, follow-up studies indicated lasting behavioural effects of their isolation in the Romanian orphanages, suggesting that a secure, warm environment and a greatly improved diet were insufficient compensations for the severe disruption in the former orphans' social lives.

53　Porges, S. W. (2011), 190.

54　Porges, S. W. (2011), 161.

Chapter 6　The evolving self

1　Braby, M. F. (2018). http://theconversation.com/curious-kids-do-butterflies-remember-being-caterpillars-99508.

2 Braby, M. F. (2018).

3 Braby, M. F. (2018).

4 Blackiston, D. J., Casey, E. S. and Weiss, M. R. ((2008). 'Retention of memory through metamorphosis: can a moth remember what it learned as a caterpillar?' PLoS ONE 3(3): e1736. https://doi.org/10.1371/journal.pone.0001736

5 Blackiston, D. J., Casey, E. S. and Weiss, M. R. (2008), p. 1.

6 Blackiston, D. J., Casey, E. S. and Weiss, M. R. (2008), p. 4.

7 Howe, M. L. (2014). 'The co-emergence of the self and autobiographical memory: an adaptive view of early memory'. In *The Wiley Handbook on the Development of Children's Memory* (Bauer, P. J. and Fivush, R., eds), pp. 545–567, John Wiley & Sons, Chichester. See also Fivush, R. et al. (2011). 'The making of autobiographical memory: intersections of culture, narratives and identity'. *International Journal of Psychology*, Vol. 46(5), pp. 321–345.

8 Howe, M. L. (2014), p. 545.

9 Howe stresses that he makes no claims for the development of the individual organism (ontogeny) that might supplant its biological and phylogenetic, i.e., physical development, only that 'it may be more than mere coincidence that these characteristics (self-consciousness and self or autobiographical memory), co-occur' in evolution. Howe, M. L. (2014), p. 548.

10 Howe, M. L. (2014), p. 558.

11 Howe, M. L. (2014), p. 561.

12 Damasio, A. (2000). *The Feeling of What Happens: Body, Emotion and the Making of Consciousness*. Vintage Books, London. Also Damasio, A. (2012). *Self Comes to Mind: Constructing the Conscious Brain*. Vintage Books, London. Also Damasio, A. (2018). *The Strange Order of Things: Life, Feeling, and the Making of Cultures*. Pantheon Books, London.

13 Damasio, A. (2000), p. 8.

14 Damasio, A. (2000), p. 12. Anticipating the criticism that, in linking consciousness and the self together, Damasio is only concerned with self-consciousness as a particular form of consciousness, he vigorously asserts that 'if the term "self-consciousness" is taken to mean "consciousness with a sense of self", then all human consciousness is necessarily covered by the term – there is just no other kind of consciousness as far as I can see'. Ibid, p. 19.

15 Damasio, A. (2012), pp. 15–16.

16 Damasio, A. (2012), p. 25.

17 Panksepp, J. and Northoff, G. (2009). 'The trans-species core SELF: the emergence of active and neuro-ecological agents through self-related processing within subcortical-cortical midline networks'. In *Consciousness and Cognition*, Vol. 18(1) March, pp. 193–295.

18 Panksepp, J. and Northoff, G. (2009), p. 194.

19 Panksepp, J. and Northoff, G. (2009), p. 205.

20 Panksepp, J. and Northoff, G. (2009), p. 198.

21 Panksepp, J. and Northoff, G. (2009), p. 202.

22 Vaal, F. de (2016). *Are We Smart Enough to Know How Smart Animals Are?* Granta, London. In his introduction, de Vaal himself quotes Darwin's confident assertion heading this chapter, that, as great as the difference between the human mind and that of other animals might appear, it 'certainly is one of degree and not of kind'. Ibid, p. 1.

23 Vaal, F. de (2016), p. 5.

24 Vaal, F. de (2016), pp. 240–241.

25 Quoted in Vaal, F. de (2016), p. 234.

26 Vaal, F. de (2016), p. 273.

27 Godfrey-Smith, P. (2016). *Other Minds: The Octopus and the Evolution of Intelligent Life.* Harper Collins, London.

28 Godfrey-Smith, P. (2016), p. 9.

29 Over the same period, Godfrey-Smith explains, different kinds of animals played key roles in shaping each other's lives via a circular process known as 'predation', where, when one kind of evolving organism changes, it changes the environment other organisms have to deal with, which in turn evolve in response to those changes; each cycle promoting further differences between species while also promoting mutual interdependence.

30 Godfrey-Smith, P. (2016), p. 98.

31 The same ability – no doubt honed in the hunt for and capture of fast moving or well-hidden prey – has also been confirmed, Godfrey-Smith writes, in laboratory experiments testing the ability of an octopus to identify different sized objects presented to them at different distances, which they did so correctly every time.

32 Godfrey-Smith, P. (2016), p. 141.

33 Vygotsky, L. S. (1978). *Mind in Society: The Development of Higher Psychological Processes.* Harvard University Press, Cambridge, MA.

34 Quoted in Godfrey-Smith, P. (2016), p. 146.

35 Godfrey-Smith, P. (2016), p. 150.

36 Godfrey-Smith, P. (2016), p. 156.

37 Tomasello, M. (1999).

38 Tomasello, M. (1999), pp. 4–5.

39 Tomasello, M. (1999), p. 5.

40 See Flavell, J. H. (1963). *The Developmental Psychology of Jean Piaget.* Van Nostrand Reinhold, New York.

41 Tomasello, M. (2014). *A Natural History of Human Thinking.* Harvard University Press, Cambridge, MA.

42 Tomasello, M. (2014), p. x.

43 Presumably imagining a future situation in which they would need it. The manoevre suggests the addition of a further cognitive trait to the great ape repertoire – the ability to anticipate future actions – previously thought exclusive to humans. Recall also the speculation by Elizabeth Marozzi and Kathryn Jeffrey quoted in the previous chapter that using the same cognitive structure for both space and memory creates the potential for imagined as well as experienced events.

44 Tomasello, M. (2014), p. 20.

45 Tomasello, M. (2014), p. 25.

46 Tomasello, M. (2014), p. 37.

Chapter 7   Tacit nexus

1 Gibson, K. R. (1993a). 'Animal minds, human minds'. In *Tools, Language and Cognition in Human Evolution* (Gibson, K. R. and Ingold, T. eds), pp. 3–19, Cambridge University Press, Cambridge. Also Gibson, K. R. (1993b). 'Overlapping

neural control of language, gesture and tool-use'. In *Tools, Language and Cognition in Human Evolution* (Gibson, K. R. and Ingold, T. eds), pp. 187–192, Cambridge University Press, Cambridge. Also Gibson, K. R. (1993c). 'Tool use, language and social behavior in relationship to information processing power'. In *Tools, Language and Cognition in Human Evolution* (Gibson, K. R. and Ingold, T. eds), pp. 251–269, Cambridge University Press, Cambridge.

2 Gibson, K. R. (1993a), p. 9. See also Langer, J. (1993). 'Comparative cognitive development'. In *Tools, Language and Cognition in Human Evolution* (Gibson, K. R. and Ingold, T. eds), pp. 300–313, Cambridge University Press, Cambridge.

3 As we have seen, that idea is not new and is commonly the subject of 'chicken and egg' questions as to which came first, bigger brains followed by faster and more complex development, or was it that the latter just *required* bigger brains?

4 Gibson, K. R. (1993c), p. 251.

5 Calvin, W. H. (1993). 'The unitary hypothesis: a common neural circuitry for novel manipulations, language, plan-ahead, and throwing?' In *Tools, Language and Cognition In Human Evolution*. (Gibson, K. R. and Ingold, T. eds), pp. 230–250, Cambridge University Press, Cambridge.

6 Calvin, W. H. (1993), p. 230.

7 Calvin, W. H. (1993), p. 231.

8 Moreover, Calvin writes, 'both inputs and outputs tend to be broadly wired in the cerebral cortex; the functional maps may suggest segregation, but the anatomy is one big smear'. Calvin, W. H. (1993), p. 232.

9 Calvin also relates the work of the neurosurgeon George Ojemann, who repeated Penfield's classic brain mapping techniques for conscious epileptic patients, but with more advanced tests for language and related sensory- and movement-sequencing functions in exploring the language cortex, which includes premotor and prefrontal regions of the brain. Ojemann found that part of the language cortex where functions were disrupted 'was always related to sequencing'. Moreover, tests for sound sequences unrelated to language could be disrupted from the same brain regions as tests of non-language related oral-facial movement sequences, suggesting that the same cortex region also serves both receptive and expressive sequencing: 'So it would appear that the brain has some regions which are particularly specialized for generating and analyzing sequences, and they may be used by multiple sensory and motor systems' Calvin, W. H. (1993), p. 234.

10 Calvin, W. H. (1993), p. 232.

11 One of the fastest loops is from arm sensors to spinal cord and back out to arm muscles: it takes 110 milliseconds for feedback corrections to be made to an arm movement. Dart throwing does not take much longer.

12 Calvin, W. H. (1993), p. 234.

13 Calvin, W. H. (1993), p. 235.

14 Addressing the question of how the brain might accumulate sufficient promising candidate sequences to choose from and then decide – out of all those possible trains straining to be released – which sequence should be chosen for enactment, Calvin draws upon more familiar models. Describing the brain as a 'Darwin machine', he argues the availability of many ready-made neural sequencers for the brain's selection would suggest the brain employs something like Darwinian natural selection in searching through all those potential winners, testing them out in remembered environments in split seconds rather than in normal evolutionary time. A more

likely, if equally speculative, scenario might suggest that experience had already made its best choice of response for each form of action and that the brain–body system instinctively decides without further investigation which sequence is best for the job.

15 Calvin, W. H. (1993), p. 248.

16 Lock, A. (1993). 'Language development and object manipulation: their relation in ontogeny and its possible reference for phylogenetic questions'. In *Tools, Language and Cognition in Human Evolution* (Gibson, K. R. and Ingold, T. eds), pp. 279–299, Cambridge University Press, Cambridge.

17 Lock, A. (1993), p. 283.

18 Lock, A. (1993), p. 284.

19 Vygotsky, L. S. (1978), p. 21.

20 Vygotsky, L. S. (1978), p. 21.

21 Vygotsky, L. S. (1978), p. 22.

22 Vygotsky, L. S. (1978), p. 24.

23 Quoted in Vygotsky, L. S. (1978), p. 7.

24 Vygotsky, L. S. (1978), p. 7. Much has changed since Vygotsky, writing in the 1920s and 1930s – he died prematurely of tuberculosis in 1934 – formulated his theory of practical intelligence, most obviously the discovery that, contrary to Engels' belief, humans are not the only tool-using creatures on this Earth. Similarly, the assumption that only humans are capable of changing the natural environment to suit their own ends has also taken a beating with the accumulated evidence of animal niche construction, if thankfully, on a far lesser scale than the destructive impact of human activity on nature. As we have seen, other formerly cut-and-dried distinctions between humans and other animals have since been undermined by more recent studies in animal cognition and social behaviour, including strong evidence of self-awareness, empathy and even a capacity amongst some primates to monitor their own actions and imagine possible alternative plans – all achievements previously thought to have been exclusive to humans. None of the above, however, diminishes Vygotsky's core insights into the vital role of practical intelligence in human development and the acquisition of language, both in its early and later stages. Vygotsky's Marxist-inspired belief that the development of first the infant and child followed by the maturing adult is fundamentally influenced by the social and cultural environment with which the individual interacts, has likewise stood the test of time. His explication of practical intelligence has also been substantiated by the peripersonal spaces and other discoveries of neuroscience of the way mind, body and the handling of physical objects meld together in everyday experience.

25 Vygotsky, L. S. (1978), p. 7. The editors also write: 'In stressing the social origins of language and thinking, Vygotsky was following the lead of influential French sociologists, but to our knowledge he was the first modern psychologist to suggest the mechanisms by which culture becomes a part of each person's nature'. Vygotsky, L. S. (1978), p. 6.

26 Wilson, F. R. (1998). *The Hand: How Its Use Shapes the Brain, Language, and Human Culture*. Vintage Books, New York.

27 Wilson, F. R. (1998), p. 7.

28 Wilson, F. R. (1998), p. 38.

29 Quoted in Wilson, F. R. (1998), p. 41.

30 Quoted in Wilson, F. R. (1998), p. 47. The social and communicative behaviour of pre-hominid primates and hominids in the early stages of this evolution was limited to what Donald describes as an 'episodic culture', comprised of a series of short-term, concrete responses to the immediate environment. There came a time, however, somewhere between the appearance of *Homo erectus* and that of *Homo sapiens* 200,000 ago when *Homo's* ability to make and use tools rose to a new level of sophistication. Moreover, as Donald writes, that improvement in technical skills was accompanied by other, crucial developments: 'Innovative tool use could have occurred countless thousands of times without resulting in an established tool making industry, unless the individual who "invented" the tool could remember and re-enact or reproduce the operations involved and then communicate them to others'. Those vital further developments were the emergence of what Donald called a 'mimetic culture' – the copying and repetition of habits and skills – and language. Gestural language, he speculates, certainly preceded spoken and syntactic language as the primary means of communication and would have served to support mimetic behaviour. But it took the development of formal language and speech to complete the integration of mind, body and technical skills begun with our primate ancestors.

31 Wilson, F. R. (1998), p. 51. Plotkin offers the example of a bullfighter who, in addition to all the physical and mental skills of his profession he acquired in his training, bears the scars of his previous encounters on his body as well as the memory of those events. For Plotkin, *all* these different facets of his experience constitute the 'bullfighter's *knowledge* of the bull'.

32 Wilson, F. R. (1998), p. 53.

33 Wilson, F. R. (1998), p. 54.

34 Quoted in Wilson, F. R. (1998), pp. 54–55.

35 Wilson, F. R. (1998), p. 57.

36 Wilson, F. R. (1998), pp. 58–59. It is not known, Wilson observes, exactly when the physiological transformation in pre-human hominid evolution began resulting in the opposition of the fourth and fifth fingers (forefinger and thumb) and the twisting (ulnar deviation) of the wrist – both of which are unique to modern humans. However, as the final development in a host of preceding changes involving the whole of the upper body from shoulder to fingertips, 'it may well have unleashed the final stage of a unique mammalian strategy for long-term species survival'. Certainly, Wilson argues, the early combination of these changes, which enables the holder to not only grip a stick or other tool firmly in the hand but also to align that tool along the axis of the arm, would have greatly increased the striking power of the hominid holder, whether the purpose was to strike an enemy or prey or to hammer something into better shape.

37 Wilson, F. R. (1998), p. 193.

38 Wilson, F. R. (1998), p. 195. Wilson also finds strong evidence for the communicative as well as manipulative powers of the dexterous human hand in the sign language now commonly used by the deaf, the development of which leapt forward in the 1970s with the work of Harlan Lane, a psycholinguist, on the American Sign Language (ASL). In 1973 Lane was shown the work on sign language that Ursula Bellugi, another psycholinguist, was doing with several deaf people at her lab in San Diego. Bellugi explained to the astonished Lane that sign language was *not* a simple matter of encoding English or any other spoken language into hand signs: 'It seems

like a language. There are rules for making up words and rules for making sentences out of the words, *but the rules have to do with space and shape – its an entirely different way of doing language* [emphasis added]'. Ibid., p. 198.

39 Wilson, F. R. (1998), p. 307.

40 Kuhn, T. (1962). *The Structure of Scientific Revolutions*. University of Chicago Press, Chicago.

41 Kuhn, T. (1977). *The Essential Tension: Selected Studies in Scientific Tradition and Change*. University of Chicago, Chicago. Especially Chapters 9 and 12.

42 Kuhn, T. (1977), p. 234.

43 Kuhn, T. (1977), pp. 226–227.

44 Kuhn, T. (1977), p. 226.

45 Kuhn, T. (1977), p. 293. See also Masterman, M. (1970). 'The Nature of a Paradigm'. In *Criticism and the Growth of Knowledge* (Lakatos, I. and Musgrave, A. eds), pp. 59–89, Cambridge University Press, Cambridge.

46 In this respect, as Margaret Masterman writes, Kuhn is unique amongst other historians of science in that he dispels 'the worry which so besets the working scientist confronted for the first time with professional philosophy-of-science, "How can I be using a theory which isn't there?"' Masterman, M. (1970), pp. 59–89.

47 See also Barbour, I. G. (1974). *Myths, Models and Paradigms*. Harper & Row, New York.

48 Kuhn, T. (1977), p. 308.

49 Baird, D. (2004). *Thing Knowledge: A Philosophy of Scientific Instruments*. University of California Press, Berkeley CA.

50 Baird, D. (2004), p. 69.

51 Hyde, L. (1979). *The Gift: Imagination and the Erotic Life of Property*. Vintage Books, New York.

52 Baird, D. (2004), p. 223.

PART III   The self in the world

1 Lewin, K. (1951; 1964). *Field Theory in Social Science: Selected Theoretical Papers*. Harper Torchbooks, New York, p. 241.

Chapter 8   Technically extended selves

1 The subtitle refers to the Greek god Prometheus, who, according to mythology, together with his brother Epimetheus was entrusted by the other gods to gift all mortal creatures on Earth with appropriate powers to enable each species to survive. However, eager to fulfil his task ahead of his brother, Epimetheus distributed all the available gifts to other species, leaving none for humans. Obliged to complete their assignment, Prometheus was compelled to steal some of the other gods own special gifts, namely fire and skills in the arts, giving them instead to humans for their own exclusive use. Thus it was that, beginning with fire – the very first and possibly most important early technology to be employed by humans – our species eventually came to rule the earth.

2 Rudofsky, B. (1977). *The Prodigious Builders: Notes Towards a Natural History of Architecture*. Harcourt Brace Jovanovich, New York.

3 Rudofsky, B. (1964). *Architecture Without Architects*. Doubleday, New York.

4 Rudofsky, B. (1977), p. 9.

5 Since the publication of Rudofsky's books there has been a growing, if overdue, interest amongst professional architects in vernacular architecture, matched by well-documented examples around the world, the basic form and materials of which have changed little over hundreds of years. Though now in retreat with the global expansion of urbanism, such dwellings are still common in rural areas and small towns and villages, both in developed and developing regions. Paul Oliver, a renowned authority on vernacular architecture, points out that, out of a possible billion or more dwellings in the world – nobody knows exactly how many there are – 'only a miniscule proportion were designed by architects; one per cent may well be an overestimate'. Oliver, P. (2003). *Dwellings: The Vernacular House Worldwide*. Phaidon, London, p. 15. To that modest figure he adds all the suburban estates and apartment blocks constructed by commercial builders or housing corporations which, he estimates, might push the grand total of professionally sanctioned and produced homes to one in ten. This still leaves the vast majority of homes on this planet built by communities and individuals for themselves using the kind of traditional methods and techniques described by Rudofsky. See also Oliver, P. ed. (1998). *Encyclopedia of Vernacular Architecture of the World*. Architectural Press, Oxford.

6 Rudofsky, B. (1977), p. 59.

7 Rudofsky, B. (1977), p. 61.

8 Rudofsky, B. (1977), p. 61.

9 While, in anthropocentric fashion, we might well judge animal constructions by the same standards we judge human artistic creations, we need to understand them, as Frans de Vaal advises above, with respect to studies of animal cognition, from their creators' viewpoints, and not just ours. It might also be argued that all animal constructions are species specific: the purpose, form and construction techniques generally restricted to particular geographical and ecological habitats, are 'light on progress' as Rudofsky puts it, and therefore are not to be compared with the incredibly diverse and fast-changing architectural and engineering works of humans across the world.

10 Rudofsky, B. (1977), p. 64.

11 Hansell, M. (2007). *Built by Animals: The Natural History of Animal Architecture*. Oxford University Press, New York. For a complementary, photographic study of some of the most impressive animal constructions see Arndt, I. and Tautz, J. (2013). *Animal Architecture*. Abrams, New York.

12 Griffin, D. (1976). *The Question of Animal Awareness*. The Rockefeller University Press, New York. See also Turner, J. S. (2002). *The Extended Organism: The Physiology of Animal-Built Structures*. Harvard University Press, Cambridge, MA. As a physiologist, Turner takes a different but equally radical approach to argue that 'the edifices constructed by animals are properly constructed external organs of physiology [added emphasis]', an idea similar to Richard Dawkins' evolutionary concept of the extended phenotype. See Dawkins, R. (1982; 1999). The Extended Phenotype: The Long Reach of the Gene. Oxford University Press, Oxford. However, Turner contends that, whereas an evolutionary biologist and neo-Darwinian like Dawkins sees the extended phenotype as primarily existing to give genes a helping hand forward, a physiologist 'sees an extended phenotype in terms of mechanism and asks how it works, how it alters the flow of matter, energy, and information through

the organism and between the organism and its environment'. Ibid, p. 2. In short, a physiologist is more concerned with how such structures actually function to serve the living animals that build them.

13 Hansell, M. (2007), p. 9. While pursuing that end, Hansell also cautions us not to equate animal intelligence *only* with those animals that build, which is just another form of anthropocentrism – as the now popular term 'animal architecture' suggests – since we think of ourselves as the supreme building species, and therefore take animal constructions as proof of higher forms of animal behaviour. As we have seen, there is plenty of evidence of advanced levels of thought amongst primates and other creatures that do *not* involve building shelters, impressive as those achievements may be.

14 Hansell, M. (2007), p. 22.

15 A function similar in principle to the 'wind towers' common to traditional dwellings along the Gulf Coast in the Middle East, which capture overhead air movements in the hot climate of the region to draw out stale air from the rooms below. The same principle has been effectively deployed by contemporary architects for such projects as the Aga Khan University and Hospital in Karachi.

16 A comparable principle, Hansell adds, is also used by some burrow-dwelling fish and mud shrimps in flowing-water systems. Though he does not provide any further explanation it may be assumed that differential pressures in the flow of water perform a similar function of replacing stale water inside the burrows with fresh water.

17 Hansell, M. (2007), p. 62.

18 Hansell, M. (2007), p. 63.

19 This too, Hansell describes as an emergent process in the acquisition of specialist building skills unique to ants as a social species, for which they have developed equivalent cognitive skills of their own according to which specialised task evolution has assigned them. Here one might think, he suggests, that specialisation of body morphology is the key factor in job specialisation: 'Their body is their toolkit; each specialist has its own'. However, it transpires that *specialisation by age* is more important for social insects, including termites, than specialisation by body shape – the reason being that, as helpless grubs, their offspring need looking after by the young adults, who are therefore only able to devote sufficient time to developing other skills in the later stages of adult life (we are talking here of days in what are mostly short lives).

20 Hansell, M. (2007), pp. 108–109.

21 Hansell, M. (2007), p. 112. See also Schowalter, T. D. (2000; 2016 4th edn). *Insect Ecology: An Ecosystem Approach*. Academic Press, London. In a manner similar to other descriptions in this book of the functional self-organisation of organisms, Schowalter characterises complex ecosystems as nested hierarchies of subsystems : 'An important part of this functional hierarchy is the "emergence" of properties that are not easily predictable by simply adding the contributions of constitutive components. Emergent properties include feedback processes at each level of the hierarchy [...] The apparent ability of many organisms to *reduce variation in structure and function* [added emphasis] suggests that ecosystems are self-regulating, that is, they behave like cybernetic systems [...] This developing concept of ecosystem self-regulation has major implications for ecosystem responses to anthropogenic change in environmental conditions and our approaches to managing insects and ecosystem resources'. Ibid, pp. 10–11.

22 Hansell, M. (2007), p. 113. An argument that Rudofsky himself would certainly have found persuasive in explaining the methods of the animal and home builders he describes.

23 Beck, B. B. (1980). *Animal Tool Behavior*. Garland, New York.

24 Shumaker, R. W., Walkup, K. R. and Beck, B. B. (2011). *Animal Tool Behavior: The Use and Manufacture of Tools by Animals*. The John Hopkins University Press, Baltimore, MD.

25 Shumaker, R. W. et al. (2011), p. 5.

26 The first are basically all movements (motor actions) performed in the execution of the tool use, such as 'Throw' and 'Drop', which have an aerial trajectory, or 'Drag, Roll, Kick, Slap, Push Over', which entail moving objects along the ground. Modes of manufacture likewise involve distinct actions required to fabricate the desired tool from the original objects and/or materials from which they are formed: namely 'Detach', 'Subtract', 'Add, Combine' and 'Reshape'. Both lists are, in turn, conveniently boiled down to seven common *functions* of tool use, including: 'extends user's reach'; 'amplifies mechanical force', and aids 'bodily comfort', and just one common function of manufacture, defined as the 'structural modification of an object or an existing tool by the user or a conspecific so that the object/tool serves, or serves more effectively, as a tool'.

27 Shew, A. (2017). *Animal Constructions and Technological Knowledge*. Lexington Books, Lanham, MD.

28 Shew, A. (2017), pp. 1–2.

29 Shew, A. (2017), p. 13.

30 See Ryle, G. (1949). *The Concept of Mind*. Barnes & Noble, New York, pp. 25–61.

31 It should be noted that, in making the distinction, Ryle makes no reference to comparisons of any sort with the behaviour of other species, but is solely concerned to rebalance what he believes to be a much neglected aspect of human knowledge and behaviour: 'Theorists have been so preoccupied with the task of investigating the nature, the source and the credentials of the theories that we adopt that they have for the most part ignored the question what it is for someone to know how to perform tasks. In ordinary life, on the contrary, as well as in the special business of teaching, we are much more concerned with people's competences than with their cognitive repertoires, with the operations than with the truths that they learn'. Ryle, G. (1949), p. 28.

32 Shew, A. (2017), p. 28.

33 Vincenti, W. (1990). *What Engineers Know and How They Know It*. John Hopkins University Press, Baltimore, MD.

34 Shew, A. (2017), p. 28.

35 Shew, A. (2017), p. 50.

36 Shew, A. (2017), p. 55.

37 Hunt, G. R. (1996). 'Manufacture and use of hook-tools by New Caledonian crows'. *Nature*, Vol. 379, pp. 249–251.

38 Later studies of NC crows in laboratory settings confirm the tool-making versatility of the species. Young crows with no previous opportunity to observe the manufacture of hook tools by adult crows were nevertheless able to fashion usable twig-and-leaf tools from pandanus leaves given to them, leading the researchers to suggest a possibly innate (i.e., genetically inherited) capacity of the species for tool making. NC crows have even outperformed chimpanzees in some tool-making tests

using unfamiliar materials, such as bending a straight wire into a hook to retrieve food in a tiny bucket from the bottom of a narrow tube; a process requiring a degree of innovation as well as an understanding of the relation of tool to problem. Other research suggests that, while some basic types of tool use by the species may be standardised, significant variations in the form and materials used in the wild may be the outcome of *sociocultural factors* (i.e., *learned* habits) influencing the design and use of the tools; a conclusion reinforced by observation of the young crows in captivity paying close attention to the researchers' demonstrations of tool use.

39 Hunt, G. R. and Gray, R. D. (2003). 'Diversification and cumulative evolution in New Caledonian crow tool manufacture'. *Proceedings of the Royal Society, London,* Vol. B 270, pp. 867–874.

40 Quoted by Shew, A. (2017), pp. 82–83.

41 Quoted by Shew, A. (2017), p. 82.

42 Schick, K. D. and Toth, N. (1993). *Making Silent Stones Speak: Human Evolution and the Dawn of Technology.* Touchstone, New York.

43 Schick, K. D. and Toth, N. (1993), p. 18.

44 Schick, K. D. and Toth, N. (1993), p. 133.

45 Schick, K. D. and Toth, N. (1993), p. 51.

46 Schick, K. D. and Toth, N. (1993), p. 143.

47 Taylor, T. (2010). *The Artificial Ape: How Technology Changed the Course of Human Evolution.* Palgrave Macmillan, New York.

48 Taylor, T. (2010), p. 72.

49 Taylor, T. (2010), p. 2.

50 The earliest species of *Homo* as an upright walking ape, *Homo habilis,* which, though otherwise greatly changed, was still possessed of small, chimpanzee-sized brains, emerged around 2.5 million years ago. That is approximately 190,000 years after the first-known use of stone tools. Not a great amount of time in the evolutionary scale of life on the planet, Taylor concedes, but enough to suggest that the use of tools *preceded* and may well have spurred the development of human intelligence, rather than the other way around.

51 Recent research suggests at least 13 per cent less than that required for carrying an infant without any artificial aids. Taylor, T. (2010), p. 119; 123.

52 Taylor, T. (2010), p. 124.

53 Arthur, W. B. (2009). *The Nature of Technology: What It Is and How It Evolves.* Allen Lane, London.

54 Arthur employs three definitions of technology throughout his book, each of which delineates a different level of development. The first and most basic of these is 'technology as a means to fulfill a human purpose', be it a method, process or device, simple or complex. Next is technology as 'an assemblage of practices and components', a plural definition which covers technologies such as electronics or biotechnology and other collections of individual technologies and practices. Finally, at the broadest level close to Stiegler's concept of 'technics', there is technology as 'the entire collection of devices and engineering practices available to a culture'. At this level, much like Stiegler, Arthur writes: 'We use this collective meaning when we blame "technology" for speeding up our lives', or perhaps like more optimistic writers, 'talk of "technology" as a hope for mankind'. Arthur, W. B. (2009), p. 28.

55 Arthur, W. B. (2009), p. 13.

56 Arthur, W. B. (2009), p. 19.

57 Arthur, W. B. (2009), pp. 20–21.

58 Arthur, W. B. (2009), p. 22.

59 Arthur, W. B. (2009), p. 145.

60 Arthur, W. B. (2009), p. 189.

61 Clark, A. (2003). *Natural-Born Cyborgs: Minds, Technologies, and the Future of Human Intelligence*. Oxford University Press, Oxford.

62 Clark, A. (2003), p. 3.

63 Clark, A. (2003), p. 198.

64 Clark, A. (2003), p. 175.

Chapter 9   Self-images

1 Goffman, E. (1959; 1990). *The Presentation of Self in Everyday Life*. Penguin Books, London.

2 See also Rosenberg, M. (1965). *Society and the Adolescent Self-Image*. Princeton University Press, Princeton, NJ. As broad as the subject is, most studies of self-images have approached the matter as mainly a problem of *self-esteem*, with varying mixtures of psychological and social content, depending on whether the principal concerns are with body images or social position or any other more specific phenomena. Working at a different level, Morris Rosenberg focuses on the diverse social factors, including family background, social class and education systems, shaping those images, and which could influence an individual's self-esteem: 'At first glance [the self-image] would appear to be a purely private, personal, and idiosyncratic phenomenon. And yet it is equally plain that the individual's self-picture is not purely non-objective art, reflecting the impulses and inspiration of the creator, but is rather a more or less clear portrait based upon the information provided by his social experience'. Ibid, p. vii. Like Goffman and Bourdieu's work, Rosenberg's insights into the effect of differential perceptions of esteem according to which social or racial group a person belongs to, combined with other influences arising from a person's background and relationships, suggest an approach to self-images close to a field-theoretic perspective.

3 Goffman, E. (1959; 1990), p. 28.

4 Goffman also cites cases of American college girls consciously *playing down* their own intelligence and abilities to accord with stereotypical beliefs in male superiority. Thus, in addition to hiding their own superior record in mathematics or other subjects from their dates and purposefully losing at any games they might play together, one college girl reports that 'one of the nicest techniques' she uses, is to deliberately misspell some long words from time to time in her messages to her boyfriend; a tactic which invariably gets a patronising but pleased response, that she certainly doesn't 'know how to spell'. Goffman, E. (1959; 1990), p. 48.

5 Even, Goffman notes, when a person does not fully believe in those standards: 'The individual may privately maintain standards of behavior which he does not personally believe in, maintaining these standards because of a lively belief that an unseen audience is present and will punish deviations from these standards. In other words, *an individual may be his own audience or may imagine an audience to be present*' [emphasis added]. Goffman, E. (1959; 1990), p. 87.

6 Goffman, E. (1959; 1990), p. 91.

7   Goffman, E. (1963). *Behavior in Public Places: Notes on the Social Organization of Gatherings.* The Free Press, New York.

8   Goffman, E. (1963), p. 33.

9   See also Hall, E. T. (1969). *The Hidden Dimension.* Anchor Books, New York.

10 Bourdieu, P. (1984; 2010), p. 188.

11 Bourdieu, P. (1984; 2010), p. 188. Offering the example of the choice of fish as a typical expression of differences of eating habits between classes, Bourdieu suggests 'the whole body schema' is involved in the manner of eating the dish. Regarded as an unmanly choice by the working classes, not only for being too light – suitable perhaps for invalids and children in need of healthy foods – but also for being too 'fiddly', handling a fish on the plate, he explains, compels men to do things, picking out any bones and so forth, that their workers' hands cannot easily handle, making them look weak and helpless. The very way of actually eating fish, delicately and in small mouthfuls, involving the front of the mouth and teeth, also contradicts workers' masculine habits of 'whole hearted male gulps and mouthfuls', which involve the back or whole of the mouth.

12 Bourdieu, P. (1984; 2010), p. 191. Most of the empirical research on which Borudieu based his analyses of bodily images and behaviour, like his other extensive researches on the habitus, was carried out between the 1950s and early 1970s. It is tempting, therefore, to fault such characterisations as portraying outdated social and sexual stereotypes. However, Bourdieu's meticulous approach to the personal habits and manners of different social groups is equally applicable to more recent times and offers a rich and detailed picture of a society at both the most general and intimate levels of experience.

13 Kelly, G. A. (1963). *A Theory of Personality: The Psychology of Personal Constructs.* W. W. Norton, New York. Also Kelly, G. A. (1970). 'A brief introduction to personal construct theory'. In *Perspectives in Personal Construct Theory* (Bannister, D. ed.), pp. 1–30, Academic Press, London. For later, related, developments in construct theory and environmental topics, see Adams-Webber, J. R. (1979). *Personal Construct Theory: Concepts and Applications.* John Wiley & Sons, Chichester. Also Honikman, B. (1980). 'Personal construct theory and environmental evaluation'. In *Meaning and Behavior in the Built Environment* (Broadbent, G., Bunt, R. and Llorens, T. eds.): pp. 79–91, John Wiley & Sons, Chichester.

14 Laing, R. D. (1961; 1969). *Self and Others.* Penguin Books, Harmondsworth.

15 Rejecting all previous approaches to understanding human issues as 'unscientific', Skinner advocates a 'technology of behaviour' based upon a human science equivalent to the rigorous physical and biological sciences, in which individual behaviour is purposefully controlled and modified by controlling the environment in which individuals live. See Skinner, B. F. (1971). *Beyond Freedom and Dignity.* Alfred N. Knopf, New York. Also Skinner, B. F. (1974). *About Behaviorism.* Alfred N. Knopf, New York.

16 Kelly, G. A. (1963), p. 46.

17 For more on Kelly's theory and methodology see Bannister, D. and Mair, J. M. M. (1968). *The Evaluation of Personal Constructs.* Academic Press, London. Also Bannister, D. ed. (1970). *Perspectives in Personal Construct Theory.* Academic Press, London.

18 Kelly, G. A. (1963), p. 95.

19 Kelly, G. A. (1963), p. 96.

20 Laing, R. D. (1961, 1969), p. 82.

21 Laing, R. D. (1961, 1969), p. 82.

22 See Laing, R. D., Phillipson, H. and Lee, A. R. (1966). *Interpersonal Perception: A Theory and a Method of Research*. Tavistock Publications, London. Especially Chapter 3, pp. 23–34.

23 The research at MIT was conducted whilst on leave from the Portsmouth School of Architecture in the UK. Other key influences on that work over the same period included the philosophy of George Herbert Mead, whose definition of the self as a 'social structure' is quoted at the beginning of this book, and the 'conversation theory' and research on cybernetic teaching machines of Gordon Pask. See Pask, G. (1976). *Conversation Theory*. Elsevier, Amsterdam. As a regular consultant and inspiration to the MIT group, Pask also provided personal support for my assignment to the group. For a full account of the theoretical aspects and technical operation of ARCHITRAINER, see Abel, C. (1975a). 'Instructional simulation of client construct systems'. Paper presented to the 1975 Architectural Psychology Conference. University of Sheffield, 3–5 July.

24 See Negroponte, N. (1975). *Soft Architecture Machines*. The MIT Press, Cambridge, MA. The book includes an illustration and brief description of ARCHITRAINER and the equipment involved, primitive by today's computer standards, but which worked well enough to test the theory and methodology. A fuller description, together with illustrations of the project set up at Portsmouth Polytechnic and related studies of cognitive structures, is included in Abel, C. (1997, 1st edn.). *Architecture and Identity: Responses to Cultural and Technological Change*. Architectural Press, Oxford, Chapter 3, pp. 33–36. Prior to being attached to Negroponte's group, in addition to the research in other disciplines mentioned above I had also conducted my own earlier investigations into computer-based methods of architectural production, the potential social and cultural impacts of which were then little understood. See Abel, C. (1969). 'Ditching the dinosaur sanctuary'. *Architectural Design*, Vol. 38, August, pp. 419–24.

25 Asked to discriminate amongst three randomly chosen photos of different house designs, the subject might describe two of those designs as 'modern' or 'stylish', in contrast to the third, 'traditional' or 'old-fashioned' design, following which the subject goes through the whole collection attaching a score from 1 to 5 according to where each design lies along the same construct dimension, from one pole to the other. The procedure is then repeated until the subject has exhausted his or her customary repertoire of constructs for that particular topic. The end product of the test is a grid of numbers indicating how each photo scores on each construct dimension, the systemic relations between which can be further examined by various statistical methods. For more on Kelly's repertory grid method, see Fransella, F. and Bannister, D. (1977). *A Manual for Repertory Grid Technique*. Academic Press, New York.

26 The first phase of the programme requires that, building on the initial information offered on each construct, the student correctly predicts how the client rates any of the various designs along each construct dimension. The second, higher-level phase requires understanding the relations *between* the different constructs. These are relationships that online statistical analysis has identified as *types* and classification systems in the client's mind and which the architect is also invited to identify through a final sequence of exercises, involving the grouping of designs across the display.

27 ARCHITRAINER was purposefully designed to better prepare architecture students for understanding the architectural and environmental values of others that do not necessarily share all their own professionally inculcated values. However, there is no reason why, taking advantage of the more advanced computer technologies and cognitive research now available, similar educational programmes might not be designed for other professions.

28 See Abel, C. (1975b). 'A note on the direct elicitation of construct links'. Unpublished research monograph, School of Architecture, Portsmouth Polytechnic. Also Abel, C. (1976). 'Landscape studies project: Portsmouth Polytechnic/Hampshire County Council'. Report to the Centre for Educational Research and Innovation of the OECD, June, 1976.

29 Hinkel, D. N. (1965). 'The change of personal constructs from the viewpoint of a theory of implications'. Unpublished PhD thesis, Ohio State University.

30 Bieri, J. (1955). 'Cognitive complexity–simplicity and predictive behaviour'. *Journal of Abnormal Psychology*, Vol. 51, pp. 263–268. Also Bieri, J. (1966). 'Cognitive complexity and personality development'. In *Experience Structure and Adaptability* (Harvey O. J. ed.), pp. 13–37, Springer, Berlin. Also Bieri, J. et al. (1975). *Clinical and Social Judgement: The Discrimination of Behavioural Information*. Krieger, New York. Especially Chapter 7, 'Cognitive structure and judgement', pp. 182–206. Amongst the first in the field to advance Kelly's theory in new directions, Bieri was dissatisfied with the then commonly accepted definition of the differentiation of cognitive structures as simply meaning a progressive development of more specific concepts and categories, and instead focused his work on cognitive complexity as a measure of the differentiation of *dimensions* of judgment: 'Cognitive complexity may be defined as the tendency to *construe social behaviour in a multidimensional way* [emphasis added], so that a more cognitively complex individual has available a more versatile system for perceiving the behavior of others than does a less cognitively complex person'. Bieri, J (1966), p. 14. See also Crockett, W. H. (1965). 'Cognitive complexity and impression formation'. In *Progress in Experimental Personality Research, Vol. 2* (Maher, B. A. ed.), pp. 47–90, Academic Press, New York. Also Adams-Webber, J. R. (1969). 'Cognitive complexity and sociality'. *British Journal of Social and Clinical Psychology*, Vol. 8, pp. 211–216.

31 For an illustrated description, see Abel, C. (1997, 1st edn), pp. 33–36.

32 Bachelard, G. (1964; 1994). *The Poetics of Space*. Transl. Maria Jolas. Beacon, Boston.

33 Bachelard, G. (1964; 1994), p. xxxvi.

34 Bachelard, G. (1964; 1994), p. 91.

35 See, for example, Blunt, A. and Dowling, R. (2006). *Home*. Routledge, London.

36 Marcus, C. C. (1997). *House as a Mirror of Self: Exploring the Deeper Meaning of Home*. Nicolas Hayes, Berwick.

37 Marcus, C. C. (1995; 2006), p. 15.

38 Marcus, C. C. (1995; 2006), p. 2. There are vital social dimensions, too, she notes, to having a home to call your own. Anyone living without a fixed address is liable to be denied access to many of the employment and financial opportunities those with homes take for granted, not to mention voting rights – the loss of which, along with their associated social and psychological costs, can cripple the lives of young and old.

39 See Cooper, C. (1974). 'The House as Symbol of the Self', in *Designing for Human Behavior: Architecture and the Behavioral Sciences* (Lang, J., Burnette, C., Moleski, W.

and Vachon, D. eds), pp. 130–146, Dowden, Hutchinson & Ross, Stroudsburg. As a former architectural researcher, Marcus had grown dissatisfied with what she had learnt about the purely functional aspects of house design, and sought inspiration in Jung's own personal reflections on the deeper meanings in the way his own home was structured from one level to the next.

40 A very different approach to Kelly's carefully structured investigations, reflective perhaps of the Californian culture of her own time as much as its Gestalt heritage.

41 Marcus, C. C. (1995; 2006), p. 8. Given Marcus's approach to interviewing her subjects, a behavioural psychologist or social scientist trained in more orthodox methodologies might want to question the empirical value of her research. It is also the case that, in addition to living in the same area, all her subjects are neither rich nor poor, but, to judge from their own stories, belong to an educated middle-class of apparently sufficient means to make decisions, express themselves and exert a level of control over their lives that others of lesser means and different backgrounds may not be capable of. However, that would miss the point of Marcus's work. From a field theoretical perspective, Marcus's case studies vividly illustrate much of the psychological and autobiographical territory covered in any evolving self-field, set within the homes and places individuals grow up in, share with others and generally conduct much of their personal lives – homes and places the memory of which their inhabitants may carry with them long after moving on. As we have seen, neither is the idea of wholeness the sole property of Gestalt psychology, but recurs again and again throughout this book, whether as an emergent feature of self-organising systems and evolving organisms, or any of their physical, social or cultural manifestations.

42 Marcus, C. C. (1995; 2006), p. 8. Hardly surprising, since most people rent or buy homes on the open market and then do their best to adapt them to suit their personal tastes.

43 See Cieraad, I. ed. (1999). *At Home: An Anthropology of Domestic Space*. Syracuse University Press, New York.

44 See, for example, Miller, D. ed. (2001). *Home Possessions: Material Culture Behind Closed Doors*. Berg, Oxford. Also Shove, E. (1999). 'Constructing home'. In *At Home: An Anthropology of Domestic Space* (Cieraad, I. ed.), pp. 130–143, Syracuse University Press, New York. Also Tilley, C., Keane, W., Kuchler, S., Rowlands, M. and Spyer, P. (2006). *Handbook of Material Culture*. Sage, London.

45 Miller, D. (2008). *The Comfort of Things*. Polity, Cambridge.

46 Miller, D. (2008), p. 1.

47 Miller, D. (2008), p. 29.

48 Miller, D. (2008), p. 286.

49 Bourdieu argued that, as with other societies chiefly governed by tradition and religion, the Berber people did not need any kind of formal education to learn how to be a Berber, since everything they touch and do is imbued with the same underlying order, from which they acquire their expectations of life, and which are characteristic of their particular society. Thus, the cultural education and socialisation of individuals rests primarily *in the order of things in their daily lives* – how to behave, worship, dress and farm the land – all of which have material dimensions that are typical of their people.

50 Barthes, R. (2013). *The Language of Fashion*. Transl. Stanford, A., Bloomsbury, London.

51 Saussure, F. de (1959). *Course in General Linguistics*. Transl. Baskin, W., Philosophical Library, New York.

52 Barthes, R. (2013), pp. 67–68.

53 Barthes, R. (2013), p. 68. In a later interview on the subject, he also explains the reason why he chose women's fashion magazines as his primary source of knowledge was because, given the lack of any applied semiological research at the time, they offered him as 'pure' a source for semiotic analysis as possible, one that rested entirely upon a single media: 'I studied fashion clothing as it is refracted through the written language of specialist magazines'. Ibid, p. 93.

54 Barthes, R. (2013), p. 58.

55 Entwistle, J. (2000; 2015, 2nd edn). *The Fashioned Body: Fashion, Dress & Modern Social Theory*. Polity, Cambridge.

56 Entwistle, J. (2000; 2015, 2nd edn), p. 7.

57 Entwistle, J. (2000; 2015, 2nd edn), p. 29.

58 Entwistle, J. (2000; 2015, 2nd edn), p. 37. See also Davis, F. (1992). *Fashion, Culture, and Identity*. The University of Chicago Press, Chicago IL. Describing the ambivalence of personal and social identities typical of modern societies as 'fashion's fuel', Davis also suggests the Western fashion industry is adept at finding new ideas in the cultural 'fault lines' and ambiguities that exist between the principle sources of identity – age, gender, class and race – which customers in turn exploit for their own self-expression. Were it not for such ambiguities, he argues, the fashion industry would have a good deal less to draw upon for inspiration than it does, given the almost perpetual fluctuations in those fault lines. Moreover, he suggests, the same persistent ambiguities of identity in modern Western societies may explain why no comparable changes in the manner of dress occur in the more stable societies of the past or present, where personal and social identities are more firmly inscribed in durable traditions.

59 Woodward, S. (2016). '"Humble" blue jeans: Material culture approaches to understanding the ordinary, global, and the personal'. In *Fashion Studies: Research Methods, Sites, and Practices* (Jenss, H. ed.), pp. 42–57, Bloomsbury, London.

60 Woodward, S. (2016), p. 43.

61 Barthes, R. (1957; 1973). *Mythologies*. Trans. A. Lavers, Paladin, St Albans.

62 Barthes, R. (1957; 1973), p. 88.

63 Barthes, R. (1957; 1973), p. 89.

64 Stevenson, H. (2008). *American Automobile Advertising, 1930–1980: An Illustrated History*. McFarland, Jefferson, NC. See also Bajracharya, A., Morin, L. K. and Radovich, K. H. (2014). 'Analysis of automobile advertisements in American magazines'. *Student Publications*. www.cupola.Gettysburg.edu/student_scholarship/225.

65 Stevenson, H. (2008), p. 1. For a lavishly illustrated coverage of both American and European automobile advertisements produced during the last century, see Heimann, J. and Patton, P. (2015). *20th Century Classic Cars: 100 Years of Automotive Ads*. Taschen, Koln.

66 Stevenson, H. (2008), p. 3.

67 Stevenson, H. (2008), p. 81.

68 Baudrillard, J. (1968; 2005). *The System of Objects*. Trans. J. Benedict, Verso, London.

69 Baudrillard, J. (1968; 2005), p. 152.

70 Baudrillard, J. (1968; 2005), p. 151.

71 Brandon, R. (2002). *Auto Mobile: How the Car Changed Life*. Macmillan, London.

72 Brandon, R. (2002), p. 120.

73 Brandon, R. (2002), p. 123.

74 Volti, R. (2004). *Cars and Culture: The Life Story of a Technology*. John Hopkins University Press, Baltimore.

75 Volti does not explain the reasons for the fall in fatalities which, given the continued lax safety standards in the industry over previous decades, probably had more to do with improved driving skills and road conditions as the country accustomed itself to the new form of transportation.

76 Nader, R. (1965). *Unsafe at Any Speed: The Designed-In Dangers of the American Automobile*. Grossman, New York.

77 See Burns, R., Ferrell, J. and Orrick, E. (2005). 'False advertising, suggestive persuasion, and automobile safety: Assessing advertising practices in the automobile industry'. *The Southwest Journal of Criminal Justice*, Vol. 2(2), pp. 132–152.

Chapter 10   Self and group identity

1 See McRae, M. (2011). *Tribal Science: Brains, Beliefs & Bad Ideas*. University of Queensland Press, St Lucia.

2 Haidt, J. (2012). *The Righteous Mind: Why Good People Are Divided by Politics and Religion*. Penguin Books, London.

3 Plato (n.d.). *Plato's Republic*. Transl. Henry Davis. Universal Classics, New York.

4 Quoted in Haidt, J. (2012), p. 84.

5 Haidt, J. (2012), p. 85.

6 Haidt, J. (2012), p. 86.

7 Bloom, P. (2016). *Against Empathy: The Case for Rational Compassion*. The Bodley Head, London.

8 Bloom, P. (2016), pp. 2–3.

9 Bloom, P. (2016), p. 7.

10 Sunstein, C. R. (2009). *Going to Extremes: How Like Minds Unite and Divide*. Oxford University Press, Oxford.

11 Achen, C. H. and Bartels, L. M. (2016). *Democracy for Realists: Why Elections do not Produce Responsive Government*. Princeton University Press, Princeton, NJ.

12 Sunstein, C. R. (2009), p. 110.

13 Festinger, L. (1957). *A Theory of Cognitive Dissonance*. Stanford University Press, Stanford, CA.

14 Festinger, L. (1957), p. 3.

15 Festinger, L. (1957), p. 6.

16 Festinger, L. (1957), p. 182.

17 Bloom, P. (2016), p. 15. Bloom notes at the time of writing there are over 1,500 books available on Amazon.com with the word 'empathy' in their title.

18 Bloom, P. (2016), p. 31. Bloom is careful to distinguish between 'emotional empathy' and 'cognitive empathy', which emerge from different brain processes and 'influence us in different ways'. The former involves an *automatic* internal reflection of the experience or actions of another person – which Bloom is mostly interested in – while the latter, he writes, falls under 'what psychologists describe as social cognition, social intelligence, mind reading, theory of mind, or mentalizing'. Ibid., p. 17.

19 See Castells, M. (1997). Also Stokes, G., ed. (1997). *The Politics of Identity in Australia.* Cambridge University Press, Cambridge.

20 Bloom, P. (2016), p. 5. The issue of altruism arouses similar concerns for the need to overcome instinctive rejections of other groups and races – especially when it comes to perceived matters of self-preservation – in favour of empathy and compassion. See, e.g., Oliner, P. M. et al., eds (1992). *Embracing the Other: Philosophical, Psychological and Historical Perspectives on Altruism.* New York University Press, New York.

21 Gebauer, G. (2014). 'Self, certainty and collective emotions'. In *Understanding Collective Pride and Group Identity: New Directions in Emotion Theory, Research and Practice* (Sullivan, G. B. ed.), pp. 34–42, Routledge, Abingdon.

22 Gebauer, G. (2014), p. 36.

23 Gebauer, G. (2014), p. 37.

24 Allport, G. W. (1954; 1978). *The Nature of Prejudice.* Addison-Wesley, Reading, MA.

25 Allport, G. W. (1954; 1978), p. 41.

26 Allport, G. W. (1954; 1978), p. 42.

27 Allport, G. W. (1954; 1978), p. 42.

28 Beyer, M., von Scheve, C. and Ismer, S. (2017). 'The social consequences of collective emotions: national identification, solidarity and out-group derogation'. In *Understanding Collective Pride and Group Identity: New Directions in Emotion Theory, Research and Practice* (Sullivan, G. B. ed.), pp. 67–79, Routledge, Abingdon.

29 For a well-illustrated history of the murals created by both sides, see Borthwick, S. (2015). *The Writing on the Wall: A Visual History of Northern Ireland's Troubles.* Bluecoat Press, Liverpool. Also Rolston, B. (2013). *Drawing Support 4: Murals and Conflict Transformation in Northern Ireland.* Beyond the Pale, Belfast.

30 McKittrick, D. and McVea, D. (2012). *Making Sense of the Troubles: A History of the Northern Ireland Conflict.* Viking, London.

31 McKittrick, D. and McVea, D. (2012), p. 2.

32 As the authors explain, the creation in 1920 of a new state and parliament of Northern Ireland, where most of the settler community was concentrated, together with the reluctant acceptance by the British Government of an independent Irish Free State (now the Republic of Ireland) in the rest of the island a year later, brought only a partial and temporary peace. Discrimination against the Catholic minority for jobs and housing in the new state remained rampant and was regarded as the norm by the Protestant majority. Most employers in the private sector were Protestant and generally recruited employees by word of mouth or on the personal recommendation of other Protestant employers. The situation in the public sector was no better; for their own part, Catholics believed that applying for positions in the public services was a waste of time since almost all such positions were held by Protestants. The supply of low-cost public housing, which was mostly administrated by Protestant-controlled local councils, was also a matter of much discontent amongst Catholics, the more so since owning a house carried with it voting and other civil rights.

33 Shirlow, P. and Murtagh, B. (2006). *Belfast: Segregation, Violence and the City.* Pluto Press, London.

34 Shirlow, P. and Murtagh, B. (2006), p. 3.

35 Quoted in Shirlow, P. and Murtagh, B. (2006), p. 15.

36 There is even an *underground* wall in Belfast City Cemetery built to separate the Protestant and Catholic dead.

37 Shirlow, P. and Murtagh, B. (2006), p. 1.

38 Shirlow, P. and Murtagh, B. (2006), p. 174.

39 Shirlow, P. and Murtagh, B. (2006), p. 174.

Chapter 11   Occupational identity

1 Stiglitz, J. (2013). *The Price of Inequality*. Penguin Books, London, p. xxii. See also Piketty, T. (2015). *The Economics of Inequality*. Trans. A. Goldhammer, Harvard University Press, Cambridge, MA. Stiglitz wryly observes: 'It shouldn't, of course, come as a surprise that some of the wealthiest Americans are promoting an economic fantasy in which their further enrichment benefits everyone. It is, perhaps, a surprise that they've done such a good job of selling these fantasies to so many Americans'.

2 Freeman, J. B. (2018). *Behemoth: A History of the Factory and the Making of the Modern World*. W.W. Norton, New York.

3 Freeman, J. B. (2018), p. 1.

4 Much of that growth reflects a shifting of labour-intensive jobs from the developed to the developing world, where labour costs are generally much lower.

5 Freeman, J. B. (2018), p. 5.

6 Freeman, J. B. (2018), p. 60.

7 Freeman, J. B. (2018), p. 73.

8 There was a catch, however, since the increase was not automatically awarded to every worker, but only to those who Ford deemed 'qualified' for it. The stringent terms excluded women entirely and involved a mandatory programme of re-education, including language training and 'acceptable behavior' both on and *off* the company plant. In short, for all the material benefits to participants, Ford's programme amounted to nothing less than a coordinated effort, as Freeman writes, 'to shape the behavior and mindset of employees to make them fit for a factory regime'. Freeman, J. B. (2018), p. 131.

9 Freeman, J. B. (2018), p. 119.

10 Notable exceptions include the French architect Jean Prouve. See Abel, C. (1969). 'Ditching the dinosaur sanctuary'. *Architectural Design*, Vol. 38, August, pp. 419–424. Also Davidson, C. (1965). 'Jean Prouve: l'habitation de notre epoque'. *Arena: Journal of the Architectural Association*, London, Vol. 81, December, pp. 128–129.

11 Corbusier, Le (1927; 1946). *Towards a New Architecture*. Transl. F. Etchells, The Architectural Press, London, Frederick A. Praeger, New York.

12 Corbusier, Le (1927; 1946), pp. 12–13.

13 Such as the need for controlled *tolerances* between components, without which interchangeability between different components and large-scale production and innovation was impossible. For a critique of Modernist conceptions of mass production and design, see Abel, C. (1969). See also Eden, J. F. (1967). 'Metrology and the module'. *Architectural Design*, Vol. XXXVII, March, pp. 148–150.

14 Banham, R. (1965). 'A clip-on architecture'. *Architectural Design*, Vol. 35, No. 11, pp. 534–535.

15 The invention of Molins' chief production engineer, D. T. N. Williamson, who really *did* know something about the technology of mass production – enough to understand its limitations as well as its advantages – System 24 built upon existing but relatively primitive, computer-based technologies for batch production of metal components, involving discrete, numerically controlled (NC) machines. Expensive and limited to carrying out one of a fixed range of cutting and shaping operations of varying complexity at a time, each of which had to be reprogrammed, NC machines were no match for the speed and continuous operation of the mass-production line, as restrictive as it was in its own way. Williamson's innovation, like Ford's, was to combine existing technologies – once again much as Arthur describes the evolution of all new technologies – by stringing together *several* NC machines, each of which is designed to perform a different operation, in a *single computer-controlled line*, moving the block of metal (aluminium because it is easier to cut than steel) on an automated conveyor between each machine, cutting and shaping it as required to produce the finished component.

16 Beer, S. (1962). 'Towards the cybernetic factory'. In *Principles of Self-Organization* (Von Foerster, H. and Zopf, Jr., G. W. eds), pp. 25–89.

17 Unhappily for Molins, System 24 also proved to be a classic case of an idea being too far ahead of its time. Neither the coordinated information and marketing systems, nor the more advanced systems of computer and managerial control envisaged by Beer as key elements of the cybernetic factory, though theoretically achievable, were yet in place. The result was that, as advanced as System 24 was, the potential combination of variable, high-volume production promised by Williamson's revolutionary system could not be achieved – not yet, anyway, in the particular industry in which Molins was engaged.

18 See Abel, C. (1986). 'Ditching the dinosaur sanctuary: twenty years on'. In *CAD and Robotics in Architecture and Construction*. Proceedings of the 1986 Joint International Conference at Marseilles, 25–27 June, Kogan Page, London, pp. 123–132. For an edited version of the former paper, see Abel, C. (1988). 'Return to craft manufacture'. *The Architects' Journal: Information Technology Supplement*, 20 April, pp. 53–57.

19 By the 1980s, specialised robots were also coming into individual use on construction sites, each of which, unlike their general-purpose factory cousins, was designed to perform a particular task of assembly or finishing of floors or walls in variable interior and exterior conditions, often running around the building under their own volition; all situations placing extra demands on semi-autonomous and highly sensitive control systems as well as the physical design of the robots themselves. Explanations offered at the time for the use of robotics in these exposed and strenuous conditions included a reduction in human accidents on building sites as well as increases in productivity and improvements in the quality of the work. Contemporary studies also suggested that most aspects of the construction process were also amenable to the use of similar technologies. See Abel, C. (1986).

20 See Abel, C. (1988).

21 Carr, N. (2015). *The Glass Cage: Where Automation is Taking Us*. The Bodley Head, London.

22 Carr, N. (2015), pp. 14–15.

23 Carr, N. (2015), p. 15.

24 Carr, N. (2015), p. 16. See also Bensman, J. and Rosenberg, B. (1960). 'The meaning of work in a bureaucratic society'. In *Identity and Anxiety: Survival of the Person in*

Mass Society (Stein, M. R.,Vidich, A. J. and White, D. M. eds), pp. 181–197, Free Press of Glencoe, Illinois.

25 Frey, C. B. and Osborne, M. A. (2013). 'The future of employment: how susceptible are jobs to computerization?' Paper presented to the 'Machines and Employment' Workshop, University of Oxford, 17 September.

26 Kurenkov, A., Liang, J. and Ramanauskas, B. (2019). 'Job loss due to AI – how bad is it going to be?' *Skynet Today*, 4 February. www.skynettoday.com/editorials/ai-automation-job-loss.

27 Kurenkov, A., Liang, J. and Ramanauskas, B. (2019), p. 1.

28 For the impacts of computerisation on office work and labour see Greenbaum, J. (2004). 'Windows on the workplace: technology, jobs, and the organization of office work'. *Monthly Review Press*, New York.

29 Carr does not acknowledge Polanyi's work in his book, but the debt is clear enough from his explanation of the difference between the two forms of knowledge.

30 Carr, N. (2015), p. 9.

31 Carr, N. (2015), p. 11.

32 See also Russell, S. (2019). *Human Compatible: AI and the Problem of Control*. Allen Lane, London.

33 World Health Organization (2018). 'Road traffic injuries'. 7 December, www.who.int/news-room/fact-sheets/detail/road-traffic-injuries.

34 For a discussion of the use of AI techniques in architectural design, or 'design by artificial selection', as I call it, see Abel, C. (2007) 'Virtual evolution: A memetic critique of genetic algorithms in design'. In *Techniques and Technologies: Transfer and Transformation. Proceedings of the 4th International Conference of the Association of Architectural Schools of Australia, 2007* (Orr, K, and Kaji-O'Grady, S. eds). University of Technology, Sydney. Republished under the title, 'Genetic designs'. Also Abel, C. (2015), *The Extended Self: Architecture, Memes and Minds*. Manchester University Press, Manchester, pp. 254–256.

35 Collinson, P. (2019). 'Automation threatens 1.5 million workers in Britain, says ONS'. *The Guardian*, 25 March. https://theguardian.com/money/2019/mar/25/automation.

36 Carr, N. (2015), p. 18.

Chapter 12   Selves online

1 McLuhan, M. (1964). *Understanding Media: The Extensions of Man*. Routledge & Kegan Paul, London.

2 Lasch, C. (1978). *The Culture of Narcissism: American Life in An Age of Diminishing Expectations*. W. W. Norton, New York.

3 Lasch, C. (1978), p. 30.

4 Lasch, C. (1978), p. 7.

5 Quoted in Lasch, C. (1978), p. 7.

6 Lasch, C. (1978), p. 7

7 Though Lasch's choice of witness may not represent the more seriously committed participants in the Chicago demonstrations, his analysis of the personal gratification that involvement in mass gatherings of this kind can give to individuals, fits with the more recent studies by Gebauer and others described in the previous chapter.

Amongst his other targets, Lasch also examines the widespread impact on the daily lives of workers of the emergence of a new kind of managerial class, motivated solely by narcissistic concerns. Citing a study of 250 managers across twelve major companies, he describes the archetypal new manager as being more interested in scoring *victories* over rivals than building industrial empires or accumulating wealth: 'Instead of pitting himself against a material task or a problem demanding a solution, he pits himself against others' Lasch, C. (1978), p. 44.

8   See also Storr, W. (2017). *Selfie: How the West Became Self-obsessed*. Picador, London.

9   Lasch, C. (1978), p. 47.

10   Carr, N. (2010). *The Shallows: How the Internet is Changing the Way We Think, Read and Remember*. Atlantic Books, London.

11   Carr, N. (2010), p. 85.

12   Greenfield, P. M. (1984; 2014). *Mind and Media: The Effects of Television, Video Games, and Computers*. Psychology Press, Hove.

13   Greenfield, P. M. (1984; 2014), p. xv.

14   Greenfield, P. M. (1984; 2014), p. xvi.

15   Greenfield, P. M. (1984; 2014), p. xvi.

16   Given that Greenfield's original research was conducted in the early 1980s, when computers and video games were a novelty and the Internet was still a decade away, it is hardly surprising that the issue of addiction does not feature in the 1984 publication. However, the omission of any reference to the growing problem in her introduction to the new edition cannot be so easily explained.

17   Griffiths, M. D., Kuss, D. J. and King, D. L. (2013). 'Video game addiction: past, present and future'. *Current Psychiatry Reviews*, Vol. 8, No. 4, pp. 1–11.

18   Griffiths, M. D., Kuss, D. J. and King, D. L. (2013), p. 2.

19   In addition to players' online self-reports, studies included a range of other personal data, such as visual and verbal memory tests, medical histories and examinations, physical as well as psychiatric (pathological) findings, functional Magnetic Resonance Imaging (fMRI) tests, and even genotyping.

20   However, the course and severity of the problem within these groups, Griffiths et al note, is also less certain and may be a result of sampling biases or the fact they just play more *often* than other socio-demographic groups.

21   Griffiths, M. D., Kuss, D. J. and King, D. L. (2013), p. 4. There are also many reported cases of actual *physical harm* to players and other serious health and medical effects arising from uncontrolled video game playing, including many familiar as well as unfamiliar symptoms, such as: epileptic seizures; obesity; wrist and neck pain; blisters, calluses and sore tendons; numbness of fingers; hand–arm vibration syndrome, sleep abnormalities and repetitive strain injuries.

22   Kuss, D. J. (2013). 'Internet gaming addiction: Current perspectives'. *Psychology Research and Behavior Management*, No. 6, 125–137.

23   Kuss is also careful to distinguish between *excessive* or 'problem gaming', which may still be controllable by individual players, and actual addiction, which is not.

24   For more on avatars and related online games, see Johnson, P. (2010). *Second Life, Media, and the Other Society*. Peter Lang, New York.

25   As widespread as Internet gaming addiction of this sort is across the world, however, estimates of the prevalence of addiction amongst gamers vary widely from region to region – from as little as 0.2% in Germany to 50% amongst Korean teenagers. While much of that difference may be due to differences in approaches and methodology,

Kuss reports, research also suggests that self-diagnosis by gamers is more reliable than expected, and that individual players' perception of any problems they may be having 'can be relatively accurate'. Whatever the differences in approach and research methodology, the steep rise in the number of cases of Internet gaming addiction in the 2000s has led to a mushrooming of treatment centres across the world; especially in Southeast Asian countries like South Korea and Japan where governments take the negative effects of gaming amongst the young – including many children – particularly seriously, but also in Europe and the US, where in- and out-patient hospitalisation and 'detoxification' programmes are now common.

26 Kuss, D. J. (2013), p. 129.

27 O'Connor, C. (2014). *Control the Controller: Understanding and Resolving Video Game Addiction*. Free Association Books, London.

28 O'Connor, C. (2014), p. 78.

29 O'Connor, C. (2014), p. 79. 'In the business, these players are called whales. Whales are the high spending one percent of an audience that are funding the game for everyone else to enjoy either free or at minimal cost. A company with a healthy attitude considers whales to be dedicated and wealthy fans of the game that get the most out of their experience by paying. A company with a less healthy attitude considers them the rich addicts'. Ibid, p. 79.

30 O'Connor, C. (2014), p. 80.

31 O'Connor, C. (2014), p. 81.

32 O'Connor, C. (2014), p. 169.

33 Castells, M. (1996). *The Rise of the Network Society. Vol. I, The Information Age: Economy, Society and Culture*. Blackwell, Oxford. See also, Castells, M. (1997) *The Power of Identity. Vol. II, The Information Age: Economy, Society and Culture*. Blackwell, Oxford.

34 Castells, M. (1996), p. 3.

35 Castells, M. (1996), p. 3.

36 Dijck, J. van (2013). *The Culture of Connectivity: A Critical History of Social Media*. Oxford University Press, Oxford.

37 Dijck, J. van (2013), p. 7.

38 Dijck, J. van (2013), p. 7. For a typically optimistic, business-orientated response to the opportunities presented by the Net, see Dyson, E. (1997). *Release 2.0: A Design For Living in the Digital Age*. Viking, London. In characteristically buoyant style, Dyson writes, perhaps prematurely: 'The Net offers us a chance to take charge or our own lives and to redefine our role as citizens of local communities and of a global society'. Ibid, p. 2. See also Coyne, R. (2016). *Mood and Mobility: Navigating the Emotional Spaces of Digital Social Networks*. The MIT Press, Cambridge, MA. Coyne offers a subtle analysis of the emotional effects that smartphones have upon their users.

39 Dijck, J. van (2013), p. 10.

40 Dijck, J. van (2013), p. 51.

41 Dijck, J. van (2013), p. 51.

42 Dijck, J. van (2013), p. 55.

Chapter 13   Transformations

1 Turkle, S. (2011). *Alone Together: Why We Expect More From Technology and Less From Each Other*. Basic Books, New York.

2 Turkle, S. (1984). *The Second Self: Computers and the Human Spirit*. Simon & Schuster, New York; and Turkle, S. (1997). *Life on the Screen: Identity in the Age of the Internet*. Simon & Schuster, New York.

3 Turkle, S. (2011), p. xii.

4 Turkle, S. (2011), p. 152.

5 Turkle, S. (2011), p. 152.

6 Turkle, S. (2011), p. 153.

7 Turkle, S. (2011), pp. 155–156. Turkle offers some amusing anecdotes recalling her all-too familiar – and generally irritating, if not excruciating – experiences stuck next to someone on a train or bus who, apparently oblivious to everyone else within hearing distance, is loudly detailing their personal travails on their phone to some remote listener. Pondering whether the self-absorbed speaker presumes he will be ignored by Turkle and the other travellers, or whether, in fact, it is those on the phone who think of themselves as being absent, in either case, she observes, the disconnection of speaker from his surroundings is palpable.

8 Turkle, S. (2011), p. 177.

9 Turkle, S. (2011), p. 177.

10 Turkle, S. (2011), p. 23.

11 Turkle, S. (2011), p. xiv. While the number of individuals finding pleasure and consolation in the company of robot pets and other automated companions may be presently small compared to online gamers or Facebook members, Turkle regards the substitution of formerly concrete human relationships by remote online contacts and robotic companions, as two sides of the same coin. The evidence she presents from numerous case studies, that many elderly people as well as young subjects are apparently ready to accept robot substitutes into their lives, is a troubling indicator of just how far digital technologies have come to penetrate, and even to *displace* human relationships.

12 Wolf, M. (2008). *Proust and the Squid: The Story and Science of the Reading Brain*. Icon Books, Cambridge.

13 Wolf, M. (2008), p. 6.

14 Wolf, M. (2008), p. 6.

15 Wolf, M. (2008), p. 5.

16 Wolf, M. (2008), p. 5.

17 Just how much restructuring, Wolf explains, is a matter of some debate, however, since some major written languages like Chinese are still based upon earlier scripts numbering thousands of characters. The issue revolves around the question of whether alphabet-based writing systems are more *efficient* than other systems in using the brain's resources needed to understand and memorise a writing system to the point of fluency, the answer to which depends largely upon *which parts* of the brain are involved in processing signs and characters, which may differ between languages. While alphabet readers rely upon a *decreased* amount of cortical space and specialised functions located in the rear portion of the left hemisphere, the brains of Chinese readers compensate for the far greater number of characters they need to assimilate by employing many more areas across *both* hemispheres for specialised, automatic processing. Different writing systems may, therefore, result in the development of their own distinctive and functionally efficient neural networks for reading.

18 Wolf, M. (2008), p. 65.

19 Wolf, M. (2008), p. 66.

20 Wolf, M. (2018). *Reader, Come Home: The Reading Brain in a Digital World*. Harper Collins, New York.

21 Wolf, M. (2018), p. 39.

22 Quoted in Wolf, M. (2018), p. 63.

23 Wolf, M. (2018), p. 63.

24 Carr, N. (2010). *The Shallows: How the Internet is Changing the Way We Think, Read and Remember*. Atlantic Books, London. See also Callil, C. et al. (2011). *Stop What You're Doing and Read This!* Vintage Books, London.

25 Carr, N. (2010), p. 6. Drawing a colourful metaphor, Carr likens the feeling to the scene in Stanley Kubrick's classic movie *2001: A Space Odyssey*, where the surviving astronaut slowly but methodically disconnects the malevolent supercomputer HAL's memory circuits: 'Over the last few years I've had an uncomfortable sense that someone, or something, has been tinkering with my brain, remapping the neural circuitry, reprogramming the memory. My mind isn't going – so far as I can tell – but its changing'. Ibid, p. 5.

26 Carr, N. (2010), p. 6.

27 Carr, N. (2010), p. 191.

28 Carr, N. (2010), p. 192.

29 Carr, N. (2010), p. 196.

30 Greenfield, S. (2008). *ID: The Quest for Identity in the 21st Century*. Sceptre, London.

31 Greenfield, S. (2014). *Mind Change: How Digital Technologies are Leaving Their Mark on our Brains*. Rider Books, London.

32 Greenfield, S. (2014), p. 123.

33 Greenfield, S. (2014), p. 256.

34 Greenfield, S. (2014), p. 267.

35 Quoted in Greenfield, S. (2014), p. 268.

Chapter 14   Loss of the private self

1 Lasch, C. (1978), *The Culture of Narcissism: American Life in An Age of Diminishing Expectations*. W. W. Norton, New York p. 30.

2 Zuboff, S. (2019), *The Age of Surveillance Capitalism: The Fight For a Human Future at the New Frontier of Power*. Profile Books, London, p. 376.

3 Orwell, G. (1949; 1992). *Nineteen Eighty-Four*. Everyman's Library, New York.

4 Snowden, E. (2019). *Permanent Record*. Macmillan, London.

5 Wylie, C. (2019). *Mindf*ck: Inside Cambridge Analytica's Plot to Break the World*. Profile Books, London.

6 Wylie, C. (2019), p. 18.

7 Wylie, C. (2019), p. 11.

8 Wylie, C. (2019), p. 13.

9 Wylie, C. (2019), p. 14.

10 It may be assumed that, like the leaders of the Liberal Democratic Party in London he later worked for, accustomed as they were to door-to-door personal canvassing, the LPC found his methods too radical.

11 For details, see Wylie, C. (2019), p. 40.

12 Wylie, C. (2019), p. 34. A pilot study he ran comparing the scores of Lib Dem voters with Labour and Tory voters on the five-factor test, indicated Lib Dems were indeed different in kind from the other voters, and did not fall so easily into the monolithic groups generally favoured by pollsters. Presenting his conclusions to the party office, he warned them of a fundamental discrepancy between what he had learned of the character of their voters as 'ideological' and 'stubborn' individuals who 'hated compromise', and the party of endless compromise they had become since joining with the dominant Tories in a coalition government: 'a betrayal of Lib Dem voter's ideals', as he described it, that 'was bound to drive people out of the party'. It was not what the party's leaders were expecting, nor wanted to hear, especially from a young, North American outsider they had specifically hired to deliver some winning, high-tech polling tools. Wylie's work with the LDP ended shortly afterwards.

13 In fact, the SCL never did set up a permanent office in Cambridge but, respecting his liking of the city, they simply hired an office space in the city and temporary workers for the day whenever they met with Bannon on his visits from the US.

14 Mercer would invest $15 million in the new company, which bought him the lion's share of ownership of Analytica, while SCL, as the nominal parent of the new company, which was to be registered in the US, took just 10 per cent. The arrangement enabled Analytica to operate in the US as an American company while SCL's defence division continued operating in the UK as a British company – an important consideration in view of the joint venture's future work on both sides of the Atlantic.

15 Wylie, C. (2019), p. 92.

16 Wylie, C. (2019), p. 95. It should be noted that, according to Wylie, the University of Cambridge 'strongly denies that it was involved with any Facebook data projects'. Ibid, p. 104.

17 Wylie, C. (2019), p. 106.

18 Wylie, C. (2019), p. 107.

19 Wylie, C. (2019), p. 110. As related by Wylie, Nix could not resist the temptation to phone the lady herself to check their information, pretending to conduct an actual survey from Cambridge University. To everyone's delight her response to every question he asked – voting record, TV favourites, which school her children went to, etc. – matched exactly the information they had on her file. After which Bannon and everyone else in the room took a turn checking their data on the phone with other unwitting individuals selected at random.

20 Preferring to keep his options open, Wylie claims he had been offered but had always refused an official contract with SCL, which clearly left him vulnerable to such moves.

21 Wylie, C. (2019), p. 121.

22 Wylie, C. (2019), p. 121.

23 Wylie, C. (2019), p. 144.

24 See Kaiser, B. (2019). *Targeted: My Inside Story of How Cambridge Analytica and Trump, Brexit and Facebook Broke Democracy*. HarperCollins, London.

25 Wylie, C. (2019), p. 153.

26 O'Toole, F. (2018). *Heroic Failure: Brexit and the Politics of Pain*. Head of Zeus, London.

27 O'Toole, F. (2018), p. 190.

28 In fact, every existing Member State has the right of veto over the admission of any new country applying to join the EU, so there never was a genuine threat of being overwhelmed by immigrants from other countries, either from Turkey – a much-touted threat by Brexiter campaigners – or any other country wanting to join (Turkey has, in any case, now dropped its application and shows no more interest in the idea).

29 Turow, J. (2011). *The Daily You: How the New Advertising Industry Is Defining Your Identity and Your Worth.* Yale University Press, Yale.

30 Turow, J. (2011), p. 4. See also Shermer, M. (2008). *The Mind of the Market: How Biology and Psychology Shape Our Economic Lives.* Henry Holt, New York.

31 Accustomed as we are to the use of the word 'publisher' for newspapers and other printed media, the terminology can be confusing, but includes online search engines like Google and other firms who provide information and news online. As used by Turow, the term 'marketers' in turn refers to firms advertising goods or services they have to sell online, but can also include firms marketing the personal data of social media members and other Net users.

32 Turow, J. (2011), p. 10.

33 Turow, J. (2011), p. 88.

34 Turow, J. (2011), p. 89.

35 Foroohar, R. (2019). *Don't Be Evil: The Case Against Big Tech.* Allen Lane, London.

36 Foroohar, R. (2019), p. xii.

37 Quoted in Foroohar, R. (2019), p. 58.

38 Foroohar, R. (2019), p. xiv.

39 Zuboff, S. (2019), p. 31.

40 Zuboff, S. (2019), pp. 31–32.

41 Zuboff, S. (2019), p. 32.

42 Zuboff, S. (2019), pp. 477–478.

43 Standing, G. (2011; 2016). *The Precariat: The New Dangerous Class.* Bloomsbury, London.

44 Standing, G. (2011; 2016), p. x.

45 See Stiglitz, J. (2013).

46 Zuboff, S. (2019), p. 480.

47 Zuboff, S. (2019), p. 482.

48 Amnesty International (2019). *Surveillance Giants: How the Business Model of Google and Facebook Threatens Human Rights.* Amnesty International, London.

49 Quoted in Amnesty International (2019), p. 8.

50 Amnesty International (2019), p. 7.

51 Amnesty International (2019), p. 49.

52 Amnesty International (2019), p. 49.

53 Berners-Lee, T. et al. (2019). *Contract for the Web.* Web Foundation, Geneva.

54 Google has also announced that, since the UK is leaving the EU, the data handling of its UK-based users will, in future, be transferred to a branch of the company in the US where UK customers would no longer enjoy either the protection of the GDPR or the UK's own Data Protection Act 2018, both of which offer far more protection than current US regulations – hardly an encouraging development.

55 Zuboff, S. (2019), p. 488.

PART IV   Summation

1 Vygotsky, L. S. (1978). *Mind in Society: The Development of Higher Psychological Processes.* Edited by Cole, M., John-Steiner, V., Scribner, S. and Souberman, E. Harvard University Press, Cambridge, MA, p. 65.

Chapter 15   Instinctive and fuzzy selves

1 Gray, J. (2015). *The Soul of the Marionette: A Short Enquiry into Human Freedom.* Allen Lane, London, p. 144.

2 For recent assessments of the full gravity of the situation, see McKibben, B. (2019). *Falter: Has the Human Game Begun to Play Itself Out?* Wildfire, London. Also Wallace-Wells, D. (2019). *The Uninhabitable Earth: A Story of the Future.* Allen Lane, London. There have also been many, far earlier and equally grave warnings of impending catastrophe, however, of which James Lovelock's 'Gaia' theory of the whole biosphere of the planet as an integrated, cybernetic system, which he first formulated in 1967, is amongst the most influential. See Lovelock, J. E. (1979; 1987). *Gaia: A New Look at Life On Earth.* Oxford University Press, Oxford. Also Lovelock, J. (2009). *The Vanishing Face of Gaia: A Final Warning.* Penguin Books, London.

3 Inevitably, as neurobiologists firmly focused on pinning down the finer mechanisms of the brain and its many functions, it is in the nature of their discipline that they should also be mostly orientated towards physicalist explanations of those functions and their location in different parts of the brain and nervous system.

4 For general guidance on interdisciplinary collaborations involving the neurosciences, see Callard, F. and Fitzgerald, D. (2015). *Rethinking Interdisciplinarity Across the Social Sciences and Neurosciences.* Palgrave Macmillan, Basingstoke.

5 As Porges explains, the polyvagal system underlying the expression of those emotions involves a complex integration of self-regulating, autonomic bodily functions and nervous systems with a more extended network of neuronal and sensory systems responsive to environmental factors.

6 Zadeh, L. (1975). 'Fuzzy logic and approximate reasoning'. Synthese, No. 30, pp. 407–428. For the relevance to psychology, see Belohlavek, R. and Klir, G. J. eds (2011). *Concepts and Fuzzy Logic.* The MIT Press, Cambridge, MA. For a general account, see also Kosko, B. (1994). *Fuzzy Thinking: The New Science of Fuzzy Logic.* Harper Collins, London.

7 Quoted in Belohlavek, R. and Klir, G. J. eds (2011), p. 4.

8 Belohlavek, R. and Klir, G. J. eds (2011), p. 4. The most important of those fresh approaches, the editors suggest, may be a new way of looking at concepts expressed in natural language, which they and other contributors, who include mathematicians as well as researchers in psychology like themselves, pursue in their collection of essays.

9 The typically assertive behaviour of the male leader of a group of large apes who senses his authority is being challenged by a rival, for example, is surely defending a self-image, if only unconsciously.

10 Gray, J. (2002), p. 56.

11 A feature that Darwin also recognised is as vital to the social lives of other primates as it to human lives. See Darwin, C. (1872; 1965).

12 See Foroohar, R. (2019), *Don't Be Evil: The Case Against Big Tech*. Allen Lane, London, p. xvi.

13 See also Klein, (2015). *This Changes Everything: Capitalism vs. the Climate*. Penguin Books, UK.

14 See Diamond, J. (2005). *Collapse: How Societies Choose to Fail or Survive*. Allen Lane, London.

15 Robins, N. (2012). *The Corporation that Changed the World: How the East India Company Shaped the Modern Multinational*. Pluto Press, London.

16 Oreskes, N. (2004). 'The scientific consensus on climate change'. *Science*, Vol. 306, 3 December, p. 1686.

17 At an international conference in June 2011, for example, organised by the Heartland Institute, an American right wing, so-called 'thinktank', speaker after speaker rose to condemn and vilify any proposals to act upon and alleviate climate change, the existence of which they all furiously denied. Most of all, however, repeated variations were heard of the opinion of one county official in the audience, who expressed the view: 'that climate change is a Trojan House, designed to abolish capitalism and replace it with some kind of "green communitarianism"'. Klein, N. (2015), p. 33. See also Marshall, G. (2014). *Don't Even Think About It: Why Our Brains Are Wired to Ignore Climate Change*. Bloomsbury, New York. In addition to confirmation bias, Marshall draws upon much evidence from neuroscientists in explanation of the factors influencing climate change denial. However, as with similar approaches cited here, the outcome is an aggregate of different neurological mechanisms and processes, rather than an explanation of what integrates them and holds them all together.

18 See Turner, J. H. (2003). *Human Institutions: A Theory of Societal Evolution*. Rowman & Littlefield, Lanham. Turner offers a sweeping macro-evolutionary approach to human institutions, limited however, by a Darwinian theory of natural selection: 'At first, selection pressures came from the biophysical environment, but as the complexity of social structure and culture increased, selection pressures came from the very sociocultural systems that had been used to increase adaptation to the biophysical environment. Thus, as institutional systems evolve, they constantly create new environments generating new kinds of second-order selection pressures that push institutional evolution toward ever more complex formations'. Ibid, p. 53.

19 See Lynas, M. (2008). *Six Degrees: Our Future on a Hotter Planet*. National Geographic, Washington, D.C. Setting out the projected effects of global warming in terrifying detail, degree by degree, Lynas reminds us it has all happened before at the end of the Permian Period, 251 million years ago, when as much as 95 per cent of all living species – on land and in the sea – were wiped out in the 'worst mass-extinction of all time'. A key turning point in what he describes as a clear case of runaway climate change, was the release of vast quantities of deadly methane gas previously locked up in the ocean depths and in the frozen tundras of the artic regions – a process already detected in some of the same areas in our own time.

20 Ripple, W. J. et al. (2019). 'World Scientists' Warning of a Climate Emergency'. *Bioscience*, biz088, https://doi.org/10.1093/biosci/biz088. See also Lenton, T. M. et al. (2019). 'Climate tipping points – Too risky to bet against'. *Nature*, Vol. 575, 28 November, pp. 592–595. In the same year, those impacts, which were all widely publicised, included: record-breaking temperature rises around the globe and associated widespread droughts; deadly, out-of-control and larger-than-ever

bush fires in Australia and North America; an unprecedented loss of land-based ice sheets in Greenland and Antarctica, contributing directly to a rise in sea levels, and equally dramatic increases in the number and severity of extreme weather conditions and related loss of life and economic damage.

21 There has been no shortage of practical proposals for a more respectful and enduring relationship with nature. All offer alternative pathways to the future, from the indigenous traditions of building that Rudofsky urged professional architects to learn from and the countless projects based on renewable energy technologies and ecologically sensitive models of development, to the Grameen Bank's radical approach to low-cost credit for the poor. For examples and related proposals, see Abel, C. (2017). Especially Chapter 19, 'Towards a global eco-culture', pp. 284–301 (first published in the Proceedings of the 1992 Conference of the International Association for the Study of Traditional Environments, IASTE).

22 McKibben, B. (1989). *The End of Nature*. Random House, New York.

23 McKibben, B. (1989), pp. 60–61.

Bibliography

Abel, C. (1969). 'Ditching the dinosaur sanctuary'. *Architectural Design*, Vol. 38, August, pp. 419–424.

Abel, C. (1975a). 'Instructional simulation of client construct systems'. Paper presented to the 1975 Architectural Psychology Conference. University of Sheffield, July 3–5.

Abel, C. (1975b). 'A note on the direct elicitation of construct links'. Unpublished research monograph, Portsmouth Polytechnic.

Abel, C. (1976). 'Landscape studies project: Portsmouth Polytechnic/Hampshire County Council'. Report to the Centre for Educational Research and Innovation of the OECD, June, 1976.

Abel, C. (1979). 'The language analogy in architectural theory and criticism: Some remarks in the light of Wittgenstein's linguistic relativism'. *Architectural Association Quarterly*, Vol. 12, December, pp. 39–47.

Abel, C. (1981). 'The function of tacit knowing in learning design'. *Design Studies*, Vol. 2, October, pp. 209–214.

Abel, C. (1982b). 'The case for anarchy in design research'. In *Changing Design* (Evans, B., Powell, J. A. and Talbot, R. J. eds), pp. 295–302, John Wiley & Sons, Chichester.

Abel, C. (1986). 'Ditching the dinosaur sanctuary: Twenty years on'. In *CAD and Robotics in Architecture and Construction*. Proceedings of the 1986 Joint International Conference at Marseilles, 25–27 June, Kogan Page, London, pp. 123–132.

Abel, C. (1988). 'Return to craft manufacture'. *The Architects' Journal: Information Technology Supplement*, 20 April, pp. 53–57.

Abel, C. (1991). 'The essential tension'. *Architecture and Urbanism*, July, 1991. Republished in Abel, C. (2017 3rd edn). *Architecture and Identity: Responses to Cultural and Technological Change*. Routledge, Abingdon, pp. 196–213.

Abel, C. (1997, 1st edn). *Architecture and Identity: Responses to Cultural and Technological Change*. Architectural Press, Oxford, Chapter 3, pp. 33–36.

Abel, C. (2007). 'Virtual evolution: A memetic critique of genetic algorithms in design'. In *Techniques and Technologies: Transfer and Transformation. Proceedings of the 4th International Conference of the Association of Architectural Schools of Australia, 2007* (Orr, K. and Kaji-O'Grady, S. eds). University of Technology, Sydney. Republished under the title, 'Genetic designs' in Abel, C. (2017 3rd edn), pp. 98–109.

Abel, C. (2013). 'The extended self: Tacit knowing and place identity'. In *Rethinking Aesthetics: The Role of Body in Design* (Bhatt, R. ed.), pp. 100–139, Routledge, New York.

Abel, C. (2015). *The Extended Self: Architecture, Memes and Minds.* Manchester University Press, Manchester.

Abel, C. (2017, 3rd edn). *Architecture and Identity: Responses to Cultural and Technological Change.* Routledge, Abingdon.

Achen, C. H. and Bartels, L. M. (2016). *Democracy for Realists: Why Elections do not Produce Responsive Government.* Princeton University Press, Princeton.

Adam, D. (2018). *The Genius Within: Smart Pills, Brain Hacks and Adventures in Intelligence.* Picador, London.

Adams-Webber, J. R. (1969). 'Cognitive complexity and sociality'. *British Journal of Social and Clinical Psychology*, Vol. 8, pp. 211–216.

Adams-Webber, J. R. (1979). *Personal Construct Theory: Concepts and Applications.* John Wiley & Sons, Chichester.

Allman, J. M., Tetreault, N. A., Hakeem, A. Y. and Park, S. (2010). 'The von Economo neurons in apes and humans'. *American Journal of Human Biology*, Vol. 23, pp. 5–21.

Allport, G. W. (1954; 1978). *The Nature of Prejudice.* Addison-Wesley, Reading, MA.

Amnesty International (2019). *Surveillance Giants: How the Business Model of Google and Facebook Threatens Human Rights.* Amnesty International, London.

Ananthaswamy, A. (2015). *The Man Who Wasn't There: Tales From the Edge of the Self.* Dutton, New York.

Andersen, P. B., Emmeche, C., Finnemann, N. O. and Christiansen, P. V. eds (2000). *Downward Causation: Minds, Bodies and Matter.* Aarhus University Press, Arrhus.

Arndt, I. and Tautz, J. (2013). *Animal Architecture.* Abrams, New York.

Arthur, W. B. (2009). *The Nature of Technology: What It Is and How It Evolves.* Allen Lane, London.

Ashby, R. (1962). 'Principles of the self-organizing system'. In *Principles of Self-organization* (Von Foester, H. and Zopf, Jr., G. W. eds), pp. 255–278, Pergamon Press, London.

Bachelard, G. (1994). *The Poetics of Space.* Beacon, Boston.

Baird, D. (2004). *Thing Knowledge: A Philosophy of Scientific Instruments.* University of California Press, Berkeley, CA.

Bajracharya, A., Morin, L. K. and Radovich, K. H. (2014). 'Analysis of automobile advertisements in American magazines'. *Student Publications.* www.cupola.Gettysburg.edu/student_scholarship/225.

Banham, R. (1965). 'A clip-on architecture'. *Architectural Design*, Vol. 35, No 11, pp. 534–535.

Bannister, D. and Mair, J. M. M. (1968). *The Evaluation of Personal Constructs.* Academic Press, London.

Bannister, D. ed. (1970). *Perspectives in Personal Construct Theory.* Academic Press, London.

Barbour, I. G. (1974). *Myths, Models and Paradigms.* Harper & Row, New York.

Barthes, R. (1957; 1973). *Mythologies.* Paladin, St Albans.

Barthes, R. (2013). *The Language of Fashion.* Transl. A. Stanford, Bloomsbury, London.

Baudrillard, J. (1968; 2005). *The System of Objects.* Trans. J. Benedict, Verso, London.

Beck, B. B. (1980). *Animal Tool Behavior.* Garland, New York.

Beer, S. (1962). 'Towards the cybernetic factory'. In *Principles of Self-Organization* (Von Foerster, H. and Zopf, Jr., G. W. eds), pp. 25–89.

Belohlavek, R. and Klir, G. J. eds (2011). *Concepts and Fuzzy Logic.* The MIT Press, Cambridge, MA.

Bensman, J. and Rosenberg, B. (1960). 'The meaning of work in a bureaucratic society'. In *Identity and Anxiety: Survival of the Person in Mass Society* (Stein, M. R., Vidich, A. J. and White, D. M. eds), pp. 181–197, Free Press of Glencoe, Illinois.

Berners-Lee, T. et al. (2019). *Contract for the Web.* Web Foundation, Geneva.

Bertalanffy, L. von. (1950). 'The theory of open systems in physics and biology'. *Science,* 13 January, Vol. 111, pp. 23–29.

Bertalanffy, L. von. (1968). *General System Theory: Foundations, Development, Applications.* George Braziller, New York.

Beyer, M. von Scheve, C. and Ismer, S. (2017). 'The social consequences of collective emotions: National identification, solidarity and out-group derogation'. In *Understanding Collective Pride and Group Identity: New Directions in Emotion Theory, Research and Practice* (Sullivan, G. B. ed.), pp. 67–79, Routledge, Abingdon.

Bieri, J. (1955). 'Cognitive complexity – simplicity and predictive behaviour'. *Journal of Abnormal Psychology,* Vol. 51, pp. 263–268.

Bieri, J. (1966). 'Cognitive complexity and personality development'. In *Experience Structure and Adaptability* (Harvey, O. J. ed.), pp.13–37, Springer, Berlin.

Bieri, J., Atkins, A. L., Briar, S., Leaman, R. L., Miller, H. and Tripodi, T. (1975). *Clinical and Social Judgement: The Discrimination of Behavioural Information.* Krieger, New York.

Blackiston, D. J., Casey, E. S. and Weiss, M. R. (2008). 'Retention of memory through metamorphosis: Can a moth remember what it learned as a caterpillar?' PLoS ONE 3(3): e1736. www. doi.org/10.1371/journal.pone.0001736.

Blakeslee, S. and Blakeslee, M. (2007). *The Body Has a Mind of Its Own.* Random House, New York.

Blackmore, S. (1999). *The Meme Machine.* Oxford University Press, Oxford.

Bloom, P. (2016). *Against Empathy: The Case for Rational Compassion.* The Bodley Head, London.

Blunt, A. and Dowling, R. (2006). *Home.* Routledge, London.

Bonduriansky, R. and Day, T. (2018). *Extended Heredity: A New Understanding of Inheritance and Evolution.* Princeton University Press, NJ.

Borthwick, S. (2015). *The Writing on the Wall: A Visual History of Northern Ireland's Troubles.* Bluecoat Press, Liverpool.

Bouchard Jr. T. J. (1999). 'Genes, environment and personality'. In *The Nature-Nurture Debate: The Essential Readings* (Ceci, S. J. and Williams, W. M. eds), pp. 98–103, Oxford, Blackwell.

Bourdieu, P. (1984; 2010). *Distinction: A Social Critique of the Judgement of Taste.* Trans. R. Nice, Routledge, Abingdon.

Bourdieu, P. (1990). *In Other Words: Essays Towards a Reflexive Sociology.* Trans. M. Adamson, Stanford University Press, Stanford, CA.

Braby, M. F. (2018). http://theconversation.com/curious-kids-do-butterflies-remember-being-caterpillars-99508

Brandon, R. (2002). *Auto Mobile: How the Car Changed Life.* Macmillan, London.

Brozzoli, C., Gentile, G., Bergoulgan, L. and Ehrsson, H. H. (2013). 'A shared representation of the space near oneself and others in the human premotor cortex'. *Current Biology,* Vol. 23, September, pp. 1764–1768.

Burns, R., Ferrell, J. and Orrick, E. (2005). 'False advertising, suggestive persuasion, and automobile safety: Assessing advertising practices in the automobile industry'. *The Southwest Journal of Criminal Justice,* Vol. 2 (2), pp. 132–152.

Callard, F. and Fitzgerald, D. (2015). *Rethinking Interdisciplinarity Across the Social Sciences and Neurosciences*. Palgrave Macmillan, Basingstoke.

Callil, C. et al. (2011). *Stop What You're Doing and Read This!* Vintage Books, London.

Calvin, W. H. (1993). 'The unitary hypothesis: A common neural circuitry for novel manipulations, language, plan-ahead, and throwing?' In *Tools, Language and Cognition In Human Evolution*. (Gibson, K. R. and Ingold, T. eds), pp. 230–250, Cambridge University Press, Cambridge.

Capra, F. (1975). *The Tao of Physics*. Fontana/Collins, London.

Carey, N. (2012). *The Epigenetics Revolution: How Modern Biology is Rewriting Our Understanding of Genetics, Disease and Inheritance*. Icon Books, London.

Carr, N. (2010). *The Shallows: How the Internet is Changing the Way We Think, Read and Remember*. Atlantic Books, London.

Carr, N. (2015). *The Glass Cage: Where Automation is Taking Us*. The Bodley Head, London.

Carson, R. (1962; 2000). *Silent Spring*. Penguin Books, London.

Cassirer, E. (1955). *The Philosophy of Symbolic Forms; Vol. 1: Language*. Yale University Press, New Haven, CT.

Cassirer, E. (1962). *An Essay on Man*. Yale University Press, New Haven, CT.

Castells, M. (1996). *The Rise of the Network Society. Vol. I, The Information Age: Economy, Society and Culture*. Blackwell, Oxford.

Castells, M. (1997). *The Power of Identity. Vol. II, The Information Age: Economy, Society and Culture*. Blackwell, Oxford.

Chen, I. (2009). 'Brain cells for socializing'. *Smithsonian Magazine*, June. www.smithsonianmag.com/science-nature/The-Social-Brain.html?c=y&story=fullstory

Cieraad, I. ed. (1999). *At Home: An Anthropology of Domestic Space*. Syracuse University Press, New York.

Clark, A. (2003). *Natural-Born Cyborgs: Minds, Technologies, and the Future of Human Intelligence*. Oxford University Press, Oxford.

Clark, B. and Hansen, M. B. N. (2009). 'Introduction: Neocybernetic emergence'. In *Emergence and Embodiment: New Essays in Second-order Systems Theory* (Clarke, B. and b Hansen, M. B. N. eds), pp. 1–25, Duke University Press, London.

Collinson, P. (2019). 'Automation threatens 1.5 million workers in Britain, says ONS'. *The Guardian*, 25 March. https://theguardian.com/money/2019/mar/25/automation Accessed September, 2019.

Cooper, C. (1974). 'The house as symbol of the self', in *Designing for Human Behavior: Architecture and the Behavioral Sciences* (Lang, J., Burnette, C., Moleski, W. and Vachon, D. eds), pp. 130–146, Dowden, Hutchinson & Ross, Stroudsburg.

Corbusier, Le (1927; 1946). *Towards a New Architecture*. Transl. F. Etchells, The Architectural Press, London, Frederick A. Praeger, New York.

Corradini, A. and O'Connor, T. eds (2010). *Emergence in Science and Philosophy*. Routledge, New York.

Coveny, P. and Highfield, R. (1995). *Frontiers of Complexity: The Search for Order in a Chaotic World*. Faber and Faber, London.

Coyne, R. (2016). *Mood and Mobility: Navigating the Emotional Spaces of Digital Social Networks*. The MIT Press, Cambridge, MA.

Crockett, W. H. (1965). 'Cognitive complexity and impression formation'. In *Progress in Experimental Personality Research, Vol. 2* (Maher, B. A. ed.), pp. 47–90, Academic Press, New York.

Damasio, A. (2000). *The Feeling of What Happens: Body, Emotion and the Making of Consciousness.* Vintage Books, London.

Damasio, A. (2012). *Self Comes to Mind: Constructing the Conscious Brain.* Vintage Books, London.

Damasio, A. (2018). *The Strange Order of Things: Life, Feeling, and the Making of Cultures.* Pantheon Books, London.

Darwin, C. (1972; 1859, 1st edn). *On the Origin of Species: A Facsimile of the First Edition.* Antheum, New York.

Darwin, C. (1871; 2009). *The Descent of Man, and Selection in Relation to Sex.* Vol. 1. Cambridge University Press, New York, pp. 104–105.

Darwin, C. (1872; 1965). *The Expression of Emotions in Man and the Animals.* University of Chicago Press, Chicago, IL.

Davidson, C. (1965). 'Jean Prouve: l'habitation de notre epoque'. *Arena: Journal of the Architectural Association,* London, Vol. 81, December, pp. 128–129.

Davis, F. (1992). *Fashion, Culture, and Identity.* The University of Chicago Press, Chicago, IL.

Dawkins, R. (1982; 1999). *The Extended Phenotype: The Long Reach of the Gene.* Oxford University Press, Oxford.

Dawkins, R. (1989, 2nd edn). *The Selfish Gene.* Oxford University Press, Oxford.

Denes, G. (2016). *Neural Plasticity Across the Lifespan: How the Brain Can Change.* Routledge, London.

Dennett, D. C. (1991). *Consciousness Explained.* Penguin Books, London.

Diamond, J. (2005). *Collapse: How Societies Choose to Fail or Survive.* Allen Lane, London.

Diamond, J. (1999). 'War babies'. In *The Nature-Nurture Debate: The Essential Readings* (Ceci, S. J. and Williams, W. M. eds), pp. 14–22.

Dijck, J. van (2013). *The Culture of Connectivity: A Critical History of Social Media.* Oxford University Press, Oxford.

Dupre, J. (1993). *The Disorder of Things: Metaphysical Foundations of the Disunity of Science.* Harvard University Press, Cambridge, MA.

Durham, W. H. (1991). *Coevolution: Genes, Culture, and Human Diversity.* Stanford University Press, Stanford, CA.

Dyson, E. (1997). *Release 2.0: A Design For Living in the Digital Age.* Viking, London.

Eden, J. F. (1967). 'Metrology and the module'. *Architectural Design,* Vol. XXXVII, March, pp. 148–150.

Eler, A. (2017). *The Selfie Generation: How Our Self Images Are Changing Our Notions of Privacy, Sex, Consent, and Culture.* Skyhorse Publishing, New York.

Entwistle, J. (2000; 2015, 2nd edn). *The Fashioned Body: Fashion, Dress & Modern Social Theory.* Polity, Cambridge.

Feyerabend, P. (1975). *Against Method.* New Left Books, London.

Ferretti, G. and Alai, M. (2016). 'Enactivism, representations and canonical neurons'. *Argumenta,* Issue 2, pp. 195–217.

Festinger, L. (1957; 1962). *A Theory of Cognitive Dissonance.* Stanford University Press, Stanford, CA.

Festinger, L. (1964). *Conflict, Decision, and Dissonance.* Stanford University Press, Stanford, CA.

Fivush, R. et al. (2011). 'The making of autobiographical memory: Intersections of culture, narratives and identity'. *International Journal of Psychology,* Vol. 46 (5), pp. 321–345.

Flavell, J. H. (1963). *The Developmental Psychology of Jean Piaget.* Van Nostrand Reinhold, New York.

Foroohar, R. (2019). *Don't Be Evil: The Case Against Big Tech.* Allen Lane, London.

Fransella, F. and Bannister, D. (1977). *A Manual for Repertory Grid Technique.* Academic Press, New York.

Francesco, M. Di (2010). 'Two varieties of causal emergentism'. In *Emergence in Science and Philosophy* (Corradini, A. and O'Connor, T. eds), pp. 64–77, Routledge, New York.

Francis, R. C. (2011). *Epigenetics: How Environment Shapes Our Genes.* W. W. Norton & Co., New York.

Freeman, J. B. (2018). *Behemoth: A History of the Factory and the Making of the Modern World.* W. W. Norton, New York.

Frey, C. B. and Osborne, M. A. (2013). 'The future of employment: How susceptible are jobs to computerization?' Paper presented to the 'Machines and Employment' Workshop, University of Oxford, 17 September.

Frith, C. D. (2015). *The Cognitive Neuropsychology of Schizophrenia.* Psychology Press, Hove.

Gallagher, S. (2000). 'Self-reference and schizophrenia: A cognitive model of immunity to error through misidentification'. In *Exploring the Self* (Zahavi, D. ed.), pp. 203–239.

Gazzaniga, M. S. (1970). *The Bisected Brain.* Appleton-Century-Crofts, New York.

Gebauer, G. (2014). 'Self, certainty and collective emotions'. In *Understanding Collective Pride and Group Identity: New Directions in Emotion Theory, Research and Practice* (Sullivan, G. B. ed.), pp. 34–42, Routledge, Abingdon.

Gibson, K. R. and Ingold, T. eds (1993). *Tools, Language and Cognition In Human Evolution.* Cambridge University Press, Cambridge.

Gibson, K. R. (1993a). 'Animal minds, human minds'. In *Tools, Language and Cognition in Human Evolution* (Gibson, K. R. and Ingold, T. eds), pp. 3–19, Cambridge University Press, Cambridge.

Gibson, K. R. (1993b). 'Overlapping neural control of language, gesture and tool-use'. In *Tools, Language and Cognition in Human Evolution* (Gibson, K. R. and Ingold, T. eds), pp. 187–192, Cambridge University Press, Cambridge.

Gibson, K. R. (1993c). 'Tool use, language and social behavior in relationship to information processing power'. In *Tools, Language and Cognition in Human Evolution* (Gibson, K. R. and Ingold, T. eds), pp. 251–269, Cambridge University Press, Cambridge.

Giddens, A. (1991). *Modernity and Self-Identity: Self and Society in the Late Modern Age.* Polity, Cambridge.

Gillett, C. (2010). 'On the implications of scientific composition and completeness: Or, the troubles, and *troubles,* of non-reductive physicalism'. In *Emergence in Science and Philosophy* (Corradini, A. and O'Connor, T. eds), pp. 25–45, Routledge, New York.

Godfrey-Smith, P. (2016). *Other Minds: The Octopus and the Evolution of Intelligent Life.* Harper Collins, London.

Goffman, E. (1959; 1990). *The Presentation of Self in Everyday Life.* Penguin Books, London.

Goffman, E. (1963). *Behavior in Public Places: Notes on the Social Organization of Gatherings.* The Free Press, New York.

Gold, M. (1992). 'Metatheory and field theory in social psychology: Relevance or elegance?' *Journal of Social Issues,* Vol. 48, No. 2, pp. 67–78.

Goodwin, B. C. (1987). 'Developing organisms as self-organizing fields'. In *Self-Organizing Systems: The Emergence of Order* (Yates, F. E. ed.), pp. 167–180, Plenum Press, New York.

Gould, S. J. (1987). 'Is a new and general theory of evolution emerging?' In *Self-Organizing Systems: The Emergence of Order* (Yates, F. E. ed.), pp. 113–130, Plenum Press, New York.

Gray, J. (2002). *Straw Dogs: Thoughts on Humans and Other Animals.* Granta Books, London, p. 123.

Gray, J. (2015). *The Soul of the Marionette: A Short Enquiry into Human Freedom.* Allen Lane, London.

Graziano, M. S. A. and Gross, C. G. (1994). 'The representation of extrapersonal space: A possible role for bimodal, visual-tactile neurons'. In *The Cognitive Neurosciences* (M. Gazzaniga, M. ed.), pp. 1021–1034, The MIT Press, Cambridge, MA.

Greenbaum, J. (2004). *Windows on the Workplace: Technology, Jobs, and the Organization of Office Work.* Monthly Review Press, New York.

Greenfield, P. M. (1984; 2014). *Mind and Media: The Effects of Television, Video Games, and Computers.* Psychology Press, Hove.

Greenfield, S. (2008). *ID: The Quest for Identity in the 21st Century.* Sceptre, London.

Greenfield, S. (2014). *Mind Change: How Digital Technologies are Leaving Their Mark on our Brains.* Rider Books, London.

Griffin, D. (1976). *The Question of Animal Awareness.* The Rockefeller University Press, New York.

Griffiths, M. D., Kuss, D. J. and King, D. L. (2013). 'Video game addiction: Past, present and future'. *Current Psychiatry Reviews,* Vol. 8, No. 4, pp. 1–11.

Haidt, J. (2012). *The Righteous Mind: Why Good People Are Divided by Politics and Religion.* Penguin Books, London.

Hall, E. T. (1969). *The Hidden Dimension.* Anchor Books, New York.

Hamilton, C. (2010). *Requiem For a Species: Why We Resist the Truth About Climate Change.* Allen & Unwin, Crows Nest.

Hansell, M. (2007). *Built by Animals: The Natural History of Animal Architecture.* Oxford University Press, New York.

Harre, R. (1972). *The Philosophies of Science.* Oxford University Press, Oxford.

Harre, R. (1974). 'Some remarks on "rule" as a scientific concept'. In *Understanding Other Persons* (Mischel, T. ed.), pp. 143–184, Basil Blackford, Oxford.

Hensel, M., Menges, A. and Weinstock, M. eds (2004). *Emergence: Morphogenic Design Strategies.* Wiley Academy, Chichester.

Heimann, J. and Patton, P. (2015). *20th Century Classic Cars: 100 Years of Automotive Ads.* Taschen, Koln.

Hickok, G. (2014). *The Myth of Mirror Neurons: The Real Science of Communication and Cognition.* W. W. Norton, New York.

Hilgers, M. and Mangez, E. (2015). *Bourdieu's Theory of Social Fields: Concepts and Applications.* Routledge, Abingdon.

Hinkel, D. N. (1965). 'The change of personal constructs from the viewpoint of a theory of implications'. Unpublished PhD thesis, Ohio State University.

Holmes, N. P. and Spence, C. (2004). 'The body schema and the multisensory representation(s) of peripersonal space'. *Cognitive Process,* Vol. 5, June, pp. 94–105.

Honikman, B. (1980). 'Personal construct theory and environmental evaluation'. In *Meaning and Behavior in the Built Environment* (Broadbent, G., Bunt, R. and Llorens, T. eds), pp. 79–91, John Wiley & Sons, Chichester.

Hood, B. (2011). *The Self Illusion: Who do You Think You Are?* Constable, London.

Howe, M. L. (2014). 'The co-emergence of the self and autobiographical memory: An adaptive view of early memory'. In *The Wiley Handbook on the Development of Children's Memory* (Bauer, P. J. and Fivush, R., eds), pp. 545–567, John Wiley & Sons, Chichester.

Hubbard, R. and Elijah W. (2000). *Exploding the Gene Myth: How Genetic Information is Produced and Manipulated by Scientists, Physicians, Employers, Insurance Companies, Educators, and Law Enforcers.* Beacon Press, Boston, MA.

Huttenlocher, P. R. (2002). *Neural Plasticity: The Effects of Environment on the Development of the Cerebral Cortex.* Harvard University Press, Cambridge, MA.

Hunt, G. R. (1996). 'Manufacture and use of hook-tools by New Caledonian crows'. *Nature, Vol. 379,* pp. 249–251.

Hunt, G. R. and Gray, R. D. (2003). 'Diversification and cumulative evolution in New Caledonian crow tool manufacture'. *Proceedings of the Royal Society, London, Series B* 270, pp. 867–874.

Hyde, L. (1979). *The Gift: Imagination and the Erotic Life of Property.* Vintage Books, New York.

Jablonka, E. and Lamb, M. J. (2005). *Evolution in Four Dimensions: Genetic, Epigenetic, Behavioral, and Symbolic Variation in the History of Life.* The MIT Press, Cambridge, MA.

Jenss, H., ed. (2016). *Fashion Studies: Research Methods, Sites, and Practices.* Bloomsbury, London.

Johnson, P. (2010). *Second Life, Media, and the Other Society.* Peter Lang, New York.

Kaiser, B. (2019). *Targeted: My Inside Story of Cambridge Analytica and How Trump, Brexit and Facebook Broke Democracy.* Harper Collins, London.

Kauffman, S. A. (1993). *The Origins of Order: Self-organization and Selection in Evolution.* Oxford University Press, New York.

Keller, E. F. (2000). *The Century of the Gene.* Harvard University Press, Cambridge, MA.

Kelly, G. A. (1963). *A Theory of Personality: The Psychology of Personal Constructs.* W. W. Norton, New York.

Kelly, G. A. (1970). 'A brief introduction to personal construct theory'. In *Perspectives in Personal Construct Theory* (Bannister, D. ed.), pp. 1–30, Academic Press, London.

Key, C. A. and Aiello, L. C. (1999). 'The evolution of social organization'. In *The Evolution of Culture: An Interdisciplinary View* (Dunbar, R., Knight, C. and Power, C. eds), pp. 15–33, Edinburgh University Press, Edinburgh.

Keysers, C. (2011). *The Empathic Brain.* Social Brain Press, Cambridge, MA

Kirshner, M. W. and Gerhart, J. C. (2010). 'Facilitated variation'. In *Evolution – The Extended Thesis* (Pigliucci, M. and Muller, G. B. eds), pp. 253–280, The MIT Press, Cambridge, MA.

Klein, N. (2015). *This Changes Everything: Capitalism vs. the Climate.* Penguin Books, UK.

Koestler, A. (1964). *The Act of Creation.* Macmillan, New York.

Koestler, A. and Smythies, J. R. eds (1971). *Beyond Reductionism: New Perspectives in the Life Sciences.* Macmillan, London.

Kosko, B. (1994). *Fuzzy Thinking: The New Science of Fuzzy Logic.* Harper Collins, London.

Kosslyn, S. M. (2002). *Neural Plasticity: The Effects of Environment on the Development of the Cerebral Cortex.* Harvard University Press, Cambridge, MA.

Kuhn, T. (1962). *The Structure of Scientific Revolutions.* University of Chicago Press, Chicago, IL.

Kuhn, T. (1977). *The Essential Tension: Selected Studies in Scientific Tradition and Change.* University of Chicago, Chicago, IL.

Kurenkov, A., Liang, J. and Ramanauskas, B. (2019). 'Job loss due to AI – how bad is it going to be?' *Skynet Today*, 4 February. www.skynettoday.com/editorials/ai-automation-job-loss Accessed September, 2019.

Kuss, D. J. (2013). 'Internet gaming addiction: Current perspectives'. *Psychology Research and Behavior Management*, No. 6, 125–137.

Laing, R. D. (1961, 1969). *Self and Others*. Penguin Books, Harmondsworth.

Laing, R. D., Phillipson, H. and Lee, A. R. (1966). *Interpersonal Perception: A Theory and a Method of Research*. Tavistock Publications, London.

Laland, K. N. (2017). *Darwin's Unfinished Symphony: How Culture Made the Human Mind*. Princeton University Press, Princeton.

Langer, J. (1993). 'Comparative cognitive development'. In *Tools, Language and Cognition in Human Evolution* (Gibson, K. R. and Ingold, T. eds), pp. 300–313, Cambridge University Press, Cambridge.

Lasch, C. (1978). *The Culture of Narcissism: American Life in An Age of Diminishing Expectations*. W. W. Norton, New York.

Leatherdale, W. H. (1974). *The Role of Analogy, Model and Metaphor in Science*. North Holland/American Elsevier, Amsterdam and New York.

LeDoux, J. (1998). *The Emotional Brain: The Mysterious Underpinnings of Emotional Life*. Phoenix, London.

Lenton, T. M. et al. (2019). 'Climate tipping points – too risky to bet against'. *Nature*, Vol. 575, 28 November, pp. 592–595.

Lerner, R. M. (2012). 'Genes and the promotion of positive human development: Hereditarian versus developmental perspectives'. In *Nature and Nurture: The Complex Interplay of Genetic and Environmental Influences on Human Behaviour and Development* (Coll, C. G., Bearer, E. L. and Lerner, R. M. eds), pp. 1–33, Psychology Press, New York.

Lewin, K. (1935; 2013). *A Dynamic Theory of Personality: Selected Papers*. Read Books, Milton Keynes.

Lewin, K. (1951; 1964). *Field Theory in Social Science: Selected Theoretical Papers*. Harper & Row, New York.

Lewin, R. (1993). *Complexity: Life on the Edge of Chaos*. Phoenix, London.

Lewis, S. L. and Maslin, M. A. (2018). *The Human Planet: How We Created the Anthropocene*. Pelican Books, London.

Lock, A. (1993). 'Language development and object manipulation: Their relation in ontogeny and its possible reference for phylogenetic questions'. In *Tools, Language and Cognition in Human Evolution* (Gibson, K. R. and Ingold, T. eds), pp. 29–79, Cambridge University Press, Cambridge.

Lovelock, J. E. (1979; 1987). *Gaia: A New Look at Life On Earth*. Oxford University Press, Oxford.

Lovelock, J. E. (2009). *The Vanishing Face of Gaia: A Final Warning*. Penguin Books, London.

Lumsden, C. J. and Wilson, E. O. (1981). *Genes, Mind, and Culture: The Coevolutionary Process*. Harvard University Press, Cambridge, MA.

Lumsden, C. J. and Wilson, E. O. (1983). *Promethean Fire: Reflections on the Origin of Mind*. Harvard University Press, Cambridge, MA.

Lynas, M. (2008). *Six Degrees: Our Future on a Hotter Planet*. National Geographic, Washington, DC.

MacWhinney, B. ed. (2008). *The Emergence of Language*. Psychology Press, Hove.

Marcus, C. C. (1995; 2006). *House as a Mirror of Self: Exploring the Deeper Meaning of Home*. Nicolas Hayes, Berwick.

Marozzi, E. and Jeffrey, K. J. (2012). 'Place, space and memory cells'. *Current Biology*, Vol. 22, November, pp. R939–R942.

Marshall, G. (2014). *Don't Even Think About It: Why Our Brains Are Wired to Ignore Climate Change*. Bloomsbury, New York.

Masterman, M. (1970). 'The nature of a paradigm'. In *Criticism and the Growth of Knowledge* (Lakatos, I. and Musgrave, A. eds), pp. 59–89, Cambridge University Press, Cambridge.

Maturana, H. R. (1980). 'The biology of cognition'. In *Autopoiesis and Cognition: The Realization of the Living* (Maturana, H. R. and Varela, F. J.), pp. 5–58. Kluwer, Boston.

Maturana, H. R. and Varela, F. J. (1980). *Autopoiesis and Cognition: The Realization of the Living*. Kluwer, Boston.

Maturana, H. R. and Varela, F. J. (1987; 1998). *The Tree of Knowledge: The Biological Roots of Human Understanding*. Shambala, Boston, MA.

McKibben, B. (1989; 2003). *The End of Nature: Humanity, Climate Change and the Natural World*. Bloomsbury, London.

McKibben, B. (2019). *Falter: Has the Human Game Begun to Play Itself Out?* Wildfire, London.

McKittrick, D. and McVea, D. (2012). *Making Sense of the Troubles: A History of the Northern Ireland Conflict*. Viking, London.

McLuhan, M. (1964). *Understanding Media: The Extensions of Man*. Routledge & Kegan Paul, London.

McRae, M. (2011). *Tribal Science: Brains, Beliefs & Bad Ideas*. University of Queensland Press, St Lucia.

Mead, G. H. (1934; 1962). *Mind, Self, & Society: From the Standpoint of a Social Behaviorist, Vol. 1.* The University of Chicago Press, Chicago, IL.

Merleau-Ponty, M. (1962). *Phenomenology of Perception*. Trans. C. Smith. Routledge and Kegan Paul, London.

Metzinger, T. (2009). *The Ego Tunnel: The Science of the Mind and the Myth of the Self*. Basic Books, New York.

Mey, H. (1972; 2015). *Field Theory: A Study of its Application in the Social Sciences*. Transl. D. Scott, Routledge, Abingdon.

Miller, D. ed. (2001). *Car Cultures*. Berg, Oxford.

Miller, D. ed. (2001). *Home Possessions: Material Culture Behind Closed Doors*. Berg, Oxford.

Miller, D. (2008). *The Comfort of Things*. Polity, Cambridge.

Mingers, J. (1995). *Self-producing Systems: Implications and Applications of Autopoiesis*. Plenum Press, New York.

Moreno, A. and Umerez, J. (2000). 'Downward causation at the core of living organization'. In *Downward Causation: Minds, Bodies and Matter* (Andersen, P. B., Emmeche, C., Finnemann, N. O. and Christiansen, P.V. eds), pp. 99–117, Aarhus University Press, Arrhus.

Moser, E. I., Kropff, E. and Moser, M. B. (2008). 'Place cells, grid cells, and the brain's spatial representation system'. *Annual Review of Neuroscience*, Vol. 31, pp. 69–89.

Muller, G. B. (2010). 'Epigenetic innovation'. In *Evolution – The Extended Synthesis* (Pigliucci, M. and Muller, G. B. eds), pp. 307–332, The MIT Press, Cambridge, MA.

Nader, R. (1965). *Unsafe at Any Speed: The Designed-in Dangers of the American Automobile*. Grossman, New York.

Negroponte, N. (1975). *Soft Architecture Machines*. The MIT Press, Cambridge, MA.

Newton, D. E. (2013). *The Animal Experimentation Debate: A Reference Handbook.* ABC-CLIO, Santa Barbara, CA.

O'Connor, C. (2014). *Control the Controller: Understanding and Resolving Video Game Addiction.* Free Press Publishing, NY.

Odling-Smee, F. J., Laland K. N. and Feldman M. W. (2003). *Niche Construction – The Neglected Process in Evolution.* Princeton University Press, Princeton, NJ.

Odling-Smee, J. (2010). 'Niche inheritance'. In *Evolution – The Extended Synthesis* (Pigliucci, M. and Muller, G. B. eds), pp. 175–207, The MIT Press, Cambridge, MA.

Oliner, P. M. et al., eds (1992). *Embracing the Other: Philosophical, Psychological and Historical Perspectives on Altruism.* New York University Press, New York.

Oliver, P. (2003). *Dwellings: The Vernacular House Worldwide.* Phaidon, London.

Oliver, P. ed. (1998). *Encyclopedia of Vernacular Architecture of the World.* Architectural Press, Oxford.

Oreskes, N. and Conway, E. M. (2010). *Merchants of Doubt: How a Handful of Scientists Obscured the Truth on Issue from Tobacco Smoke to Global Warming.* Bloomsbury, New York.

Oreskes, N. (2004). 'The scientific consensus on climate change'. *Science*, Vol. 306, 3 December, p. 1686.

Orwell, G. (1949; 1992). *Nineteen Eighty-Four.* Everyman's Library, New York.

O'Toole, F. (2018). *Heroic Failure: Brexit and the Politics of Pain.* Head of Zeus, London.

Overton, W. F. (2004). 'Embodied development: Ending the nativism–empiricism debate'. In *Nature and Nurture: The Complex Interplay of Genetic and Environmental Influences on Human Behaviour and Development* (Coll, C. G., Bearer, E. L. and Lerner, R. M. eds), pp. 201–223, Psychology Press, New York.

Panksepp, J. and Northoff, G. (2009). 'The trans-species core SELF: The emergence of active and neuro-ecological agents through self-related processing within subcortical-cortical midline networks'. In *Consciousness and Cognition*, Vol. 18, 1, March, pp. 193–295.

Parfit, D. (1979). 'Personal identity'. In *Philosophy As It Is* (Honderich, T. and Burnyeat, M. eds), pp. 186–211, Penguin Books, Harmondsworth.

Parfit, D. (1984). *Reasons and Persons.* Oxford University Press, Oxford.

Pask, G. (1976). *Conversation Theory.* Elsevier, Amsterdam.

Pattee, H. H. (2000). 'Causation, control, and the evolution of complexity'. In *Downward Causation: Minds, Bodies and Matter* (Andersen, P. B., Emmeche, C., Finnemann, N. O. and Christiansen, P. V. eds), pp. 63–77, Aarhus University Press, Arrhus.

Paul, E. F., Miller, F. D. and Paul, J. eds (2005). *Personal Identity.* Cambridge University Press, Cambridge.

Pelligrino, G. di and Ladavas, E. (2015). 'Peripersonal space in the brain'. *Neuropsychologia*, Vol. 66. January, pp. 126–133.

Pigliucci, M. and Muller, G. B. (2010). 'Elements of an extended evolutionary synthesis'. In *Evolution – The Extended Synthesis* (Pigliucci, M. and Muller, G. B. eds), pp. 3–17, The MIT Press, Cambridge, MA.

Piketty, T. (2015). The Economics of Inequality. Trans. A. Goldhammer, Harvard University Press, Cambridge, MA.

Plato (no date). *Plato's Republic.* Transl. H. Davis. Universal Classics, New York.

Plomin, R. and Defries, J. C. (1999). 'The genetics of cognitive abilities and disabilities'. In *The Nature–Nurture Debate: The Essential Readings* (Ceci, S. J. and Williams, W. M. eds), pp. 178–195, Blackwell, Oxford.

Plomin, R. (2018). *Blueprint: How DNA Makes Us Who We Are.* Allen Lane, London

Polanyi, M. (1958). *Personal Knowledge: Towards a Post-critical Philosophy*. University of Chicago Press, Chicago.

Polanyi, M. (1967). *The Tacit Dimension*. Anchor Books, New York.

Polanyi, M. (1969). *Knowing and Being*. University of Chicago Press, Chicago.

Porges, S. W. (2011). *The Polyvagal Theory: Neurophysiological Foundations of Emotions, Attachment, Communication, Self-Regulation*. W. W. Norton, New York.

Prigogine, I. and Stengers, I. (1985). *Order Out of Chaos: Man's New Dialogue With Nature*. Flamingo, London.

Protevi, J. (2009). 'Beyond autopoiesis: Inflections of emergence and politics in Francisco Varela'. In *Emergence and Embodiment: New Essays in Second-order Systems Theory* (Clarke, B. and Hansen, M. B. N. eds), pp. 95–112, Duke University Press, London.

Ramachandran, V. S. and Blakeslee, S. (2005). *Phantoms in the Brain: Human Nature and the Architecture of the Mind*. Harper Perennial, London.

Ridley, M. (2003). *Nature via Nurture: Genes, Experience and What Makes Us Human*. Fourth Estate, London.

Ripple, W. J. et al. (2019). 'World scientists' warning of a climate emergency'. *Bioscience*, biz088, https://doi.org/10.1093/biosci/biz088

Rizzolatti, G. and Sinigaglia, C. (2011). 'Through the looking glass: Self and others'. *Consciousness and Cognition*, 20, pp. 64–74.

Robins, N. (2012). *The Corporation that Changed the World: How the East India Company Shaped the Modern Multinational*. Pluto Press, London.

Rolston, B. (2013). *Drawing Support 4: Murals and Conflict Transformation in Northern Ireland*. Beyond the Pale, Belfast.

Rose, H. and Rose, S. (2012). *Genes, Cells and Brains: The Promethean Promises of the New Biology*. Verso, London.

Rosenberg, M. (1965). *Society and the Adolescent Self-Image*. Princeton University Press, Princeton, NJ.

Rudofsky, B. (1964). *Architecture Without Architects*. Doubleday, New York.

Rudofsky, B. (1977). *The Prodigious Builders: Notes Towards a Natural History of Architecture*. Harcourt Brace Jovanovich, New York.

Russell, S. (2019). *Human Compatible: AI and the Problem of Control*. Allen Lane, London.

Ryle, G. (1949). *The Concept of Mind*. Barnes & Noble, New York.

Saussure, F. de (1959). *Course in General Linguistics*. Transl. Baskin, W. Philosophical Library, New York.

Schellenberg, J. A. (1978). *Masters of Social Psychology: Freud, Mead, Lewin, and Skinner*. Oxford University Press, New York.

Schick, K. D. and Toth, N. (1993). *Making Silent Stones Speak: Human Evolution and the Dawn of Technology*. Touchstone, New York.

Schowalter, T. D. (2000; 2016 4th edn). *Insect Ecology: An Ecosystem Approach*. Academic Press, London.

Sennett, R. (2008). *The Craftsman*. Penguin Books, London.

Shellenberg, J. A. (1978). *Masters of Social Psychology: Freud, Mead, Lewin, and Skinner*. Oxford University Press, New York.

Shermer, M. (2008). *The Mind of the Market: How Biology and Psychology Shape Our Economic Lives*. Henry Holt, New York.

Shew, A. (2017). *Animal Constructions and Technological Knowledge*. Lexington Books, Lanham, MD.

Shirlow, P. and Murtagh, B. (2006). *Belfast: Segregation, Violence and the City*. Pluto Press, London.

Shove, E. (1999). 'Constructing home'. In *At Home: An Anthropology of Domestic Space* (Cieraad, I. ed.), pp. 130–143, Syracuse University Press, New York.

Shumaker, R. W., Walkup, K. R. and Beck, B. B. (2011). *Animal Tool Behavior: The Use and Manufacture of Tools by Animals*. The John Hopkins University Press, Baltimore, MD.

Skinner, B. F. (1971). *Beyond Freedom and Dignity*. Alfred N. Knopf, New York.

Skinner, B. F. (1974). *About Behaviorism*. Alfred N. Knopf, New York.

Snowden, E. (2019). *Permanent Record*. Macmillan, London.

Sperber, D. (2000). 'An objection to the memetic approach to culture'. In *Darwinizing Culture: The Status of Memetics as a Science* (Aunger, R. ed.), pp. 163–173, Oxford University Press, Oxford.

Standing, G. (2011; 2016). *The Precariat: The New Dangerous Class*. Bloomsbury, London.

Stevenson, H. (2008). *American Automobile Advertising, 1930–1980: An Illustrated History*. McFarland, Jefferson, NC.

Stiegler, B. (1998). *Technics and Time, I: The Fault of Epimetheus*. Trans. Richard Beardsworth and George Collins. Stanford University Press, Stanford, CA.

Stiglitz, J. (2013). *The Price of Inequality*. Penguin Books, London.

Stokes, G. ed. (1997). *The Politics of Identity in Australia*. Cambridge University Press, Cambridge.

Storr, W. (2017). *Selfie: How the West Became Self-obsessed*. Picador, London.

Sunstein, C. R. (2009). *Going to Extremes: How Like Minds Unite and Divide*. Oxford University Press, Oxford.

Taylor, T. (2010). *The Artificial Ape: How Technology Changed the Course of Human Evolution*. Palgrave Macmillan, New York.

Tilley, C., Keane, W., Kuchler, S., Rowlands, M. and Spyer, P. (2006). *Handbook of Material Culture*. Sage, London.

Tomasello, M. (1999). *The Cultural Origins of Human Cognition*. Harvard University Press, Cambridge, MA.

Tomasello, M. (2014). *A Natural History of Human Thinking*. Harvard University Press, Cambridge, MA.

Tomasello, M. and Slobin, D. I. eds (2015). *Beyond Nature and Nurture: Essays in Honor of Elizabeth Bates*. Psychology Press, Hove.

Turkle, S. (1984). *The Second Self: Computers and the Human Spirit*. Simon & Schuster, New York.

Turkle, S. (1997). *Life on the Screen: Identity in the Age of the Internet*. Simon & Schuster, New York.

Turkle, S. ed. (2007). *Evocative Objects: Things We Think With*. The MIT Press, Cambridge, MA.

Turkle, S. (2011). *Alone Together: Why We Expect More From Technology and Less From Each Other*. Basic Books, New York.

Turner, J. H. (2003). *Human Institutions: A Theory of Societal Evolution*. Rowman & Littlefield, Lanham, MD.

Turner, J. S. (2002). *The Extended Organism: The Physiology of Animal-Built Structures*. Harvard University Press, Cambridge, MA.

Turow, J. (2011). *The Daily You: How the New Advertising Industry Is Defining Your Identity and Your Worth*. Yale University Press, New Haven, CT.

Vaal, F. de (2016). *Are We Smart Enough to Know How Smart Animals Are?* Granta, London.

Varela, F. J., Thompson, E. and Rosch, E. (1993). *The Embodied Mind: Cognitive Science an Human Experience.* The MIT Press, Cambridge, MA.

Veale, D., Willson, R. and Clarke, A. (2009). *Overcoming Body Image Problems, Including Body Dysmorphic Disorder: A Self-Help Guide Using Cognitive Behavioral Techniques.* Robinson, London.

Vincenti, W. (1990). *What Engineers Know and How They Know It.* John Hopkins University Press, Baltimore, MD.

Volti, R. (2004). *Cars and Culture: The Life Story of a Technology.* John Hopkins University Press, Baltimore, MD.

Vygotsky, L. S. (1978). *Mind in Society: The Development of Higher Psychological Processes.* Harvard University Press, Cambridge, MA.

Wagner, G. P. (2014). *Homology, Genes, and Evolutionary Innovation.* Princeton University Press, Princeton, NJ.

Wallace-Wells, D. (2019). *The Uninhabitable Earth: A Story of the Future.* Allen Lane, London.

Ward, B. and Dubos, R. (1972). *Only One Earth: The Care and Maintenance of a Small Planet.* Pelican Books, Harmondsworth.

Weinstock, M. (2010). *The Architecture of Emergence: The Evolution of Form in Nature and Civilization.* Wiley, Chichester.

Wells, S. (2010). *Pandora's Seed: The Unforeseen Cost of Civilization.* Allen Lane, London.

Wilkins, J. S. ((2009). *Species: A History of the Idea.* University of California Press, Berkeley, CA.

Williamson, D. T. N. (1967). 'New wave in manufacturing'. *American Machinist*, 11 September, pp. 143–154.

Wilson, F. R. (1998). *The Hand: How Its Use Shapes the Brain, Language, and Human Culture.* Vintage Books, New York.

Winch, P. (1958). *The Idea of a Social Science and its Relation to Philosophy.* Routledge & Kegan Paul, London.

Wise, C. (2004). 'Drunk in an orgy of technology'. In *Emergence: Morphogenetic Design Strategies* (Hensel, M., Menges, A. and Weinstock, M. eds), pp. 54–57, Wiley Academy, Chichester.

Wittgenstein, L. (1953, 3rd edn). *Philosophical Investigations.* Transl. G. E. M. Anscombe, Macmillan, New York.

Wohlleben P. (2015). *The Hidden Life of Trees.* Trans. Jane Billinghurst, William Collins, London.

Wolf, M. (2008). *Proust and the Squid: The Story and Science of the Reading Brain.* Icon Books, Cambridge.

Wolf, M. (2018). *Reader, Come Home: The Reading Brain in a Digital World.* Harper Collins, New York.

Woodward, S. (2016). '"Humble" blue jeans: Material culture approaches to understanding the ordinary, global, and the personal'. In *Fashion Studies: Research Methods, Sites, and Practices* (Jenss, H. ed), pp. 42–57, Bloomsbury, London.

World Health Organization (2018). 'Road traffic injuries'. 7 December, www.who.int/ news-room/fact-sheets/detail/road-traffic-injuries

Wylie, C. (2019). *Mindf*ck: Inside Cambridge Analytica's Plot to Break the World.* Profile Books, London.

Yates, G. B. (1987). 'Differentiation, morphogenesis, and death of organisms'. In *Self-Organizing Systems: The Emergence of Order* (Yates, F. E. ed.), pp. 131–132, Plenum Press, New York.

Zadeh, L. A. (1975). Fuzzy logic and approximate reasoning'. *Synthese*, No. 30, pp. 407–428.

Zahavi, D. ed. (2000). *Exploring the Self: Advances in Consciousness Research*. John Benjamins Publishing Company, Amsterdam.

Zuboff, S. (2019). *The Age of Surveillance Capitalism: The Fight For a Human Future at the New Frontier of Power*. Profile Books, London.

Index